Kirtley Library
Columbia College
8th and Rogers
Columbia, MO. 65201

D1556927

WITHDRAWN

Turkey, the Straits
and U.S. Policy

Turkey, the Straits
AND
U.S. Policy

HARRY N. HOWARD

Published in cooperation with
the Middle East Institute

THE JOHNS HOPKINS UNIVERSITY PRESS

Baltimore and London

Copyright © 1974 by The Johns Hopkins University
Press.
All rights reserved. No part of this book may be re-
produced or transmitted in any form or by any means,
electronic or mechanical, including photocopying,
recording, xerography, or any information storage or
retrieval system without permission in writing from
the publishers.
Manufactured in the United States of America

The Johns Hopkins University Press, Baltimore,
Maryland 21218
The Johns Hopkins University Press Ltd., London

Library of Congress Catalog Card Number 74-6826
ISBN 0-8018-1590-8
Library of Congress Cataloging in Publication data
will be found on the last printed page of this book.

327.73
HOW
6124

To Virginia
and our grandchildren

Contents

Foreword

Two types of writing in the field of foreign affairs go hand in hand and are essential elements in the making and recording of diplomatic history.

The first is the reduction to writing of current activity in all aspects of international affairs, or what might be called operational drafting. Despite the inroads of electronics which too often lead to stress on speed of transmission to the detriment of excellence of presentation, the need for clear and accurate writing remains, and is in fact enhanced, in the increasingly complex world in which we find ourselves.

The other and companion type of writing to which I referred is of a recording and analytical nature—historical if you will—and it picks up where the operational leaves off. To be sure, documentation does become available in various ways in official publications, presidential libraries, and other sources, but it is still in raw material form and requires intensive refining before it can be put to practical use.

This refinement may, of course, take various forms, but it can have special usefulness and value when it is focused on a particular subject of past significance and potential future concern. And it may be of added utility if the author has had the opportunity to supplement scholarly endeavor with a liberal dash of official experience conducive to an outside-inside viewpoint.

It is this type of work which we find in Dr. Harry Howard's *Turkey, the Straits and U.S. Policy.*

First of all, although Dr. Howard began his career in the academic world and is still active in it, his mid-career period was largely devoted to service in various capacities in the Department of State, where his vast fund of knowledge and sound judgment as developed in the academic field were put to good use in meeting the problems of the day, much as his official work has contributed to his subsequent academic endeavors.

Second, his choice of the Straits as his subject is of special utility and interest as a problem which has been the focus of power diplomacy for many years and which can be expected to continue to be so in the years to come. What Dr. Howard has done here is to compress the essential elements of the matter between the covers of a single volume which constitutes a definitive work upon which those who follow him can draw as a documentary starting point for future study and action.

I might add that in the many years of my association with Dr. Howard I have been aware of his constant interest in, and study of, the Straits question, and I am sure that many will join me in expressing their happiness that we are now able to share the fruit of his labors in the form of his book.

RAYMOND A. HARE

Preface

Many books have been written about the problem of the Turkish Straits—an issue which, in varying forms, may be traced back at least to the Trojan Wars (1194-84 B.C.). Relatively few have appeared in recent years, and fewer still have treated of American policy and interest in the question. One American diplomatic historian, the late Bernadotte E. Schmitt, confessed to me some years ago that he was unaware that the United States had a policy, much less an interest, until the beginnings of World War II. Since the area was on the periphery of American interest, not at the center, his unawareness was, of course, entirely understandable. A recent British writer gives no attention to the development of American policy until he comes to the period of the Paris Peace Conference in 1919—and not much then.

Like practically all of his students, I came essentially to work on the question of the Straits under the direction of the late Professor Robert J. Kerner at the University of California, when I prepared a doctoral dissertation dealing with the partition of the Ottoman Empire immediately after World War I. During World War II, as a member of the Department of State, in preparation for a possible peace conference, I made a number of studies covering not only the standard subjects of the "Eastern Question," Imperial Russia (the USSR), Great Britain, France, and the Straits, but the development of U.S. policy and interest. The subject was intriguing. Leaving the technicalities of the various conventions aside, the United States, during the nineteenth century, insisted on complete freedom of transit and navigation for American vessels regardless of restrictions in treaties and conventions to which it was not a party, and the Ottoman government seemed to put the United States in a special category, although there were limits beyond which it could not go without risking its position.

I fully realize that there are elements in the American-Turkish relationship other than those of the Straits. I make no pretence to duplicating what others have written on a wider plane. I am also aware that over the centuries other states have been more heavily involved. I have, nevertheless, taken American policy and interest in the Straits as a thread, and have attempted to tell the story of the

xi

American concern with the problem, which became of special significance following World War II. It is still possible that the problem
contains elements of importance, even in a period of instant communications and guided missiles.

The work begins with the foundations of American policy, carries
the account through World War I, the Paris Peace Conference, and the
Lausanne Conference of 1922-23, when the first of the postwar
regimes of the Straits in which the United States acquiesced was
adopted. The later chapters discuss the elaboration of the Montreux
Convention, the entry of Turkey into World War II, the "great debate"
on the question of the Straits during 1945-46, and the development
of the problem of the Straits since World War II.

Many have made helpful suggestions over the years and during
the preparation of this book, including former colleagues in the Department of State. The writer wishes to thank especially Majid
Khadduri, The School for Advanced International Studies of the
Johns Hopkins University; Rouhollah K. Ramazani, of the University
of Virginia; and William Sands, editor of the *Middle East Journal*
who read the manuscript through and contributed to its revision. I
am also grateful to Kay Manalo, managing editor of the *Journal*, for
all the work she has done in the tedious task of editing the manuscript
for publication. Peter Nulty, editorial assistant, was also most helpful
in the work of editing. As usual, I am especially grateful to my wife,
Virginia, for her long-suffering patience, understanding, and inspira-
tion. I alone, of course, assume full responsibility for all errors of
omission or commission. All others are hereby exonerated.

Turkey, the Straits
and U.S. Policy

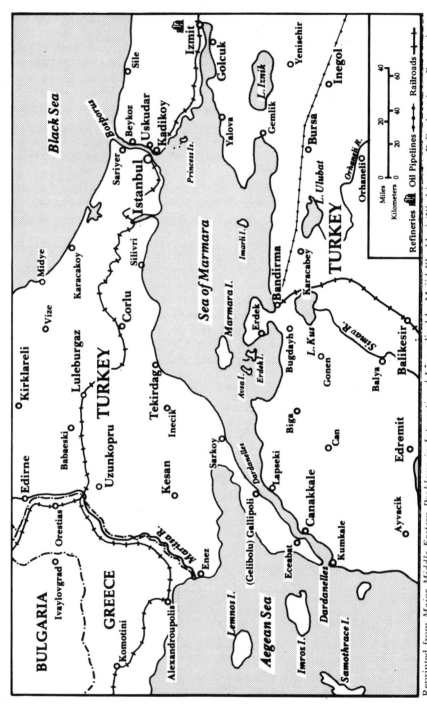

Reprinted from *Major Middle Eastern Problems in International Law*, edited by Majid Khadduri (Washington, D.C.: American Enterprise Institute for Public Policy Research, 1972).

Chapter I
The Foundations of American Policy (1830-1914)

The modern history of the problem of the Turkish Straits, essentially, begins with the Treaty of Küçük Kaynarca between Imperial Russia and the Ottoman Empire, on July 10, 1774, under which Russian commercial vessels received the right of passage through the Straits to and from the Black Sea. Subsequently, similar rights were granted to the commercial vessels of other nations as well.[1] The problem of that strategic waterway is as old as the Trojan Wars (1194-84 B.C.). The European Powers, Imperial Russia, Austro-Hungarian Empire, France, and Great Britain, had long been interested in the Ottoman Empire, and the question of the Turkish Straits was one of abiding interest. But it was not until May 7, 1830 that the United States made its first treaty with the Sublime Porte, although one had been signed with the Sultan of Morocco as early as 1787. Throughout the nineteenth century the American interest was peripheral in character, very much less than that of the European Powers, and so it remained until World War II in 1939, despite the professed American interest during 1917-18, the Wilsonian principle of the internationalization of the Straits in the Fourteen Points, and the discussions at the Paris Peace Conference.

It is well to recall that the United States sent only observers to the Lausanne Conference during 1922-23 and refused to assume any responsibilities under the Convention of the Straits, even if it did acquiesce in that instrument, and that it sent no observers at all to

[1]For convenience see Harry N. Howard, *The Problem of the Turkish Straits* (Washington, D.C.: USGPO, 1947), pp. 14 ff.; J. C. Hurewitz, *Diplomacy in the Near and Middle East*, vol. 1, *A Documentary Record, 1535-1914* (Princeton, N.J.: D. Van Nostrand, 1956), pp. 54-61. See also Alan W. Fisher, *The Russian Annexation of the Crimea, 1772-1783* (Cambridge, England: Cambridge University Press, 1970).

the Montreux Conference in 1936, once it was clear that the principle of freedom of transit and navigation in the Straits would remain unimpaired. Not until December 3, 1941, four days prior to the attack on Pearl Harbor, did the United States declare the defense of Turkey essential to its own, when it extended lend-lease assistance to that country. By this time, indeed, the problem of the Straits was becoming of much political significance to the United States, and it was of concern in the postwar years. The problem was discussed at Tehran, Yalta, and Potsdam conferences. During the summer and fall of 1946, the United States entered into the great diplomatic debate with the Soviet Union concerning the elaboration of a new regime of the Straits. By February 18, 1952, upon their entry into the North Atlantic Treaty Organization, Turkey and Greece became allies of the United States. In the years following World War II, to maintain the principle of freedom of transit through the Straits and into the Black Sea, despite Soviet protests, the United States regularly sent frigates or destroyers on routine visits. But this was a matter of the unanticipated, far-off future, in the mid-twentieth century and beyond. True, even during the nineteenth century, the United States was interested in the principle of freedom of transit and navigation, both for ships of commerce and of war, as it was in the case of other international waters. But there was relatively little American commerce in the Straits, and political interests were hardly the focus of serious attention.

The Foundations of American Policy: The Treaty of May 7, 1830

While diplomatic relations between the United States and the Ottoman Empire were not established until 1831, in 1799 President Adams appointed William Smith, of South Carolina, then minister to Portugal, to be minister to the Sublime Porte, with full authority to negotiate a treaty of commerce and amity. That mission was soon abandoned. But the American flag was displayed as early as November 9, 1800, flying from the mast of the United States frigate (USF) *George Washington*, under the command of Commodore William Bainbridge, who had been sent to Algeria with the annual American tribute to the Bey, who compelled Bainbridge to carry it to the Sultan, along with a number of passengers. Following the usual courtesies, Bainbridge was well received. His vessel was conducted to the inner harbor and the negotiation of a treaty was proposed. Bainbridge informed the Ottoman official that the President had already appointed a minister, who expected to arrive within six months, and the Capudan Pasha wrote a letter for the minister, to be carried as protection in his travels in the Ottoman Empire.[2] American merchant ships ventured into Ottoman waters even in colonial days, Izmir being the major port of call, and between 1811 and November 1820, except for the war period of 1812, no less than thirteen American vessels, on the average, arrived annually at Izmir. But the first American vessel to penetrate the Black Sea, evidently, was the *Calumet* of Boston although there was no appreciable trade with Constantinople until after the treaty of 1830.[3]

The Treaty of Commerce and Navigation, signed at Constantinople on May 7, 1830,[4] among other things, essentially secured for the United States the rights which had been granted to other states as to commercial passage of the Straits. Article VII, for example, declared: "The merchant vessels of the United States, either in ballast or laden with the production of their countries or with productions and merchandise not prohibited of the countries of the Ottoman Empire, may pass from the waters of the Imperial residence and go and come in the Black Sea like the aforesaid nations [most favored nations]." Nothing, of course, was said as to the passage of American warships, although this was not a matter of particular significance to the United States at the time. Moreover, according to "the ancient rule" of the Sultan's empire, entrance of men-of-war into the Dardanelles and the Bosphorus in time of peace was prohibited.

Development of the American Position, 1830-1862

President Andrew Jackson sent the treaty of May 1830, with its principle of freedom of commerce, to the U.S. Senate on December 15, 1830, and it was approved on February 2, 1831. On March 2, 1831, the Congress made appropriations for a legation in Constantinople

[2]Leland J. Gordon, *American Relations with Turkey, 1830-1930: An Economic Interpretation* (Philadelphia: University of Pennsylvania Press, 1932), chap. 1. See also James A. Field, *America and the Mediterranean World, 1776-1882* (Princeton, N.J.: Princeton University Press, 1969), passim.

[3]David H. Finnie, *Pioneers East: The Early American Experience in the Middle East* (Cambridge: Harvard University Press, 1967), chap. 2, notes that 12,000,000 gallons of New England rum went through Ottoman ports in the first six months of 1830. See also Sydney N. Fisher, "Two Centuries of American Interest in Turkey," in a *Festschrift for Frederick B. Artz* (Durham, N.C.: Duke University Press, 1964), pp. 113-38.

[4]See House Document No. 250, 22d Congress, 1st Session, *Negotiation of the Treaty of 1830*; D. H. Miller, *Treaties and Other International Acts of the United States of America* (Washington, D.C.: USGPO, 1931 ff.), 3: no. 69, p. 549. A secret article, ac-

and, on April 15, the President commissioned Commodore David Porter, then consul-general at Algiers, as chargé d'affaires. Porter, who was authorized to exchange ratifications, took passage on the USF *John Adams*, which passed the Dardanelles without dismounting her guns, and ratifications were duly exchanged on October 3, 1831.

THE PROBLEM OF AMERICAN WARSHIPS
IN THE STRAITS

American commerce in the Straits was not extensive, although clippers plied the Mediterranean and, in any case, occasioned few difficulties between the United States and the Sublime Porte. Interestingly enough, however, the problem of the passage of U.S. warships through the Straits,[5] although not one of major significance at all, did raise problems with the Sublime Porte, and also served to develop American policy relative to the rules governing international waterways. Moreover, the policy developed concerning the Straits underwent no essential change, in principle, prior to the outbreak of World War I, or even until 1923, when the United States acquiesced in the principles enshrined in the Lausanne Convention.

Without entering into all the details, it will be recalled that Imperial Russia had sought a special position in the Black Sea and the Straits, which included closure of the Straits to nonriverain warships, but opening to those of Russia, as indicated in the Russo-Ottoman treaties of 1798, 1805, and 1833 (Hünkâr Iskelesi), although what it achieved in 1833 was the Sultan's promise to close the Straits to all foreign warships whenever Russia was engaged in a defensive war. The London Conventions of July 15, 1840, and July 13, 1841 reaffirmed commercial freedom in time of peace and closure to foreign warships "at all times." So long as the Porte was at peace, no foreign warships were to enter the Straits, and the signatories agreed to conform to this rule. As in the past, the Sultan reserved the right

---

cording to which certain ships were to be built for the Ottoman Empire in the United States, was rejected by the Senate. Commodore John Rodgers, who was authorized to negotiate secretly in 1825 with the Capudan Pasha and instructed to secure freedom of movement through the Dardanelles, visited Constantinople with his squadron in July 1826. See also Finnie, *Pioneers East*, chap. 3, on the negotiations and the work of Henry Eckford and Foster Rhodes in rebuilding the Ottoman fleet after the disaster at Navarino (1827).

[5]When Commodore Patterson requested permission for passage of the USF *United States* in the fall of 1835, on advice of the Russian Embassy, the Porte rejected the request to avoid a precedent. See, especially, Serge Goriainov, *Le Bosphore et les Dardanelles. Etude Historique sur la Question des Détroits. D'après la correspondance diplomatique déposée aux archives centrales de Saint-Petersbourg et à celles de L'Empire*, Preface de M. Gabriel Hanotaux, de l'Academie française (Paris: Plon, 1910), p. 45.

to deliver *firmans* of passage for light warships, employed in the service of foreign missions in the Ottoman Empire. Subsequently, these principles were confirmed in the Treaty of Paris, March 30, 1856, following the Crimean War, and the Black Sea was demilitarized, the flag of war being prohibited "in perpetuity," although the contracting parties were to have two *stationnaires* at the mouth of the Danube, and the Ottoman Empire and Russia were to have six 800-ton steam vessels and four 200-ton vessels.[6]

The United States was not a party to any of these international instruments and did not intend to accept the restrictions which they imposed on passage of the Straits by American warships. American warships had passed the Dardanelles on a number of occasions. One noteworthy case in the period just prior to the outbreak of the Crimean War, which had led to the Treaty of 1856, was concerned with the journey of Louis Kossuth, the Hungarian patriot and rebel, to the United States, following the defeat of the Hungarian revolutionaries in 1849. Kossuth obtained asylum in the Ottoman Empire, and on February 28, 1851, Secretary of State Daniel Webster, who was much interested in bringing Kossuth to the United States, instructed George P. Marsh, the American minister to the Sublime Porte, that "compliance with the wishes of the Government and people of the United States in this respect will be regarded as a friendly recognition of their intercession, and as a proof of national good will and regard." The Ottoman government was, indeed, well disposed, and on September 7, 1851 the USF *Mississippi* sailed up the Dardanelles and was met by an Ottoman frigate at Gemlik, where Kossuth embarked. There was evidently considerable rejoicing, for we are told: "When the sea had trembled to the shouts, Captain Long began to speak, but the accents died away in "three cheers more for Kossuth!'" Tranquillity soon returned to the deck of the noble bark, and Kossuth retiring with his

[6]E. Hertslet, *Map of Europe by Treaty* (London, 1875-91), 2: 925-28, 1008-12, 1024-26, 1250-65; Gabriel Noradoughian, *Recueil d'Actes Internationaux de l'Empire Ottoman* (Paris, 1900), 2: 230, 303 ff.; C. C. Hyde, *International Law* (Boston: Houghton Mifflin, 1945), 1: 519-21. See also Goriainov, *Le Bosphore et les Dardanelles*, pp. 25-81; Hurewitz, *Diplomacy in the Near and Middle East*, 1: 72-77, 105-06; "Russia and the Turkish Straits: A Revaluation of the Origins of the Problem," *World Politics* 14, no. 4 (July 1962): 605-32; "The Background of Russia's Claims to the Turkish Straits," *Belleten* 28, no. 111 (1964): 459-503; R. J. Kerner, "Russia's New Policy in the Near East After the Peace of Adrianople," *Cambridge Historical Journal* 5, no. 3 (1937): 280-90; A. N. Mandelstam, *La Politique Russe d'Accès à la Méditerranée au XXeme Siècle* (The Hague: Academie de Droit International, *Recueil des Cours* 47 [1934]), 1: 603-798; P. E. Mosely, *Russian Diplomacy and the Opening of the Straits Question in 1838 and 1839* (Cambridge: Harvard University Press, 1934); V. J. Puryear, *England, Russia and the Straits Question* (Berkeley: University of California Press, 1931); *France and the Levant* (Berkeley: University of California Press, 1941); *Napoleon and the Dardanelles* (Berkeley: University of California Press, 1951).

family to his comfortable and pleasant rooms, the *Mississippi* struck with her strong arms the romantic waters of the Dardanelles; the foaming wake lengthened swiftly, and the minarets of the Sultan's domain disappeared in the haze of the distance, while a greater than Czesar was borne away amid the perils of the sea!'"[7]

Passage of the *Mississippi* in September 1851 had constituted no problem. The case of the USF *Wabash* in 1858, two years after the signature of the Treaty of Paris, did.[8] The United States sought in 1858, and subsequently obtained, a *firman* from the Sultan for the service of the United States legation. When the somewhat large frigate, the USF *Wabash*, carrying more than fifty guns, arrived at Constantinople in the autumn of 1858, however, the representatives of France, Great Britain, and Russia protested to the Porte which, in turn, made representations to the American minister, James Williams. The *Wabash* soon departed for Mediterranean waters, after having received the Sultan on board, since he wished to display special courtesy toward the Americans for the reception which Ottoman naval officers had received in the United States in 1857.[9] Prince Gorchakov, the Russian chancellor, explained that the Imperial Russian government was not animated by any unfriendly sentiments toward the United States, but

---

[7]P. C. Headley, *The Life of Louis Kossuth, Governor of Hungary, Including Notices of the Men and Scenes of the Hungarian Revolution; to Which Is Added an Appendix Containing His Principal Speeches, etc. With an Introduction by Horace Greeley* (Auburn: Derby and Miller, 1852), pp. 228–29. See also Samuel Flagg Bemis, *A Diplomatic History of the United States* (New York: Holt, 1950), pp. 311–12; David Lowenthal, *George Perkins Marsh: Versatile Vermonter* (New York: Columbia University Press, 1958), passim; Y. T. Kurat, "The European Powers and the Question of the Hungarian Refugees of 1849" (Ph.D. dissertation, University of London). Kossuth left the *Mississippi* at Gibraltar in order to visit London prior to coming to the United States. Captain George C. Read visited Constantinople during 1832 in the USF *Constellation*; Commodore Daniel T. Patterson paid a month's visit in the fall of 1833 in the USF *United States*, although no frigate of that size of any nation previously had been permitted to pass unless carrying a minister or ambassador. In 1837 the USF *Constitution* cruised the Mediterranean and visited Constantinople. The brig *Truxton* passed the Dardanelles in 1843 to bring home the body of the first American minister resident, Commodore David Porter, and in 1844 the USF *Plymouth* passed the Dardanelles, but was not allowed to sail into the Black Sea. Between 1831 and the outbreak of the Crimean War American warships passed the Straits on thirteen occasions. See Field, *America and the Mediterranean World*, pp. 165–75, 195–98.

[8]For a general analysis of passage of warships during this period, see Erik Brüel, *International Straits: A Treatise on International Law* (London: Sweet and Maxwell, 1947), vol. 2, *Straits Comprised by Postive Regulations*, pp. 269, 285–89. Puryear, *Napoleon and the Dardanelles*, p. 362, notes no archival records as to navigation of the Straits by warships up to 1809, except those of Russia as an active ally from 1798 to 1805. There were some exceptions, including the Russian vessel, the *Kriepost*, in April 1699, and some American vessels, as noted above.

[9]Goriainov, *Le Bosphore et les Dardanelles*, pp. 292–93; Coleman Phillipson and Noel Buxton, *The Question of the Bosphorus and Dardanelles* (London: Stevens and Haynes, 1917), pp. 151–52.

was solely concerned with the principles embodied in the Treaty of
Paris concerning the passage of warships through the Straits. In a
dispatch of January 14, 1859, to St. Petersburg, Secretary of State
Lewis Cass advised the American minister, Francis W. Pickens, that
since the United States was not a party to the Treaty of Paris, it could
not "be expected to act in conformity with the views of any other of
those parties than the Sublime Porte."[10]

THE TREATY OF 1862

American relations with the Ottoman Empire during the Civil War
were very friendly. Edward Joy Morris, who arrived in Constantinople
as minister resident in 1861, was cordially received.[11] Throughout the
war the Ottoman government looked with favor upon the Union cause,
and on March 26, 1862 an order was issued prohibiting the entrance of
privateers or any class of vessels into the ports and waters of the
Ottoman Empire fitted out for the purpose of preying upon American
commerce and exempting U.S. warships from any restrictions.[12] Morris
considered the Ottoman action, taken at his request, as a "sign of the
determination of the Turkish Government to discountenance the
hostile designs of the rebels against the integrity of the republic of the
United States." He noted that the Sublime Porte never recognized the
Confederate States of America as a belligerent, despite the action of
Great Britain and France in so doing. Nor did it, "at any time, directly
or indirectly, manifest any sympathy with their efforts for the destruction of the American Union." To the contrary: "During the whole
period of the war the war vessels of the United States enjoyed unlimited hospitality of the Turkish ports, and they were never put upon
a level with the rebel cruisers, and subject to an odious and unjust
restriction of twenty-four hours' stay in the harbors of this empire.
The above order was issued in good faith, and it would have been en-
forced to its full extent had occasion required it."

Moreover, as early as February 25, 1862, the United States and the
Ottoman Empire signed a new treaty of commerce and navigation,

[10]See, especially, John Bassett Moore, *A Digest of International Law* (Washington,
D.C.: USGPO, 1906), 1: 664 ff.; Marjorie M. Whiteman, ed., *Digest of International Law*
(Washington, D.C.: USGPO, 1965), 4: 307–43, 417–80.

[11]Harry N. Howard, "President Lincoln's Minister Resident to the Sublime Porte:
Edward Joy Morris (1861-1870)," *Balkan Studies* 5 (1964): 205–20.

[12]Department of State, *Foreign Relations of the United States, 1862* (Washington,
D.C.: USGPO, 1861 ff.), p. 788, hereafter referred to as *USFR*. See also Morris's dispatch of July 13, 1865, in which he cites the date of this order as April 23, 1862, and
provides a text. *Papers Relating to Foreign Affairs, Accompanying the Annual Message
of the President to the First Session, Thirty-Ninth Congress* (Washington, D.C.:
USGPO), 3: 297–98.

which was proclaimed on July 2, 1862. Among other things, the new treaty stipulated:

All rights, privileges, and immunities, which have been conferred on the citizens or vessels of the United States of America by treaty already existing between the United States of America and the Ottoman Empire, are confirmed, now and forever, with the exception of those clauses of the said treaty which it is the object of the present treaty to modify; and it is moreover expressly stipulated that all rights, privileges, or immunities, which the Sublime Porte now grants, or may hereafter grant to, or suffer to be enjoyed by the subjects, ships, commerce, or navigation of any foreign power, shall be equally granted to and exercised and enjoyed by the subjects, ships, commerce, or navigation of any other foreign power, shall be equally granted to and exercised and enjoyed by the citizens, vessels, commerce, and navigation of the United States of America.[13]

The United States formally thanked Sultan Abdul Aziz, and on June 24, 1862, Secretary of State William H. Seward declared that it would be "to the honor of the Sultan of Turkey that he took the lead in conceding to the United States rights which, it is now expected, will soon be conceded by all the other maritime powers."

The Basic American Position, 1866–1871

Following the American Civil War, on January 22, 1866, Morris advised Secretary of State Seward that he had joined his colleagues in a note to the Porte requesting permission for sailing vessels to pass through the Bosphorus and Dardanelles during the night. Similarly, on February 28, 1866, he advised the Department of State that, although American commerce therein was "inconsiderable," he had joined in a note to the Sublime Porte about the position of commerce in the Black Sea, in order to obtain protection for lives and property "on this 'tempestuous sea." Since this was a very limited approach to the problem, Seward approved.[14]

Later in the year, on September 7, 1866, the USF *Ticonderoga*, under the command of Commodore Steedman, arrived at Constantinople for an eleven-day visit.[15] Commodore Steedman was received by the Grand Vizier, presented to the diplomatic corps, and dined with the British and Russian ambassadors. Morris duly noted that there had

---

[13]Article I. See W. M. Malloy, *Treaties, Conventions, International Acts, Protocols and Agreements between the United States of America and Other Powers, 1776–1909* (Washington, D.C.: USGPO, 1910), 2: 1321–28.

[14]*USFR* (1866), 2: 236–40. Total American–Ottoman trade in 1876 was less than $4,000,000.

[15]Ibid., p. 252.

been no untoward incidents during the visit and that the *Ticonderoga* was "the second U.S. man-of-war which has been admitted to Constantinople since the formation of treaties excluding war vessels above the size of naval despatch boats from the Dardanelles and the Bosphorus. The moral and political effects of the visit cannot fail to be of the most salutary character; and it is the more remarkable as no vessel of her dimensions belonging to any European power is admitted to pass through the Straits to Constantinople."

But Morris was also concerned with Russian pretensions to control of Constantinople and the Straits. Commenting, on February 28, 1868, on the developments in the Danubian Principalities of Moldavia and Wallachia, which looked ultimately toward the establishment of an independent and unified state of Rumania, he wrote that "the absorption of the principalities by Russia would put that power in possession of all the available routes of access to Constantinople" and "render it almost impossible to defend the capital with any prospect of success."[16] Later, on November 2, 1866, Morris advised the Department of State of the recognition of Prince Karl von Hohenzollern-Sigmaringen as Hospodar of the Danubian Principalities and of the fact that the project for union did not please St. Petersburg. That would "throw obstacles in the way of Russian progress to Constantinople, and it is therefore questionable if Roumania will enjoy, even under Prince Hohenzollern, the tranquillity and repose necessary to its development into an independent national existence."

On the other hand, Cassius Marcellus Clay, the American minister in St. Petersburg,[17] who did not doubt that some persons in high places in the Russian capital desired "the possession of Constantinople and the Straits," speculated that the "ruling minds" looked upon the project, not as something to be fought for, "or bought at a great price of money or blood." It was acceptable, however, "if good fortune should throw it into their power." Russia did not desire war, but it would not permit "any great power to take Constantinople without a great war." On the other hand, Russia might carry on a war for the protection of the Balkan Slavs and the Greeks and, if a Greek Empire should be established on the Hellespont and the Black Sea, Russia, in Clay's view, would hope "to find in it a permanent and grateful ally, and not a jealous enemy." Indeed, that might prove to be "the ultimate and peaceable solution of the eastern problem." In sum, Russian policy seemed to call for: "First the gradual autonomy of the Sclave and Greek provinces, till the Turkish rule ceases; and then the Straits in

---

[16]Ibid., pp. 237–38, 254–55.
[17]For Clay see Jay Monaghan, *Diplomat in Carpet Slippers* (Indianapolis: Bobbs Merrill, 1945), passim.

the hands of a petty power, protected by all the great rivals, or ultimately a respectable Greek empire or kingdom, absorbing all the
Greek and Sclave subjects now belonging to Turkey."[18]

CONGRESSIONAL PRINCIPLES ON FREEDOM OF NAVIGATION IN THE STRAITS

No doubt the action of the U.S. House of Representatives relative
to passage of the Straits reflected something of a general interest in
the problem, based largely on the rather vague principles of freedom
of the seas. On Monday, July 6, 1868, Representative William D.
Kelley of Pennsylvania, by unanimous consent, submitted the following resolution, which was read and approved, evidently without
serious discussion, if any at all, of the issues and treaties involved, if
the record of the proceedings reflects accurately the deliberations:

> Resolved, that the President be requested to instruct the Minister of the
> United States to the Sublime Porte to urge upon the Government of the Sultan
> the abolition of all restrictions through the Straits of the Dardanelles and
> Bosphorus to the Black Sea, and to endeavor to procure the perfect freedom of
> navigation through those Straits to all classes of vessels.[19]

Morris, the minister to Constantinople, was rather favorably impressed with this unanimous expression of congressional sentiment,
although the resolution in fact made little, if any, practical sense. He
advised the Secretary of State on July 20 that the time had come when
the restrictions on warships "should be abolished altogether and when
their navigation" in the Straits and the Black Sea "should be open to
all the navies of the world." Later he wrote to Seward with considerable prescience:[20] "During the Crimean War, the American shipping interest in the region was quite large. It is now inconsiderable,
but the future of the United States is so vast and the enterprise of the
American people so great, that our commerce may take quite a large
development in this part of the East at no distant period. In this aspect
the restrictions and regulations in question seem to deserve consideration." Morris felt that the restrictions imposed by existing treaties, to
which, in any event, the United States was not a party, were harmful
to commerce and contrary to the American–Ottoman treaty of 1862,
which he had negotiated.

---

[18]USFR (1867), 1: 384–85, for Clay's dispatch of March 20, 1867. See also Domna
Dontas, Greece and the Great Powers, 1863–1875 (Thessaloniki: Institute for Balkan
Studies, 1966).

[19]Congressional Globe, 74, pt. 4, 40th Congress, 2nd Session (1867–68), pp. 3764–65.

[20]See his Despatch No. 263, July 20, 1868; National Archives, Turkey No. 20, E. J.
Morris, May 3, 1867–March 3, 1869, pp. 205–394, Department of State. See also his
dispatch of August 1868.

On the other hand, an anonymous brochure of the time, written by the Ottoman consul general in New York, Christopher Oscanyan, an Armenian Christian, as if he were an American citizen, observed that the restrictions on the passage of warships had served both the interest of "guaranteeing the integrity of the Ottoman Empire, and of insuring a safeguard to European peace." It also noted that, by signing the treaty of 1830, the United States had accepted the restrictions and that, as to commercial passage, the Sublime Porte had "always shown a readiness to remove all causes of hindrance thereto, and to lessen the obstacles which interfere with navigation." As the author put the matter:

> Do we not also discover the object of the Kelley proposition? Whatever this may be, should we find ourselves forced to a choice between the false, equivocal, and dangerous policy which this proposition seems to indicate; where interests of natures so different, that they could not be mingled save by a resort to diplomacy, or complications still more weighty, are confused and confounded, whether unintentionally or by design; were we called to choose between this proposition and the course of the American statesmen of 1830, who were so careful to exclude from their treaty all that could call in question its strictly commercial character—while we do not impugn the intention of the honorable Representative from Pennsylvania—we should not hesitate to avow our preference for the policy, at once wise, loyal, and dignified, of Van Buren, Clay, and John Quincy Adams.[21]

Beyond instructing the minister to obtain such information as he could relative to the various restrictions or obstructions to which commercial vessels were subjected, however, no action appears to have been taken under this congressional resolution.[22] Secretary of State Seward sent an instruction to Morris on July 11, 1868, and a similar one was addressed to Clay in St. Petersburg who, however, failed to obtain the desired information. On October 5, nevertheless, Baron Stoeckl, the Russian minister in Washington, was informed that it was "uncertain" whether President Johnson would take any action under the resolution. At the same time, the Russian minister was advised that, in principle, the United States favored the "largest freedom of navigation and commerce compatible with the rights of individual nations" and, therefore, could be expected to favor "the removal of the restrictions upon the navigation of the Bosphorus and Dardanelles within the limits of international law."

---

[21] *The United States and Turkey* (Washington, D.C.: McGill and Witherow, 1868), pp. 1–17. See also Christopher Oscanyan, *The Sultan and His People, by a Native of Turkey* (New York: Derby and Jackson, 1857).

[22] Moore, *Digest of International Law*, 1: 664 ff.

THE VISIT OF ADMIRAL FARRAGUT TO CONSTANTINOPLE, AUGUST 1868

Meanwhile, the visit of Admiral David Glasgow Farragut to Constantinople on the USF *Frolic*, which Morris reported on August 24, 1868, served to test the principles governing the passage of foreign warships through the Straits.[23] Since the *Frolic* was well within the tonnage limitations prescribed in the Treaty of Paris (1856), the application for a *firman* of passage was promptly granted. Some days later, however, Admiral Farragut's flagship, the USF *Franklin*, on which he was making a round-the-world trip, was reported at the entrance of the Dardanelles awaiting the Admiral's orders on his departure from Constantinople. Since Morris thought so eminent an officer of the United States Navy should have exceptional honors, he conferred with Ali Pasha, the grand vizier, and Fuad Pasha, the foreign minister, regarding a *firman* to suspend the rules of the Treaty of Paris, "by which vessels of war of the dimensions of the *Franklin*" were excluded from the Straits. Informed, at first, that exceptions "were only made in favor of princes of the blood," Morris promptly replied that under such a rule, the United States, a democracy with no royalty, "would not enjoy the same privileges as the aristocratic states of Europe, and that this provision of the treaty was partial in its application, and to the derogation of our dignity." Morris was a Philadelphia lawyer! Advised to make formal application, he did so, and was "pleased to know that His Majesty the Sultan desired the entrance of the *Franklin*." On August 18, Morris made application and, two days later, on August 20, he received the reply of the Sublime Porte: "As you have been pleased to recognize in the said note, the existing treaties have established the principle of the closing of the Straits. Although the dimensions of the vessel in question exceed the limits expressly fixed by the treaty of Paris, His Majesty the Sultan, my august sovereign, desirous nevertheless of giving proof of his deferential regard for a distinguished personnage of the great American republic, has been pleased for this purpose, and in a manner altogether exceptional, to grant the permission asked for the passage of the frigate *Franklin*."[24]

Fuad Pasha begged Morris to take "note of the exceptional character of the granted authorization." At about the same time, August 19, the Porte sent a circular note to the signatories of the Treaty of Paris represented at Constantinople, stating:

[23] *USFR* (1868), 2: 114–15.

[24] Ibid., p. 116. See also Charles Lee Lewis, *David Glasgow Farragut: Our First Admiral* (Annapolis: United States Naval Institute, 1943), pp. 359–85.

The flag-ship of Admiral Farragut having arrived at the Dardanelles, the United States Legation, admitting the principle of the closing of the Straits as established by the treaties, has expressed to us the desire that the said vessel should be permitted to pass through the Straits to Constantinople. The dimensions of the naval vessel in question are, it is true, beyond the limitations stipulated in the Treaty of Paris; but his Imperial Majesty the Sultan, wishing to testify his regard for the great American republic, and to see this magnificent frigate, has for this purpose, and in a manner altogether exceptional, granted the requested permission. I have deemed it my duty to bring this fact to the knowledge of the representatives of the powers parties to the above treaty and I beg them to take notice of the exceptional character of the granted authorization, which, I have no doubt, they will find sufficiently justified.[25]

On August 23, Morris advised Fuad Pasha of his pleasure that the exception had been made and a *firman* for passage granted.

Morris felt, indeed, that Admiral Farragut was treated with "rare courtesy" and "in a manner altogether unexceptional." The Admiral was presented to the Sultan, was given a dinner by the Grand Vizier, and the British and Russian ambassadors gave dinners in his honor, the French Ambassador being ill. All told, Morris believed that the visit of Admiral Farragut to Constantinople, accompanied by the arrival of his flagship, would "prove a most auspicious one in every respect." One interesting and incidental byproduct of the visit was that Admiral Farragut was instrumental in obtaining an imperial charter for Robert College.[26] Farragut entertained the Grand Vizier and the Minister for Foreign Affairs, together with the diplomatic corps, on his flagship on August 26, although the Sultan was unable to attend, and the Ottoman authorities extended "every civility." He sailed on August 29 for the Piraeus with the *Franklin* and the *Frolic*.[27]

But the visit did raise problems, and some weeks after Farragut's departure, on September 28, 1868, Savfet Pasha circularized the Powers, including the United States, on the prohibition of the passage of the Dardanelles and the Bosphorus by foreign warships, recalling the ancient rule of closure and the conventions of 1841 and 1856. Among other things, the note stated:

This principle has always been maintained; and if on rare and exceptional occasions it has been permitted to some vessels of war to pass the straits, it was always in virtue of a special authorization accorded out of deference to the distinguished personnages on board of them.

[25] *USFR* (1868), 2: 118.
[26] See Cyrus Hamlin, *My Life and Times* (Boston: Pilgrim Press, 1893, 1924), pp. 432, 443-50; George Washburn, *Fifty Years in Constantinople* (Boston: Houghton Mifflin, 1909), pp. 12-13; Lewis, *Farragut*, pp. 262-63; Cyrus Hamlin, *Among the Turks* (New York: Robert Carter, 1878), passim. See also Robert L. Daniel, *American Philanthropy in the Near East, 1820-1960* (Athens, Ohio: Ohio University Press, 1970), pp. 71 ff.
[27] *USFR* (1868), 2: 116.

The Sublime Porte, however, recognizes that a relaxation in the strict application of the aforesaid principle with respect to vessels of war, apart from the exceptions provided by articles 2 and 3 of the convention of March 30, 1856, would not be compatible with the declaration contained in the aforesaid treaty of Paris.

It has, therefore, been decided that, henceforward, there will positively be no exception but for vessels of war which have on board a sovereign or the chief of an independent state.

The preceding decision having been sanctioned by his Imperial Majesty the Sultan, I have the honor to beg you to report it to the Government of the United States for its information.[28]

Morris did so on October 2, 1868, and he sent the various exchanges concerning the problem to the Department of State in a dispatch of October 29, 1868.[29]

THE BASIC PRINCIPLES OF AMERICAN POLICY, 1871-1872

An intense era in the development of the "Eastern Question" opened in the 1870s, and the question of the Straits played a prominent role at the time. It was altogether fitting that the United States, which seemed so remote from the problem, should be somewhat interested. During the Franco-Prussian war of 1870-71, namely, on October 31, 1870, the Russian government repudiated the restrictive clauses as to naval armament in the Black Sea, which had been "demilitarized," if not "neutralized," in the Treaty of 1856. While Bismarck's Germany supported St. Petersburg and France was unable to act, Great Britain and Austria-Hungary strongly protested the Russian move. On December 6, 1870, Wayne MacVeagh, the American minister to the Sublime Porte, indicated that a conference on the "Eastern Question" had been proposed, and that "the peaceable solution of the difficulty" was regarded as certain.[30] Some weeks later, on December 31, MacVeagh wrote of "the unsettled state of the public mind" in Constantinople, referred to various problems, and stated that he hoped to send a dispatch "of some interest by the next mail on the subject of the Straits of the Dardanelles and the Bosphorus," since he had heard a rumor that "the approaching conference" would "consider the question of their use by foreign powers." He added that "their importance is increasing day by day," and the time could not "be very far distant when an authoritative determination of their status" would "be required alike in the interest of commerce and of peace."[31]

[28]Ibid., p. 117. de Martens, *Nouveau Recueil*, 64: 268-69.
[29]*USFR* (1868), 2: 117.
[30]*USFR* (1871): 887. For a recent study see M. S. Anderson, *The Eastern Question, 1774-1923* (New York: St. Martin's, 1966), chaps. 6 and 7. See also Barbara Jelavich, *The Ottoman Empire, the Great Powers and the Straits Question, 1870-1887* (Bloomington: Indiana University Press, 1973), especially chaps. 2 and 3.
[31]*USFR* (1871): 888-89.

A few days later, on January 5, 1871, Secretary of State Hamilton Fish advised MacVeagh concerning an "absurd newspaper report of a letter from President Grant to the Emperor of Russia congratulating the latter upon his denunciation of the clause of the treaty of Paris which restricts freedom of navigation in the Black Sea." He noted:

The occasions are rare which are conceived to warrant or require a deviation on the part of the President from the rule which limits his communications to foreign sovereigns to mere letters of ceremony. The occasion adverted to was not deemed sufficient to call for any such communication. It is true that the United States, not having been a party to the treaty of Paris, may have more or less reason to complain of any curtailment of their rights under the law of nations which it may have effected. No formal complaint on the subject, however, has as yet been addressed to either of the parties to that instrument, though the restriction which it imposes on the right of our men-of-war to the passage of the Dardanelles and the Bosphorus is under serious consideration.[32]

MacVeagh sent the Department of State a long dispatch on January 24, 1871, analyzing the development of the treaty position concerning the regime of the Straits,[33] since the Conference of London was then considering the problem with the Russians, which, among other things, commented on the politico-strategic situation of the Straits:

On the west the narrow Straits of the Dardanelles connect the Sea of Marmora with the Greek Archipelago; on the east the narrow Straits of the Bosphorus connect the Sea of Marmora with the Black Sea. From the beginning of one strait to the end of the other the shores on both sides belong exclusively to the Ottoman Empire; and its capital and chief city is at the meeting of the waters of the Straits of the Bosphorus and of the Sea of Marmora. This site is asserted to be practically incapable of defense against an attack by a naval force, except at the two entrances . . . , and it is also asserted that the absolute necessity of fortifying and defending these entrances, as the only means of securing the safety of Constantinople from attacks by sea, was recognized centuries before the conquest of the country by Ottoman Sultans, and that the same necessity has been constantly asserted and maintained ever since. In this view all the waters connecting the Greek Archipelago with the Black Sea are *mare clausum*, and are navigable by the consent of and under the restrictions imposed by the Government of the Ottoman Empire.

[32]Ibid., p. 890. In view of the general position relative to freedom of passage through the Straits, the United States was somewhat sympathetic to the Russian move, but it did not offer an offensive and defensive alliance to Russia, as Goriainov suggests, if the latter would support the United States in the *Alabama* case, and it was inconceivable that it was ready to force the issue by sending an American fleet through the Dardanelles. See Goriainov, *Le Bosphore et les Dardanelles*, p. 193; Phillipson and Buxton, *Question of the Bosphorus and Dardanelles*, pp. 111-12; James T. Shotwell and Francis Deak, *Turkey at the Straits: A Short History* (New York: Macmillan, 1940), pp. 51-52.
[33]*USFR* (1871): 892-96. For excerpts from the protocols of the Conference of 1871, see Great Britain, Foreign Office, Turkey No. 16 (1878), *Treaties and Other Documents Relating to the Black Sea, the Dardanelles, and the Bosphorus: 1535-1877* (translations), Cmd. 1953, pp. 54-57, 57-59, 61-67. For convenience see also Harry N. Howard, *The Problem of the Turkish Straits*, 14 ff.

MacVeagh also observed that, both as to commercial passage and that of warships, the Ottoman government alleged "that its policy has been uniform and as liberal as a proper regard for its own safety would allow; and that its conduct in the exercise of its undoubted rights of control over these connecting waters has often received, as it has always deserved, the approval of all friendly powers." MacVeagh then reviewed the treaties governing passage of the Straits, going back to 1535, but laying special stress on the treaties of Küçük Kaynarca (1774), Adrianople (1829), and Hünkàr Iskelesi (1833). He added that the Ottoman-American treaty of May 7, 1830

was concluded with the Porte, securing to us all the privileges of the most favored nations, and providing that "the merchant vessels of the United States shall have liberty to pass the canal of the imperial residence, the Bosphorus, and go and come in the Black Sea." Our treaty of commerce— 1862—contains upon this subject only the clause usually inserted in commercial treaties concluded in recent years with the Porte. "The firmans required for merchant vessels of the United States on passing through the Dardanelles and the Bosphorus shall always be delivered in such manner as to occasion to such vessels the least possible delay." It will thus be seen that the fullest liberty exists for the navigation of all these connecting waters by the merchant vessels of all nations.

MacVeagh felt, however, that the regulations were antiquated and "unnecessarily vexatious," particularly in view of the required sanitary inspections and the delays occasioned thereby. He thought that while there was no serious objection to the rights claimed by the Porte, "the mode of asserting and exacting them" was "objectionable." But a contrary situation existed with regard to the passage of warships, in view of the "ancient rule of the Ottoman Empire" against free passage, sanctioned by the Anglo-Ottoman treaty of 1809, and in the secret clause of the treaty of Hünkàr Iskelesi, as well as in the treaty of 1840. MacVeagh also referred to a circular delivered by the Porte on March 5, 1842,[34] requesting the Powers to observe the "ancient rule," which had been confirmed in 1850 and 1861:

This circular was transmitted to Washington by Commodore Porter, then occupying this mission, April 16, 1842. It only remains to add that the Convention of the Dardanelles was reenacted in terms, and annexed to the Treaty of Paris of 1856, and that an exception has always existed to the "ancient rule" in question in favor of armed vessels of moderate size visiting the Porte, by special permission, on missions of friendship, or attached to the service of foreign legations at Constantinople. It will be seen, therefore, that the closing of these straits to ships of war has never been rested upon the agreement of the powers recognizing it, but always upon the undoubted rights of the Ottoman Empire, and while six great powers at Paris in 1856 recognized this usage it is

[34]For text, see *Cmd. 1953* (1878): 22.

not known that any power at any time has ever questioned either its propriety or its validity.

In the end, the London Conference, on March 13, 1871,[35] accepted the Russian position concerning remilitarization of the Black Sea, although it declared against breaches of such international agreements. Among other things, the new convention, signed by Austria-Hungary, France, Germany (Prussia), Great Britain, Italy, Russia, and the Ottoman Empire, not only abrogated the restrictive Black Sea clauses, but stipulated:

> *Article II.*—The principle of the closing of the Straits of the Dardanelles and the Bosphorus, such as it has been established by the separate Convention of March 30, 1856, is maintained, with power to His Imperial Majesty the Sultan to open the said Straits in time of peace to the vessels of war of friendly and allied powers, in case the Sublime Porte should judge it necessary to secure the execution of the stipulation of the Treaty of Paris of March 30, 1856.
>
> *Article III.*—The Black Sea remains open, as heretofore, to the mercantile marine of all nations.

In view of the dispatch of Hamilton Fish, of January 5, 1871, MacVeagh, on March 27, sent another long communication concerning the problem,[36] pointing out that the "ancient rule of the exclusion of ships of war" was maintained "except when the Porte deems it necessary to open them to allied and friendly fleets to secure the objects of the treaty of Paris of 1856; in other words, to resist the attack of an enemy." It might, therefore, "become important at any moment" for the Department of State to consider the question of "the denial of the passage of these straits to our ships of war," as the Secretary of State had hinted. While the Sublime Porte's position, according to MacVeagh, in this respect did not rest on treaties, it did rest solely "upon the imperial usage of this empire; a usage explicitly recognized by the authoritative treatise of our own Wheaton, sanctioned by the recognition and respect of all nations at peace with the Porte since the possession of Constantinople by the Ottoman Sultans, and whose validity and prosperity are not known to have been ever seriously questioned." But the mode of exercising this right had, from time to time, been the subject of treaties and agreements, as noted above. Moreover, "if, therefore, the Porte has the right of closing these straits to vessels of war, the mode of the exercise of that right would seem to be wholly unobjectionable at the present time, for, unlike the Russian treaty of 1833, the present treaty operates upon all nations with perfect equality. The recognition of this right of the Porte by the Government of the United States has been frequent and uniform."

[35]Hertslet, *Map of Europe*, 3: 1920-21.   [36]*USFR* (1871): 897-900.

MacVeagh then gave a brief history, down to 1871, of the passage, or attempted passage, of American warships through the Straits, indicating that "during the forty years of friendly intercourse" hardly a year had passed without an application for the passage of an American warship, in virtue of the exception to which he had alluded. He noted the pleasure expressed by the United States in 1868 on the occasion of the Farragut visit. But the Minister went on to state: "The passage of our vessels of war has uniformly been requested in writing, and either as within the exception to the rule, or as an act of special courtesy in suspension of it. In the latter case, it has uniformly been followed by the thanks of our Government for the favor. . . . We began our intercourse with Turkey by a treaty which secured for our vessels of commerce the right of passing these straits; and thus excluding the idea that we possessed the same right for our ships of war. In the long interval we have uniformly recognized, in all the modes known to diplomatic intercourse, the continued existence of the distinction."[37] But American practice and policy, thus far, had been consonant with that of other Powers, and it was felt that any deviation therefrom "would certainly require very grave reasons for its justification," although the United States was not following the general policies of the European Powers and was not bound to do so in this respect. MacVeagh indicated that he had taken every opportunity to assert a sincere American friendship for the Ottoman Empire, that the United States was a partisan of "no power, whether friendly or hostile" to the Ottoman Empire, and that it "remembered with gratitude the unswerving fidelity of the Porte during our great struggle." At the same time, however, he stated frankly that "in the interest of our general policy we would rejoice at the opening of these waters to the unrestricted navigation of the globe, and that we would continue to cherish the hope that it would before long appear to the government of the Sultan to be compatible in every way with its interest and its safety to abandon in this respect the ancient usages of the empire. In the meantime, however, I have added, it would be grossly unjust to the United States to imagine for a moment that it would suffer itself to be used as the agent or ally of any other subject."

Secretary of State Fish replied on May 5, 1871, in a communication which laid down the basic policy of the United States which, granted the changes of time and circumstance, was to be followed, essentially and in principle, until the Lausanne Convention of July 24, 1923. Among other things, he wrote:

[37]MacVeagh noted, of course, that "in time of peace no war vessel of any nation is allowed to enter these connecting waters. On the east the fortresses of the Bosphorus, and on the west the fortresses of the Dardanelles, prohibit and deny such entrances to the war flag of any nation, however friendly to the Sublime Porte."

This Government is not disposed to prematurely raise any question to disturb the existing control which Turkey claims over the Straits leading into the Euxine. It has observed the acquiescence of other Powers whose greater propinquity would suggest more intimate interests in the usage of other powers from the passage of those straits.

But while this Government does not deny the existence and the usage, and has had no occasion to question the propriety of its observance, *the President deems it important to avoid recognizing it as a right under the law of nations.*

The position of Turkey with reference to the Euxine may be compared to that of Denmark with reference to the Baltic, with the difference that the former is sovereign over the soil on both sides of the straits, while Sweden owns the territory on the east of the sound leading to the Baltic.

We are not aware that Denmark claimed the right to exclude foreign vessels of war from the Baltic merely because in proceeding thither they must necessarily pass within cannon-shot of her shores. If this right has been claimed by Turkey in respect of the Black Sea, it must have originated at a time when she was positively and comparatively in much more advantageous position to enforce it than she now is. The Black Sea, like the Baltic, is a vast expanse of waters, which wash the shores not alone of Turkish territory, but those of another great power who may, in time of peace, at least, expect visits from men-of-war of friendly states. It seems unfair that any such claim as that of Turkey should be set up as a bar to such an intercourse, or that the privileged should in any way be subject to her sufferance.

There is no practical question making it necessary at present to discuss the subject, but should occasion arise when you are called upon to refer to it, *you will bear in mind the distinction taken above, and be cautious to go no further than to recognize the exclusion of the vessels as a usage.*[38]

In other words, the United States was prepared to accept the usage, but it did not recognize it as a principle of international law restricting passage, even of warships, through the Turkish Straits, and had no intention of doing so.[39] Further statements of American views were occasioned when the USS *Congress*, under Captain Rhind, and the USS *Shenandoah*, sought passage in November and December 1872. Thus, on November 30, the American minister to the Sublime Porte, George H. Boker, raised a question concerning the request of Captain Rhind for the *Congress* to pass the Straits. Secretary Fish replied on January 3, 1873 that Captain Rhind's application for a *firman* had been unauthorized, that he had been unaware of the obstacles and precedents, and more particularly of Fuad Pasha's circular of August 19, 1868, during the visit of Admiral Farragut to Constantinople. But Fish observed: "The abstract right of the Turkish Government to obstruct the navigation of the Dardanelles even to vessels of war in time of peace,

[38]Ibid., pp. 902-03; Moore, *Digest of International Law*, 1: 666-67. For the Danish Sound, see, especially, Brüel, *International Straits*, 2: part I (italics added).
[39]See also the dispatch of John P. Brown to Secretary of State Fish, on November 24, 1871, in which he reported concerning the new facilities granted by the Sublime Porte to merchant ships passing through the Straits, which were considered very satisfactory. *USFR* (1872): 667-68, 669.

is a serious question. The right, however, has for a long time been claimed and has been sanctioned by treaties between Turkey and certain European states. A proper occasion may arise for us to dispute the applicability of the claim to United States men-of-war. Meanwhile, it is deemed expedient to acquiesce in the exclusion."[40] In connection with the unauthorized and subsequently countermanded request of the captain of the *Shenandoah* for permission to pass the Dardanelles, Fish wrote to Boker: "The United States are not a party to the convention which professed to exclude vessels of war from the Dardanelles; and while it is disposed to respect the traditional sensibility of the Porte as to that passage, the shot which it is supposed may have been intended for a national vessel of this Government might if it had been directed to the supposed intention have precipitated a discussion if not a serious complication." Although the United States was "disposed to respect" the position of the Sublime Porte, that was not to be taken as implying any direct recognition of the "ancient rule" of the Ottoman Empire on the part of the United States. Not a signatory of the conventions regulating passage of the Straits, the United States insisted that it was in an exceptional position, and the Ottoman government seemed inclined to accept its position. In a certain sense, the United States today follows the principles outlined in 1871, when it sends destroyers or frigates into the Black Sea for annual "trips north" as spring or fall descends upon these strategic waters.

Persistence in the American Policy

No serious question appears to have arisen to passage of the Straits, insofar as the United States was concerned, between 1873 and the latter part of 1895, although there were important developments affecting the Ottoman Empire. The Balkan revolt against the Ottoman Empire in 1875, for example, led ultimately to the Russo-Turkish war in 1877–78, with all the consequences which these events entailed. Victorious Russia dictated the peace of San Stefano, of March 3, 1878, Article XXIV of which stipulated: "The Bosphorus and the Dardanelles shall remain open in time of war, as in time of peace, to the merchant vessels of neutral states arriving from or bound to Russian ports. The Sublime Porte consequently engages never henceforth to establish at the ports of the Black Sea and the Sea of Azov a fictitious

---

[40]Moore, *Digest of International Law*, 1: 667–68; Brüel, *International Straits*, 2: 307. According to an article in *The Levant Herald*, accompanying Boker's dispatch of December 17, 1872, a shot was fired at a French steamer under somewhat uncertain circumstances.

blockade at variance with the spirit of the Declaration signed at Paris, April 4/16, 1856."[41]

Pressure was brought to bear against Russia, however, primarily by Great Britain and Austria-Hungary, with the result that the Treaty of Berlin, July 13, 1878, "revised" the work of San Stefano. So far as the Straits were concerned, according to Article LXIII, the provisions of the Treaty of Paris (1856) and the Treaty of London (1871) were maintained. Nevertheless, on July 11, Lord Salisbury, the British representative declared that the obligations of the British government did "not go further than an engagement with the Sultan to respect in this matter His Majesty's independent determinations in conformity with the spirit of existing treaties." Count Shuvalov, the Russian representative, on the other hand contended that the principle "of the closing of the Straits" was "a European principle" and that, therefore, the stipulations of 1841, 1856, and 1871, confirmed at Berlin, were "binding on the part of the Powers, in accordance with the spirit and letter of the existing treaties not only as regards the Sultan but also as regards all the Powers signatory to these transactions."

AMERICAN WARSHIPS

Between 1878 and 1914, of course, the situation in the Balkans changed quite radically, with Serbia and Rumania becoming independent, while Bulgaria declared its independence in 1908, during the Bosnian crisis. Imperial Russia supported the small Slavic states in their attempts to supersede the Ottoman Empire in Europe, for its own secular reasons, and the Young Turk Revolution in 1908 was unable to stem the rising tide of Balkan nationalism.[42] The Italo-Turkish war (1911–12) and the Balkan wars which followed (1912–13) threatened the very existence of the Ottoman Empire.

In view of the Armenian disorders, American missionaries in the Ottoman Empire and other American citizens as well were apprehen-

---

[41]Hertslet, *Map of Europe*, 4: 2674–94, 2727–28. It may be noted in passing, as well, that the Suez Canal was opened in 1869 and that in 1875 Great Britain purchased the Khedive's shares of the stock in the Suez Canal Company. The Constantinople Convention of October 29, 1888, which came to regulate passage of the Canal, served as a model for the regulations established later for the Panama Canal, except in time of war, and also had some influence in connection with the Turkish Straits. See, especially, Norman J. Padelford, *The Panama Canal in Peace and War* (New York: Macmillan, 1942), pp. 34–35, 37; Hurewitz, *Diplomacy in the Near and Middle East*, 1: 202–04; B. Boutros-Ghali et Youssef Chlala, *Le Canal de Suez, 1854–1957: Chronologie, Documents* (Alexandria, Egypte: Société Egyptienne de Droit International, 1958). For a Turkish view of the general period, see Y. T. Kurat, *Henry Layard' in Istanbul Elçiligi, 1877–1880* (Ankara, 1968).

[42]E. E. Ramsaur, *The Young Turks: Prelude to the Revolution of 1908* (Princeton, N.J.: Princeton University Press, 1957).

sive of danger, and there were appeals for protection. The American minister in Constantinople, A. W. Terrell, had been much concerned with the problem, had taken it up with the Sublime Porte, and had advised the Department of State on March 13, 1895, as to the desirability of having an American warship in Ottoman waters. The Minister was informed on April 4 that the Navy Department had been approached with respect to having the USS *Marblehead*, of 2,000 tons, then at Gibraltar, visit Smyrna, Adalia, Alexandretta, and Beirut to ascertain what foundations there were for "the alarming apprehensions expressed in that quarter." At the same time, Rear Admiral W. A. Kirkland, commander of the European station, was ordered to proceed immediately with the USS *San Francisco* from Palermo to Smyrna and to direct vessels under his command to touch at Alexandretta and Adalia.[43] Both the Ottoman minister in Washington, Mavroyani Bey, and the Sublime Porte were apprehensive as to the meaning of these developments, but were assured that the visits were "without any unfriendly purpose," but that their presence at the ports of "the Syrian, Aleppan and Adanan coasts" would afford an opportunity "to learn whether there is just ground for the apprehensions of insecurity of life and property which our citizens in that region have expressed." While the *Marblehead* and the *San Francisco* left Turkish waters at the end of April 1895, they were back in the autumn, since the difficulties had not abated, and remained substantially until the end of the year. Richard Olney, President Cleveland's secretary of state, was glad to have assurances from Mavroyeni Bey as to American lives, and on October 15, he advised the Ottoman Minister: "The visit of the *Marblehead* to Turkish waters at this juncture is in pursuance of a long-established usage of this Government to send its vessels, in its discretion, to the ports of any country which may for the time being suffer perturbation of public order and where its countrymen are known to possess interests. This course is very general with all other Governments, and the circumstances that a transient occasion for such visits may exist does not detract from their essentially friendly character."[44]

Rear Admiral Thomas O. Selfridge appears no sooner to have arrived at Marseilles to assume command of the European station when, on November 15, 1895, he wrote to Terrell in Constantinople requesting that, since it was "very desirable" that he confer with the Minister

---

[43]*USFR* (1895): 1242–43. See also Daniel, *American Philanthropy*, pp. 99, 115–16; Joseph L. Grabill, *Protestant Diplomacy and the Near East: Missionary Influence on American Policy, 1810–1927* (Minneapolis: University of Minnesota Press, 1971), chap. 1.

[44]*USFR* (1895): 1324.

concerning the disturbances in the Ottoman Empire, he "procure a firman from the Porte for me to visit Constantinople in the *Marblehead*, the smallest vessel of our squadron." Terrell advised Admiral Selfridge on November 20 that he had applied for the *firman*, and noted that there was "a feeling here of much apprehension, and the news from the interior of Asia is fearful." He added: "The cooperative action of European Powers, if agreed on, is not known here. If there should be an effort by their boats to rush the Dardanelles and reach this city, the interval between the effort and the arrival of the fleet here would be one of much danger to resident Christians. Other Governments have dispatch boats on which their people could take refuge. Ours has none."[45] Terrell cabled the Department of State on November 21 that Admiral Selfridge's request had been rejected by the Sultan, who "feared that other powers would seek to follow the example, and especially requests that Admiral Selfridge should not come to the Dardanelles."[46] Accordingly, Terrell cabled Admiral Selfridge at Smyrna and requested him to keep the Legation "informed from time to time of his place of anchorage in the eastern Mediterranean," and he hoped that Admiral Selfridge had been instructed to inform the Ottoman "functionaries with whom he may have official intercourse that his naval force" would not be "used to protect revolutionists bearing American passports in entering Turkey from Cyprus." Evidently the Secretary of State was also somewhat puzzled as to the application for a *firman*, for Olney inquired of the Legation at Constantinople on December 5: "What application did you make in respect of *Marblehead*? Why? To whom? . . . Had you any reason to think other treaty powers would consent? Explain fully."[47] Terrell cabled on December 6 that he had made the application at the Admiral's request, that he knew "nothing of his instructions," but "supposed he was authorized," and noted that "our war vessels have come here since the treaty which closed Dardanelles. I had reason to believe that the *Marblehead's* coming would not be objected by the treaty Powers." At the same time, to be more explicit no doubt, Terrell wrote a brief dispatch to the Department of State making a complete explanation, stating that the Sultan had very politely "declined to grant permission for the *Marblehead* to visit Constantinople for the alleged reason that similar applications would then be made by the representatives of other Powers, which he could not possibly grant." He added that he "had not been favored with any knowledge of the instructions to the Admiral," and presumed, naturally, that he was authorized to request "permission to come here with his boat."[48]

45Ibid., p. 1383.   46Ibid., p. 1344.   47Ibid., p. 1380.
48Ibid., p. 1383.

Somewhat later, Terrell asked the Ottoman government for permission for the USS *Bancroft* to pass the Straits, since it had been authorized to remain at the disposal of the American Legation at Constantinople. On January 16, 1896, however, Mavroyeni Bey, the Ottoman minister in Washington, informed the Department of State that the Sublime Porte would not comply with this request. He stated: "Your Excellency knows perfectly well the earnest and sincere desire of the Imperial Government to do all in its power to strengthen if possible the ties of friendship which unite the two countries, but in this case a certain fact is involved, to wit, that only the signatory powers of the treaty of Paris enjoy the right to have vessels of war permanently at Constantinople at the orders of their respective embassies. Now, the United States Government does not appear in the number of the signatories of that treaty. I am, consequently, sure that your Excellency will be pleased to take the foregoing into consideration."[49] Meanwhile, the American warships remained in Ottoman waters during the disturbances, and on November 27, 1895, the *Minneapolis* was ordered to Smyrna, where it was soon expected to meet the *Marblehead* and the *San Francisco*.[50]

TOWARD WORLD WAR I

There were no further incidents of major significance in the development of U.S. policy toward the problem of the Turkish Straits in the period of 1896 to 1914, when World War I broke out, although it was an era of grave importance for all the peoples of the Eastern Mediterranean and the world at large.[51] By the end of the nineteenth century the German Empire had become a powerful factor in the Middle East, with increasing influence at Constantinople, both economically and politically. At the same time, Great Britain, hitherto a staunch defender of Ottoman integrity, began to think in terms of the division of the Sultan's estate into spheres of influence and interest, centering on the Arab world and Egypt, and by 1914 Great Britain, France, and Germany were ready to strike bargains. Moreover, in view of the German menace, as early as 1903 the British government was reaching the conclusion that "the exclusion of Russia from the Straits was not for Great Britain a primary naval or military interest."[52] There were

[49]Ibid., p. 1481.

[50]Ibid., pp. 1355–56, 1404.

[51]For the general American interest and policy, see John A. DeNovo, *American Interests and Policies in the Middle East, 1900–1939* (Minneapolis: University of Minnesota Press, 1963), chaps. 2–3.

[52]See the decision of the Committee on Imperial Defence Regarding the Straits, February 11, 1903; Memorandum by Sir Charles Hardinge. Memorandum Respecting the Passage of Russian Warships through the Dardanelles. Foreign Office, November

difficulties as to the passage of Russian warships in the Russo-Japanese War during 1904-05, and the Russian government sought to attain passage of the Straits for Russian warships in 1908-09, while excluding nonriverain warships from the Black Sea. While the British government agreed "in principle" to the passage of Russian warships, it insisted on reciprocity and no agreement was reached. During the Italo-Turkish War, owing to an Italian bombardment, the Straits were closed from April 18 to May 18, 1912.

The United States was not seriously involved in these complications, or did not so consider itself. On September 28, 1908, however, Acting Secretary of State Robert L. Bacon advised the American ambassador, J. G. A. Leishman, that the U.S.S. *Scorpion*, a schooner and converted yacht of 800 tons displacement and 200 feet in length, with light saluting artillery, had been detailed for early dispatch to Constantinople as a *stationnaire*. A request for permission to pass the Straits was to be made, with the understanding that the *Scorpion* was to be stationed at Constantinople. But in the absence of informal prior intimation of Ottoman approval the Department of State hesitated to make the request.[53] Leishman informed the department in October that permission had been granted. Two days later he was directed to convey to the Sultan President Roosevelt's "great satisfaction" with this "courteous permission," which was considered additional proof of the friendship existing between the Ottoman Empire and the United States. Leishman was advised that the *Scorpion*, under the command of Lt. Commander George W. Logan, would sail on October 22 and that Logan would telegraph from Malta or some other convenient port and settle the formalities of passage. Formal Ottoman approval, with an *iradé* authorizing "the passage through the Dardanelles of the yacht *Scorpion*," which was to "arrive at the port of Constantinople to serve as a stationnaire," was received on October 21.[54]

During the Italo-Turkish and Balkan wars there were fears of disorders and on November 9, 1912, the USS *Tennessee* and the *Montana* were ordered to sail on November 12, to arrive off Smyrna and Beirut at the end of the month. The British, French, and Russian govern-

16, 1906. Great Britain, Foreign Office, *Documents on the Origins of the War, 1898-1914* (London: HMSO, 1924-26), 4: 59-60. For changes in British policy, see also George S. Papadopulos, *England and the Near East, 1896-1898* (Thessaloniki: Institute for Balkan Studies, 1969). See also Edward Mead Earle, *Turkey, The Great Powers and the Baghdad Railway* (New York: Macmillan, 1923).

[53]*USFR* (1908): 751.

[54]Ibid., p. 752. Logan was to be under the direction of the ambassador and his position was to be assimilated to that of naval attaché, although he was not "to discharge any diplomatic functions," subject to the advice of the Ambassador. In view of disorders in 1909, Leishman, on August 14, cabled that the *Scorpion*, temporarily away from Constantinople, should return as soon as possible. *Ibid.* (1909): 562.

ments, which had ships in the Straits, promised protection to Americans, and with American vessels in the Mediterranean this was thought sufficient, although a naval auxiliary, the USS *Brutus*, was ordered to leave Norfolk for Smyrna on November 20. Generally speaking, however, the early appearance of a large fleet of warships in the Bosphorus assured the protection of foreigners, the presence of the *Scorpion* was sufficient to represent U.S. interests, and U.S. cruisers were free to act along the Mediterranean coasts, if the numerous American interests around Smyrna and Beirut were threatened.

The persistence of American policy is well illustrated by events immediately following the outbreak of World War I when, as will be seen in the next chapter, the United States refused to recognize the right of the Ottoman Empire to close the Straits even to American warships. Despite all the vicissitudes of European and world politics in the nineteenth and early twentieth centuries, American policy relative to the Turkish Straits remained unaltered, and the position adopted in September 1914 was merely a reiteration of the policy set forth by Secretary of State Hamilton Fish in 1871. It is clear from the record that while the United States never admitted the legal principle involved in the right of the Ottoman Empire, the riparian state, to close the Straits, even to warships, it did reluctantly acquiesce in the Ottoman practice and usage and did not press matters to an issue.

The problem of the Turkish Straits in all its ramifications was well on the periphery of American interest, not at the focus of attention, and the American commercial, economic, and political interests were certainly not vital, although the missionary-educational enterprise was one of abiding concern. Nevertheless, it may be important to note that the principles enunciated were part and parcel of the long-standing tradition with respect to freedom of commerce and freedom of the seas. This, moreover, was a theme which would recur in the years to come in connection with the development of American policy regarding the Turkish Straits and other bodies of water in the Middle East.

Chapter II

The Turkish Problem during World War I (1914-1918)

It was upon the foundations of these earlier traditional policies in the nineteenth century that later American policies were developed in the twentieth century, when the problem of the Straits moved from the periphery of American interest and became one of more active concern. No change occurred in American policy relative to the Turkish Straits in the years immediately prior to the outbreak of World War I in August 1914, the basic principles having been laid down in the nineteenth century and more specifically elaborated by Secretary of State Hamilton Fish during 1871-72.[1] Nor did the coming of the war itself alter American policy. Imperial Germany literally dragged the Ottoman Empire into the war on October 28-29, 1914, with an attack on Russian Black Sea installations, on the basis of the secret treaty of August 2, 1914, and the later passage of the two German battle cruisers, the *Goeben* and *Breslau*, through the Straits. Entry of the Ottoman Empire into the war was one of the decisive factors leading to the downfall of the Russian Empire, but it also brought about the end of the Sultan's empire as well.[2] President Wilson, in his address of January 8, 1918, called for freedom of passage for commerce through the Turkish Straits under international guarantees. At both the Lausanne and the Montreux conferences the primary American con-

---

[1] For a brief review, see Harry N. Howard, "The United States and the Problem of the Turkish Straits," *Middle East Journal* 1, no. 1 (January 1947): 59-78; "The United States and the Problem of the Turkish Straits: The Foundations of American Policy (1830-1914)," *Balkan Studies* 3, no. 1 (1962): 1-28.

[2] On the *Goeben* and *Breslau*, see, especially, Barbara W. Tuchman, *The Guns of August* (New York: Macmillan, 1962), chap. 10, pp. 137-62. Admiral Souchon's purpose was "to force the Turks, even against their will, to spread the war to the Black Sea coast against their enemy, Russia." Quoted from Admiral Wilhelm von Souchon, *La Percée de SMS Goeben et Breslau* (Paris: Payot, 1930).

27

cern lay in maintenance of the principle of freedom of commerce. Following World War II, as already indicated, the American interest was much more direct, and it is noteworthy that the United States government participated in the great debate concerning the fate of the Straits after the war at Yalta and Potsdam. Nor was it merely a commercial interest in the postwar years. Great events were taking place in the Eastern Mediterranean and the Aegean, and it was clear enough that the fate of nations in the neighborhood of the historic waterway might well be determined by the outcome. But the story of the development of American policy in these eventful and fateful years remains to be told.

The United States and the War

Although the United States was not to declare war on the Ottoman Empire, relations were not pleasant even during the period of American neutrality. The Ottoman government informed the United States on August 8, 1914, a bare six days after the signature of a secret alliance with Germany, of its intention to remain neutral.[3] In Constantinople, Ambassador Henry Morgenthau, Sr., kept the Department of State informed as to developments, including all the rumors afloat and the facts concerning the *Goeben* and *Breslau*, which had arrived at the Golden Horn on August 11, indicating that a German naval mission would now reinforce the military mission of General Liman von Sanders, who had arrived in the Ottoman capital in December 1913.[4]

Morgenthau was instructed on August 26, 1914 that under no circumstances was he to offer suggestions to the Sublime Porte concerning the position of the Ottoman Empire in the war. If asked, he was to state that the United States was very desirous that the war spread no farther and that the Empire remain neutral.[5] Baron von Wangenheim, the German ambassador, indeed, told Morgenthau on August 27 that Germany, too, wanted Ottoman neutrality, but

[3]Department of State, *The Foreign Relations of the United States, 1914 Supplement, The World War* (Washington, D.C.: USGPO), p. 52. Hereafter referred to as *USFR*. See also Harry N. Howard, *The Partition of Turkey: A Diplomatic History, 1913-1923* (Norman: University of Oklahoma, 1931; New York: Howard Fertig, 1966), pp. 83-102.

[4]See Alan Moorehead, *Gallipoli* (New York: Ballantine, 1956); Ulrich Trumpener, *Germany and the Ottoman Empire, 1914-1918* (Princeton, N.J.: Princeton University Press, 1968), chaps. 1-3; F. G. Weber, *Eagles on the Crescent* (Ithaca, N.Y.: Cornell University Press, 1970), chaps. 1-3; Howard, *Partition of Turkey*, chap. 3; Caleb F. Gates, *Not to Me Only* (Princeton, N.J.: Princeton University Press, 1940), chap. 13.

[5]*USFR, 1914 Supplement, The World War*, p. 77.

intended to "prevent Russia from taking Constantinople," which Germany considered to be "the prize that Russia will demand if victorious." Nevertheless, Admiral von Souchon, who had arrived with the *Goeben* and *Breslau*, thought the Straits as well fortified as Cuxhaven, impregnable against an Anglo-French naval attack, and that they would not be closed to commerce unless attacked. Morgenthau repeated all this to the British Ambassador who, in turn, authorized him to state that the British would not attack Smyrna, "but would force the Dardanelles if closed against commerce."[6] The next day, Morgenthau, when advised that 50 German naval officers and 700 sailors had arrived from Germany to enter the Ottoman navy, stated that if the USS *North Carolina* came to Constantinople, permission would have to be secured for passage of the Straits.[7] The Dardanelles were, in fact, closed on September 27, and on September 28 the British fleet off the Dardanelles compelled Turkish destroyers to return to the Straits, since they were thought to have German officers or sailors aboard. Weber Pasha, German commandant in the Dardanelles, thereupon placed additional mines completely closing the Straits. The grand vizier, Prince Said Halim, "greatly agitated," affirmed the closure to Ambassador Morgenthau on September 28, and stated that the empire did not desire to enter the war. Ambassador Morgenthau, in conformty with established American policy, informed him that the United States "did not admit" the legal right of the Ottoman government to close the Dardanelles in time of peace. The Grand Vizier hoped the incident would be settled shortly and the Dardanelles reopened, but to Morgenthau the situation appeared "extremely critical."[8]

Meanwhile, there were rumors as to the abolition of the capitulatory regime in the Ottoman Empire, a measure which was carried out on October 1, despite the opposition of the United States, although the British, French, and Russian governments were willing to concede the point, provided Ottoman neutrality were preserved and the German military and naval missions were sent home.[9] In the end, the empire was brought into the war, as observed above, by the

[6]Meanwhile, in an interview with the Ottoman ambassador in Washington, Rustem Bey, in *The Washington Star*, September 8, 1914, the Ambassador not only criticized American attitudes toward his government, but gratuitously referred to "lynchings" in the United States and the "water cure" in the Philippines. Rustem Bey thereafter took a voluntary extended leave, although President Wilson was reluctant to ask for his recall. See *USFR, The Lansing Papers (1914–1920)*, 1: 68–75.

[7]*USFR, 1914 Supplement, The World War*, pp. 79–80.

[8]Ibid., pp. 113–14.

[9]Ibid., pp. 767–68. See also Nasim Sousa, *The Capitulatory Regime of Turkey: Its History, Origin and Nature* (Baltimore: The Johns Hopkins University Press, 1933), chaps. 10 and 11.

German–Ottoman naval attack against the Russian Black Sea coast off Odessa on October 28-29, 1914.[10] Morgenthau summed up the situation on November 7, stressing German control of the Straits. By December 19, he advised Secretary of State William Jennings Bryan that it might produce "good results" if he were willing to warn Germany of its responsibility if any Christian massacres occurred in the Ottoman Empire, since Germany had "absolute control" of the Ottoman fleet and almost controlled the army, and von Wangenheim had declared that if the British complied with the Russian request to force the Dardanelles and enter Constantinople, a massacre of non-Muslims was "inevitable." Morgenthau added that Ottoman officials and von Wangenheim were much concerned about the Dardanelles and had sent soldiers and guns to the Prinkipo Islands and the Asiatic shore of the Marmara.[11] Three days later, on December 22, Ambassador Gerard, in Berlin, was so instructed.

While the government at Washington had been kept informed as to developments following the Ottoman entry into the war and was much concerned with all that went on, Ambassador Morgenthau summed up his views later on from his vantage point in Constantinople.[12] Among other things, he observed that the real power in the Ottoman capital lay not in the hands of the Sultan, whom he considered "absolutely powerless," but in those of the Committee of Union and Progress, and more particularly of Enver, Talat, and Cemal Paşa, although the party, in his view, had few followers among the people. Alarmed and anxious at the possible forcing of the Dardanelles, when the British fleet attacked on February 19, 1915, preparations had been made to move the capital from Constantinople to Eskişehir. Enver, however,

took advantage of their depression and conferred with Liman von Sanders and determined that they would concentrate their entire forces in the defense of the Dardanelles. He reassured the doubting ones and gave positive orders that the Government should not be removed from Constantinople. As the Sultan and also the German and Austrian Ambassadors had also opposed the removal, Enver's action promptly rehabilitated him; and when they successfully repulsed their enemies at the Straits early in the spring, their courage arose, and the crowd—that was trembling with fear and had

---

[10]*USFR, 1914 Supplement, The World War*, pp. 120 ff.

[11]Ibid., pp. 136-43, 789; Joseph L. Grabill, *Protestant Diplomacy and the Near East: Missionary Influence on American Policy, 1810-1927* (Minneapolis: University of Minnesota Press, 1971), chaps. 3 and 4.

[12]*USFR, The Lansing Papers, 1914-1920*, 1: 762-66, 766-69. Letters of Morgenthau to Secretary of State Lansing, November 4, 18, 1915. See also Trumpener, *Germany and the Ottoman Empire*, chaps. 3 and 4.

practically abandoned all hopes of retaining Constantinople and had even pleaded for safety zones which should be exempted from bombardment when the fleet would enter the harbor—gradually dropped its terror and changed into a self-reliant, and later on defiant, nation.

Considered irresponsible in 1908-09, the Ottoman triumvirate had now "become dizzy from success" and justly claimed that they had "compelled England and France to employ 500,000 troops to try and force the Dardanelles and to use a tremendous fleet, sacrifice numerous ships and spend millions of pounds worth of ammunition, all of which greatly diminished their power to defeat Germans. They feel at present that they have successfully kept the Great Powers at bay and are very proud of the achievement."

Intoxicated with their "apparent success," those in power were beginning to underestimate completely the assistance given by the Germans. They were, indeed, "very touchy on that point and want no one to give the Germans any credit for the defense of the Dardanelles. There has already developed considerable feeling between the Turks and the Germans. . . . All the prominent Turkish officials emphatically object to Germany's bringing an army into Turkey. They do not say so openly but I know that they fear that if the Germans ever come here, they will not leave the country again. As it is, the Germans are now gradually making a bloodless occupation of this country." After the futile Anglo-French attempt on March 18, 1915, to force the Dardanelles, the Ottoman authorities "became convinced of the almost impregnability of the Dardanelles" and began, according to Morgenthau, "to develop the plan of exterminating the Armenians to punish them for their alleged perfidy towards the Turks in November and December 1914 at the Caucasus boundary."[13]

The Problem of the Straits and the Partition of the Ottoman Empire

With Ottoman participation in the war on the side of Germany, the destiny of the empire was now in play. A great polyglot empire at the intercontinental crossroads, it was natural that its fate should concern the Great Powers of the world, including even the United States of

[13]On the Armenian problem see Trumpener, *Germany and the Ottoman Empire*, chap 7; James B. Gidney, *A Mandate for Armenia* (Kent, Ohio: Kent State University Press, 1967), chaps. 2-4. See also Stanley E. Kerr, *The Lions of Marash: Personal Experiences with American Near East Relief, 1919-1922* (Albany, N.Y.: State University of New York Press, 1973).

America. Some of the decisive campaigns of World War I were fought in the Middle East, and during the course of the struggle there were serious discussions as to the future of that region and its peoples once the war was over.

THE AMERICAN INTEREST

Within less than a year after the beginning of the war, as a matter of fact, those discussions, which led to a number of secret interallied agreements outlining the future status of the Middle East as the Allied statesmen of the day, engaged as they were in a great world struggle, envisaged it.[14] There had been some talk as early as September 1914, and Ambassador Page reported from London on January 15, 1915 his understanding that Russia would have Constantinople.[15] Colonel Edward M. House, President Wilson's special emissary, who visited London during February 1915, reported Sir Edward Grey's view on February 9, that "Russia might be satisfied with Constantinople," and indicated that they had discussed the matter in some detail. On March 7, Sir Edward advised House that, although "he did not know the mind of Russia," he believed that if given Constantinople and the Straits, the Russians "would be willing to acquiesce in almost any other terms that might be agreed upon."[16]

THE SECRET AGREEMENTS CONCERNING THE OTTOMAN EMPIRE

The first of the secret interallied agreements looking toward the partition of the Ottoman Empire was the Anglo-Russian accord of March 12, 1915, according to which Great Britain accepted the Russian demand for control of Constantinople and the Straits, with the necessary European and Asiatic hinterlands. In return, Constantinople was to be a free port and the Straits were to be open to commercial vessels. Moreover, the 1907 neutral zone in Iran was to pass under British control.[17] It was not until April 10, 1915 that France

---

[14]In general, see H. N. Howard, *Partition of Turkey*, chaps. 4–6; Robert J. Kerner, "Russia, the Straits and Constantinople, 1914-1915," *Journal of Modern History* 1, no. 3 (September 1929): 400–15; and "Russia and the Straits, 1915-1917," *Slavonic Review* 8, no. 24 (March 1930): 589–93. See also E. A. Adamov, *Konstantinopol i Prolivy* (2 vols.; Moscow, 1925-26), [French translation: *Constantinople et les Détroits* (2 vols.: Paris, 1930)]; *Razdel Aziatskoi Turtsii* (Moscow, 1924).

[15]Charles Seymour, *Intimate Papers of Colonel House* (Boston: Houghton Mifflin, 1926), 1: 354–55.

[16]Ibid., 2: 363, 393.

[17]See Great Britain, Foreign Office, *Documents on British Foreign Policy, 1919-1939*, edited by E. L. Woodward and Rohan Butler, first series (London: HMSO, 1962), 4: 635–38. Hereafter cited as *British Documents, 1919-1939*. See also C. Jay Smith, Jr., "Great Britain and the 1914-1915 Straits Agreement with Russia: The British Promise of November 1914," *American Historical Review* 70, no. 4 (July 1965):

reluctantly agreed to the Russian proposition, while the St. Petersburg government approved the French project for control over Syria. The agreements concerning Constantinople and the Straits, therefore, were to initiate the discussions concerning the rest of the Ottoman estate.

By this time Italy was preparing to join forces with the Entente. According to the Treaty of London, of April 26, 1915, Italy was to receive its share of the Ottoman legacy—retention of the Dodecanese Islands, occupied since 1912, and the vilayet of Adalia.[18] Italy, in fact, entered the war on August 21, 1915. Ambassador Page, commenting on the Italian situation as it related to the Balkan and Turkish problems, wrote the Secretary of State on August 21[19] that the "Balkan muddle" was "so great that no one appears to know what the final result there will be." Bulgaria, had already essentially decided to join the Central Powers by May 1915, signed a treaty in September, and entered the war in October.[20] Page felt that the Allies would have to do everything in their power by promises "and whatever means are at their disposal to induce Bulgaria to join them." If Bulgaria did join the Entente, Ambassador Page thought

it would probably settle Turkey's fate in a very short time, as she is generally believed to be very short of all means of defense and to be dependent on Germany by way of Bulgaria for nearly everything. . . .
  While it is said that Russia was promised possession of Constantinople and the Dardanelles, and undoubtedly has looked forward to this, and while France is believed to have been acquiescent in this plan, so far as I can find out, none of the other Powers, either among the Allies or in the Eastern Mediterranean have been desirous of such a digestion of this apple of discord on which they all look with longing eyes.
  I myself feel that the most probable solution of the whole matter will be that in the end Constantinople will be left in the hands of the Porte with a

1015-34; Laurence Evans, *United States Policy and the Partition of Turkey, 1914-1926* (Baltimore: The Johns Hopkins University Press, 1965), chaps. 1 and 2; R. R. James, *Gallipoli: The History of a Noble Blunder* (New York: Macmillan, 1965).
  [18]René Albrecht-Carrié, *Italy at the Paris Peace Conference. The Paris Peace: History and Documents* (New York: Columbia University Press, 1938), chap. 1, pp. 334-39.
  [19]*USFR, The Lansing Papers,* 1: 723-24.
  [20]Ambassador Penfield wrote from Vienna on November 4 (ibid., pp. 640-41) that the reason for Bulgaria's action was simple: "England announced months ago that an Entente victory meant that Constantinople would be given to Russia. Every Bulgarian with whom I have talked has stoutly maintained that his country preferred to have Turkey in command at the Golden Horn and the Dardanelles. Russia was not wanted at any price, not with the practical certainty of the eventual absorption of Bulgaria by Russia once she was established in Constantinople. Besides, in Bulgarian opinion, Russia's setback was a serious one, from which there was no evidence that she could rally. Germany was victorious. And the King of Bulgaria was a German prince, be it remembered." See also Harry N. Howard, "L'entrée de la Bulgarie dans la guerre mondiale (1914-1915)," *Les Balkans* 6, no. 7 (July 1934): 213-42.

modest hinterland and the city and the Straits will be neutralized and put under the protection of the Powers; otherwise it will almost certainly prove, what I have said, an apple of discord, and no one knows what difficulties will arise over it at the close of the present war.

Within a year after the agreement with Italy, more definite blueprints for the partition of the Ottoman Empire were ready. On April 26, 1916, a tripartite agreement among France, Great Britain, and Russia was signed, during the visit of Sir Mark Sykes and Georges Picot to the Russian capital. This important diplomatic exchange stipulated that Imperial Russia should have Armenia, a portion of Kurdistan, and Northern Anatolia west of Trabzon. The French sphere included Syria, the vilayet of Adana, southern Kurdistan, and Cilicia, together with Harput. If an independent Arab community were to be established, Great Britain was to have a sphere in Mesopotamia, with Baghdad, and access to the ports of Acre and Haifa in Syria. Palestine, or Southern Syria, was to be placed under an international regime. By the Sykes–Picot agreement of May 9–16, 1916, between Great Britain and France, the Anglo-French spheres were specifically delineated, although the general outlines of the earlier tripartite agreement were observed and the agreement looked toward the establishment of an Arab state or confederation with the Anglo-French spheres. Less than a year later, on April 19–21, 1917, by the agreement of St. Jean de Maurienne, Italy was promised concessions both in Smyrna and Adalia in return for its recognition of the Sykes–Picot agreement of 1916.[21]

SOME DIFFICULTIES WITH THE SECRET AGREEMENTS: THE ARABS

There were to be serious difficulties with these secret agreements, however. In certain aspects they were contradictory. But more serious, perhaps, they seemed incompatible with certain agreements which Great Britain and the government of India had made with the Arabs. As early as October 31, 1914, Lord Kitchener had given the

[21]Albrecht-Carrié, *Italy at the Paris Peace Conference*, pp. 345–48. Ambassador Page, in Rome, who had heard various rumors and reports as to the Poincaré promise of Constantinople and the Straits as early as 1912, and of the inducement of Constantinople and the Straits in 1914 to keep Russia from signing a separate peace, reported his views on January 22, 1917, that "the handing over to Russia of all the provinces therein listed with the cession of Constantinople and the Dardanelles, will undoubtedly give her tremendous, if not overwhelming power in Europe and make her very strong in the Orient," *USFR, The Lansing Papers*, 1: 750–51. See also *USFR, Supplement I, 1915*, p. 17. For the Sykes-Picot Agreement, see also *British Documents, 1919–1939*, first series, 4: 241–51; St. Jean de Maurienne Agreement, ibid., pp. 638–43. See also Fayez A. Sayegh, "British Pledges on Palestine," *Arab Outlook* 2, nos. 4 and 5 (April–May 1964): 1–12.

Amir Husayn, the grand sherif of Mecca and the ruler of the Hijaz, a guarantee of independence, but it was not until July 14, 1915, that the real negotiations between Great Britain and the Hijaz got under way. They were carried on through the office of the high commissioner in Egypt, Sir Henry McMahon. In the very first note, Husayn expressed his willingness to fight the Turks provided Great Britain recognized Arab independence south of the 37th parallel. After some inconclusive negotiations in the summer of 1915, the British reply came on October 24, 1915. Sir Henry opposed Husayn's claims to the Mersin-Alexandretta region and to that portion of Syria west of Damascus, Hama, Homs, and Aleppo. In general, however, the rest of the future Arab boundaries were accepted "within those frontiers wherein Great Britain" was "free to act without detriment to the interests of her ally, France." Naturally, too, agreement with Husayn was to be without prejudice "to our existing treaties with Arab chiefs." Husayn's letter of November 5, 1915, accepted the British proposition concerning Mersin and Alexandretta, but still held out for Aleppo and Beirut, not to mention Basrah and Baghdad. He was willing, however, to recognize a temporary British occupation of Basrah and Baghdad. There were still items to be determined, but by January 30, 1916, the British had substantially accepted Husayn's terms, although definitive disposition of Baghdad and Basrah, as well as the French claim in Syria, remained undetermined.[22]

It is interesting to observe, however, that the government of India had begun negotiations with the Amir Ibn Sa'ud of the Najd in December 1915, leading to an agreement which was ratified on July 18, 1916.[23] The accord with Ibn Sa'ud was to cause grave difficulties in the years to come and seemed clearly in opposition to that between London and Husayn, for it recognized Ibn Sa'ud's sovereignty over the Najd, Qatif, Jubail, and lands along the Persian Gulf.

Such, in broad terms, were the so-called "secret treaties" partitioning the Ottoman Empire, initiated on the basis of the accords concerning the question of Constantinople and the Straits. Such were the conflicting claims and interests based thereon. That the United States government was considerably interested in these matters, although not precisely informed, had now become clear.

[22]See United Kingdom, Foreign Office, Miscellaneous No. 3 (1939), *Correspondence between Sir Henry McMahon, G.C.M.G., G.C.V.O., K.C., I.E., C.S.I., H.M. High Commissioner at Cairo and the Sherif Husayn of Mecca, July 1915–March 1916* (with a map), Cmd. 5967; George Antonius, *Arab Awakening* (London: H. Hamilton, 1938), chap. 13 and pp. 413 ff.; King Abdallah of Jordan, *Memoirs* (New York: Philosophical Library, 1950), chaps. 12-14.
[23]Howard, *Partition of Turkey*, pp. 188-93. See also H. C. Armstrong, *Lord of Arabia: Ibn Saud: An Intimate Study of a King* (Penguin, 1938), passim.

The United States Enters the War

But these were only the beginnings of conflicting promises, disillusion, and disappointment. In March 1917, shortly before the United States entered the war against Imperial Germany, revolution came to Russia and the Tsar was forced to abdicate. Although the United States broke diplomatic relations with Germany on February 3, 1917, it assumed that friendly relations with the Ottoman Empire would continue—a position also taken by the Ottoman government, provided war did not break out between the United States and Germany.[24] On March 2, 1917, Ambassador Abram I. Elkus, who had succeeded Morgenthau in October 1916, reported similar sentiments from Talat Pasa and Cavid Bey and a friendly attitude on the part of the Sultan. There was considerable feeling against the Germans, but an Ottoman minister told Elkus:

The way the Entente Powers had published their terms of peace was a most stupid piece of business. There were thousands of people in this country, who were against the war and longed for peace, and yet the Entente Governments say that they want to give Constantinople to Russia. All these people now want the continuation of the war.

[An Ottoman minister] knew that there were no diplomats in Germany, that it was only through force that the Germans wanted to deal with every nation, but he had believed that in England and France there were good diplomats. The way the latter acted in this matter showed him that there is a penury of statesmanship in those countries.[25]

SOME AMERICAN VIEWS

As relations with Germany worsened, on March 31, 1917, Secretary of State Lansing advised Elkus that the United States had "no controversy with Turkey" and desired "to maintain the friendly relations which have always existed."[26] On April 2, Ambassador Elkus sounded out the Ottoman Minister for Foreign Affairs as to whether the Sublime Porte would follow the German lead in case of war between the United States and Germany, and received the reply that "the relations of the United States and Turkey were friendly, more

---

[24]*USFR, 1917, Supplement 1*, pp. 113, 148-49. On December 18, 1916, Balfour sent a note to President Wilson stating that among the British war aims was: "The setting free of the populations subject to the bloody tyranny of the Turks; and the turning out of Europe of the Ottoman Empire so decidedly foreign to western civilization." See Harold Nicholson, *Curzon: The Last Phase, 1919-1925: A Study in Post-War Diplomacy* (Boston: Houghton Mifflin, 1934), p. 98.

[25]Letter from Elkus to Lansing, March 2, 1917; *USFR, The Lansing Papers*, 1: 787-91.

[26]*USFR, 1917, Supplement 1*, pp. 191-92.

so now than for some time." There was no reason why they should not
so continue, and the Ottoman government, therefore, had "not taken
into consideration the emergency of a war with the United States."
Elkus had the impression that the Germans, who were apprehensive
about the possibility of internal disturbances in the Ottoman Empire,
desired the presence of American diplomats as a guarantee against
possible massacres of Christians, although he did not personally
credit it.[27]

Although there was a strong desire for peace among many Turks,
German influence was strong, and there was no assurance that the
Entente Powers were willing to enter the negotiations for a separate
peace with the Ottoman Empire. Elkus reported his conviction on
April 5[28] that the Ottoman leaders were placing all their hopes in a
peace between the Central Powers and Russia, and it was hinted
"that Turkey was ready to open the Straits and to make other concessions." An interview in *Tanin* by the Grand Vizier, on April 5, stated
that the long-standing enmity between the Ottoman Empire and
Russia "was due to ambitious aims of the Russian Empire [against]
Turkey and that should liberal Russia abandon those aims" there was
no reason "why the Russian and Turkish relations should not be
cordial." Elkus thought it might be wise, if the Department of State
thought fit, "to suggest to the Entente Powers that Russia state
categorically" that it would "not conclude a separate peace with the
Central Powers," and he believed it "likely that Turkey" might "then
abandon Germany and offer to negotiate with the Entente Powers."

Nevertheless, following the entry of the United States into the war
on April 6, 1917, the Ottoman Empire was obliged to break with the
United States, as it did on April 10,[29] although there were assurances
"that American citizens and institutions should be treated as hereto-
fore, without having any official relations with the American consuls.
While there was some agitation in favor of an American declaration of
war against the Ottoman Empire, spearheaded by Senators Henry
Cabot Lodge and William H. King, President Wilson resisted these
pressures. Following a discussion with Alsberg, private secretary to
Ambassador Elkus, who had left Constantinople on April 6, Secretary
Lansing wrote to President Wilson on May 17[30] concerning Turkish

[27] Ibid., pp. 206-07.
[28] *USFR, 1917, Supplement 2,* 1: 16-17; Trumpener, *Germany and the Ottoman
Empire,* chaps. 4 and 5.
[29] *USFR, 1917, Supplement 1,* pp. 598-606; Grabill, *Protestant Diplomacy,* chap. 4;
R. R. Trask, *The United States Response to Turkish Nationalism and Reform, 1914-
1939* (Leiden: Brill, 1971), chap. 1.
[30] *USFR, The Lansing Papers,* 2: 17-19. On May 24, 1917, Boghos Nubar Pasa,
president of the Armenian National Delegation, wrote to Secretary Lansing outlining

irritation at German arrogance and the hope of American friendship and assistance in reconstruction. Lansing also reported the belief that if Enver, Talat, and Cemal were appropriately approached, either by promises or bribery, "they would allow some submarines to enter the Dardanelles and destroy the German vessels, and that if that was done and the Turks relieved of their fear of the Germans, they would be willing to make peace on very favorable terms for the Allies." It would be "a tremendous blow to the Central Powers to have Turkey withdraw as no doubt Bulgaria would be forced to follow the same course."

By this time the U.S. government was receiving some detailed, if not always accurate, information concerning the secret treaties partitioning the Ottoman Empire. Hints had come in from Rome, Vienna, and London, as observed above, and as early as February 14, 1916, Colonel House, in London for talks with Sir Edward Grey and others in the British government, noted: "We all cheerfully divided up Turkey, both in Asia and Europe. The discussion hung for a long while around the fate of Constantinople. George and Balfour were not enthusiastic over giving it into the hands of Russia, Grey and Asquith thinking if this were not done material for another war would always be at hand. I suggested the neutralization of Constantinople."[31]

With the overthrow of the Tsar in Russia and the advent of the provisional government in March 1917, there was much discussion and agitation concerning the problem of the Straits, with Paul Miliukov, the minister of foreign affairs, taking the acquisition of the Straits as the primary thread of his policy. But there was considerable opposition, especially from the left-wing Socialist Revolutionaries and the Bolsheviki. The American consul at Petrograd, North Winship, reported on April 10, 1917, concerning the agitation against the secret treaties, noting that agitators were opposed to the agreement among the Allies "providing for the transfer of Constantinople to Russia, as this would involve the enslavement of the Turks."[32]

When Arthur James Balfour came to Washington during April–May 1917, there was considerable discussion of the problems of the peace and the question of the future of the Ottoman Empire was raised. Balfour talked at length with Colonel House and told President

the Armenian claims in the partition of the Ottoman Empire, including the six vilayets of Erzurum, Bitlis, Van, Diyarbekir, Mammuret-Elaziz, and Sivas, together with Cilicia and the ports of Mersin and Alexandretta on the Mediterranean and of Trabzon on the Black Sea. *USFR, 1917, Supplement 2,* 1: 792–96.

[31]Seymour, *Intimate Papers of Colonel House,* 2: 181.

[32]*USFR, 1918, Russia,* 1: 23; Howard, *The Partition of Turkey,* pp. 195–96. There was much talk of internationalization of the Straits region. Ramsay MacDonald stated in the House of Commons on February 12, 1917: "There are two points on the continent of Europe which I venture to say this empire ought not willingly to surrender to the

Wilson of the general nature of the secret agreements, informally and personally. In discussions of April 22 and 28, for example, Balfour and House agreed that attempts at a separate peace might be made with both Austria and Bulgaria. It was agreed that Serbia should receive Bosnia and Herzegovina, and return part of Macedonia to Bulgaria. Rumania, it was thought, should have Bessarabia and the Banat, while Austria might be composed of Bohemia, Hungary, and Austria proper. The next point was Constantinople: "We agreed that it should be internationalized. Crossing the Bosphorus we came to Anatolia. It is here that the secret treaties between the Allies come in prominently. They have agreed to give Russia a sphere of influence in Armenia and the northern part. The British take in Mesopotamia (and the region) which is contiguous to Egypt. France and Italy each have their spheres embracing the balance of Anatolia up to the Straits."[33] Colonel House told Balfour that it was "all bad," and Balfour was somewhat vague in his explanation of just what the treaties included. On April 30, House, Wilson, and Balfour were in conference at the White House when the question of Constantinople and the Straits arose, and specifically the problem of internationalization. House sensed the heart of the problem when, although agreeing in principle, he pointed out the difficulties which would ensue in connection with a consequent attempt to internationalize the Danish Sound, and the Suez and Panama canals. But neither Wilson nor Balfour, despite the obvious similarities, thought that "the two questions had much in common."

During the Balfour visit, the British statesman made available a copy of certain minutes of the Imperial Council in which, among other things, he had stated: "The practical destruction of the Turkish Empire is undoubtedly one of the objects which we desire to attain. The Turks may well be left—I hope they will be left—in a more or less independent position in Asia Minor. If we are successful unquestionably Turkey will be deprived of the most important portions of the Valley of the Euphrates and the Tigris; she will lose Constantinople; and Syria, Armenia and the southern parts of Asia Minor will, if not annexed by the Entente Powers, probably fall more or less under their domination."[34]

---

possession of a Great Power. One of them is Belgium. And the other is Constantinople. . . . I venture to say that if a Great Power has taken possession of Constantinople and has fortified it and the Dardanelles, this country will be busy with an attempt to solve the problem of imperial communication in a form which it has never had to face before." *Parliamentary Debates, House of Commons,* 90, col. 348.

[33] Seymour, *Intimate Papers of Colonel House,* 3: 43–45.

[34] Balfour to Lansing: *USFR, The Lansing Papers,* 2: 23. For the Balfour visit, see Blanche E. C. Dugdale, *Arthur James Balfour, First Earl of Balfour, K.G., O.M., F.R.S., 1960–1930* (New York: Putnam, 1937), 2: 144–51; David Lloyd George, *War Memoirs of David Lloyd George, 1916–1917* (Boston: Little Brown, 1934), 3: 549–50.

THE REVOLUTION IN RUSSIA

On May 3, 1917, the Russian charge d'affaires, K. M. Onou, advised the Department of State of Russian war aims.[35] He also talked with Balfour on May 3, who in turn related the general results of his mission to the United States, with which he expressed satisfaction, confirming that the United States did not count on signing any agreement with the Allies, which did not, in any case, diminish the sincerity of American cooperation.[36]

Some days later, Winship reported from Petrograd on May 8 that "it must be stated plainly that Milyukov, who has always been an advocate of certain solution of the Dardanelles and Bosporus question, expresses only his personal opinion and not that of the Temporary Government itself."[37] He also cited the *Workers' Gazette*, in which it was stated that the Socialists must not only fight against Lenin but also "against the advocates of the annexation of the Dardanelles as represented by Milyukov and the English and French newspapers."[38] The provisional government proclaimed a peace based on no annexations and no indemnities and the principle of the "self-determination of peoples," on May 18, 1917, and Miliukov was forced to resign as foreign minister. But Onou learned on May 27 that the text of this latest declaration of Russian policy was not known in Washington and he transmitted it to the Department of State officially. Onou found the department "particularly disturbed" by the words "a peace without annexations and without indemnities," since there was a question whether one would consider as annexations the reunion of Alsace-Lorraine to France, the liberation of the provinces of Bosnia and Herzegovina, and the Armenian territories of Asia Minor. The question of indemnities was also somewhat disturbing. M. I. Tereschenko, the new Russian foreign minister, advised the Russian ambassador in Washington, B. A. Bakhmetev, on July 4, 1917,[39] that in view of British and French statements there was now some question of a revision of the interallied accords, but he saw "no particular necessity for America to enter into the number of powers bound by the agreements." Nevertheless, the provisional government would willingly accept American adherence to the agreement on the nonconclusion of a separate peace. On August 18,[40] Tereschenko advised Bakhmetev that the Italian government had

[35] *USFR, Russia, 1918*, 1: 38–39.
[36] Adamov, *Konstantinopol i Prolivy*, 1: 395–96; (French edition), 1: 369–70.
[37] *USFR, Russia, 1918*, 1: 44.   [38] Ibid., p. 48.
[39] Adamov, *Konstantinopol i Prolivy*, 1: 396–97, 398–400; (French edition), 1: 370–72, 372–75.
[40] Adamov, *Konstantinopol i Prolivy*, 1: 403–04; (French edition), 1: 379–80. For the Root Mission see *USFR, Russia, 1918*, 1: 107–53.

manifested a "pressing desire to obtain from us a recognition of Italian rights in certain regions of Asia Minor, in case of a fortunate conclusion of the war." As the Ambassador knew, conversations had taken place on a number of occasions for the purpose of partitioning Asia Minor. During the visit of Elihu Root to Russia, Tereschenko had explained that it would be out of place to "enter into any examination of this question," whoever took the initiative in such discussions. Tereschenko asked Bakhmetev, in case Italy or any other Allied state did desire to enter into conversations concerning the "projected territorial annexations as a consequence of the present war," to discuss the matter confidentially with the Department of State in order to get it to accept the Russian point of view. He added: "Having reasons to suppose that the general orientation of the policy of the United States concerning Turkey and its future is similar to the principles placed by us thenceforth at the basis of the international community, we attach a great importance that the question be settled by the voice of America, which enjoys, of course, a certain authority in Turkey. Also we think the moment favorable for a confidential exchange of views with the Washington cabinet on Turkish affairs, in order to see that the conduct of Russia and America, after the war will agree as much as possible." Bakhmetev replied on August 31[41] that the Italians had not submitted the question to the United States. He had learned from Secretary of State Lansing that any such attempt would find no sympathy. The growing "reciprocal understanding" with the United States had enabled Bakhmetev cautiously to broach the subject of Turkey. In talks with Lansing and William Gibbs McAdoo, the secretary of the treasury, he had gained the impression that it was "possible to exercise a certain pressure on the Allies to get them to renounce their desire of conquest in Turkey, which might serve to get Turkey out of the war and thus to facilitate its end and the triumph of democratic ideas. The same idea seemed to be developing also in regard to the Balkans, and particularly to Bulgaria."

Likewise, in June and August 1917, there were further detailed bits of information from German statements concerning the war. President Wilson advised Colonel House, who was in London as a special representative of the United States at the Inter-Allied Conference, on December 1, 1917,[42] that the American people would "not fight for any selfish aim on the part of any belligerent, with the possible exception of Alsace-Lorraine, least of all for the divisions of territory such as have been contemplated in Asia Minor." By the end

[41]Adamov, *Konstantinopol i Prolivy*, 1: 404; (French edition), 1: 380–81.
[42]*USFR, 1917, Supplement 2*, 1: 104–06, 169–70, 331; *USFR, Russia, 1918*, 1: 39, 52, 66, 76–77, 228, 365, and 421 for secret agreements.

of 1917 further information was available and, on December 27, Ambassador Francis's dispatch from Petrograd, containing the texts of some of the communications concerning Constantinople and the Straits and the treay with Italy (1915), was received in Washington.

DEVELOPMENT OF THE ALLIED POSITION

With the Bolshevik Revolution of November 1917 and the denunciation and publication of the "secret treaties" concerning the Middle East,[43] the world had come to know something of the understandings concerning the Ottoman Empire, although not necessarily the whys and wherefores of the interallied diplomacy of which they were the product. Meanwhile, Prime Minister David Lloyd George, in December 1917, had sent Field Marshal Jan Christian Smuts and Philip Kerr (later Lord Lothian) to Switzerland, unofficially to investigate the possibilities of peace with Austria-Hungary and the Ottoman Empire. Kerr, in particular, handled the Ottoman problem, reporting on December 19. He discussed the situation with Sir Horace Rumbold in Berne, and also with Parodi in Geneva, since the latter had had several conversations with the Turkish Red Crescent Mission then in Switzerland. He learned that there were divergent views within the Committee of Union and Progress and that there was a small group well disposed toward the Entente, although it did not include Enver Paşa, "a pure militarist Germanophile." But Parodi indicated that a number of well-known Turks, such as Cemal Paşa, Lutfi Fikri Bey, a deputy from Adana, Kemal Bey, and others had told him that, although they disliked the Germans intensely, they were hard pressed to reply to the Germanophile propaganda that "whereas the Germans" were "pledged to recover the Empire, the Allies" were "pledged to destroy it." According to Parodi, the Ententophile section of the Committee of Union and Progress would be ready to consider a settlement along the following lines:

1. Acknowledgement by the Ottoman Empire of "the complete political independence of the Kingdom of Hedjaz and of the rest of Arabia."
2. Establishment of Syria, Mesopotamia and Palestine as autonomous provinces "either as separate entities or federated together under the Turkish flag."

[43] USFR, 1918, Supplement 2, 1: 493–516. Acting Secretary of State Frank L. Polk informed Congressman Heflin (Alabama) on March 12, 1918, that the United States was not and had not been concerned "in any way with the secret arrangements or treaties between European powers in regard to war settlements." He also disclaimed knowledge of the secret treaties "except through reports emanating from the Bolshevik press." On March 22, Lansing repeated to Heflin that the Department of State had "no actual proof of the existence of these treaties. The information it has in regard to them is derived from rumors and reports, most of which have appeared in the press."

3. The decision as to Armenia to be left to the European Powers, with the Kurds of Armenia transferred to a separate Kurdish vilayet.
4. But Constantinople "must remain Turk." On this they lay the utmost stress, and it would have the most enormous moral effect in Turkey if it became known that the Allies would be willing that Constantinople should remain Turkish. The Allied declarations which still hold the field are those of Miliukoff. These have never yet been amended. They also wish for a strategic rectification of their frontiers with Bulgaria. They are extremely bitter about the part they surrendered to Bulgaria as the price of getting her into the War and fiercely demand it back. As to the Straits, Bosphorus and Dardanelles, they would agree that they should be neutralised—a special International Commission to be appointed to control the waterways, quays, etc. They would dismantle the forts and make no new ones within a certain radius.[44]

Kerr thought there were possibilities in an approach through Parodi and Muhtar Bey, who was in Switzerland at the time in connection with the exchange of prisoners. Moreover, he made an unofficial communication to Muhtar Bey which indicated that the Allied Powers were not animated by all the hostile intentions which had been attributed to them, that they were willing to free Turkey of the public debt in respect of certain territories to be liberated, and that they were determined that Ottoman authority should be withdrawn from Armenia, Syria, Mesopotamia, Palestine, and Arabia. In the event that an immediate peace with the Allies was prepared, "provided the Dardanelles, Sea of Marmora and the Bosphorus were neutralized," Constantinople was to "remain the capital of Turkey." Neutralization was "to consist of the dismantlement of all forts and the withdrawal of troops within a certain distance of the waterway, and the handing over of the control of the waterway between the Mediterranean and the Black Sea and of any quays and docks which might be necessary to an International Commission, as in the case of the Suez Canal." Nothing, however, came of this unofficial overture, and the war with the Ottoman Empire, after the terrible Allied losses in the Dardanelles campaign, continued on until the end of October 1918.[45]

THE BALFOUR DECLARATION

Meanwhile, on November 2, 1917, the British government announced the very controversial Balfour Declaration, stating that it viewed "with favour the establishment in Palestine of a national home for the Jewish people" and would endeavor to achieve this object, although it was understood "that nothing shall be done which may prejudice the civil and religious rights of existing non-Jewish

[44]See Lloyd George, *War Memoirs*, 5: 55–62.
[45]See also William Yale, "Morgenthau's Special Mission of 1917," *World Politics* 1, no. 3 (1948): 308–20.

communities in Palestine or the rights and political status enjoyed by Jews in any other country."[46] While this problem and others dealing with the broader aspects of the partition of the Ottoman Empire need not detain us here, since our primary concern is with the question of the Straits, it may be said that the policy concerning Palestine had been discussed for a long while, although its launching in 1917 was for "propagandist reasons." David Lloyd George has indicated that the policy of the British government with regard to Palestine and Zionist colonization was officially communicated to the Amir Husayn as early as January 1916 and that the Arab leaders offered no objections "so long as the rights of the Arabs in Palestine were respected."[47]

But the Arabs were disturbed by the Balfour Declaration. Commander David Hogarth, the distinguished British authority on the Middle East, was sent on January 4, 1918 to convey a reassuring message to the Amir Husayn, now King Husayn of the Hijaz, whose forces had rendered excellent service in the war against the Ottoman Empire.[48] Hogarth announced the determination of the Entente Powers "that the Arab race shall be given full opportunity of once again forming a nation in the world," although a special regime would have to be established in Palestine. In that connection, "the friendship of Jewry to the Arab cause" was "equivalent to support in all states where Jews" had "a political influence." Zionist leaders were determined to achieve success for their movement through "friendship and co-operation with the Arabs, and such an offer" was "not one to be lightly thrown aside." Hogarth talked with King Husayn and found him believing that Arab unity and his own kingship were synonymous. However, he thought the problem of international control over the Palestinian holy places not as settled, but as one to be resolved after the peace conference. Interestingly enough, Hogarth doubted that Husayn had abated any "of his original demands on behalf of the Arabs, or in the fullness of time, of himself." Somewhat later,

[46]Parliamentary Debates, House of Commons 99, col. 838. See also Chaim Weizmann, Trial and Error: The Autobiography of Chaim Weizmann (New York: Harper, 1949), chap. 18; Leonard Stein, The Balfour Declaration (London: Valentine, Mitchell, 1961); William I. Cargo, "The Origin of the Balfour Declaration," Papers of the Michigan Academy of Science, Arts, and Letters, 28 (1942): 597–612.

[47]David Lloyd George, Memoirs of the Peace Conference (New Haven: Yale University Press, 1939), 2: 733.

[48]See United Kingdom, Foreign Office, Miscellaneous No. 4 (1939), Statements made on behalf of H.M. Government during the year 1918 in regard to the future status of certain parts of the Ottoman Empire, Cmd. 5964. See also reports of William Yale in USFR, 1918, Supplement 1, 1: 237–38, 241–44, 282. See also Conférence des Préliminaires de Paix, British Delegation, Memorandum on British Commitments to King Husayn.

in June 1918, Hogarth conveyed a declaration to seven Arab representatives in Cairo, giving assurances of independence.

Peace Aims and Statements: 1918

Meanwhile, there were other statements of policy concerning the Middle East. The Soviet denunciation of the secret treaties and the Russian withdrawal from the war gave Prime Minister Lloyd George the occasion to declare, on December 20, 1917, that "of course, the fact that Russia has entered into separate negotiations absolutely disposes of any question there may be about Constantinople."[49] Some days later, the British Labor Conference passed important resolutions on war aims. With regard to the Ottoman Empire, the Labor Conference opposed "handing back to the universally execrated rule of the Turkish Government any subject people which has been freed from it. Thus whatever may be proposed with regard to Armenia, Mesopotamia and Arabia they cannot be restored to the tyranny of the sultan and his pashas." On the other hand, the Labor Conference was opposed to any imperialistic schemes and suggested that these territories be placed under "supernational authority, or league of nations." As for Constantinople, that city "should be made a free port, permanently neutralized, and placed (together with both shores of the Dardanelles and possibly some or all of Asia Minor) under the same impartial administration."[50] On January 5, 1918, Prime Minister Lloyd George, in an important address to the Labor Conference, declared that the Allies were not fighting to deprive the Turkish people of their homelands: "While we do not challenge the maintenance of the Turkish Empire in the homelands of the Turkish race with its capital at Constantinople—the passage between the Mediterranean and the Black Sea being internationalized and neutralized—Arabia, Armenia, Mesopotamia, Syria and Palestine are in our judgment entitled to a recognition of their separate national conditions."[51]

DEVELOPMENT OF THE AMERICAN POSITION

Lloyd George had foreshadowed—and even "scooped"—President Wilson's Fourteen Points address of January 8, 1918, Point XII of

---

[49]*Parliamentary Debates, House of Commons*, 100, col. 2220.

[50]*World Peace Foundation* 1, no. 3 (February 1918): 121. See also Leonard Wolf, *The Future of Constantinople* (London, 1917), passim.

[51]See Lloyd George, *War Memoirs of David Lloyd George, 1917-1918*, 5: 70; Lawrence Zetland, Earl of Ronaldshay, *Life of Lord Curzon* (New York: Boni and Livewright, 1928), 3: 151-61; Laurence Evans, *United States Policy and the Partition of Turkey, 1914-1924* (Baltimore: The Johns Hopkins University Press, 1965), chap. 2.

which was devoted to the Ottoman Empire: "The Turkish portions of
the Ottoman Empire should be assured a secure sovereignty, but the
other nationalities which are now under Turkish rule should be assured an undoubted security of life and an absolutely unmolested opportunity of autonomous development and the Dardanelles should be
permanently opened as a free passage to the ships and commerce of
all nations under international guarantees."[52]

There was some feeling in official quarters that the United States
should declare war against the Ottoman Empire and, on May 2, 1918,
Secretary of State Lansing reported to President Wilson that, indeed,
a majority of the Senate Committee on Foreign Relations favored a
declaration of war against both the Ottoman Empire and Bulgaria.[53]
On May 7, General Tasker H. Bliss indicated that the Supreme
Council favored such a declaration against the Ottoman Empire, but
not against Bulgaria at the time. Both Italy and France favored such
action against both. Lansing advised the President that, while all the
Entente Powers favored action against the Ottoman government, the
British government felt that it would be wise to delay action against
Bulgaria, a view which General Bliss shared.[54]

Late in the summer, on September 21, 1918, Secretary Lansing
prepared a memorandum for the guidance of the American peace
commissioners, in which he dealt with the problem of the Ottoman
Empire, which was to be reduced to Anatolia, perhaps with no
European possessions at all. Constantinople and the Straits were to
be placed under an international protectorate or a government acting
as a mandatory. Greece was to have the Dodecanese Islands and possibly territory on the coast of Asia Minor. Armenia and Syria were to
be placed under the protectorate of such Powers as seemed "expedient from a domestic as well as an international point of view."
Palestine was to be placed under an autonomous or international
protectorate or under a mandatory Power. Great Britain was to be
full sovereign over Egypt or to exercise a complete protectorate, while
the Arabs were to receive consideration as to full or partial sovereignty over such state or states as they might establish.[55]

On October 14, 1918, through the Spanish Ambassador in Washington, the Ottoman government indicated its readiness to negotiate

[52]Ray Stannard Baker and W. E. Dodd, *The Public Papers of Woodrow Wilson* (New
York: Harpers, 1927), 3: 160-61. See also report made in January 1918 by The
American Inquiry to President Wilson regarding "War Aims and Peace Aims," R. S.
Baker, *Woodrow Wilson and World Settlement* (Garden City: Doubleday and Page,
1922), 3: 25-41. For origins of The American Inquiry, see *USFR, Paris Peace
Conference* (1919), 1: 9 ff. Hereafter cited as *PPC*.
[53]*USFR, The Lansing Papers*, 2: 121-22.
[54]Ibid., pp. 124-30. See also *USFR, 1918, Supplement 1*, 1: 213, 215, 227.
[55]Robert Lansing, *Peace Negotiations* (Boston: Houghton Mifflin, 1921), pp. 192-97.

peace with the Entente, accepting as a basis for the negotiations the program "laid down by the President of the United States in his message to Congress of January 8, 1918 and in his subsequent declarations, especially the speech of September 27."[56] It was learned on October 29 that the Ottoman government was "very anxious" to renew "friendly and diplomatic relations" with the United States and, indeed, on October 30, 1918, one month after Bulgaria had surrendered, an armistice was signed with the Ottoman Empire at Mudros, the terms of which, among other things, guaranteed access to the Black Sea and provided for Allied occupation of the forts along the Dardanelles and Bosphorus.[57]

Meanwhile, the official American commentary on President Wilson's Fourteen Points, which was prepared by October 1918, dealt in detail with the Turkish problem.[58] Constantinople and the Straits, under this elaborated statement, were to be internationalized, the Turks were to be restricted to Anatolia, while the coastal region, "where the Greeks predominate," was to be placed under international control, with Greece as the probable mandatory. Armenia was to be given a Mediterranean port under some protecting power. Despite the French claim, it was felt that the Armenians might prefer a British protectorate. Syria had already been allotted to France, in any event. The best mandatory for Mesopotamia and the Arabs appeared to be Great Britain, whose armed forces had already conquered most of these territories. Palestine, likewise, would probably go under a British mandatory. Guarantees for the mandates were to be written into the peace treaties, containing protection for minorities, the open door, and the internationalization of the railway trunk lines.

Just two days before the armistice with Imperial Germany, on November 9, 1918, Great Britain and France issued a joint declaration which embodied vague and general promises, stating that their aim in the Middle East was "the complete and final emancipation of all those peoples so long oppressed by the Turks, and to establish

---

[56] *USFR, 1918, Supplement 2*, 1: 360.

[57] Ibid., p. 416. For the "Five Points" of September 27, 1918, see Baker and Dodd, *Public Papers of Woodrow Wilson*, 3: 257; *USFR, 1918, Supplement 1*, 1: 441-43. See also Lloyd George, *War Memoirs*, 6, chap. 6.

[58] See Seymour, *Intimate Papers of Colonel House*, 4: 199-200. See also David Hunter Miller's draft memorandum of July 31, 1918, a portion of which deals with the Ottoman Empire. Miller argued that Point XII excluded complete sovereignty over certain portions of the Empire, but not necessarily required its abandonment over Armenia, Syria, Palestine, and Arabia. Internationalization of the Straits was recommended. David Hunter Miller, *My Diary at the Conference of Paris, with Documents*, (22 vols., New York, 1928), vol. 2, Document 85, pp. 428-57. See also Henri Barbusse, ed., *The Soviet Union and Peace* (New York: International Publishers, 1930), pp. 48-57, for Soviet comments on the Wilson position.

national governments and administrations which shall derive their authority from the initiative and free will of the peoples themselves. To realize this, France and Great Britain are in agreement to encourage and assist the establishment of native governments in Syria and Mesopotamia, now liberated by the Allies, as also in those territories for whose liberation they are striving, and to recognize those governments immediately after they are effectively established."[59]

TOWARD THE PEACE CONFERENCE

The Amir Faysal, son of the Amir Husayn, had entered Damascus with his forces on October 1, 1918, and it now appeared that at last the Arabs had come into their own.[60] Undoubtedly, however, the Arabs had expected rather too much from the Anglo-French declaration and the promises which had been made to them. They took the November declaration to be a more or less precise definition of their status when the peace conference assembled in Paris in January 1919. Meanwhile, on the eve of the conference, at a meeting of the British cabinet in December 1918, there was much discussion of Middle Eastern problems.[61] It was after the cabinet meeting that Lloyd George made an arrangement with Clemenceau, whereby the vilayet of Mosul was transferred from the French sphere of influence and Palestine was to come under the control of Great Britain instead of being internationalized. The formal consent of France to these changes was completed on February 15, 1919.[62]

Other claimants, as already noted, were also pressing their demands as to the Ottoman estate, among them the Armenians, to say nothing of the Greeks, and the American minister in Athens, Garrett Droppers, saw no solution of the Ottoman question, "as France, Italy, England will all have a slice if Greece takes hers, so I much prefer to

[59]J. C. Hurewitz *Diplomacy in the Near and Middle East* (Princeton: N.J. D. Van Nostrand, 1956), 2: 28; *PPC*, 2: 274-75. On October 17, 1918, General Sir Edmund Allenby advised Faysal "that whatever measures might be taken during the period of military administration they were purely provisional and could not be allowed to prejudice the final settlement by the peace conference, at which no doubt the Arabs would have a representative. . . . I reminded the Emir Feisal that the Allies were in honour bound to endeavour to reach a settlement in accordance with the wishes of the people concerned, and urged him to place his trust wholeheartedly in their good faith," Cmd. 5057.
[60]See, especially, Zeine N. Zeine, *The Struggle for Arab Independence: Western Diplomacy and the Rise and Fall of Faisal's Kingdom in Syria* (Beirut: Khayats, 1960), chap. 2.
[61]Lloyd George, *Memoirs of the Peace Conference*, 2: chap. 23, especially, pp. 739-46.
[62]See Secret Minutes of the Conference, March 20, 1919; Baker, *Woodrow Wilson and World Settlement*, 3: 1-19; Harry N. Howard, *The King-Crane Commission: An American Inquiry in the Middle East* (Beirut: Khayats, 1963), ch. 1.

see the country remain as a unit, giving to non-Turish population every guarantee, and removing police and finance from native hands. For some years we shall have the worst passions let loose in Asia Minor unless we settle the question with a single eye to resident population."[63]

The Italian government, in December 1918, was already proposing that a strong contingent of Italian troops be sent to Constantinople, "in accordance with the agreement for the international occupation of that town," a proposition which the British government did not disapprove, although it feared that the Greeks would take similar steps if the Italians proceeded to occupy Anatolia without consultation. That the situation in the Ottoman capital was now growing quite critical was very clear from the reports of the American commissioner, Lewis C. Heck. On January 4, 1919, he reported that ordinary government activities were "badly disorganized," the food problem in Constantinople "uncertain," and the financial situation "more and more critical." As to the problems about to face the Ottoman Empire, the American Commissioner stated:

The Armenians have on the whole behaved well and have been moderate in their claims avoiding all agitation which might provoke further trouble in the interior. Such prudence is essential in view of poor public security and danger of further outrages. The landing at Mersina of a large number of Armenians with French troops is claimed by the Turkish Armistice Commission to be a direct provocation and very likely will lead to troubles in the Asia Minor District where Turkish population is much aroused. If an independent Armenia is to be established, official announcement should be kept in abeyance until a large number of the persons guilty of the previous massacres have been placed under arrest in order to show to the Turkish population the danger of indulgence in further massacres.

On the other hand, the Greeks are very extravagant in their claims which include the city of Constantinople. They have sent here Naval and Military forces, and local Greek population have been provacative towards the Turks, although so far, there have been no serious disorders between the two elements.

General attitude among Turks is one of hopeless[ness], waiting the outcome of the Peace Conference. They resent permission accorded to Armenians and other racial elements to send representatives to Paris while such permission has been refused to them. As publicly expressed, their chief hope is in the application of the President's principles of nationality and self-determination, as they feel that other Allied Powers are likely to be more severe than the United States. . . . At present Turks are trying to create friction between British and French by praising the former, and criticizing the latter at every opportunity. However, large French investments and financial interests in the country are counted on in some circles to secure French support for the future maintenance of independent Turkish Government.[64]

[63]*PPC*, 2: 271, 275.   [64]Ibid., pp. 277-78, 280-83.

Insofar as they were known, the United States government was somewhat disturbed by the Allied plans for the disposition of the Ottoman Empire which had been elaborated during World War I. As to Constantinople and the Straits, the United States favored a regime which would provide for the most complete freedom of transit and navigation, under international guarantees. This was very clear in principle from Point XII in President Wilson's well-known fourteen Point address of January 8, 1919. The enunciation of a principle, long established in the Anglo-American tradition of "freedom of the seas," however, was one thing. The establishment of a new regime, as the Paris Peace Conference was to demonstrate, and its implementation was quite another.

Chapter III

The Question of Constantinople and the Straits at the Paris Peace Conference (1919)

The Position of the Powers at the Opening of the Peace Conference

When the Paris Peace Conference formally opened on January 18, 1919, the policies to be adopted concerning the future of the Middle East were already well outlined in the secret agreements of 1915-17, as well as in the declarations which had followed in the final year of the war. The problems raised by the collapse of the Ottoman Empire were so serious and the conflict of interests, especially between France and Great Britain, so fundamental and vital that it was not until four and one-half years later, with the signature of the Treaty of Lausanne on July 24, 1923, that the Powers reached a solution.[1] The question of Constantinople and the Straits—and of American policy and interest—was only one of the great issues involved, but it raised all the other problems in the area, including the disposition of Turkey proper on the Anatolian plateau, Armenia, and the spoils of war along the Mediterranean shores and in the Arab world.

THE POSITION OF FRANCE

The French position seemed fairly clear on the eve of the discussions at Paris. When Marcel Cachin raised the question of the secret

---

[1] In general, see Harry N. Howard, *The Partition of Turkey: A Diplomatic History, 1913-1923* (Norman: University of Oklahoma Press, 1931; New York: Howard Fertig, 1966), chap. 7; *The King-Crane Commission: An American Inquiry in the Middle East* (Beirut: Khayats, 1963), chap. 1.

agreements in the Chamber of Deputies on December 27, 1918, Briand declared that the agreements would be "brought before the congress of peace," but could become treaties only when they had been ratified by the conference. Nevertheless, when Foreign Minister Pichon spoke in the Chamber the next day, he declared that France had "incontestable" rights in the Ottoman Empire. France was to stand, in other words, on the basis of the secret agreements and to insist on observance to the letter.[2]

THE POSITION OF THE UNITED STATES

From the very moment of their arrival, it would seem, and before the peace conference got under way, the Americans were engaged in conversations as to their attitude toward a Turkish settlement. As early as December 2, 1918, David Hunter Miller, the legal adviser to the United States Delegation, was engaged in discussion with Lord Eustace Percy, of the British Foreign Office, who raised the question of internationalizing Constantinople and the Straits under the League of Nations. Among other things, Lord Eustace "went so far as to suggest that if the formulation of general principles were attempted the Panama Canal would come in the same class as the Straits." So would the Suez Canal and other international waterways—as President Truman was to sense at Potsdam in 1945—but Mr. Miller replied "pleasantly" that "such a grouping seemed hardly among the possibilities," and he regarded Percy's remark concerning the Panama Canal as "an attempt to show difficulties in the way of the idealistic principles of the United States." On January 11, 1919, Miller dined with Lord Robert Cecil and Colonel T. E. Lawrence, among others, and there was much discussion of the Ottoman Empire, Miller reporting the British representatives present unanimous that "the United States should take Constantinople, and agreement, although reluctant on the part of Colonel Lawrence, that the United States would administer Syria."[3]

At about the same time, January 9, Harold Nicolson, of the British Delegation, conferred with Professors Albert H. Lybyer and Clive Day, of the United States, and found them "evidently firm about turning Turks out of Europe, but vague as to who is to be [their] successor in the Constantinople zone."[4] As to the limits of the region

[2]*Journal Officiel. Chambre* (1918:2), p. 3716; Georges Clemenceau, *Discours de Paix* (Paris: Plon, 1938), pp. 14-15.

[3]David Hunter Miller, *My Diary at the Conference of Paris, with Documents*, (22 vols.; New York, 1928). Hereafter cited as *MD*. See, especially, *MD*, 1: 27-28, 74.

[4]Harold Nicolson, *Peace-Making. 1919. Studies in Modern Diplomacy* (New York: Harcourt, Brace, 1939), pp. 228-29. Nicolson noted that the Americans "would be quite prepared to see us at Constantinople as Mandatory—but less prepared to act in

of the Straits, the Americans suggested two alternatives: (1) a restricted zone, including the Çatalca lines, Gallipoli, the Marmara Islands, and a section of the Asiatic shore, might be established; (2) an extended zone, including essentially the Enos-Midia (Enez-Midye) line in Europe, and the line from Edremit to Sakarya in Asia, might be established. Nicolson surmized that Wilson wanted "some small power, or some group of small powers, to administer this Constantinople or Straits Zone." The Americans objected and desired "either U.S.A. or Great Britain to assume the mandate. They doubt, however, whether American opinion would allow of them taking the mandate themselves. As regards Turkey in Asia they evidently expect to have to take over Armenia, but are vague about the rest."

A few days after the formal opening of the Peace Conference, on January 21, the Intelligence Section of the American Commission to Negotiate Peace had worked out the outline of a report with recommendations for the President, a considerable portion of which was devoted to the Middle East.[5] Beginning with the region of Constantinople and the Straits, the Intelligence Section recommended that "there be established in the Constantinople region an international state," that it be under a mandate of the League of Nations, and receive such a governmental organization as might "seem most expedient to the peace conference." The boundaries would include the entire coastline of the Straits and the Sea of Marmara, with the Enes-Midye line in Europe, in part the Sakarya River line, including the towns of Bursa and Bandirma on the Asiatic shore. It was also recommended that "the Bosphorus, and Dardanelles be permanently opened as a free passageway to the ships of commerce of all nations, under international guarantees." As to Turkey proper, it was proposed that "there be established a Turkish Anatolian state" and that

---

that capacity themselves. U.S. opinion not ready for this responsibility, but they 'might' be ready to assume responsibility for Armenia. They are very keen on a Greek Zone at Smyrna." Arthur D. Howden Smith, *Mr. House of Texas* (New York: Funk and Wagnalls, 1940), pp. 164–65, says that he suggested to House in January 1919 a "permanent solution of the Question of Constantinople and the Straits." That was to internationalize the city and the region of the Straits, making Constantinople the seat of the League of Nations. House finally disapproved, however, because of the climate—he was counting on being the U.S. delegate to the League of Nations. "So he plumped for Geneva, where he had always been comfortable."

[5]*MD*, 4: 249–65, Document 246. Outline of Tentative Report and Recommendations prepared by the Intelligence Section, in Accordance with Instructions, for the President and Plenipotentiaries, January 21, 1919. See also William H. Hall, "Reconstructing Turkey," *Asia* 18, no. 11 (November 1918): 945–51, and William H. Hall, ed., *Reconstruction in Turkey. A Series of Reports Compiled for the American Committee of Armenian and Syrian Relief* (New York, 1918),—for private distribution. See also Laurence Evans, *United States Policy and the Partition of Turkey, 1914–1924* (Baltimore: The Johns Hopkins University Press, 1965), chas. 3 and 4.

the mandatory principle be applied to Turkish Anatolia, although no recommendation was made "as to the Power to be selected to carry out this principle." While the Dodecanese Islands and Rhodes were to be assigned to Greece, there was no recommendation that the Smyrna region be so assigned. To give Greece "a foothold upon the mainland would be to invite immediate trouble. Greece would press her claims for more territory; Turkey would feel that her new boundaries were run so as to give her a great handicap at the very start. The harbor of Smyrna has been for centuries an outlet for the products of the Central Anatolian plateau and upland."

Several recommendations were made concerning the non-Turkish portions of the Ottoman Empire, although they need not concern us in detail. It was proposed that an Armenian state be established, under a mandate of the League of Nations, with outlets on the Mediterranean through Cilicia and on the Black Sea through Trabzon. A Mesopotamian state was proposed, but with no suggestion as to the mandatory, with a possibility of confederation with other Arab states. A similar suggestion was made as to Syria. A British mandate for Palestine, with provision for a Jewish National Home, and adequate safeguards for the Holy Places, was proposed, and it was recommended that the desert portion of the Arabian Peninsula be treated separately. Nevertheless, "the policing of the Red Sea, Indian Ocean, and Persian Gulf coasts of Arabia, and the border lands behind them," was to be left with the British Empire.

THE BRITISH POSITION

Similarly, British experts outlined the British position at the opening of the conference. A series of important memoranda set forth the position to be assumed concerning the Middle East and deserve considerable study.[6] In a memorandum of February 18, 1919, which is the definitive statement at the opening of the conference, the term "Middle East" was taken to refer to those "Middle Eastern" countries which had been in the war and which were now subject to "re-settlement at the hands of the Peace Conference." This included all European and Asiatic territories formerly under direct or indirect

[6]See, especially, Great Britain, Foreign Office, *Statement of British Policy in the Middle East for Submission to the Peace Conference (if required)*, February 18, 1919. *Statement by the British Government for the Peace Conference Concerning the Settlement of the Middle East (1st Proof for Revision)*, February 7, 1919; *Maps Illustrating Memorandum Respecting the Settlement of Turkey and the Arabian Peninsula: Appendix on Previous Commitments of His Majesty's Government in the Middle East; Memorandum on British Commitments to King Hussein*. These memoranda were prepared by and under the direction of Arnold J. Toynbee. See also Fayez A. Sayegh, "British Pledges on Palestine," *Arab Outlook* 2, nos. 4 and 5 (April–May 1964): 1–12.

Ottoman sovereignty and "territories formerly Russian, situated between the Russo-Turkish and Russo-Persian frontiers and the Caucasus Mountains—a physical frontier which may be taken roughly as the geographical boundary between the Middle East and North-Eastern Europe." The principles to be applied included the Armistice of November 11, 1918, the Wilson Fourteen Points of January 8, 1918, and subsequent addresses, "with certain reservations"—none of which concerned the Middle East, however. It was noted, nevertheless, that technically "the Allies have pledged themselves to the United States to make peace on the basis of the Fourteen Points only with Germany, and they are not bound by them to Turkey, with whom they had previously concluded an armistice on different conditions. They are, however, bound towards Germany, the United States and each other, that the settlement of Turkey shall be made on the basis of these points and of the President's subsequent pronouncements."

A number of points in Wilson's Fourteen Points Address bore on the Middle East, although Point XII specifically referred to the Ottoman Empire, and the Mt. Vernon Address of February 4, 1918, calling for a settlement on the basis of the free acceptance of the people involved, also applied in principle. While the British government agreed with these principles and had pledged itself, together with its allies, to make them the basis of the settlement, it was also bound "by certain previous treaties, agreements and understandings entered into before or during the war, but all in circumstances very different from the present, which it might be difficult or impossible to harmonise with the new situation and the new principles governing the settlement."

In applying the Wilsonian principles to the situation in the Ottoman Empire, the British statement insisted that "non-Turkish populations," or populations in which the Turkish element was in a minority, should "be liberated completely from Turkish rule, and from all political connection, even nominal, with the Ottoman Government," with the reservation of equitable participation in the prewar Ottoman debt. This principle was to apply to the Arabs and the Armenians, and possibly even to Thrace and Smyrna. But where the Turkish people were in a majority, where they had not "given the minority elements security of life, separation should follow." The rest of Turkey should be independent, although it should be required to accept foreign advisers, nominated by the various Powers under the authority of the Peace Conference, for "the more important financial and administrative departments." Otherwise, Turkey "should be independent." Moreover, "the peoples of these independent States should be at liberty to opt for the assistance of a foreign Power," but the Conference, "with due consideration for the wishes of the peoples," should define the conditions of assistance, and the assisting Power "should act as the Mandatory of the Conference or ultimately of the League of Nations." Subject to certain limitations, the principle of self-determination should be accepted. There were areas, as in Thrace, Constantinople, and Armenia, in which the people could not speak with a united voice and in which the "Assisting Power" would have "to be chosen by the Conference rather than by the people themselves." The Armenians and the Zionist Jews, it was felt, had claims "to special consideration out of proportion to their present numerical strength." Finally, there were "world interests such as the 'permanent opening of the Black Sea Straits as a free passage to the ships and commerce of all nations under international guarantees,' or access to the Holy Places in Palestine for all religious or denominations legitimately interested in each of them, which are so important that they must, if necessary, take precedence over the wishes of the inhabitants of the localities in which they are situated."

The British memorandum then proceeded to examine the disposition of the Ottoman territories specifically. For example, there was the problem of Thrace, Constantinople, and the Turkish Straits: "His Majesty's Government consider that the free passage of the Black Sea Straits, on a footing of equality for the ships of all nations, in peace or war, under international control (as stipulated in the Twelfth Point of President Wilson's address of 8th January 1918), can be secured only by removing the shores of the Bosphorus and Dardanelles, and part, at least, of the littoral of the Sea of Marmora, from Turkish sovereignty, dismantling all fortifications, and introducing some external authority to secure the maintenance of the desired conditions." The necessary authority could be provided in two alternative ways. First, a mandatory Power might be appointed to assist the administration of the region and keep the peace among the different nationalities, maintaining "the freedom of the Straits in the name of the Conference or ultimately of the League of Nations." Or, second, the same authority might be delegated to an international body by the conference or the League of Nations, with a high commissioner as executive officer. But the settlement of the problem of the Straits, naturally, would affect that of Eastern, or Ottoman, Thrace. If the unity of the Straits, including the entire shoreline, were placed under a mandatory, a portion of Ottoman Thrace would be involved. The entire province, with a mixture of Greeks and Turks, "might possibly be thrown in, a few frontier districts being assigned, on geographical and to a less extent on ethnographical grounds, to

Bulgaria." But if the zone of the Straits were to be limited to Constantinople and the immediate shoreline of the Bosphorus, the rest of the Asiatic littoral would remain to Turkey, "while the least objectionable solution for the European littoral of the Sea of Marmora and its Thracian hinterland would be to assign it to Greece."

The British hoped that the Italian and Greek governments would arrive at an agreement relative to the Dodecanese Islands, which the Italians had taken in the Tripolitan War of 1911–12, under which the wishes of the people could be given effect. Despite the Turkish character of the hinterland, it was felt that the problem of Smyrna, with its large Greek population, should be treated separately, "and that the question of its union with Greece ought to be considered by the Conference. . . . His Majesty's Government suggest that the question ought not to be decided without consultation of the various sections of the local population and expert investigation of the geographical problem."

The problem of Anatolia was a very large one, but since the major part of the population was "predominantly Turk," the British believed that "an independent Turkish national State should be left in existence in this area." As to boundaries:

"The boundaries of this State should depend on the west, upon the disposal of the Straits and the Sea of Marmora, and on the decision of the Conference in regard to Smyrna. On the East, His Majesty's Government consider that the frontier should be drawn where the more or less homogeneous Turkish population of Anatolia gives place to the mixed Turkish, Armenian, and Greek population of the northeastern vilayets of the former Ottoman Empire. They would propose a line leaving Selefke, Kasaria, and Samsun in Turkey, but excluding Mersina, Sivas and Kerasund."

In view of its bankruptcy, the British government believed the Ottoman government "should be required to appoint foreign advisers" to such financial and administrative departments as those of Finance, Customs and Internal Revenue, the Post Office, and the Audit and Establishment Office. Such advisers should be nominated by certain governments represented at the conference, and should not be removed without their consent. The Ottoman government should be bound by their advice. On the other hand, the British believed assistance could be fruitful only if it aimed "at promoting the prosperity and productivity of the country." It might extend to agriculture, woods and forests, and communications. This would mean a mandatory for the Ottoman state: "In the event of any Power being opted for by the Turkish people, the Conference should define the conditions on which that Power should co-operate in the reconstruction of Turkey with the advisers proposed above and should appoint the Power to be its mandatory, or ultimately the mandatory of the League of Nations, within these limits."

In the non-Turkish portions of the former Empire, it was recommended that the six Armenian vilayets be "independent, but under mandate." In view of the long-standing special interests of Great Britain in the Arabian Peninsula, it was proposed that the Peace Conference, or ultimately, the League of Nations, recognize the special relations existing, or which came into existence, between Great Britain and the various Arab states. Mesopotamia, together with Southern Kurdistan, it was suggested, should be placed under mandate, along with Syria and Palestine.

But the British experts were not unaware that Great Britain and France had entered into secret agreements concerning the disposition of Ottoman territories, and that some of these were contrary to the spirit of the Wilson principles, and it was so stated. This was especially true of the French claim in Syria. It is somewhat curious to observe, however, the statement that Great Britain had "no previous commitments" in the matter of "Thrace, Constantinople and the Black Sea Straits," unless the inference is that the defection of Soviet Russia as a consequence of the revolution of November 1917 simply effaced that embodied in the agreement of March 12, 1915. Moreover, the pledge to allow the Italians to remain in the Dodecanese Islands was inconsistent with the Wilson principles.

But it is also of interest to note the views of Lord Curzon concerning the possible disposition of the Ottoman Empire, for he disagreed with some of his cabinet colleagues on this important subject. In a memorandum prepared as early as January 2, 1918, but not circulated until the following year, he argued that the right of self-determination, to be accorded to the "subject races" of the Ottoman Empire, should also be given to the Turkish people, with the Anatolian Plateau to be preserved in its integrity for the future Turkish state, and no portion of "Turkey proper for the benefit of the Greeks, the French or the Italians." While either Ankara or Bursa might become the new Turkish capital, Lord Curzon would deprive Turkey of its European possessions, and Constantinople and the Straits would be internationalized under the League of Nations, "if possible under American chairmanship, charged with the task of keeping open the Straits and of safeguarding Constantinople as the 'cosmopolis or international city' of the Eastern world."[7]

[7]Harold Nicolson, *Curzon: The Last Phase, 1919-1925: A Study in Post-War Diplomacy* (Boston: Houghton Mifflin, 1934), pp. 75–78. Curzon believed that the Power "clearly indicated" as the guardian of the Straits was Great Britain, but he felt that no British government would dream of adding "so vast and perilous a charge" to its responsibilities.

Conflicting Aspirations at Paris

THE UNITED STATES AND THE MANDATES

As noted above, the Turkish problem was a very important issue at Paris, in informal exchanges of opinion between the Delegations of the United States and the United Kingdom, especially, on the eve of the Peace Conference, and it was generally agreed that the Ottoman Empire should be broken into its component national elements. President Wilson, in a first draft of the Covenant of the League of Nations, on January 10, 1919, had indicated that territories formerly belonging to the Ottoman Empire should be placed under some kind of trust under the projected League of Nations and not be the subject of annexation by any Power.[8] But it was not until January 30 that formal discussion of the Ottoman problem essentially began, in connection with consideration of the mandate problem, when David Lloyd George indicated that the principle already had been accepted, although, in general, mandates were to be applied only to conquered parts, either of the Ottoman or the German Empire, which excluded Smyrna, Adalia, and Northern Anatolia. A British memorandum of January 29 called for the separation of Armenia, Syria, Mesopotamia, Palestine, and the Arabian Peninsula from Ottoman rule, and the placing of these areas under mandate, the wishes of the inhabitants being "a principal consideration in the selection of the mandatory power."[9]

But President Wilson did not share entirely the views of his British colleague and did not believe it the proper moment to discuss the partition of the Ottoman Empire. While he had heard talk of an American mandate, he felt that the American people would not be inclined to accept one: "He himself had succeeded in getting the people of America to do many things and he might succeed in getting them to accept this burden also. But even if it was suggested that American troops should occupy Constantinople, or Mesopotamia, it was evident that they could not do so as they were not at war with Turkey. Therefore, it would, in his opinion, be extremely unwise to accept any form of mandate until they knew how it was intended to work."[10] While these comments filled Lloyd George with "despair,"

---

[8]Howard, *The Partition of Turkey*, pp. 218-19; *The King-Crane Commission*, chap. 1.

[9]Department of State, *The Foreign Relations of the United States. Paris Peace Conference, 1919* (Washington, D.C.: USGPO, 1942-47), 3: 785-86, 795-96; 11: I, 5. Hereafter cited as *PPC*.

[10]*PPC*, 3: 788. Henry White, a Republican member of the United States delegation, wrote to Senator Lodge that he was much interested in Lodge's view as "to the possibility of our people's being willing to accept a mandate from the League of Nations to administer Constantinople and the Bosphorus." White had "a sort of feeling" that, "with time to educate public opinion" to "the idea that our doing so would be

President Wilson reiterated that "he could think of nothing the people of the United States would be less inclined to accept than military responsibility in Asia."[11] Finally, on January 30, the mandate principle was formally approved, and it was agreed that the Powers should apply the principle "that the well-being and development of such peoples" formed "a sacred trust of civilization," and that provisions for the performance of this trust should be written into the Covenant of the League of Nations, as had been proposed by the British Delegation. It was thought that the tutelage of such peoples should be entrusted to certain "advanced" nations, although the character of the mandate was to vary with differing conditions. Certain peoples, formerly a part of the Ottoman Empire, had already reached such a stage of development that their independence could be recognized provisionally, "subject to the rendering of administrative advice and assistance by a mandatory power until such time as they are able to stand alone." Moreover, the desires of the communities were to be "a principal consideration in the selection of the mandatory power."[12]

VOICES OF THE PEOPLES

Within a few days the Supreme Council was ready to hear the claims and counterclaims of the Middle Eastern peoples, although the voice of the Turkish people was relatively inaudible in Paris, even if it thundered on the Anatolian Plateau.[13] First came Venizelos, the premier of Greece, on February 5, 1919,[14] who asked for Northern Epirus, the Aegean Islands, Thrace, and Western Asia Minor, with the city and vilayet of Smyrna, and cast a longing eye toward Constantinople, which he considered a "Greek city," without formally claiming it. When Venizelos concluded the next day, Lloyd George, who was anxious to maintain control of the Straits, proposed the examination of the Greek demands by an expert committee, which reported on March 6, accepting in part the claim to Northern Epirus, although the Italian representative opposed. All delegations accepted the Greek claims to Thrace, although Italy would make no recommendation for Western Asia Minor, because it could not be separated from the problem of Anatolia as a whole. Moreover, Greek and Italian

---

for the world's good and the promotion of peace, our people might possibly not be unwilling to assume that amount of responsiblity, and I am exceedingly glad to know that you are inclined to that opinion." See Allen Nevins, *Henry White: Thirty Years of American Diplomacy* (New York: Harper and Brothers, 1930), p. 376.

[11]*PPC*, 3: 789-90, 805, 807, 817.
[12]*MD*, 4: 130-31.
[13]Howard, *The Partition of Turkey*, pp. 222-31.
[14]*PPC*, 3: 859-66, 868; 11: 20.

ambitions clashed in the Smyrna region. Amir Faysal presented the case for Arab independence and unity on February 6, and Chaim Weizmann presented the Zionist claims to Palestine on February 27, while Boghos Nubar Pasha appeared for the Armenian Delegation on February 26.[15]

As the Arabs were opposed to the Zionist claims to Palestine, so were the Turks opposed to those of the Armenians. But there were other Turkish elements at Paris, aside from those who were to represent the Ottoman government at the conference. The Congress of Liberal Turks, represented by General Şerif Paşa, presented a number of memoranda for the consideration of the conference. Essentially, this group desired the preservation of the territorial integrity of the Ottoman Empire, including Constantinople. Moreover, on the eve of the conference, the Turkish Wilsonian League,[16] one of the founders of which was Hüseyin Bey, of Robert College, prepared a program asking President Wilson for American supervision of Turkish affairs for a period of some fifteen to twenty-five years. Essentially the Turkish Wilsonian League called for the preservation of the sovereignty of the sultan under a constitutional monarchy, protection of the rights of minorities, appointment of "an American Adviser-in-Chief" with expert assistance in various key ministries, supervision of the police and *gendarmerie* in each province, and "assurance by an international guarantee of the complete neutrality of Turkey during the period of American supervision."

Such were the complicated problems involved in the future of the Middle East when the Peace Conference began its deliberations in January and February 1919. How the problems were to be met, especially in regard to the Turkish Straits, will be examined in the pages which follow.

The Problem of Constantinople and the Straits

Detailed discussion of the disposition of Constantinople and the Straits, as we have seen, began very early at Paris, and there was constant consideration of the problems involved for a number · of weeks. But no solution was actually to be reached until the signature

---

[15]*PPC*, 3: 888-94, 1015-20; 11: 61, 63, 66-67, 72, 76-77, 79, 85, 87, 99, 116, 133-34, 140, 145-46, 150, 155; 4: 169ff., 147-57. See Great Britain, Foreign Office, *Documents on British Foreign Policy 1919-1939*, edited by E. L. Woodward and Rohan Butler, first series (London: HMSO, 1962), 4: 920-24. Hereafter cited as *British Documents, 1919-1939*. See also *MD*, 3: 188-89; 4: 297-99; J. C. Hurewitz, *Diplomacy in the Near and Middle East* (Princeton, N.J.: D. Van Nostrand, 1956), 2: 38-39.

[16]Howard, *The King-Crane Commission*, pp. 28-29.

of the Treaty of Lausanne, on July 24, 1923, along lines substantially different from those contemplated at the Paris Peace Conference in 1919.

THE QUESTION OF MANDATES

Throughout March and April 1919 the experts labored on the project of a Constantinopolitan state. This was an exceedingly difficult and complicated business. It was intimately related to a host of other basic issues involving the disposition of the Ottoman Empire. But until its structure and boundaries were determined, it appeared impossible to formulate the outlines of the rest of Thrace, Anatolia, and the Smyrna region of Asia Minor.[17]

It was during this period that Italy became especially nervous both about Fiume and the problem of Asia Minor. David Lloyd George and Clemenceau suggested on April 21 that Rome might compromise on the Adriatic question if given a mandate in Asia Minor, which, Clemenceau thought might cover a part of Anatolia, bordering on the territory assigned to Greece in the Smyrna region, and the Constantinopolitan and Armenian mandates.[18] President Wilson opposed the idea for a number of reasons, while Lloyd George proposed an Italian sphere such as Great Britain had in various parts of the world. Because of President Wilson's opposition on the Adriatic question, the Italians left Paris on April 24 and did not return until May 5.[19] On April 30 it was announced that an Italian warship had gone to Smyrna, and it was suggested that all the Powers send warships to that troubled area.

These developments, of course, were of deep concern to the Paris peacemakers and, on May 5, at a meeting of the Council of Four, Lloyd George suggested the impossibility of an immediate settlement of the mandate problem in the Ottoman Empire and a redistribution

[17]Howard, *The Partition of Turkey*, p. 232; *MD*, 6: 284-86, 320; *PPC*, 5: 1-14, for Council of Four discussion, March 20, 1919, of project for interallied commission to investigate conditions of peace in the Ottoman Empire.

[18]On April 1 Wilson, Clemenceau, Lloyd George, and Orlando agreed that Turkey had only to recognize the territorial limits of Armenia, that a strictly ethnographic limit should be applied between Greece and Turkey, and Constantinople and the Straits were to be placed under a separate mandate of the League of Nations. It remained to be determined whether Turkey would be independent or placed under a mandate separate from that of Constantinople. See Paul Mantoux, *Les Délibérations du Conseil des Quatres. 24 Mars-28 Juin 1919*, I, *Jusqu'à la Rèmise Allemande des Conditions de Paix* (2 vols.; Paris: Editions du Centre National de la Recherche Scientifique, 1955), 1: 114. See also *PPC*, 5: 106-09.

[19]On May 5, 1919, Lloyd George announced Italian occupation of the harbor of Marmaris as a coaling station. A battalion was at Konya by agreement, and troops had been landed at Adalia, and possibly at Alaja. For Italian policy, January-October 1919, see *MD*, 19: 557-59; Mantoux, *Deliberations*, 1: 484-88.

of troops. In his view, the United States would send troops to Armenia and Constantinople, Great Britain would evacuate the Caucasus, France would garrison Syria, and the Greeks could occupy Smyrna. The Italians were overlooked in this scheme, and Lloyd George's announced intention to withdraw troops from the Caucasus was "in order to have them ready to counteract any move by the Italians." At the end of the session, the British statesman repeated that he was "very anxious to settle the question of the mandates before the Treaty of Peace," but President Wilson felt it could hardly be settled within two days, and remarked that "in regard to Turkey in particular, it was impossible for him to give a decision at present as to whether the United States would take a mandate," a difficulty which Lloyd George much appreciated. The next day, President Wilson stated definitely that the United States could not send troops to the Ottoman Empire, since it had not been at war with that country. Italy might be compelled to get out of Anatolia, however, because of its dependence on the United States for credits. An Italian mandate for Anatolia, in the President's view, would be a cause for grave friction. At the same time, Wilson thought that the only advantage in allowing Italy to keep Fiume was that it would break the Treaty of London, which gave the Dodecanese Islands to Italy. On May 7, Premier Venizelos was brought into the discussion, especially as to the disposition of Greek troops.[20]

The Council of Four pondered the Italian situation on May 13, when Lloyd George once more raised the mandate problem and rather naively suggested that an Italian mandate in Anatolia might solve the immigration question in the United States. President Wilson favored uniting the Smyrna district and the Dodecanese Islands with Greece. Harold Nicolson indicated a line on the map excluding the Baghdad railway from the Italian zone. Again, Lloyd George brought forward his proposal: "The United States should take a mandate for Armenia; France should take a mandate for Northern Anatolia; Italy for Southern Anatolia; and Greece should be dealt with as' proposed by President Wilson. The United States, he earnestly hoped, would also take a mandate for Constantinople." But the Italians demanded Scală Nǔova (Makri–Mersin area) in addition, and President Wilson, true to his earlier pronouncements, would not promise American acceptance of a mandate for any part of the Ottoman Empire. Moreover,

[20]*PPC*, 5: 465–66, 472, 482–84, 501–05; Mantoux, *Déliberations*, 1: 510. On May 6, Lloyd George stated that "it ought to be decided that M. Venizelos should be allowed to land two or three divisions at Smyrna to protect his fellow-countrymen in Turkey." Wilson pointed out that the Greek Commission "was unanimously in favour of giving this area to Greece."

the President reminded his colleagues that "certain influential and important elements in Turkey were very anxious that Turkey should not be divided, but that it must be subjected to guidance. There should be a single mandate for the whole. The principle was the same as that which he had contended for the case of the Arabs, namely, that the mandate should not be divided. He felt there was much to be said for this proposal." Lloyd George thought this would be difficult in practice, while Clemenceau could see little difference between a "mandate for development and administration, and a mandate for guidance."[21]

On May 14 Lloyd George presented his plan for the reorganization of the Ottoman Empire, which had been worked out by Harold Nicolson. It involved (1) an American mandate for Constantinople and Armenia; (2) full Greek sovereignty over Smyrna and Aivali (Ayvalik), the Dodecanese Islands and Castellorizo; and (3) spheres of influence in the rest of Asia Minor, with a Greek mandate for the territory adjacent to Smyrna. Italy was to have the mandate for the southern seaboard, from west of Makri to the point where Armenia was to strike the Mediterranean. France was to receive the mandate for the rest of the "future Turkish state." President Wilson favored a "loose" French mandate over a Turkish state in northern Anatolia, as it would be better not to have the French and Italians mixing in southern Anatolia—both with advisers at the Turkish capital. Lloyd George urged this as "the great argument against dividing up Anatolia." According to Wilson, southern Anatolia should be a self-governing unit with Konya as the capital and an elected governor-general. As an alternative, Lloyd George proposed that the sultan remain in Constantinople, as sovereign over all Turkey, leaving France, Italy, and Greece to overlook parts of Anatolia, while the United States supervised the activities of the sultan at Constantinople. Subject to senatorial approval, the President now agreed to two proposals, originally drafted by Nicolson.[22] He accepted the principle of an American mandate over Armenia. The second proposal provided for "a mandate over the city of Constantinople, the Straits of the Bosphorus and Dardanelles, the Sea of Marmora and a small con-

---

[21]*PPC*, 5: 579–83, 584, 812; Mantoux, *Délibérations*, 2: 58–63. Lloyd George stated that he "would like to add Cyprus to Greece, although there were considerable difficulties," since such an act "would deprive the whole transaction of any atmosphere of 'grab.' " Wilson thought "it would be a great thing if Mr. Lloyd George could accomplish that." On May 22, Lloyd George noted that "it had also been proposed that we should give up Cyprus, although that was not in any bargain or treaty."

[22]See *PPC*, 5: 614–20; Mantoux, *Délibérations*, 2: 73–77; *British Documents, 1919–1939*, first series, 4: 857–69. See also Howard M. Sachar, *The Emergence of the Middle East, 1914–1924* (New York: Knopf, 1969), passim.

tiguous territory, the frontiers of which shall be determined by agreement between the United States, British, French and Italian Delegations, whose recommendations, if unanimous, shall be accepted without further reference to the Council." A second set of proposals which, like the first, was to be submitted to the Italian Delegation, resolved that "Turkish sovereignty shall cease over Constantinople, Turkey in Europe, the Straits and the Sea of Marmora," and provided, as noted above, for the distribution of the rest of Anatolia.

But another very important decision was also reached on May 14. On April 12, Premier Venizelos had reported serious troubles in Smyrna and Aydin and had urged strong, immediate measures. The Greeks had made preparations for a landing at Smyrna. May 14 witnessed a landing of Greek forces under cover of British and French warships and the USS *Arizona* and five American destroyers. This was the beginning of the terrible Greco-Turkish tragedy of 1919–22 which ended so disastrously for the dreams of a greater Hellas in Asia Minor.

THE DIFFICULTIES WITH ITALY

The Italian landings on the coast of Asia Minor thoroughly angered President Wilson, Lloyd George, and Clemenceau, and the problem was discussed in detail with Orlando at the meeting of the Council of Four on May 17. A complaint was presented to Orlando, and on the morning of May 16, Lloyd George circulated a memorandum by Balfour, protesting against the partition of Anatolia.[23] Balfour did not believe that the Ottoman Empire had been so rotten as to warrant such treatment, despite what he was to draft for Clemenceau's signature for the Ottoman Delegation on June 23. He was particularly fearful that the partition would "deeply shock large sections of Mohammedan opinion." He felt that "we must admit

---

[23]*PPC*, 5: 668–72, 686–89; *MD*, 19: 563; Charles Seymour, *Intimate Papers of Colonel House* (Boston: Houghton Mifflin, 1926), 4: 467; Mantoux, *Délibérations*, 2: 88–89; R. S. Baker, *Woodrow Wilson and World Settlement* (Garden City: Doubleday and Page, 1922), 3: 302–07; René Albrecht-Carrié, *Italy at the Paris Peace Conference. The Paris Peace: History and Documents* (New York: Columbia University Press, 1935), passim; Maxwell H. H. Macartney and Paul Cremona, *Italy's Foreign and Colonial Policy, 1870–1937* (London and New York: Oxford University Press, 1938), chap. 3. Nicolson noted in his diary, May 19 (*Peace-Making*, p. 343): "Most of the Cabinet have come over from London to discuss the future of Turkey . . . . Curzon pressed for ejection of Turk from Europe, and accepts Greek zone at Smyrna although with deep regret. Montagu and Milner are all against disturbing the Turks still further. Winston wants to leave him as he is, but to give America the mandate over Constantinople at the Straits, with a zone extending as far as Trebizond. A. J. B. wants Constantinople under an American mandate, Smyrna and the rest of Turkey as an independent kingdom, suprevised by foreign 'advisers.' Ll.G. is non-committal. No decision come to in so far as, through the glass darkly, I can ascertain."

that no such scheme would ever have been thought of, if it had not been necessary to find some method of satisfying Italian ambitions." Under the Balfour scheme, Turkey would remain an undivided state without a mandatory, with much diminished territories, but with substantially the same status as that of the old empire. The Ottoman sultan would "reign at Brusa or Konia as his predecessors had formerly reigned at Constantinople." But since something had to be found for the Italians in Asia Minor, "at the smallest cost to mankind," something might have to be found in the Adalia region. It is interesting to note, of course, that British interests were well taken care of, for Constantinople would not be the Turkish capital, Turkey would not control the Straits, and Great Britain would retain what it had gained and desired in Mesopotamia and Palestine.

On the afternoon of May 17, Lloyd George introduced a number of prominent Indian Muslims, including the Aga Khan, under the sponsorship of the secretary of state for India, E. S. Montagu, and all protested particularly against the detachment of Constantinople and the region of the Straits, primarily because Constantinople was the seat of the Caliphate.[24] Aftab Ahmad, for example, earnestly appealed to the principles of President Wilson and Lloyd George "as regards Constantinople, Thrace and Asia Minor." Yusuf Ali, formerly a member of the Indian government, desired "that full consideration be given to the feelings and sentiments of the Indian Mohammedans on the question of the retention by the Turks of Constantinople and Thrace and Asia Minor, where they have substantially a Turkish population, and that the interests of the Mohammedans in all the other provinces should be so safeguarded that they have a reasonable hope of making further and further progress and entering into that committee of nations which is typified by admission when the time comes to the League of Nations."

Partly in view of the position of the Muslim League, Lloyd George suggested on May 19 that the Italian mandate proposal be withdrawn and the Italians get out of Asia Minor entirely. When Wilson, seemingly much surprised at the Muslim sentiment, proposed leaving the Sultan in Anatolia and perhaps even in Constantinople, under French advice, Lloyd George declared that if France were to be the single adviser of Turkey, "he would have to ask for a re-examination of the whole question of mandates in the Turkish Empire." The Prime Minister wanted a solution, but not one which would place France in prospective control of Constantinople and the Straits. Later, on May 19, when the Italians had employed the usual pretext of

[24]*PPC*, 5: 690–701; Mantoux, *Délibérations*, 2: 96–104.

"anarchy" as the reason for their landing of troops, Lloyd George informed them that if they did not remove their troops, he would disinterest himself entirely in Italian claims in Asia Minor.[25]

Lloyd George came forth with another mandate scheme for the Ottoman Empire on May 21, which called for an American mandate over the region of Constantinople and the Straits, Armenia, and Cilicia. Anatolia would remain undivided, except for the region to be united with Greece. Unless the United States would take the mandate over Anatolia, there would be none for that territory. On the other hand, France was to have a provisional mandate for Syria, until the report of the Interallied Commission, which was to proceed to the Middle East, while Great Britain would assume a similar mandate for Mesopotamia. Until Russia's reorganization, the United States was to have a mandate over the Caucasus. Italy was entirely excluded from any mandate over any portion of the former Ottoman Empire.[26] While Indian Muslim objection was said to have been the basic reason for excluding Italy, there was also the British desire to preserve the freedom of the Straits through an American mandate, without French or Italian interference. The British forces had done nine-tenths of the fighting against the Ottoman Empire, and the British government had now decided that it was not good policy to partition the Turkish Anatolian homelands. However, since an independent Turkey would require some sort of foreign supervision, that control should be exercised by the United States. The Turks would distrust a European mandate, fearing that Turkey might become "a mere colony." Moreover, it was "impossible to make Italy sole mandatory in Anatolia and if France alone exercised this power Italy would be jealous." It was also perfectly clear that Great Britain would oppose any other mandatory. The United States alone must assume that obligation.

While there was much to justify the British position concerning an American mandate, President Wilson went to the essence of the project when he announced once more that he questioned American willingness to accept an Anatolian mandate. Moreover, he declared that even "if the United States were the mandatory of the Straits they would not in the least object if the Sultan were advised in stipulated matters by other Powers on the subject of the government of Anatolia." Thereupon, Lloyd George replied that "if the United States could not take a Mandatory over Anatolia, it would be better

[25]See, especially, *PPC*, 5: 705-11, 716-23, 726; Mantoux, *Délibérations*, 2: 110-13; David Lloyd George, *Memoirs of the Peace Conference* (New Haven: Yale University Press, 1939), 2: 782-94, 805-06.
[26]*PPC*, 5: 755-68, 769-71; Mantoux, *Délibérations*, 2: 133-43.

for the Sultan to clear out of Constantinople." Clemenceau, like Wilson, but on entirely different grounds, also objected to the British scheme and urged that France "surely ought not to be expelled from Asia Minor on two such grounds as the Musulman question and the Italian question," and he was very bitter concerning alleged British bad faith in connection with the Syrian problem.[27]

THE GREEK PROBLEM

Meanwhile, the Greek occupation of Smyrna during May 14-18, 1919, produced a furore in Paris.[28] As a consequence the Turkish cabinet had resigned and Admiral Mark Bristol, the American high commissioner in Constantinople, cabled the American Commission in Paris on May 17 that everybody was surprised by the occupation and that the Turks considered it a "humiliation," a sentiment which might be "changed to resentment and general discontent."[29] A storm of protest from various groups of Turkish citizens went to President Wilson, including members of the Ottoman League of National Unity and the Central Bureau of the National Congress of Turkey, during the latter part of May, charging that "the decisions of which Smyrna is to be the object are in flagrant contradiction with the high principles for whose triumph the United States went to war." On May 19, Mustafa Kemal landed at Samsun and began the odyssey which led to the foundation of the Turkish republic and the emergence of the Turkish nation. Admiral Bristol cabled on May 22 that "the disturbed feelings" in Turkey were increasing and he begged for a statement regarding the Greek occupation, "or else occupation by associated military forces." On May 31, after a conference with leading Turkish citizens, including the former grand vizier, Izzet Paşa, Bristol cabled that if the United States became the mandatory for Turkey, "the support and cooperation of Turkish military forces could be relied upon" and that only a small U.S. military force would be necessary. But he complained that, while the British and French were making desperate rival efforts to control the Ottoman Delegation to the Peace Conference, nothing was being done in behalf of the United States and stressed that in the selection "no

---

[27]*PPC*, 5: 756-66, 770-71. When Lloyd George challenged Clemenceau concerning the naming of the French members of the proposed inter-allied commission, the latter indicated that "he was ready for the French representatives to go, as soon as the British troops in Syria had been replaced by French."

[28]For a justification of the Greek position, see A. A. Pallis, *Greece's Anatolian Venture—and After* (London: Methuen, 1937).

[29]The material which follows comes from the papers of Admiral Mark Bristol, contained in the files of the King-Crane Commission. For the views of Lord Curzon, who opposed the Smyrna venture, see Nicolson, *Curzon: The Last Phase*, chap. 4.

American influence" was being brought to bear in any way. Damat Ferid Paşa, who later headed the Ottoman Delegation, evidently represented French sentiment. Bristol was much troubled by the Greek action in Smyrna, and also noted that the French and the Italians had exerted every effort to extend their influence in that region. While he did not question the wisdom of the Peace Conference, he wanted to provide correct information, because he felt "that those who made the decision could not have known all the facts beforehand."

OTTOMAN VIEWS

When President Wilson reported on May 28 that, despite the protests of the Powers, Italy was still sending troops to Asia Minor, Lloyd George stressed that he "had made it quite clear that, if Italy did not withdraw her troops, he would disinterest himself altogether in Italian claims in Asia Minor." By May 30 an application had come from the Grand Vizier to send a delegation to the Peace Conference, and it was agreed that Philip Kerr should draft Clemenceau's reply. Wilson believed that the "first object would be to protest against what had been done in Smyrna." A cable was approved the next day, expressing the willingness of the Council to receive an Ottoman Delegation, and a hearing was set for June 17.[30]

When Damat Ferid Paşa appeared before the Council of Ten on June 17 he did not condone the crimes of the Ottoman government during the war, but insisted on a peace in accordance with the Wilson principles, based on the *status quo ante bellum*, a proposition which was hardly realistic within the context of the times.[31] In Thrace, the Ottoman Delegation asked for a line northwest of Constantinople, a frontier for the defense of both Constantinople and Adrianople (Edirné). In Asia Minor, it claimed territory bounded on the north by the Black Sea, on the east by the Tigris River and the Ottoman–Persian frontier before the war. This would include the vilayets of Mosul and Diyarbekir, as well as part of Aleppo to the Mediterranean.

[30]*PPC*, 6: 83, 116, 134, 215–18, 222, 232, 370; *British Documents, 1919–1939,* first series, 4: 254–55; Mantoux, *Déliberations,* 4: 257; M. Cambon, *Correspondence, 1870–1924* (Paris, 1940), 3: 237–38. In a discussion with Lord Curzon on May 30, Ambassador Cambon indicated that a British representative had "practically offered to France the undisputed mandate for Constantinople, the whole of Anatolia, Armenia (if it were not given to the Americans), and Syria." Two days, later, however, he had submitted the rival proposition that the United States should receive the mandate for the whole of Turkey, both in Europe and Asia, including Syria, but excluding Mesopotamia and Palestine, which had excited the wrath of Clemenceau, who then continued the discussion of control at Constantinople, with European Turkey to be in French control and Asiatic Turkey in British military control.

[31]*PPC,* 4: 509–12; Mantoux, *Déliberations,* 2: 327–28, 445–46.

While the Ottoman government would discuss the Armenian frontiers, the islands near the coast should remain Ottoman to protect the
mainland. Autonomy would be granted to the Arab communities
under Ottoman sovereignty, and the Ottoman government would
negotiate with Great Britain concerning Egypt and Cyprus. But the
Ottoman people would never accept the partition of the Empire,
which would upset the Eastern balance. While the Ottoman Delegation, to put it mildly, was not well received, it submitted a
memorandum of its views, and on June 23 received a stinging reply
from Clemenceau.[32]

WILSON'S DEPARTURE FROM PARIS

In view of President Wilson's imminent departure, Lloyd George
raised the Turkish issue again on June 25,[33] outlining the future frontiers, but leaving the final disposition of the territories until the
American attitude concerning a mandate was definitely known.
Wilson agreed that final disposition of the Ottoman Empire ought
not to be delayed for the next two months and asserted that the
amputations would involve Mesopotamia, Syria, and Armenia, while
Clemenceau observed that the question of Constantinople was involved. The President proposed to "cut off all that Turkey was to give
up; and to oblige Turkey to accept any conditions with regard to over-
sight or direction which the Allied and Associated Governments
might agree to." Although some Power "ought to have a firm hand,"
he thought a mandate over Turkey would be a mistake. "Constantinople and the Straits should be left as a neutral strip for the
present," and it was already in Allied occupation. Wilson "would
make the Sultan and his Government move out of Constantinople and
he would say what was ceded to the Allied and Associated Powers."
Lloyd George thought it involved "the question of whether the Turk
was to go out of Constantinople," while Wilson considered that
question decided. He had "studied the question of the Turks in
Europe for a long time, and every year confirmed his opinion that
they ought to be cleared out."

The next day President Wilson agreed to present the plan for an
American mandate over Constantinople and the Straits to the United
States Senate, and he noted that "Constantinople was not a Turkish
city, other races there were in the majority."[34] The difficulties in respect

[32]*PPC*, 6: 576, 577-80, 617, 688-91, 691-94; Mantoux, *Délibérations*, 3: 473.
In general, see also Howard, *The King-Crane Commission*, pp. 154-61.
[33]*PPC*, 6: 675-77; Mantoux, *Délibérations*, 2: 516-18; *British Documents, 1919-
1939*, first series, 4: 643-51.
[34]*PPC*, 6: 711-13; Mantoux, *Déliberatons*, 2: 530-35.

to the Asiatic settlement arose, he said, from the Italian attitudes. Clemenceau would refuse to discuss matters with the Italians, while Lloyd George feared that Italian intervention would cause unrest among Muslims the world over. Wilson was so exasperated that he thought the Italians "should be asked clearly to state whether they remained in the Entente or not." If so, Italy must participate with the Allies "and do nothing independently." It was agreed on June 27 that further consideration of the treaty with Turkey should be suspended until "such time as the Government of the United States of America could state" whether it was "able to accept a mandate for a portion of the former Turkish Empire." The next day, the United States, Great Britain, and France warned Rome that, unless curbed, its action would mean "the loss of all claim to further assistance or aid from those who were once proud" to be its associates.[35]

President Wilson and the American Delegation left a few days after signature of the Treaty of Versailles with Germany, although a few members remained to work on the treaties which were yet to be concluded. But even a provisional settlement with Turkey was delayed until 1920, the problem of the Turkish Straits being of special significance. As David Lloyd George remarks:

> It was impossible to contemplate any peace settlement which would leave so vital an international waterway to be dominated by the guns of a country that had taken so disastrous an advantage of its command of an indispensable way of communication between great nations. A peace which would not secure the world against this menace would not be a peace to which any responsible or even sane statesman could append his signature. The Allies, therefore, soon after the war commenced, came to the conclusion that the freedom of the Narrows from the Bosphorus to the Dardanelles must be secured, not by paper guarantees above a Turkish signature, but by entrusting the keys to this channel to hands that could be relied upon to maintain free access along its waters to all nations that kept the rules of the Covenant of Peace.[36]

It seemed evident to the statesmen at Paris that the Straits could not be left in the hands "of a weak and venal Power like Turkey," with no special interest in freedom of access. President Wilson was

[35]*PPC*, 6: 729, 741, 755, 757, 760–62; Mantoux, *Délibérations*, 2: 549; *British Documents, 1919–1939*, first series, 4: 652–53; Howard, *The King-Crane Commission*, pp. 159–61. See also René Albrecht-Carrié, "New Light on Italian Problems in 1919," *Journal of Modern History* 13, no. 4 (December 1941): 493–516; "Documents: Italy and Her Allies, June 1919," *American Historical Review* 46, no. 4 (July 1941): 837–43.

[36]Lloyd George, *Memoirs of the Peace Conference*, 2: 807–13; Russian Political Conference (Lvov, Sazonov, Chaikovsky, Maklakov), *Memorandum Presented to the President of the Conference of Peace, Paris, July 5, 1919* (Paris, 1919); *British Documents, 1919–1939*, first series, 4: 653–54.

not opposed to an American mandate over Constantinople or Armenia or both, but "it was obvious that neither France, Britain nor Italy could undertake the task." Had not the Bolshevik Revolution intervened, Russia "would have been the most fitting choice for a mandatory," or the Straits might have been assigned to Greece, with "much historical and ethnical justification." Another alternative was to establish an international commission, with Great Britain, France, the United States, and Italy as members. To Lloyd George it seemed clear

that the best solution would be the choice of a mandatory Power not involved in the jealousies and rivalries of European States; one whose remoteness from these age-long contentions would have been a guarantee of impartiality, and whose power and position in the world would have given authority to its decisions. The same principle applied to the Armenian problem. . . . When the delegates of Great Powers assembled at the Conference examined the difficulties, it became clear that America was the only mandatory who would have been acceptable to all alike. . . . Had the President displayed any reluctance to entertain the idea, we would have been forced to contemplate the next best arrangement. In my judgment that would have been the placing of the Greeks in control of the Straits.

THE TURKISH PROBLEM, JULY–AUGUST 1919

The Council of the Heads of Delegation decided on June 30 to postpone further discussion of the treaty with the Ottoman government until the American position could be ascertained, although the problems continued to be discussed, especially in connection with attempts to determine the Greek and Bulgarian boundaries. At a meeting of the American Delegation on July 1, Herbert Hoover was "very averse" regarding the Armenian "poor-house" and felt that it would be "a terrific burden and a public act of charity for the United States to take a mandate" over Constantinople. He declared that, as a port, Constantinople served "no useful purpose except as the gateway to the Black Sea, as a coaling station, and as a home for pilots." Since it was no longer necessary for ships even to stop at Constantinople, Hoover thought its population would soon drop from 2,000,000 to 200,000, or its people would have to be supported by a Great Power. France "would be the logical power to receive a mandate over this City because of the future associations which France would undoubtedly have with Russia."[37]

[37]*PPC*, 11: 261–62. What Mr. Hoover had in mind is not at all clear. The population of Istanbul was about 2,247,630 in 1970; 83,293,840 tons of international shipping, or 19,658 ships, passed the Straits in 1973.

On July 18, Henry White, acting head of the United States Delegation until the arrival of Frank L. Polk, informed the council of a cable from President Wilson stating that there would be a very considerable delay in the Turkish treaty if the council were to await the American views as to the assumption of a mandate before proceeding with the matter. Clemenceau could not wait indefinitely and stated that when other work had been finished, the council would do its best to settle Turkish affairs. It could take note of President Wilson's statement: "President Wilson knew full well what the difficulties were. He wished to obtain a mandate in Armenia and an American Commissioner had been appointed. He asked for part of Cilicia, and was favorably disposed towards accepting a mandate for Constantinople. The question of Constantinople was one of the greatest importance for Europe. It had caused wars in the past, and required the closest study."[38]

Similarly, there was a brief discussion of the problem on July 21, in connection with the question of the Bulgarian frontiers, with Tardieu suggesting that "the internationalization of the Bosphorus and the Dardanelles" would give Bulgaria "free access to the open sea." Hence, there was no necessity for serious concessions in Thrace or an outlet on the Aegean Sea.[39] Tardieu argued further on July 31 that although Bulgaria lost its access to the Aegean Sea, it still had access to the Black Sea and to the Danube, "and the opening of the Straits would be to her advantage."[40] The argument was not especially impressive to White, who thought Dedeagaç might be developed into a good port, and pointed out the patent fact that "access to the Mediterranean from a port in the Black Sea was obviously more circuitous and less desirable." President Wilson had suggested a phraseology in the projected Bulgarian treaty whereby Bulgaria would recognize the right of the Principal Allied and Associated Powers to transfer Bulgarian Thrace, as defined in the treaty, "to the proposed International State of Constantinople" and agree "to accept and cooperate in the effectuation of such transfer" whenever it was made. But Clemenceau declared that if the territory of the proposed Constantinopolitan state were increased to this extent, "its atrribution to any mandatory power would become impossible." There might be agreement if only Constantinople and

[38]*PPC*, 7: 14, 194-98, 200-01; *British Documents, 1919-1939*, first series, 1: 11, 131-36; 4: 670-78.

[39]*PPC*, 7: 234-35, 242-43, 353, 355; *British Documents, 1919-1939*, first series, 1: 161-63.

[40]*PPC*, 7: 434-42; 11: 342-44; *British Documents, 1919-1939*, first series, 1: 258-66.

the Straits were in question, but Clemenceau saw no chance if large territories were added. In turn, Tardieu stated that "internationalized States had been invented for a definite general advantage. The State of Constantinople was considered desirable in order to safeguard the freedom of the Straits. If a large hinterland, including Thrace, were added to it, the result would be that it would include 760,000 Turks, 650,000 Greeks, 75,000 Bulgars. On what pretext could a mass of 650,000 Greeks at the very frontier of Greece be made subject to another State?"

There were no easy solutions, and on August 7, Polk reiterated the American suggestion to attribute Thrace "to an international state," which had been "scoffed at."[41] Polk seemed none too happy with his instructions concerning the problem, for he wrote to Colonel House on August 20, 1919:

> We are drifting along here in rather an unsatisfactory way owing to the fact that I am having some difficulty in getting instructions from Washington. We almost made a compromise on the Thracian situation after a hard fight against the whole "bunch" and were then told by Washington that they would not listen to any compromise whatever, but wanted East and West Thrace in an international State. That of course is out of the question, for as long as it is not known who is to have the mandate for Constantinople neither the British nor the French would be willing to run the chance of the other getting all the territory along the Aegean. I have telegraphed again to Washington and am waiting anxiously to see whether I am going to get "spanked" or whether we can close up the Bulgarian treaty. This really is the only serious question I have left.[42]

Toward the Development of an American Position

THE KING-CRANE REPORT

Meanwhile, the American Section of the International Commission on Mandates in Turkey, or the King-Crane Commission, which President Wilson had sent to investigate and report concerning conditions in the Ottoman Empire, had finished its work in Constantinople on August 21, and a copy of the report was presented to Polk and White and General Bliss on August 28, in Paris.[43] In general, the report, which was favorably received by the American commissioners, recommended (1) an Armenian mandate, excluding Cilicia, which was to go with Anatolia; (2) an international Con-

[41]*PPC*, 7: 609–11; *British Documents, 1919–1939*, first series, 4: 340–49.
[42]*PPC*, 7: 670–73; 858–59; *British Documents, 1919–1939*, first series, 1: 399–403. See also *PPC*, 11: 634–35.
[43]See *PPC*, 12: 745–863 for text. See also Howard, *The King-Crane Commission*, chaps. 7 and 8, pp. 345–61.

stantinopolitan state, under a mandatory, separate from Turkey; (3) a mandatory for a separate Turkish state; (4) no territory to be set off for the Greeks, who could be given autonomy in Smyrna under the general mandate for Turkey; (5) a single general mandate for all Asia Minor (not including Mesopotamia and Syria), with Armenia, the Constantinopolitan state, and the Turkish state; (6) the United States to assume this general mandate.

But the problem of Constantinople and the Straits is of special interest, and during its stay in Constantinople, where the report was written, the King-Crane Commission interviewed numerous people as to their ideas concerning the future of Turkey. The commission considered it necessary to have a clear view of the nature of the proposed Constantinopolitan state, which should be directly under the League of Nations and be administered by a permanent mandatory, removable only for cause. Moreover, in its view, the mandatory should be a "trustee for international interests, not a power using its position to advance its own national interests." The supervising Power, therefore, should be disinterested both territorially and strategically. While the proposed state could be administered by a body similar to the International Commission of the Danube, it was thought that a single mandatory would serve better.

Such a State should include Constantinople, and have charge of its administration. This is the more demanded, for Constantinople is a markedly cosmopolitan city, where the Turks are probably not even in the majority. This State should also have a reasonable territory on either side of the Straits. All fortifications should be abolished. This international territory would of course be open to all people for any legitimate purposes. Like the District of Columbia in America, it would be a natural place for great educational and religious foundations, so that such Moslem institutions could remain and be further built up. The Turkish population, equally, of course, would be free to stay. But Constantinople would no longer be the capital of Turkey. In the administration of the State, however, all possible consideration should be given to the Moslem sentiment, and reasonable practical adjustments arranged. The Sultan might even conceivably continue to reside at Constantinople if that were desired under the conditions named.

A number of factors dictated this solution. It was necessary to insure the permanent freedom of the Dardanelles and to remove the intrigue of plot and counterplot on the Golden Horn. There was also the opportunity to make the heavy responsibility for this world center international rather than to leave it to a single power. Creation of a separate Constantinople community would assist Turkey in developing a proper democratic form of government in the Anatolian homelands, not only through the power of example, but by relieving it of the responsibility of the control of the Straits. At the same time, the Turks within the region of the Straits would doubtless have the best government they had ever had. The establishment of an international state would avoid future difficulties between rival powers, because otherwise there would be "endless intrigues on the part of various Powers to possess or control the Straits." It was suggested that the new state include the city of Constantinople, Turkish Thrace, and a strip of Asiatic Turkey, with the shores of the Bosphorus, the Sea of Marmara, and the Dardanelles. The solution was not intended to humiliate Turkey or those who professed the Muslim faith. The purpose was to safeguard the peace of Turkey and the world, although such a readjustment would involve both disturbance and sacrifice. In the end, however, the entire world, it was thought, would "gain from a permanent solution of this vexing world question."

STEPS TOWARD PEACE

The King-Crane Report, which contained reflections and recommendations concerning the Turkish homelands, the region of Constantinople and the Straits, and Thrace, had little or no influence at Paris, although a copy was shown to the British Delegation.[44] There was continued discussion of the problem of the Straits, and on September 1, Clemenceau made it quite clear that he could not accept the Wilson proposals, since he thought it a "very dangerous proposal to ask the Commissioner at Constantinople to take charge of an area containing 700,000 Greeks and 700,000 Turks, who would be in a continual state of warfare." If the President persisted, it would be impossible to reach a settlement. Balfour thought the problem of the Bulgarian treaty most pressing, but felt that the future of Constantinople and Asia Minor could not be settled before the conclusion of that treaty.[45] In the end, it was decided that the Central Territorial Committee should determine a boundary in accordance with President Wilson's message of August 28, as the southern Bulgarian boundary, that the portion of Western Thrace to be ceded by Bulgaria would be ceded to the Allied and Associated Powers and placed under interallied occupation and later to be attributed to Greece. Finally, the treaty was to stipulate Bulgarian access to

[44]*PPC*, 11: 432-33; Lloyd George, *Memoirs of the Peace Conference*, 2: 696-97. On September 21, Buckler of the American Commission, who said the British had seen the report and were "excited" by it, wanted to know if there were "any objection to the British Commission having a copy of the Crane-King Report." Polk thought they "had better trust to their memories," but did not doubt that "very copious notes" had been made.

[45]*PPC*, 7: 839-40, 8: 35-38; *British Documents, 1919-1939*, first series, 1: 508-09, 524, 589-92.

a portion of the Aegean Sea. The next day, after an explanation by Tardieu, the frontier line was approved unanimously, and it was agreed that he should examine the question of assuring free economic access to the Aegean by river and rail to Bulgaria by means of "general guaranteeing articles" in the Bulgarian treaty.[46]

By mid-September the Bulgarian treaty was so near completion that Polk wanted to hand a copy to the Bulgarian Delegation on September 16. Lloyd George observed that with the clearing up of one or two problems only the Turkish treaty would remain, but he feared that this problem could not be settled for some months, since "at present the Conference was held up in the matter until President Wilson was able to declare the position of America in regard to Mandates." Despite Polk's reassurances, Lloyd George was not sanguine, and thought the Conference could not "found its procedure on the assumption that the American position in regard to the Turkish mandate would be cleared by October." In any event, the conference would have to be reconstituted in November or later for the consideration of the Turkish problem. At the same time, the British leader thought it impossible to discuss the mandate problem, although arrangements for military occupation of various areas could be discussed, as he had done with Clemenceau on September 13, with regard to Syria, when he arranged the withdrawal of British forces from Syria and Cilicia. In view of American objection to a purely Greek occupation, it was decided that Bulgaria should evacuate Western Thrace and the Strumitza Loop, but that the oc-cupation should be effected with Allied troops, with a few Greek troops in certain designated areas.[47]

The actions of Greek and Italian forces in Asia Minor confronted the council with problems early in October.[48] During a call at the Foreign Office on October 21, Venizelos pressed the Greek case with Lord Curzon, especially concerning Thrace and Constantinople. The Greek statesman favored an international administration for Constantinople, largely on the ground that "this was the only form of Government which could successfully withstand, at some future date, the ambitions of a resuscitated Russia." He added that "if either the British or the French were to assume the mandate, they would certainly find themselves involved, some day or other, in a

---

[46]PPC, 8: 35-37, 48-51, 55-57, 63-67.
[47]PPC, 8: 202-03, 205-08, 216-17, 263-66, 270, 279; British Documents, 1919-1939, first series, pp. 685-91, 700-01; Zeine N. Zeine, The Struggle for Arab Independence: Western Diplomacy and the Rise and Fall of Faisal's Kingdom in Syria (Beirut: Khayats, 1960), chap. 6.
[48]PPC, 8: 512-17, 531-33, 728-29, 846-47, 861-63.

bitter conflict with the secular ambitions of the Russian people. On the other hand, an international administration would be in a position to resist Russian encroachment." But Venizelos did not object to having the Sultan in Constantinople, although the capital might be moved to Bursa.[49] There was little or no discussion of the problem during November, but much of the Greek question at Smyrna, and on November 8 Clemenceau warned that the "Turkish problem was not settled," that the "Council would be more and more led to respecting the integrity of Turkish territory." In the end, the Bulgarian treaty was signed on November 27, and there was no further discussion of the Turkish problem at Paris, or of that of Constantinople and the Straits, until the negotiation of the Treaty of Sèvres in 1920. The Treaty of Neuilly gave an economic outlet to Bulgaria on the Aegean Sea, but not one through Salonika or Dedeagaç.[50]

THE REPORT OF THE HARBORD MISSION
Before concluding its work at Paris, the American Commission to Negotiate Peace received another report from the Middle East which raised many basic questions. On recommendation of Herbert Hoover and Henry Morgenthau, Sr., a military mission had gone out to Armenia in August, under the direction of Major General James G. Harbord. Completed on October 16, the report of this mission threw some additional light on the problems involved, although it made no positive recommendations.[51] Among other things, the Harbord Mission observed:

A power which should undertake a mandatory for Armenia and Transcaucasia without control of the contiguous territory of Asia Minor— Anatolia—and of Constantinople, with its hinterland of Roumelia, would undertake it under most unfavorable and trying conditions, so difficult as to make the cost almost prohibitive, the maintenance of law and order and the security of life and property an uncertainty, and ultimate success extremely doubtful. With the Turkish Empire still freely controlling Constantinople, such a power would be practically emasculated as far as real power is concerned. For generations these peoples have looked to Con-

[49]*British Documents, 1919-1939*, first series, 4: 835-37; 2: 229-30, 262 ff., 287 ff., 295 ff.

[50]See, especially, *PPC*, 8: 821-22, 870-902.

[51]Major-General James G. Harbord, *Conditions in the Near East. Report of the American Military Mission to Armenia*, 66th Congress, 2nd Session, Senate Document No. 266; Department of State, *The Foreign Relation of the United States, 1919* (Washington, D.C.: USGPO), 841-74. See also Evans, *United States Policy and the Partition of Turkey*, chaps. 7 and 8; James B. Gidney, *A Mandate for Armenia* (Kent, Ohio: Kent State University Press, 1967), chap. 8; Howard, *The King-Crane Commission*, pp. 270-76.

stantinople as the Seat of authority. . . . Before the war Constantinople was the most important part of Continental Europe, reckoned upon the basis of shipping clearances. There are well-informed business men who believe it is destined to become the third most important commercial city in the world. But, through generations of habit, unless put under a mandatory, Constantinople will continue to be a whirlpool of financial and political currents. Concession hunting, financial intrigue, political exploitation, and international rivalries will center there in the future as in the past. Concerted international action for administration of Constantinople is impracticable. . . . There must be actual control, for responsibility without authority is worse than useless in a land of oriental viewpoints.

The Mission concluded that there was "something to be said on the part of the Turk," as well as of the Armenians, and held that the problem of Armenia could not be solved without answering the questions as to the fate of Turkey and the future of Russia. Pending final solutions, the Mission believed that the Power which assumed the Armenian mandate "should also exercise the mandate for Anatolia, Roumelia, Constantinople and Transcaucasia." The divisions of the mandate were an administrative detail to be worked out by the mandatory, although a natural subdivision might include Roumelia, the city of Constantinople, Anatolia, and the Transcaucasian region, less Russian Armenia. It was simpler and more economical, in the Mission's view, to include the entire Ottoman Empire under a single mandatory than to divide it, and in all probability a plebiscite would ask for an American mandate throughout the Ottoman Empire. A strong nation should assume the mandate for at least a generation. A disinterested nation, however, would assume such a mandatory only "from a strong sense of altruism and international duty" in "this breeding place of wars and at the unanimous wish of other parties to the Covenant of the League of Nations."

PROBLEMS OF AMERICAN POLICY

Both the King-Crane Commission and the Harbord Mission posed very serious problems for the consideration of the United States in 1919, and whatever the decision there were heavy risks, whether in evasion or acceptance of responsibilities. While there were attempts to get the United States to assume some responsibility, Viscount Grey, the British ambassador in Washington, cabled Lord Curzon on October 13 that anti-Wilson feeling rendered it out of the question that the Senate would approve any mandate, although it was possible that, if elected President, General Leonard Wood might take a broad view of the matter. Grey thought it might be worthwhile, if possible, "to make temporary arrangements for Constantinople," which would

keep the door open for an American mandate later on. But the idea
should be kept secret, since if it became known, it might prejudice the
progress of the political campaign.[52]

Grey reported on October 18 that while the United Kingdom
should be willing to see an American mandate over Constantinople
and the Straits, delays were causing difficulties, and behind the
various projects were some things which he did not like. He talked
with Henry Morgenthau, Sr., on October 23. Morgenthau thought
that after Senatorial approval of a treaty it might be possible for him
and General Harbord "to create a wave of idealism in favour of
Mandate for Constantinople and Armenia." Morgenthau suggested
an Anglo-American or international control of the Straits of Gibraltar
to show that the United States was invited into full partnership in
the East. In return, Morgenthau indicated that the United States
should agree to a similar control of the Panama Canal[53]—surely a naive
position, however logical, in the light both of contemporary and
later American attitudes.

By the end of November another attempt was made to influence
American participation in the Middle Eastern settlement. An American memorandum of November 26 insisted on the need "of a definite
Turkish policy" for the United States.[54] It was assumed that the
United States would join the League of Nations and take part in the
negotiation of the Turkish treaty, not merely because of the importance of American interests in Turkey but because the settlement
affected "the success of the League of Nations and the peace of the

[52]*British Documents, 1919-1939*, first series, 4: 815, 836-37, 846-47. While Lord
Curzon advised Lord Granville on October 21 that Venizelos favored an international
administration over Constantinople, it was generally agreed that little could be done
about the peace settlement, since the Supreme Council had decided "not to discuss
the Turkish settlement until President Wilson" announced "the American policy
regardng mandates," although Lord Curzon had suggested negotiations as soon as
possible in London.

[53]*British Documents, 1919-1939*, first series, 4: 816-17, 826-27, 843. It may be
observed that, on October 17, Sir Eyre Crowe transmitted a summary of the
Harbord Report to the Foreign Office, noting that it threw no new light on the Middle
Eastern situation, although it appeared to support the recommendations of the King-
Crane Commission relative to Constantinople and the Straits, Anatolia, and Armenia,
with "an integral United States mandate, possibly subdivided in some way for the
three above regions."

[54]The American Commission to Negotiate Peace, *Memorandum on the Policy of
the United States Relative to the Treaty with Turkey*, Hotel de Crillon, Paris,
November 26, 1919 (mimeographed), from the papers of Henry Churchill King. For
other aspects of these problems, see Joseph L. Grabill, *Protestant Diplomacy and the
Near East: Missionary Influence on American Policy, 1810-1927* (Minneapolis:
University of Minnesota Press, 1971), chaps. 8-10; Robert L. Daniel, *American
Philanthropy in the Near East, 1820-1960* (Athens, Ohio: Ohio University Press,
1970), chap. 7; R. R. Trask, *The United States Response to Turkish Nationalism and
Reform, 1914-1939* (Leiden: Brill, 1971), chap. 2.

world." But it was necessary that the American negotiators know the official U.S. position, since Great Britain and France had a definite policy. Among other things, the American Delegation should know the extent to which the King-Crane and Harbord reports would be followed, or whether the United States would recognize the secret interallied agreements for the partition of the Ottoman Empire. If not, would the United States be prepared to supply money and troops to implement a more suitable policy? Would the United States co-operate "in the international control of such portions of Turkey" as were not placed under mandate? These problems arose, for example, in Thrace, Constantinople, and the Straits. Western Thrace would follow the fate of Constantinople, along with a strip on the European and Asiatic shores of the Straits. If neither the United States nor any other Power would take the mandate, the Straits would have to be placed under international control, similar to that devised for Turkish Anatolia. But how far would the United States go in assisting and guiding a government in Anatolia, where Greek, Italian, and French claims would reduce the Turkish area by about 50 percent? There were also the problems of Armenia and the Arab portions of the Ottoman Empire, and the basic question of whether the United States would assume any responsibility. The memorandum set forth both altruistic and "selfish" and material reasons for possible intervention:

(1) In the interest of peace we ought not to permit a patch-work division of Turkey based on the spoils system and callous to local sentiment, such as will certainly be made if America held aloof. No Power except the United States can prevent the carrying into effect of those notorious "secret agreements," which would lead certainly to war and probably another world war.
We ought therefore to join in the Turkish Treaty and refuse to permit such a settlement even if the refusal costs us money and trouble.
(2) If the United States takes no part, or an apathetic part, in the settle-ment of the Near East, its material interests must suffer incalculably. Com-mercial opportunities in Turkey will be lost to the United States if it keeps aloof. The only way to maintain in Turkey our traditional trade policy of the "open door" is to be on the spot and *hold* the door open.

But, while the problems had been well-stated in the King-Crane and Harbord reports, and the alternatives were well-formulated in the memorandum of November 26, 1919, events in the Middle East, and especially on the Anatolian plateau—the Turkish homelands—took a fundamentally different course. The memorandum received no response, despite the urgent plea for a statement of policy from Wash-ington. The President was already gravely ill. There was now little or no leadership in high places in the United States, which was not prepared to become involved in the Middle East. There was still some talk of a possible American mandate for Constantinople, but, as Henry White assured everyone at Paris, "the chances were a hundred to one that the Americans would never take a mandate anywhere," and the British and French governments had already arrived at that conclusion.[55] Moreover, the Turkish Nationalists under Mustafa Kemal upset the applecart.

As observed throughout this chapter, the primary interest of the United States in the Turkish Straits at the Paris Peace Conference lay in the maintenance of the principle of freedom of commercial passage under international guarantees—a principle which was to be reasserted in the years ahead. While President Wilson was somewhat inclined toward the assumption of direct responsibilities for Anatolia and the region of the Straits, and both the King-Crane and the Harbord Commissions looked toward an American mandate, the United States was clearly not ready for such a development. In the period which ensued, leading up to and including the Lausanne Conference, when a new Convention of the Straits was to be elaborated, the United States maintained this position without essential change.

[55]Nevins, *Henry White*, p. 469; Nicolson, *Curzon: The Last Phase*, pp. 110–15. A visit of Foreign Minister Pichon to London in November 1919 for a talk with Lord Curzon, led to the elaboration of a plan similar to that developed by Curzon in January 1918 and earlier in 1919, whereby Turkey would be placed under an international administration, with Turkish sovereignty over Anatolia, subject to zones of influence and foreign advisers. But the British cabinet rejected the scheme on January 6, 1920, despite the support of Balfour, Curzon, and Lloyd George.

Chapter IV
Toward Sèvres and Lausanne

Atatürk and the Nationalist Movement

While the Allied Powers considered the problems of the Middle East at Paris, the Turks themselves were much concerned with their own fate and destiny. Patriotic groups sprang up here and there, all with varying programs, all involved with the fate of the Ottoman Empire, now moving toward its doom after more than 400 years. Among the most influential and genuine was The Union for the Defense of the National Rights of the Eastern Provinces, with headquarters at Constantinople and Erzurum, which became the nucleus of the Nationalist Congress at Erzurum, headed by Mustafa Kemal. During this period there was much talk of an American mandate, especially at Constantinople, but also at the congresses at Erzurum and Sivas during July and September 1919. The Congress of Sivas adopted a Declaration on September 11, a forerunner of the Turkish National Pact of January 28, 1920, which constituted the basic political platform on which Mustafa Kemal and the Nationalists proposed to rally the country, although there were still differences of view among them. The Sivas Declaration pointed out that all Turkish territory within the Mudros armistice frontiers, inhabited by "a preponderate majority of Turkish populations," formed "an undivided and inseparable whole," and declared that they were "absolutely resolved to resist and to defend" their rights against all intermeddling or occupation on the part of any powers. On condition that the territorial integrity of the country be recognized, the Turkish people, it was stated, were willing to accept technical and economic assistance from any state which did not display "imperialistic tendencies."[1]

---

[1]In general, see John Patrick Douglas Balfour, Lord Kinross, *Atatürk: A Biography of Mustafa Kemal, Father of Modern Turkey* (New York: Morrow, 1965); Mustapha

While the Turkish people desired American assistance of some
sort, and many people, at Constantinople in particular, wanted an
American mandate, there is little evidence, other than an indirect
statement in the Harbord Report, that Mustafa Kemal himself
desired such a mandate. At least, he was opposed to a mandate,
although many prominent Turkish leaders continued to think that
Turkey could save itself only through an American mandate over the
entire country.[2]

The actions of the Nationalist Congresses at Erzurum and Sivas
were followed by renewed vigor on the part of the Ottoman government in Constantinople, and Mustafa Kemal was outlawed. On
January 28, 1920, the new Parliament at Constantinople adopted the
Turkish National Pact. On March 16 Allied Forces occupied Constantinople, although it was announced that they did not intend
either to destroy the authority of the sultanate or "to deprive the Turks
of Constantinople." The Nationalist reply followed on April 23 when
a provisional government was established, with Mustafa Kemal as
president, and the National Pact adopted.[3] This remarkable document, consisting of six brief articles, proclaimed the unity of the
Turkish people, but declared that the Arabs in enemy occupied territory and the people of Western Thrace were to choose their own
destiny in complete freedom. While the rights of minorities were
guaranteed, Turkey was to "enjoy complete independence" in the
government of the nation, to assure its development along modern
lines. For that reason, the Nationalists opposed any restriction
inimical to their political, judicial, and financial development. As to
the problem of Constantinople and the Straits, the National Pact
declared:

"The security of the city of Constantinople, which is the seat of the caliphate
of Islam, the capital of the sultanate, and the headquarters of the Ottoman

Kemal, *A Speech Delivered by Ghazi Mustapha Kemal, President of the Turkish Re-
public. October 1927* (Leipzig: Koehler, 1929); Gasi Mustafa Kemal Pascha, *Die
Dokumente zur Rede* (Leipzig: Koehler, 1929); Harry N. Howard, *The King-Crane
Commission: An American Inquiry in the Middle East* (Beirut: Khayats, 1963), chap. 9;
Howard M. Sachar, *The Emergence of the Middle East* (New York: Knopf, 1969),
passim; Jukka Nevakivi, *Britain, France and the Arab Middle East* (New York: Ox-
ford, 1969), passim; Briton Cooper Busch, *Britain, India and the Arabs, 1914–1921*
(Berkeley and Los Angeles: University of California Press, 1971), passim.

[2]Major-General James G. Harbord, *Conditions in the Near East. Report of the
American Military Mission to Armenia*, 66th Congress, 2nd Session, Senate Document
No. 266, Exhibit C. See Great Britain, Foreign Office, *Documents on British Foreign
Policy, 1919–1939*, edited by E. L. Woodward and Rohan Butler, first series (London:
HMSO, 1962), 4: 820, 823–25. Hereafter cited as *British Documents, 1919–1939*.

[3]J. C. Hurewitz, *Diplomacy in the Near and Middle East* (Princeton, N.J.: D. Van
Nostrand, 1956), 2: 74–75.

Government, and the Sea of Marmara, must be preserved from every danger. Provided this principle is maintained, whatever decision may be arrived at jointly by us and all other interested governments concerned, regarding the opening of the Bosphorus to the commerce and traffic of the world, is valid."

In other words, Turkey demanded security at Constantinople but, that being assured, the Straits were to be open to commerce in agreement with the Powers.

The Development of American Policy toward Turkey (1920-1922)

ANGLO-FRENCH POSITIONS

Meanwhile, the problem of a Turkish settlement, with all its complications, continued to occupy the Allied statesmen in London and Paris, as already observed, as well as the government in Washington, and there was much misunderstanding, misinformation, and misinterpretation concerning developments in Turkey, especially with regard to the Nationalist movement.[4] Neither the King-Crane Report, which had been filed with the White House in September 1919 and thence with the Department of State, nor the Harbord Report, had any basic influence on American policy during this period.[5] The primary aim of the United States, from the beginning of 1920 to the opening of the Lausanne Conference in 1922, was to safeguard "American interests," American lives and property, somewhat narrowly conceived. American policy, which eschewed any responsibilities in the Middle East, it must be recognized, was among the elements which prevented a settlement of the problem of the mandates for two and one-half years or more after the war.

While there was no further discussion for the time being of the Turkish problem at the Peace Conference, the British and French governments conferred constantly, whether in Paris or London. David Lloyd George and Clemenceau took up the problem of the mandates and the Turkish Straits on December 11, 1919, when Clemenceau proposed renunciation of the system of mandates "so

[4]*British Documents, 1919-1939*, first series, 4: 912-14.

[5]Excerpts from the King-Crane Report were published in R. S. Baker, *Woodrow Wilson and World Settlement* (Garden City: Doubleday and Page, 1922), chap. 35, and in *The New York Times*, December 3 and 4, 1922. The report was published in full for the first time in *The Editor and Publisher* 55, no. 27 (December 2, 1922): i–xxvii. It was published officially in 1947 in Department of State, *The Foreign Relations of the United States. Paris Peace Conference, 1919* (Washington, D.C.: USGPO, 1942-47), 12: 751-862. Hereafter referred to as *USFR*. See Howard, *The King-Crane Commission*, pp. 311-13.

far as Asia Minor" was concerned. The Ottoman Empire, in his view, "should be dealt with as a whole in the manner which seemed best," although he did not want to include the Arab part of the former Empire.[6] In the French view, the first problem was that of Constantinople, and "the Straits must be kept in the hands of an Allied force and taken altogether out of the hands of Turkey." But it would be a mistake "to take the Turks out of Constantinople," although Clemenceau would consider the city "separate from the Straits." He thought this would avoid much trouble, since, if the Sultan were to govern "in our interest," it would be easier to "govern through the Sultan as an intermediary, and for this reason it would be better to leave him in Constantinople," with Bursa as a possible alternative. The latter move, however, would cause difficulties which should be avoided.

All this had a very familiar ring, and Lloyd George thought there were "objections" to leaving Constantinople in Turkish hands. He agreed that Asia Minor "was not a suitable field in which to apply the system of mandates" and that "the Straits must be placed under some form of international control." The Prime Minister recalled that the war had probably been prolonged for some two years by closure of the Straits:

"As regards Constantinople itself, the British Government felt that complete control of the Straits would not be assured unless Constantinople also was in the hands of some international force. Constantinople was situated at the gates of the Bosphorus, even though the Dardanelles were open. Another consideration was that the Allied peoples would not wish to have placed upon them the burden of paying for the troops required to keep open the Straits. The Straits ought to be made self-supporting, but this could not be done without Constantinople. In the port and city of Constantinople it should be possible to raise sufficient taxes and dues to pay for the troops."

In the British view, there should be an international force composed of Anglo-French and perhaps Italian and Greek troops, under the direction of a neutral commissioner, since Lloyd George wished the Straits "to be really neutral." In the future, "there might be trouble with Russia, which might join itself with Germany," and for this reason the Prime Minister wanted "an inter-allied force at Constantinople," and was "unwilling to trust the Sultan." In the event of a Russo-German combination, the Germans might get hold of the Sultan, as in the past, and Lloyd George "wanted an absolute guarantee of the neutrality of the Straits" which could prevent such a possibility. The question of Constantinople also depended to some extent on the disposition of Asia Minor, where there

<hr>

[6]*British Documents, 1919–1939*, first series, 4: 727–33.

might be an independent Turkish state, or, perhaps, an Anglo-French condominium, exercising the basic authority. Both Lloyd George and Clemenceau feared the latter alternative. While Venizeloz had suggested the possibility of establishing the Sultan "in a sort of Vatican at Constantinople," Lloyd George did not want the Sultan in Constantinople, with a Turkish population of 500,000, with Russia always desirous of obtaining Constantinople, and with Germany constantly intriguing. Not unmindful of Muslim sentiment concerning Constantinople, what Lloyd George "especially wanted to avoid was trouble in Europe." Lord Curzon feared difficulties with the Greeks if the Sultan remained and observed that "the Turkish policy of the future would be strongly nationalist."

Clemenceau, no gentle cynic, thought it sufficient to have one "Pope" in the West. Even if there were no mandate system in Asia Minor, be believed there would have to be "some international control over the Turkish Government," since the Turks were incapable of self-government. Moreover, there would have to be some control over the Straits. Clemenceau "thought it was possible for the two nations to control the Straits by a joint force. As regards Asia Minor also he required a solution which would avoid friction, which was the one thing he wished to escape. He realized that the logical solution was to join Constantinople to the Dardanelles and Bosphorus under a single inter-allied European authority, and if certain objections could be surmounted he would accept it. Anyhow, the proposal certainly deserved thorough examination. He was opposed to the suggestion that the President of the United States should be asked to nominate a president of the international authority." In fact, Clemenceau felt that neither the United Kingdom nor France "would be so unreasonable as to push a quarrel too far." The United States, which was very far away, "could help much," but Clemenceau could not forget that "politically America had forced a peace system on the Allies with which she had refused to agree." In his view, it was necessary to "establish a sort of balance between the Dardanelles, the Bosphorus, Constantinople and Asia Minor." While Great Britain was first in commercial interests, France was first in "matters of local enterprise and industry," and a balance could be arranged. If the two Powers were generally agreed in Europe, "the questions of Constantinople and Bursa would be easier to solve." He favored a system in which a British president would alternate with a French, although he felt that Italy, too, would have to be included in any projected solution. Lloyd George considered the French proposal "most admirable" and suggested immediate examinàtion, although he wondered whether the Sultan at Bursa would act under international control. Clemenceau thought "financial control" should be sufficient, although there would be no spheres of influence.

There were further discussions on December 13, and later on December 22-23, when the French proposed an administration over Constantinople and the Straits under an inter-allied commission, composed of representatives of France, Great Britain, Italy, Russia (if and when reconstituted), and possibly also of Rumania and Greece, for economic (shipping) reasons.[7] The French would not object to eventual American participation, but felt that the smaller states should have only a consultative status, while the British raised the question of Bulgarian membership, and suggested that the Great Powers should have two votes and the smaller states one. Ultimately a two-year rotation in the chairmanship between Great Britain and France was accepted. It was generally agreed that the new state should be under an international regime, under the protection of the League of Nations, without direct administrative control, and there was a question as to the extent to which Turkish officials should be encouraged to participate in the government.

In the end, on December 22, it was agreed that the new Turkish state, with the capital at Konya or Bursa, should be placed under the League of Nations, have elective institutions, and that, in the event of disputes in the Commission, reference should be made to the Council of the League of Nations. Interestingly enough, it was also agreed that the Dodecanese Islands should be returned to Greece, and no difficulty was anticipated in view of the Venizelos-Tittoni agreement of July 29, 1919, although trouble was expected concerning the Italian evacuation of Southern Anatolia. There was also general approval of an independent Armenia and Greek occupation of the Smyrna region. The meeting ended with a statement of the French expert, Philippe Berthelot, that "the Nationalist movement headed by Mustapha Kemal was largely bluff, and that a show of force from the points where the Allies had troops would be sufficient to show this." Lord Curzon was not "so optimistic," although he "agreed that a way could be found of imposing those conditions if the Allies were united and determined upon it." The discussions on December 23 largely centered on the problems of Kurdistan and the Caucasus.[8]

[7]Ibid., pp. 773-74, 938, 966, 966-70; René Albrecht-Carrié, *Italy at the Paris Peace Conference. The Paris Peace: History and Documents* (New York: Columbia University Press, 1938), pp. 242-43.

[8]See also Firuz Kazemzadeh, *The Struggle for Transcaucasia (1917-1921)* (New York: Philosophical Library, 1951); Sir Olaf Caroe, *Soviet Empire: The Turks of Central Asia and Stalinism* (London: Macmillan, 1963), chaps. 6 and 7; Charles W. Hostler, *Turkey and the Soviets* (London: Allen and Unwin, 1957).

But there were grave misgivings among some British officials concerning the Anglo-French discussions. On January 4, 1920, Lord Curzon saw for the first time a paper of Edwin Montagu, secretary of state for the colonies, who was still much concerned with the issue of Constantinople.[9] Curzon sensed that the basic reason why the French government wanted the Turks to remain in Constantinople was that it had a profound distaste for a condominium like that in the Sudan, considered it certain that the British would want to get rid of the burden, and believed that France "would be left at Constantinople in practical control of the Turk and of the Turkish Nationalist movement, soon to be in the ascendant," which France would manipulate to its advantage in every part of the Eastern world. Curzon considered this to be "the insidious danger" of the original French proposal, and he hoped his colleagues would be on their guard against any attempt to revert to it. He also felt that the proposal to leave the Sultan in Constantinople did not appear in the results of the December meeting. In conclusion, he wrote:

Lastly, ought we not to look to the future? Constantinople has been for centuries, ever since a Roman Emperor moved his capital there, the prize of the Eastern world. To this day its possession is coveted by France, Greece, Russia, and I daresay Bulgaria. How are we to prevent it from becoming once more the prey of rival ambitions and the cockpit of future struggles, except by putting it under international supervision now? If we leave the Sultan there, what is to prevent the German from recommencing the old intrigues? Will not the Bulgarian and the Greek be condemned to a lifelong rivalry? Will not a resuscitated Russia once again look to the Bosphorus for the gratification of her secular ambitions? Let us suppose that you have a combination between the Bolshevik, assuming him to be victorious in Russia, and the Turk—assuming him to be left as Sovereign in Constantinople—let us suppose—what is by no means unlikely—that a recovered Germany once again takes a hand in the game—what is to prevent the repetition at some future date, perhaps in a more dangerous form, of the experience of 1914-1915? Finally—and here I repeat a warning already given—what is to prevent France from assuming the role of champion of the new Islam, and organising the Moslems of the Western World from Morocco to Syria against the Moslems of the East, i.e., Mesopotamia, Arabia, Persia, Afghanistan and India. I cannot imagine a greater danger to the peace of the world than a division between French and British Islam, of which I do not think that I am fanciful in seeing the omens already above the horizon. I call attention to the fact that on his recent return from Syria, M. Picot, the French High Commissioner, and no friend of ours, went out of his way to visit Mustapha Kemal in Sivas.

The conclusion of my argument is that in spite of the immediate risks involved in the policy of expulsion—which in my judgment will have to be encountered anyhow, whether we keep the Turk in Europe or bid him go—the longer view demands that we should not sacrifice the opportunity presented

[9]*British Documents, 1919-1939*, first series, 3: nos. 55, 62; 4: 938-70, 992-1000.

to us by the defeat of an enemy whose entrance into the war prolonged it
for at least two years and cost us millions of treasure and tens of thousands
of lives, to settle once and for all a question which more than any single
cause has corrupted the political life of Europe for nearly 500 years.[10]

Lord Curzon considered another proposal prepared by Berthelot, on
January 12, 1920, which called for maintenance of an independent
Turkish state, suppression of Turkish militarism, preservation of
absolute freedom of the Straits, under an international organization,
an independent Armenia, freedom of the Arabs from Turkish rule,
protection of minorities, and reform of the Turkish administration,
under the guarantee and control of the interested Powers. Peace
with Turkey, it was said, raised four principal problems: Constantinople and the Straits, Anatolia and Asia Minor, Armenia and
Syria, Mesopotamia and Arabia. Robert Vansittart, on the other
hand, contended that two solutions were possible in the matter of
Constantinople, under one of which the Sultan would remain at
Constantinople and under the other would be expelled. Expulsion
would be justified from both the historical and moral points of view.
In the event of expulsion, "it would be possible to create a State of
Constantinople and the Straits, comprising in Europe the territory
situated between the Sea of Marmora and the line Enos-Midia (or
confined to the Chatalja lines), and in Asia only the Asiatic shore of
the Straits of the Bosphorus (with a frontier running from Shile on the
north to Ismid on the south) and of the Dardanelles (with a frontier
running from Tenedos and following a line about 50 klom. from the
coast), the Asiatic shore and (sic) the Sea of Marmora remaining
Turkish. All the islands between the Black Sea and the Mediterranean would be included in the State."

The new state would be "neutralized" under the League of Nations
and demilitarized to a depth of 30 kilometers. The administration
would be first organized and directed by a government commission,
composed of two representatives of the Great Mediterranean
Powers (France, Italy, Great Britain), to which could be added subsequently the United States, if it desired to participate, and Russia,
as soon as it had been reconstituted, and one representative for
Greece, Rumania, and ultimately for Turkey. In the event of differences, reference was to be made to the Council of the League of
Nations. The chairmanship was to alternate every two years
between the United Kingdom and France, but after eight years, it

[10]Ibid., 4: 560–88, for Picot visit with Mustafa Kemal in November 1919. The cabinet
rejected Curzon's policy as to Constantinople, and he protested on January 7 (see
Laurence Zetlan, Earl of Ronaldshay, *Life of Lord Curzon* [New York: Boni and Livewright, 1928], 3: 270).

might be entrusted to one or the other Great Powers in rotation, by a two-thirds vote of the commission. The commission was to control the military and naval forces charged with policing the Constantinopolitan state and guarding the Straits.

If Constantinople remained the Ottoman capital, Vansittart considered that it would only be necessary to have about 30,000 troops, one-third each to be supplied by Great Britain, France, and Italy. The task would "be to guarantee the absolute liberty of the Straits and to occupy the points decided on by military experts, but which should not include Constantinople, where no Turkish troops could be maintained other than the Sultan's small personal guard." The Turkish state in Europe would be restricted to the hinterland of Constantinople, and administrative reform would be applied over the Turkish state. Vansittart would also call for the "formation of an International Straits Company, to be formed by the fusion of the French and foreign companies interested in all matters concerning navigation in the Straits. The inevitable development of traffic throughout the East after the conclusion of peace makes it possible to consider a scheme which would permanently internationalise communications between the Aegean and the Black Sea. Such internationalisation cannot fail to facilitate the settlement of questions concerning the hinterland of these communications by sea."

The Ottoman Empire would continue to exist in Asia Minor under the national Osmanli dynasty, covering essentially the Anatolian plateau, with a capital at Konya, Bursa or Ankara. Smyrna (Izmir) was to be made a free port, with Greece playing a predominant part in its control, and Greece would receive compensation in Europe, especially in sovereignty over Adrianople (Edirné), and Thrace to the Enos–Midia (Enez-Midye) line, the frontier of the Constantinopolitan state and perhaps even to the Çatalca line. Italy was to withdraw from Southern Anatolia, and it was felt that Italian consent would be obtained easily. Armenia would become independent, under the protection of the League of Nations, and it was hoped that the United States would be interested.[11] On January 13, Eric G. Forbes-Adam submitted a counter draft to the French proposal relative to Constantinople and the Straits, stressing the dangers of Pan-Turanism and Pan-Islamism, and indicated that an international control or condominium could hardly work smoothly, especially where national sentiment was strong and the interests of the controlling nations were in conflict.[12] But the same considera-

[11]*British Documents, 1919–1939*, first series, 4: 1016–25.
[12]Ibid., pp. 1026–28, 1043–44, 1044–61. See also Forbes-Adam's letter to Eric Phipps, January 20, including a Montagu draft, in which the latter pointed out that in "closing

tions, it was thought, would apply much less "to an international zone of the Straits after the removal of the Turkish Government": "The duties of the international commission would be primarily those of keeping open the Straits, maintaining order and arranging for a Government satisfactory to the mixed populations of the zone. There is no reason why any really vital or controversial issue should arise among the Great Powers on the Commission." It could hardly be hoped that the Allied occupation would be permanent, and after departure, Constantinople again would be coveted by Russia, Bulgaria, and possibly Greece. Moreover, it was doubted that Venizelos would accept the proposition concerning Izmir, and the settlement proposed "against the true interests of the Turkish population of Anatolia."

AMERICAN POLICY IN THE MIDDLE EAST

While the United States, under President Wilson's leadership, had taken a strong stand in favor of the mandate system, it would assume no official responsibility in any of the Middle Eastern countries, and little elsewhere. The United States was interested in protecting American lives and property and in asserting the principle of the "open door" in mandated territories.[13] It protested against the San Remo oil agreement between France and Great Britain (April 1920), and it was anxious to preserve the capitulatory rights of American citizens and business interests, and was concerned with the protection of Christian minorities on Turkish territories, especially Greeks and Armenians, but uncommitted as to specific measures. While the American Senate, on June 1, 1920, had

---

the Straits Turkey cut the communications of Russia with the Allies, caused Russia's political and military dissolution and prolonged the war with all its disasters; such a catastrophe cannot be allowed to be renewed." It was proposed that Turkey "hand over to the Allies the duty and the responsibility of maintaining the neutrality of the Dardanelles, the Sea of Marmara and the Bosphorus. The Allies will entrust this duty to a force of such dimensions as they may consider necessary and will assume the right to take such measures, naval, military, financial, and administrative, as they may consider necessary for the purpose of securing the safety of the Straits. Details of the organization necessary to give effect to these measures . . . will be decided by the Allies" (Ibid., pp. 1036–42). Vansittart and Forbes-Adam sketched the problem for Lord Curzon and indicated that the retention of the Turks at Constantinople would make the place a center of intrigue, "backed by a resuscitated Germany with Russia possibly behind her. This would make the task of Great Britain and France in the Straits zone a dangerous or impossible one."

[13]See United Kingdom, Miscellaneous No. 10 (1921), *Correspondence between H.M. Government and the United States Respecting Economic Rights in Mandated Territories*, Cmd. 1226; Department of State, *Mandate for Palestine*, Near Eastern Series No. 1 (Washington: USGPO, 1931); Howard, *The King-Crane Commission*, pp. 294–96; Laurence Evans, *United States Policy and the Partition of Turkey, 1914–1924* (Baltimore: The Johns Hopkins University Press, 1965), chaps. 9 and 10.

rejected a mandate over Armenia, President Wilson had been asked to help determine the boundaries, but by the time the delimitation was prepared, the fate of Armenia was sealed with the establishment of Soviet Armenia.[14]

The Anglo-French discussions of December 1919–January 1920, of course, were to lead into the more formal preparations for the treaty of peace with Turkey and, indeed, that was their purpose. The American representatives on the Peace Commission, meanwhile, had left Paris in December, as already observed, and took no formal part in the negotiation of the Treaty of Sèvres, although the American government was kept informed of developments and expressed its view unofficially concerning the pending settlement. The Supreme Council advised the United States on January 22, 1920, that if it were unable to take part in the settlement the Allies would have no other alternative but to proceed, "keeping the United States Government fully informed of the course of the discussion and taking every care compatible with the early conclusion of peace to elicit their views." But with the world in a somewhat chaotic state, time was "the most vital element."[15]

On March 12, four days before the formal British occupation of Constantinople, Jusserand, the French ambassador in Washington, transmitted the proposals for the Turkish treaty to Acting Secretary of State Polk.[16] He had already informed Secretary of State Colby that the work of drafting the treaty had gone "far enough to make it possible to consider summoning the Turkish delegates at an early date." Jusserand wanted to ascertain the American attitude and to know whether the United States would take any part in the Turkish settlement. Very significant were the provisions relative to the Turkish Straits:

> The Turkish Sultan and Government will be maintained at Constantinople, that decision, however being contingent upon the execution of the terms of peace and observance of the guarantees therein stipulated in favor of the minorities. No Turkish troops, except the Sultan's bodyguard, will remain in Constantinople.
>
> The Allies will continue to reserve the right of military occupation in Turkey-in-Europe and in a zone south of the Straits and of the Sea of Marmora.

[14]See, especially, James B. Gidney, *A Mandate for Armenia* (Kent, Ohio: Kent State University Press, 1967), chaps. 9–11; *USFR* (1920), 2: 655–59; 3: 757–73, 774–809, 924–26. See also Joseph L. Grabill, *Protestant Diplomacy and the Near East: Missionary Influence on American Policy, 1810–1927* (Minneapolis: University of Minnesota Press, 1971), chaps. 9–11; R. R. Trask, *The United States Response to Turkish Nationalism and Reform, 1914–1939* (Leiden: Brill, 1971), chap. 2.

[15]*British Documents, 1919–1939*, first series, 4: 1070–71.

[16]*USFR* (1920), 3: 748–50. See also David Lloyd George, *Memoirs of the Peace Conference* (New Haven: Yale University Press, 1939), 2: 807–08.

An international Commission will be created, with administrative and financial powers, to ensure the freedom of the straits, which will be guaranteed in time of peace as in time of war. The Commission, which will exercise its powers in the name of and by delegation from the Sultan, will have its own flag and budget, with power to borrow money on its revenues. It will collect taxes on the basis of complete equality between all countries. It will do whatever may be necessary for the improvement of navigation and will be vested with naval police rights. France, England, Italy, and in certain contingencies the United States and Russia, will each have on the Commission one representative with two votes. Rumania, Greece and ultimately Bulgaria will have a representative with one vote. The Chairmanship may be held only by a representative of one of the Great Powers. Several other questions, regarding in particular the passage of warships and the regime of the Straits in time of war are still under advisement. In case the territory of Greece should extend as far as the Sea of Marmora, the Greek shore would be subject to the same regime as the Turkish shore.

Greece was to be assigned that portion of Thrace not left to Turkey, while special guarantees would be given to the Turks in Adrianople [Edirné], and a "free port" would be assigned to Bulgaria, perhaps at Dedeagaç. Interestingly enough, "a special arrangement" was being made for Great Britain, France, and Italy, the purpose of which was to set aside spheres of influence "in the matter of furnishing advice and instructors." Armenian independence would be recognized, under assistance from the League of Nations, and Turkey was to "relinquish all rights in Mesopotamia, Arabia, Palestine, Syria and all the islands." The vilayet of Izmir, with the probable exclusion of Aydin, was to be administered "by the Greeks under the Sultan's suzerainty," although the port was to be free and part of it reserved for Turkey. There were also economic considerations, such as the liquidation of German properties, foreign concessions, and the Ottoman public debt.

This was a fairly complete program, and Secretary of State Colby replied on March 24,[17] very frankly stating that the United States now opposed "retention of the Turks at Constantinople," and did not believe that the Muslims of the world would resent their expulsion from the Golden Horn. Concerning the Straits, he observed:

The Government of the United States notes with pleasure that provision is made for Russian representation on the International Council, which it is proposed shall be established for the Government of Constantinople and the Straits. This Government is convinced that no arrangement that is now made concerning the government and control of Constantinople and the Straits can have any elements of permanence unless the vital interests of

[17]*USFR* (1920), 3: 750-53. Compare with the memorandum of the General Board of the Navy, November 10, 1922.

Russia in those problems are carefully provided for and protected, and unless it is understood that Russia, when it has a Government recognized by the civilized world, may assert its right to be heard in regard to the decisions now made.

It is noted with pleasure that the questions of passage of warships and the regime of the Straits in war time are still under advisement as this Government is convinced that no final decision should or can be made without the consent of Russia.

Aside from the zone of the Straits, the United States believed that Eastern Thrace should go to Greece, with the exception of the northern part, which was "clearly Bulgarian in population." Justice and fair dealing, therefore, demanded that "the cities of Adrianople [Edirné] and Kirk Kilisseh [Kirklareli] and the surrounding territory should become part of Bulgaria." Colby also wanted more information concerning spheres of influence and interest in Turkey proper and expressed his interest in Armenia. He also felt that Mesopotamia, Arabia, Palestine, Syria, and the islands should be placed "in the hands of the Great Powers," to be disposed of as those Powers determined. He thought a spirit of fairness would prevail as to commercial interests, although the question of concessions required study, and he understood that the territorial arrangements would "in no way place American citizens or corporations, or the citizens or corporations of any other country in a less favorable situation than the citizens or corporations of any Power party to this treaty."

The Allies concluded the San Remo agreement, together with an oil agreement, on April 24, 1920. The agreement provided for the maintenance of the Sultanate in Constantinople, the right of the Allies to occupy European Turkey and the zone of the Straits, the creation of an Armenian state with access to the Black Sea, and Turkish abandonment of Syria, Palestine, Mesopotamia, and the Aegean Islands.[18] Two days later, on April 26, the Allied Powers expressed their pleasure at having the American view, but, since the United States would take no active part in the peacemaking relative to Turkey, they did not interpret the desire for information to mean that "the negotiations with Turkey should be delayed until each of the particular points" had been discussed exhaustively with the United States, and an agreement had been reached, for that would make "fruitful negotiations impossible."[19] Because of the desire for American participation, and at grave risk, the Allies had already delayed the Turkish negotiations. The Allies shared the American

---

[18]For texts of San Remo Agreements, April 24, 1920, see *USFR* (1920), 2: 655–58; Cmd. 2226 (1921); Hurewitz, *Diplomacy in the Near and Middle East*, 2: 75–77.

[19]*USFR* (1920), 2: 753–56.

desire for justice and fair play, but many points were raised concerning the Colby note. They rejected the American position regarding ejection of the Sultan from Constantinople, although they admitted that the problem might have been different were the United States to share "the responsibilities, dangers and sacrifices" in the Middle East. The Turco-Asiatic frontiers, they contended, were based on ethnic, economic, and geographical considerations. The Powers noted that the United States welcomed provision for Russian representation on the Commission of the Straits, although the United States had wrongly assumed that the commission was to administer Constantinople. The question of the Straits had been carefully studied "with a view to safeguarding freedom of passage," and it was hoped and believed that the United States would accept the agreed provisions. But it had been obviously impossible "to defer the drafting of so vital a chapter of the Turkish treaty pending the eventual consultation with Russia." They agreed concerning Eastern Thrace, but not as to the Bulgarian character of Adrianople (Edirné) and Kirk Kilisseh (Kirklareli), which were basically Turkish. Like the United States, they were also interested in Armenia, and agreed as to the Aegean Islands, Mesopotamia, Arabia, Palestine, and Syria. But the problem of Izmir was also causing trouble, thanks to both Greek and Turkish claims. The city was intimately connected with the Turkish hinterland, as the natural outlet to the sea. Moreover, the Allies had been advised that "the immediate and complete cession" of Izmir would arouse Turkish national feeling to such a pitch as to render "the rest of the contemplated settlement of Turkey difficult if not impossible." Therefore, the Allies thought of placing Izmir under Greek administration, while retaining Turkish sovereignty until a plebiscite could be held. The economic provisions, they held, were in harmony with the principles approved in the other treaties, and the United States was assured that they had not sought to place citizens or corporations in a privileged position as compared with American citizens or corporations.

A few weeks after the San Remo meeting, on May 11, 1920, the Turkish terms were presented to Damat Ferid Paşa, the head of the Ottoman Delegation, who protested at length on June 25 concerning their severity.[20] It was not merely a matter of detaching vast terri-

---

[20]*Observations of the Ottoman Empire on the Conditions of Peace. Ottoman Delegation to the Peace Conference,* from Damat Ferid Paşa to Millerand, President of the Peace Conference, June 25, 1920, E.S.H. Bulletin No. 637. American Embassy, Paris, July 1, 1920.

tories from the old empire, but one of fundamental infringement of Ottoman sovereignty. The Ottoman Delegation could not accept the provisions concerning Constantinople and the Straits, for Constantinople was "not only the capital of Turkey," but "the vital organ of the nation, the immortal monument of Turkish history, the symbol of Ottoman ethnical unity." To deprive Turkey of Constantinople "would be to strike at her heart, to injure her in her past and to paralyze her future." The peaceful and prosperous existence of the nation could be assured only if Constantinople remained "as firmly attached to the country as the head is to the body." Similarly, it could not accept the Straits Commission, which would control the vital waterway at Constantinople and which, while seeming "to be an international Commission destined to ensure the internationalization of the Straits," would in reality "represent only certain States." Turkey and other states would be excluded, while "two votes would be attributed to each of the delegates of the Principal Powers" and other delegates would have only one vote. So the draft treaty instituted no international "juridical and political organization of the Straits," but merely created a political and military power in favor of certain nations, particularly Great Britain, with all the risks which such a regime would bring with it. Such a violation of Ottoman sovereignty was not necessary to defend "the freedom of navigation" in the Straits: "Far from ensuring the internationalization of the Straits in conformity with the object which it is proposed to attain, the regime of the Draft Treaty would favor their nationalization by another State. The internationalization of the Straits could be realized only by means of an international organism, that is to say by a juridical organism representing all the states together. The League of Nations would be quite qualified to ensure this realization if it delegated, for example, a neutral High Commissioner." The Ottoman government was willing to accept all restrictions on its sovereignty which were dictated by the necessity of assuring commercial freedom of the Straits "to all flags on a footing of complete equality." The Ottoman Delegation also rejected the provisions relative to Izmir and the principle of Armenian independence, while the situation in the Hijaz was accepted, although adjustments were held necessary in Syria and Mesopotamia. On July 8 the Ottoman Delegation bitterly condemned the Allied project for dismemberment of the empire and observed: "At Constantinople itself, Turkey would not be at home. At the side of His Imperial Majesty the Sultan and of the Turkish Government—even above them—a 'Commission of the Straits' would reign over the Bosphorus, the Sea

of Marmora and the Dardanelles. Turkey would not even be represented on this Commission, while Bulgaria would send a
delegate to it."[21] The Ottoman protests were quite futile. On July 16,
1920, the Allied Powers, which recalled Ottoman "guilt" in entering
the war on the side of the Central Powers, the misdeeds against
the minorities and the massacres of the Armenians, rejected the
Ottoman contentions. As to the regulation of the Straits, they said:
"The Powers cannot hesitate to take the necessary measures
to prevent new treachery to the cause of civilization by a Turkish
Government. They will not then modify the broad outlines of the
regime that it appeared to them legitimate and equitable to
institute in order to guarantee the liberty of the Straits. Nevertheless,
they did not think that they ought to reject entirely the observations
of the Ottoman Delegation as far as the representation of Turkey on
the Straits Commission is concerned. They have decided to grant to
Turkey, as a riparian Power, as to Bulgaria under the same conditions,
the right to send a delegate to this Commission."[22] The Allies had
resolved to "put an end forever" to Ottoman domination over other
nations, but they denied that the treaty had "the character attributed
to it by the Ottoman Delegation." True, it deprived Turkey of
sovereignty over possessions which had been badly governed. Turkey
was, however, to be a national state, and there was nothing to
prevent the Turkish nation from prospering, if reforms were
instituted. The treaty had gone so far as to retain Constantinople as
the Turkish capital, although it was doubtful that the Turks constituted "a majority of the population there." If the Ottoman government refused to sign the peace and showed itself incapable of reestablishing its authority over Anatolia or of insuring the execution
of the treaty, the Allies would have to revise the provision relative
to Constantinople and would be forced to expel the Turks from
Europe, "this time forever." The Ottoman government was given
until July 27 at midnight to signify its intentions.

---

[21]*Observations générales présentées par la délégation ottomane à la Conférence
de la Paix*, July 8, 1920. Article 40 of the Treaty of Sèvres was modified to add Turkey
to the membership of the Straits Commission, while Article 178 was modified to provide for the demolition of all fortifications in the Straits zone and in the neighboring
Greek islands. Provision was also made for the destruction of roads and railways
which could be used for bringing mobile batteries into the region of the Straits or into
the islands of Lemnos, Imbros, Samothrace, and Tenedos.
[22]*Reply of the Allied Powers to the Observations of the Ottoman Empire to the Conditions of Peace, July 16, 1920*, E.S.H. Bulletin No. 743, July 21, 1920, vol. 8, American Embassy, Paris.

THE TREATY OF SÈVRES

There was little else for the Ottoman government to do, evidently,[23] and on August 10 the Treaty of Sèvres was duly signed. The terms were severe in the extreme. The Turkish homelands were left to the Turkish nation, together with Constantinople, the shores of the Marmara, and the Gallipoli peninsula. But Turkey had to recognize the separation of Syria, Mesopotamia, and Palestine and their position as British and French mandates, while the Hijaz was to be independent and Izmir to be placed under Greek administration for five years, when a plebiscite was to be held. Greece was to have Imbros and Tenedos, which controlled entry to the Dardanelles. Armenia was to be independent, with boundaries to be determined by President Wilson, and the Ottoman government was to renounce to Great Britian all rights to Egypt, the Sudan, and Cyprus. All claims to the Dodecanese Islands were renounced in favor of Italy.

The regulations of the Turkish Straits, similarly, were drastic, under the form of internationalization of those strategic waters. Although, as promised, "the rights and title" of Turkey over Constantinople were not formally affected, if Turkey failed to live up to its treaty obligations, the provisions were to be altered still more in favor of the Allied Powers. Article 37 stipulated:

The navigation of the Straits, including the Dardanelles, the Sea of Marmora and the Bosphorus, shall in future be open, both in peace and war, to every vessel of commerce or of war and to military and commercial aircraft, without distinction of flag.
These waters shall not be subject to blockade, nor shall any belligerent right be exercised nor any act of hostility be committed within them, unless in pursuance of a decision of the Council of the League of Nations.

To assure the "freedom" of the Straits, Turkey was compelled to assign control over the Dardanelles, Marmara, and the Bosphorus to

[23]For Treaty of Sèvres, see United Kingdom, Foreign Office, Treaty Series No. 11 (1920), *Treaty of Peace with Turkey, Signed at Sèvres,* August 10, 1920, Cmd. 964; Hurewitz, *Diplomacy in the Near and Middle East,* 2: 81–90; Société pour l'Etude de l'histoire turque, *Histoire de la République turque* (Istanbul: Basimevi, 1935), pp. 61–65; Halidé Edib, *Turkey Faces West* (New Haven: Yale University Press, 1930), pp. 176–90. See also United Kingdom, Foreign Office, Treaty Series No. 12 (1920), *Tripartite Agreement between the British Empire, France, and Italy, Respecting Anatolia, August 10, 1920,* Cmd. 963. For a final Turkish appeal, see *Note from the Ottoman Delegation Requesting Certain Changes in the Conditions of the Turkish Treaty, August 1, 1920,* E.S.H. Bulletin No. 820, vol. 9, American Embassy, Paris. For a recent analysis, see Paul C. Helmreich, *From Paris to Sèvres: The Partition of the Ottoman Empire at the Peace Conference of 1919–1920* (Columbus: The Ohio State University Press, 1974).

a Commission of the Straits, which was to be given a comprehensive authority, and to be composed of representatives of the British Empire, France, Italy, Japan, the United States (if and when willing), Soviet Russia (when it became a member of the League of Nations), Greece, Rumania, Bulgaria, and Turkey (when members of the League of Nations). The Great Powers were each given two votes. The commission was to function "in complete independence of Turkish authority," of course, and in the case of interference with freedom of passage, an appeal to the Allied forces could be made. It was to perform the duties of the previous health and sanitation bodies, and necessary police forces were to be placed under its direct authority. The rules and regulations governing transit and navigation of the Straits, embodied in Articles 57–61, stipulated:

  1) Belligerent warships were not to revictual, except to complete passage of the Straits and reach the nearest port of call, and repairs only to make seaworthy were to be made;
  2) Passage of belligerent vessels was to be made with "the least possible delay";
  3) The stay was not to exceed 24 hours, except in cases of distress, and opposing belligerent vessels were to depart at an interval of 24 hours;
  4) The League of Nations was to lay down any other war rules for the Straits.

Prizes were to be subject to similar regulations. No troops were to be embarked or disembarked, "except in case of accidental hindrance of passage," nor were munitions or other war materials to be landed in the regions under the control of the International Commission. Article 60, however, declared that nothing in these provisions was to be deemed "to limit the powers of a belligerent or belligerents acting in pursuance of a decision by the Council of the League of Nations," in which the Allied Powers were the dominant voice.[24]

An annex embodied the organization of the International Commission of the Straits, the chairmanship of which was to be on a two-year rotatory basis among the United States, Great Britain, France, Italy, Japan, and Soviet Russia. Decisions were to be taken by majority, and the chairman was to have a casting vote. Abstention was to be regarded as a negative. The commission was authorized "to prepare, issue, and enforce," as well as to amend and repeal, the regulations for the Straits. Since there was little likelihood of the United States taking its position on the commission, and Soviet

---

[24]For convenience, see Harry H. Howard, *The Problem of the Turkish Straits*, Department of State Publications 2752, Near Eastern Series 3 (Washington, D.C. USGPO, 1947), pp. 19–21.

Russia was diametrically opposed to it, this placed the Straits firmly under Allied—essentially British—control, at least for the time being. In addition, it is well to recall that while the Turkish homelands were to be independent and to form the nucleus of a national state, in reality national independence was to be a farce, with the capitulatory regime still in operation and the country actually divided into spheres of economic interest.

While the Treaty of Sèvres was the high watermark of British and Allied policy concerning the Ottoman Empire, it proved abortive. Despite the Ottoman signature, the Turkish nationalists under Mustafa Kemal scorned it, and continued their struggle against the Greeks. Neither the United States nor the Soviet Union, each for its own reasons, liked the treaty. Among other things it was contended that it would serve only to promote turmoil in the Middle East, and there were fears in Washington that American economic and other interests might be seriously impaired or injured.

THE TURKISH NATIONALIST REVOLT AGAINST
THE TREATY OF SÈVRES

The Turkish Nationalists fought for two years more against the fate sketched out in the Treaty of Sèvres, although the course of that struggle need not deter us at this point.[25] Some months after the Ottoman signature, the Nationalists virtually effected a diplomatic revolution. On March 13, 1921, an agreement was signed with Italy, recognizing the latter's right of exploitation in Adalia, Aydin, Konya, and the Heraclea coal mines, and Italian forces were withdrawn from Adalia in June 1921. After preliminary moves in 1920, France and the Turkish Nationalists signed an agreement at Ankara on October 20, 1921, covering both political and economic developments.[26]

But, while renewing relations with France and Italy, the government in Ankara also moved toward Soviet Russia, which seemed on the point of returning, as it were, to the policy of Hünkâr Iskelesi (1833), developing a policy in Asia in general and the Middle East in

---

[25]For aspects of these developments, see Harry J. Psomiades, *The Eastern Question: The Last Phase: A Study in Greek–Turkish Diplomacy* (Thessaloniki: Institute for Balkan Studies, 1968); Ferenc A. Vali, *Bridge Across the Bosphorus: The Foreign Policy of Turkey* (Baltimore: The Johns Hopkins University Press, 1971), chaps. 1 and 2.

[26]See United Kingdom, Foreign Office, Turkey No. 1 (1922), *Correspondence between H.M. Government and the French Government respecting the Angora Agreement of October 20, 1921*, Cmd. 1570; Turkey No. 2 (1921). *Dispatch from H.M. Ambassador at Paris enclosing the Franco–Turkish Agreement signed at Angora on October 20, 1921*, Cmd. 1556.

particular, against Great Britain, as had Tsarist Russia prior to World War I. Partly in response to British policy, Soviet Russia developed a "security system" for protection and expansion both in Europe and in Asia. On May 7, 1920, the Republic of Georgia was brought into the Soviet system. A treaty with Iran, signed on February 26, 1921, renounced all the rights of the former Tsarist regime, although it gave the Soviet government the right to send troops to Iran to prevent an attack on Soviet Russia, should the danger occur. Under Soviet influence, Iran rejected ratification of an earlier agreement with Great Britain of August 1919. Two days after the signature of the Soviet-Iranian treaty, an agreement was signed with Afghanistan. By the end of February 1921, all three Transcaucasian republics—Armenia, Georgia, and Azerbaijan—were conquered and under Soviet control.

On March 16, 1921, Nationalist Turkey and Soviet Russia proceeded to settle their accounts, each in its own particular interest, when Yussuf Kemal Bey signed a treaty of friendship with the Moscow government. Under the new treaty, Turkey received Kars and Ardahan, while Batum was placed temporarily under a Soviet-Turkish condominium. Soviet Russia accepted Turkish abolition of the capitulations, and both parties mutually pledged not to recognize any treaty imposed on either by force. Moscow recognized the Ankara government, with all the territories claimed in the National Pact.[27] Article V was of particular importance as to the Turkish Straits; and the USSR was to revert to it after World War II: "In order to assure the opening of the Straits to the commerce of all nations, the contracting parties agree to entrust the final elaboration of an international agreement concerning the Black Sea to a conference composed of delegates of the littoral States, on condition that the decisions of the above-mentioned conference shall not be of such a nature as to diminish the full sovereignty of Turkey or the security of Constantinople, her capital." In turn, Turkey, which was now engaged in a struggle for national survival, received a certain amount of assistance from Soviet Russia in the terrible months which were ahead. On October 13, 1921, Turkey concluded the Treaty of Kars with Armenia, Georgia, and Azerbaijan, delimiting their frontiers, recognizing the provisions of the Treaty of Moscow, and ceding Batum to Georgia, the city becoming a free port for Turkey. Article

---

[27] For texts of treaties of Moscow (March 16, 1921) and Kars (October 13, 1921), see Great Britain, Foreign Office, *British and Foreign State Papers*, 1923, Part 2, 118: 990-96; 120: 906-13; Howard, *The Problem of the Turkish Straits*, p. 21. These treaties, in addition to those of 1798, 1805, and 1833, were cited in support of the Soviet thesis, expounded in 1945 and 1946, as to joint control and defense of the Straits. See also E. A. Adamov, *Izvestia*, August 24, 1946.

IX was identical with the provisions of Article V of the Treaty of Moscow as to the Straits, and this was also true of the Turco-Ukrainian Treaty of January 2, 1922.[28]

Meanwhile, following the Treaty of Sèvres, the United States carried on a spirited correspondence with Great Britain and France concerning economic rights in mandated territories. While the European Powers had no reason to question American rights *per se*, they indicated that the place for such discussion was in the Council of the League of Nations, of which the United States, of course, was not a member. Formal approval was, therefore, much delayed, essentially because of American opposition to consideration of the mandates without the express, definite, and previous approval of the United States, and by the Greco-Turkish war, and the difficulties between Turkey and Great Britain over the Mosul frontier between Iraq and Turkey. Ultimately, it was not until September 29, 1923, following the Lausanne Conference, that France's Syrian mandate went into effect, while agreement with the United States was finally achieved on April 24, 1924. The United States signed an agreement with Great Britain relative to Palestine on December 3, 1924.[29]

By this time, however, the Greco-Turkish tragedy was moving toward a Turkish victory, and Greek forces failed to take Ankara in the great battle of the Sakarya during August 24–September 16, 1921. By March 1922, the Allied Powers agreed to some revisions of the Treaty of Sèvres and attempted a settlement of the struggle, although the Turks refused an armistice until a Greek evacuation from Anatolia and further mediatory efforts failed signally. In an ultimatum to the Turkish Nationalists on July 29, Turkish occupation of Constantinople was forbidden. By late August came the Turkish counteroffensive, and by early September 1922 the Greek forces were fleeing toward the coast, and Turkish troops took Izmir on September 9–11, 1922.

The Greek defeat relieved the Turkish Nationalist government of the necessity of looking to Soviet Russia for military and diplomatic support for the moment—and Turkey and Soviet Russia were bound to disagree concerning the question of the Straits as well as economic and political problems. As Turkish forces advanced toward the region of the Straits in August 1922, the Soviet government supported the principle of Turkish sovereignty over Constantinople and the Straits and the protection of Soviet interests in the Black Sea and the

---

[28]Howard, *The Problem of the Turkish Straits*, p. 21.
[29]*USFR* (1921), 1: 87–96, 97–142; (1922), 2: 117–34, 268–310; (1923), 2: 1–8.

Straits. On September 13, Karakhan sent a note to Lord Curzon bitterly denouncing Allied policy and declared that the fate of the Straits was to be decided by a conference of the riverain Powers, as stipulated in the Treaty of Moscow:

> . . . Russia cannot consent to the Straits being opened to the battleships of any country, and, in particular, that Great Britain, with the consent of her Allies, should have control of the Straits without the consent, and against the wishes, of the Powers who have vital interests in the Black Sea, and who should have the right of decision as to the fate of the Straits.
>
> Russia, Turkey, the Ukraine, and Georgia, to whom belongs practically the whole of the Black Sea coast, cannot admit the right of any other government to interfere in the settlement of this question of the Straits and will maintain the point of view above set out even if the contrary point of view is backed by military or naval superiority.[30]

This was, of course, an old theme in Russian policy, and it was to be repeated, especially during the period of 1945-46. Muslim members of the Indian legislature protested to the Viceroy of India at the same time and cabled the British government urging neutrality in the Greco-Turkish struggle. It was suggested that as a basis for peace Turkey retain Thrace with Edirné, international control over the Straits and Constantinople be abolished, and the Sultan-Caliph be retained in Constantinople.

Already, on September 11, the Allied Commissioners in Constantinople had advised the Turkish Nationalists that they would permit no violation of the zone. of the Straits, and the next day Great Britain asked both France and Italy to assist in their defense, while British troops were already proceeding to the danger zone.[31] On September 15, the British government appealed to the Dominions and to Greece, Yugoslavia, and Rumania to help defend the Straits against a possible Turkish incursion. An official statement of September 16 explained the British position: "The approach of the Kemalist forces to Constantinople and the Dardanelles and the demands put forward by the Angora Government . . ., if assented to, involve nothing less than the loss of the whole results of the victory over Turkey in the late war. The channel of deep salt water that separates Europe from Asia

---

[30]For text see the London *Times*, September 14, 1922; *L'Europe Nouvelle*, 5, no. 39 (September 30, 1922): 1240-41. See also RSFSR, *Godovoi Otchet k IX S'ezdu Sovetov 1920 g.* (1921): 45, 123-24; *Mezhdunarodnaia Politika RSFSR v. 1922* (Moscow 1923): 56-57; A. J. Toynbee, *Survey of International Affairs (1920-1923)* (London: Oxford University Press for RIIA), p. 374; Ahmed Rustem Bey, *La Crise Proche Orientale et la Question des Détroits de Constantinople* (Geneva, 1922); Harry N. Howard, *The Partition of Turkey* (Norman: University of Oklahoma Press, 1931; New York: Howard Fertig, 1966), pp. 266-74.

[31]The London *Times*, September 12, 13, 1922.

and unites the Mediterranean and the Black Sea affects world interests, European interests, and British interests of the first order."[32] But while the French government was "absolutely in accord" with Great Britain as to the necessity of preserving freedom of the Straits, it differed fundamentally as to "the proper means to realize it."[33] On September 19 all French troops in the region of the Straits were ordered withdrawn. Of the Dominions, only Australia and New Zealand, whose troops had fought valiantly in the Gallipoli campaign, favored taking direct action and offered to send troops. Neither Yugoslavia nor Rumania was moved to fall in line, while Greece had been heavily engaged with Turkey since May 1919. On September 19, the United States, although it affirmed its interest in the principle of freedom of the Straits, refused to take any action.[34]

All these developments now had their natural and obvious climax. Lord Curzon conferred with Poincaré and Count Sforza in Paris on September 19, and it was announced the next day that a conference would be called for the settlement of the Eastern question, to which France, Great Britain, Italy, Japan, Greece, Rumania, Yugoslavia, and Turkey would be invited to send representatives. Soviet Russia and its vassals were not to be invited, but on September 23 an invitation was sent to Ankara, advising the Nationalist government of the proposed conference, on the basis of the return of Turkish Thrace to the Maritza and Edirné to Turkey. A conference was to meet at Mudanya to arrange an armistice between Greece and Turkey.

On September 24 Prime Minister David Lloyd George declared that the first and primary element in British policy was "anxiety as to the freedom of the seas between the Mediterranean and the Black Sea." He repeated that closure of the Straits had prolonged the war by some two years and had contributed to the collapse of Imperial Russia. The original program concerning Turkey had broken down, since the United States was to have undertaken the mandate for Armenia and the Constantinopolitan state, France the responsibility for Cilicia, Italy that for Adalia, and Greek forces were to have occupied the vilayet of Izmir. But things had not turned out well.

[32]Winston Churchill, *The Aftermath* (New York: Scribner's, 1928), pp. 450-54; *New York Times*, September 17, 1922; London *Times*, September 18, 1922; *L'Europe Nouvelle* 5, no. 39 (September 30, 1922): 1239-40; Ronaldshay, *Life of Lord Curzon*, 3: 300-02.

[33]See Poincaré's address of November 10, 1922, with texts of notes, in *Journal Officiel. Chambre* (1922-1923): 3056-60.

[34]London *Times*, September 19-21, 1922; Churchill, *The Aftermath*, pp. 454-56; Edouard Driault and Michel Lheritier, *Histoire Diplomatique de la Grece de 1821 à Nos Jours* (Paris: Presses Universitaires, 1926), 5: 400-14.

The United States had rejected the Armenian mandate, France had surrendered Cilicia in October 1921, the Italians had withdrawn from Southern Anatolia, and Greek hopes centering in Izmir had now been smashed.

We, therefore, have regarded it as a matter of paramount importance to the interests of European peace that the war in Asia Minor should not spread in Europe. We have . . . taken steps to strengthen our position in the Dardanelles . . ., with a view of achieving two objectives: First, that of securing the freedom of the Straits, and second, that of preventing the prairie fire, which devastated Asia, from crossing the narrow seas and lighting the dry timber in the Balkans.

We do not wish to hold Gallipoli and Chanak in the interests of Great Britain alone. We do not consider that Great Britain alone should have the sole responsibility there. We believe that those important shores should be held under the auspices of the League of Nations in the interest of all nations alike. . . .

But the freedom of the Straits remains. That is of vital interest to us as a maritime and commercial power and to civilization throughout the world. That we can maintain, and the fight that we are putting up at the present moment is the fight to insure that, whatever happens at the peace conference, we shall not abandon the policy of securing the freedom of the Straits. . . . That is why we are taking the steps which we have already taken, and we shall do our best to secure an immediate conference between all the Powers concerned in order to establish permanent peace. . . . I want to make it clear that we do not want a second Gibraltar in the Dardanelles. We want the League of Nations to keep the Straits open for all nations.[35]

Soviet Russia, of course, did not accept the British thesis concerning the Turkish Straits. On September 24, it called for a conference "of all interested Powers, in the first place—Black Sea Powers," to deal with the Turkish problem, and three days later, Azerbaijan, Armenia, and Georgia, the Transcaucasian Republics, joined Soviet Russia in a declaration that "they would not recognize any decision which would be taken without the participation of the Transcaucasian Republics and against their interests." They all expected to be represented at the forthcoming conference on Middle Eastern problems.[36]

The Turkish Nationalists accepted the conditions for an armistice on September 29 and promised not to attack the region of the Straits, provided the Allied Powers would cede Constantinople with Eastern Thrace to the Maritza River, including Edirné.[37] At the same time the

[35]*New York Times*, September 24, 1922.
[36]*L'Europe Nouvelle* 5, no. 40 (1922): 1271; *Mezhdunarodnaia Politika RSFSR v. 1922* (Moscow 1922): 57.
[37]*Asie française* 12 (1922): 354-55; M. S. Anderson, *The Eastern Question* (New York: St. Martin's, 1966), pp. 371-72. See also Harold Nicolson, *Curzon, The Last Phase, 1919-1925: A Study in Post-War Diplomacy* (Boston: Houghton Mifflin, 1934).

Turks called on the British commander at Çanak, General Harrington, to evacuate the Asiatic shore of the Straits, as the Italians and French had done, and insisted that no Greek ships pass the Straits. The British positions were being reinforced, however, and Harrington warned the Turks not to threaten them.

Secretary of State Charles Evans Hughes, on September 26,[38] expressed satisfaction at the calling of a conference, and trusted that "suitable arrangements" would "be agreed upon in the interest of peace to preserve the freedom of the Straits pending a conference to conclude a final treaty of peace between Turkey, Greece and the Allies." On the other hand, the Soviet government[39] protested its exclusion from the conference and warned that it "would recognize no decision" taken without its participation or against its interests. It favored, as it had in the past and reasserted in the future, Turkish sovereignty and control over Constantinople and the Straits, in order to protect its own interests. The Western Powers, but especially Great Britain, refused to restore sovereignty over the Straits to Turkey "in the name of freedom of the Straits, but in reality in order to maintain there their own domination." Efforts to settle the crisis in the Middle East without the participation of the interested peoples could "give no positive result nor avoid the imminent risk of a new war." Consequently, Soviet Russia proposed a conference of the Black Sea Powers to determine the regime of the Straits:

> The freedom of the Straits, in the name of which Europe is preparing a new effusion of blood, signifies only freedom for the Powers to block the Straits at a moment and under any pretext whatever, and to separate thus the entire Black Sea from the rest of the world.
> The Russian Government is also a partisan of freedom of the Straits, but a freedom which concerns only merchant ships, and which frees entirely at the same time the Straits and the Black Sea from the presence of foreign naval vessels.

An additional note from Moscow protested the blockade of the Straits and demanded removal of all limitations on commercial vessels passing through those waters.[40]

---

[38]London *Times*, September 27, 1922. See also Nicolson, *Curzon, The Last Phase*, chap. 9. The British had only 300 rifles and a single strand of wire at Çanak.

[39]Soviet Note to the British Government, September 27, 1922; *L'Europe Nouvelle* 5, no. 40 (1922): 1271.

[40]Ibid., pp. 1271-72. See also *Mezhdunarodnaia Politika RSFSR v. 1922*, p. 57; Louis Fischer, *The Soviets in World Affairs* (London: Cape, 1930), 1: 399-403; Ettore Anchiere, *Constantinopli e gli Stretti nella Politica Russa ed Europa del trattato di Qüciuk Kainargi alla Convenzione di Montreux* (Milano: Giuffre, 1948), chap. 33. Jane Degras, ed., *The Communist International, 1919-1943. Documents* (London: Oxford University Press, 1956), 1: 368-70, 380-81, 406-07.

As a result of these developments, a conference met at Mudanya to arrange an armistice between Greece and Turkey, which was signed on October 11.[41] The Turkish Nationalists had demanded immediate occupation of Constantinople and Eastern Thrace, but since the Allied Powers were now formally united once more, they were not able fully to exploit that issue to a favorable conclusion. But the armistice stipulated that Greek forces were to be withdrawn from Thrace behind the left bank of the Maritza River. Allied forces were to occupy the right bank, including Karagaç, and were to be withdrawn only when the Ankara government could take over the territory. Neutral zones, which the Turkish Nationalists promised to respect, were to be drawn up, and Turkish troops were not to be moved into Eastern Thrace until ratification of a treaty of peace. The road to Lausanne was now well paved.

Setting the Stage for the Lausanne Conference

THE AMERICAN POSITION ON THE EVE OF LAUSANNE

A few weeks after the Armistice of Mudanya, on November 20, 1922, the Lausanne Conference, which was to last until July 24, 1923, and to bring peace and stability to the Middle East for many years, formally opened. The British government, which had appealed to the United States to help defend the Straits, also raised the question of American representation at Lausanne. Secretary of State Hughes refused to comment on territorial questions, but gave his unequivocal approval of "the proposal to insure the freedom of the Straits and protection of racial and religious minorities," as long, it seemed, as the United States was to assume no responsibilities. While Admiral Bristol, the American high commissioner in Constantinople, and others questioned the desirability of American participation, Lord Curzon hoped the United States would "take as active a part as might be possible under our traditional policy of detachment from purely European affairs." With its important shipping interests, Curzon felt that the United States could properly participate in preparing "a plan for assuring the free passage of the Straits." With American cooperation, he believed it would be much easier to formulate an equitable scheme for "the proper security of the Straits." There were some uncertainties as to whether the British government desired

---

[41]Elliot G. Mears, *Modern Turkey* (New York: Macmillan, 1924), pp. 658–59; *L'Europe Nouvelle* 5: 1366–77; *Histoire de la République Turque*, pp. 110–21, 123–30.

full or limited American participation, although, in the beginning, it appeared that only limited participation was desired.[42]

Secretary Hughes advised Ambassador Herrick in Paris on October 27 that while the United States had not been at war with the Ottoman Empire it was concerned with the Middle East and not disposed to relinquish its rights.[43] It was interested in maintenance of the capitulations, protection of philanthropic, educational, and religious institutions, freedom of opportunity for business enterprise, protection of minorities, opportunities for archaeological research, and assurances concerning the Straits. The United States did not like the secret arrangements made during the war or the Tripartite Agreement of August 1920, and for itself sought only "to protect its rights and to assure the Open Door." At the same time, Herrick was informed that the United States would send observers, but would not sign a treaty, although the Americans would be ready at the first opportunity to negotiate a treaty with Turkey for the protection of American interests. The American attitude toward the problem of the Straits was both reminiscent of the traditional policy of the United States and somewhat significant in the context of 1922 and the years after World War II: "Of the two phases of this question relating to the time of peace and the time of war, the Department is not disposed to become involved in commitments concerning the latter, particularly when Turkey or the Great Powers of Europe may be the belligerents. It is of distinct interest to this Government, however, to obtain effective assurances that the Straits would be open in time of peace for both merchant ships and ships of war to proceed to Constantinople and through the Black Sea. This Sea is a highway of commerce and should not be under the exclusive control of Turkey and Russia." While it was "neither natural nor desirable" to become involved in matters not pertinent to its interests, the Department of State should be kept informed, and the American observers should be "keen for the protection of American interests." They should be "ready to throw the full weight of our influence to obtain assurances for the freedom of the Straits and the protection of minorities, candid as to our views and in a suitable time to make the separate agreement which at some time must be made with the Turkish Government recognized by the Powers. No point of advantage should be forfeited, no just influence lost, no injurious

[42]*USFR* (1923), 2: 879, 880–82; especially the memorandum of Allen W. Dulles, September 19, 1922.
[43]Ibid., pp. 884–89.

commitments made. We should maintain the integrity of our position as an independent power which has not been concerned with the rivalries of other nations which have so often made the Near East the theater of war."

On October 27, the British government officially invited the United States to be represented at Lausanne and indicated that the three Allied Powers would welcome an American observer, as at San Remo, "in a similar capacity or in a more active capacity, especially in the discussion of the question of the Straits." The next day, Hughes designated Ambassador Richard Washburn Child, at Rome, to head the American Delegation, while Joseph C. Grew, the American minister in Switzerland, and Admiral Mark Bristol, the high commissioner in Constantinople, together with Julian Gillespie, of the American Embassy in Constantinople, were also to be members of the delegation. Later on, Lord Curzon, although the decision was later reversed, denied the Soviet claim to representation, but he believed that the United States, "as a maritime power in her own interest as well as in common interest ought to participate to the full in the Straits convention." Lord Curzon hoped that the American government and people would "appreciate the propriety, wisdom and obligation of this sharing of responsibility for maintaining a great open waterway as a wide-open door." Curzon's views concerning the capitulations were practically identical with those of the United States.[44]

AMERICAN INTEREST IN THE STRAITS

The United States Navy Department had a very natural interest in the forthcoming Lausanne Conference, and on November 10 the General Board of the Navy submitted an important memorandum dealing with American policy relative to control and navigation in the Straits.[45] The region of the Straits, it pointed out, had long been a center of tension, intrigue, and conflict, and American interest therein was closely allied with any arrangements which would promote the peace of the world. That solution which would give "the greatest prospect of lasting peace in the Near East" would fit in with

---

[44]Ibid., pp. 889-91, 965-66; Joseph C. Grew, *Turbulent Years: A Diplomatic Record of Forty Years, 1904-1945* (2 vols.; Boston: Houghton Mifflin, 1952), especially 1: chaps. 18-20, for the Lausanne Conference.

[45]*USFR* (1923), 2: 893-97; Hurewitz, *Diplomacy in the Near and Middle East*, 2: 117-19. "American Policy as to Freedom of Navigation of the Dardanelles." The Senior Member President of the General Board, Department of the Navy [W. L. Rodgers] to the Secretary of the Navy [Denby]. Compare with the Colby memorandum of March 24, 1920, *supra*, pp. 00.

American interests. The Navy believed that this important water-way should not be in the possession of any single power, as it had been. It belonged "to all the world as part of the highway of trade. Any and every step to block or impede the access of sea-borne commerce to this sea,—the Black Sea—is subversive of world organization and contrary to world interests, as it will set up international pressures and tensions that will lead inevitably to renewed wars."

The significance of the Straits to Russia, one-half of whose total exports in normal times went through that waterway, was noted: "Russia, potentially one of the greatest of world powers, exports in normal times one-half of all her products *via* the Black Sea. Russia has no other outlet comparable in importance with that through the Dardanelles. The importance to Russia of this outlet will increase greatly with the growth of Russian population, and, especially with the improvement of Russia's means of internal transportation. No solution that imposes an artificial barrier between so great a power and the sea can contain within it the elements of permanency—of stability."

The problem of freedom of navigation in the Straits for warships was more complicated and less capable of "permanent settlement." Freedom of commerce would be a necessary part of any regime of the Turkish Straits, and there should be equitable treatment for the ships of all nations. Whatever rights of navigation in the Straits were granted to other non-Black Sea Powers should be granted to the Black Sea Powers. The destruction of the Russian Black Sea fleet during World War I had "entirely changed the policy of Great Britain in relation to the Dardanelles." The General Board believed that "the natural solution of the question, as well as the one most favorable to American interest and influence in world affairs" was "complete freedom of navigation of the Straits for all vessels of war." Like many American officials before and since, the board, however, could see no parallel between the status of the Turkish Straits and that of the Panama Canal. In summary, the General Board held that American interests demanded:

1) That if an international commission of control of the Straits is set up, the United States should have representation on the international commission of control and in all positions subordinate to that commission, equal to that of any other foreign power.
2) That the Straits, including the Dardanelles, the Sea of Marmora, and the Bosphorus, be open to the free navigation of the merchant ships of all flags without distinction or preference.
3) That the United States and its nationals have the same rights and privileges within and adjacent to the waters above mentioned as are

possessed or may be granted to any other foreign power or to its nationals. . . .

4) That the Straits, including the Dardanelles, the Sea of Marmora, and the Bosphorus, be open to the free navigation of the vessels of war of all flags.

5) That all fortifications commanding these waters be razed and that no new fortifications be erected.

On November 10, with the opening of the Lausanne Conference only ten days off, the British ambassador in Washington, Sir Auckland Geddes, discussed the delicate Middle Eastern situation with Secretary of State Hughes.[46] Geddes wanted to know how far Great Britain could rely on the United States to help thwart possible Turkish attempts to drive the entire Christian population from Constantinople, with the implication that force might be necessary as a deterrent. Hughes indicated that the United States would use diplomatic pressure "to the utmost extent," but was unwilling to threaten war unless it were ready to go to war. Geddes, with much justice, if little diplomatic finesse, referred to the important role which the United States had played at the Paris Peace Conference, to the leadership of President Wilson in the mandate problem, and to the delays in the peace-making in the Middle East. Secretary Hughes wanted no controversy regarding the Peace Conference, but stated pointedly that the United States "would never consent to accept a mandate over the Near East; that the American conception of the situation was quite different from what the Ambassador had stated the British conception to be." Americans desired no territorial aggrandizement and did not understand why others did. Hughes "could not for a moment assent to the view that this Government was in any way responsible for the existing conditions," although some Americans did not share his view. The United States had not sought to partition Anatolia, was not intriguing in Constantinople, and was not responsible for the Greek tragedy. That was the "American point of view," which Hughes was prepared to "elaborate and substantiate at any time." The Secretary of State also charged that what "troubled the dreams of the British statesmen was their maintenance of their imperial power," with which the United States was not concerned—the questions of India, Egypt, the Suez Canal, and imperial relations with the Middle East. When Geddes asked for cooperation on November 13, Hughes inquired: "Cooperate in what?" A threat of war, he thought, might eventuate in catastrophe.

[46]See the Hughes memoranda of November 10, 13, 1922 in ibid., pp. 952–55, 955–58.

The Lausanne Conference: The First Phase (November 1922–February 1923)

One of the most important diplomatic conclaves after World War I, the Lausanne Conference marked the triumph of the Turkish Nationalists, and it was faced with very difficult and complicated problems.[47] One of the most serious was that of the Turkish Straits and, essentially, three basic theses were presented at Lausanne: (1) the British position, designed to preserve the freedom of the ancient waterway under an international regime which, in fact, would preserve the dominant influence of British sea power; (2) the Turkish project, insuring Turkish sovereignty over the Straits, but providing a restricted freedom and (3) the Soviet plan, insisting on Turkish sovereignty, but closing the Straits to warships, with the Black Sea remaining virtually a Soviet *mare clausum*.[48]

THE AMERICAN POSITION ON THE STRAITS

The American position concerning the Straits seemed fairly well outlined when the Lausanne Conference formally opened on November 20, although it was subject to change in detail for purposes of diplomatic maneuver. Ambassador Child announced at the outset that his delegation would take no part in the negotiations, sign no documents, or assume any engagement, but would be present at all discussions and expected to be treated on a footing of perfect equality with all other delegations. Child went to Lausanne very skeptical as to its outcome, but with the "great wish to establish . . . the principle of the Open Door in the Near East." From beginning to end, the Americans expressed themselves vigorously whenever American interests seemed involved.[49]

[47]For the minutes of the conference, see Republique française, Minstère des Affaires Etrangères, *Documents diplomatiques. Conférence de Lausanne sur les affaires du proche-orient (1922-1923). Recueil des Actes de la Conférence. Prémière série*, Tomes 1-4, *Deuxième série*, Tomes 1 and 2 (Paris: Imprimerie Nationale, 1923); Great Britain, Foreign Office, Turkey No. 1 (1923), *The Lausanne Conference on Near Eastern Affairs, 1922-1923*, Cmd. 1814. See also Evans, *United States Policy and the Partition of Turkey*, chap. 14; Howard, *The King-Crane Commission*, pp. 301-10; Roderic H. Davison, "Middle East Nationalism: Lausanne Thirty Years After," *The Middle East Journal* 7, no. 3 (Summer 1953): 324-48; Psomiades, *The Eastern Question: The Last Phase*, passim. See also Grabill, *Protestant Diplomacy*, chaps. 10 and 11; Trask, *United States Response to Turkish Nationalism and Reform*, pp. 27-36.

[48]The Soviet position was already clear in the Soviet-Turkish treaties of Moscow and Kars (1921), and the Turkish-Ukrainian treaty of 1922, which provided for the elaboration of a convention by Turkey and "the Black Sea Powers."

[49]Cmd. 1814, p. 11. For a brief, general statement of the Hughes position see Merlo J. Pusey, *Charles Evans Hughes* (New York: Macmillan, 1951), 2: 571-75. See also

While the American Delegation felt that Western Thrace should go to Greece and the region around Edirné to Bulgaria, it was interested in these problems and that of the Aegean Islands only as they affected the disposition of the Straits and Constantinople. American interest in the Straits was evident from the very beginning, and on December 1, 1922, the American Mission in Lausanne raised the problem with Washington:

> The trend as we see it is that no one will controvert the general principle of freedom of the Straits in peacetime for ships of commerce. We have already received instructions not to claim freedom of passage during war. There will arise the question of passage of warships in peacetime and the administration of any zone which may be neutralized or demilitarized. We will not volunteer any comment on the first question but we may be asked for our views. We wish instructions as to the attitude of our Government, with special consideration of the bearing upon waterways such as the Panama Canal of any precedents that it may be attempted to establish here. What attitude shall we take with respect to a neutralized or demilitarized zone regarding: (1) pledges of support for the enforcement of such neutralization or demilitarization; (2) membership on any international board set up for the control of such zone? Doubtless the Department is aware that there will be a tendency to inquire as to the willingness of the Americans to assume such obligations.[50]

Hughes thought that commercial ships should be allowed passage in peacetime and "neutral commercial vessels in wartime," while warships, perhaps, should be allowed passage in peacetime for the protection of the embassy, consulates, and citizens, and, if possible, neutral warships should be allowed passage in wartime.[51] All fortifications should "be removed and none built in the future." The Secretary of State insisted that there was "no proper comparison with the Panama Canal in this matter," as the Soviet and Turkish delegations had contended emphatically, for the United States had "the right to fortify the Panama Canal as an artificial waterway," which required "protection as such." President Warren G. Harding had authorized a statement that "in view of the traditional American policy," there would be no assurances that American membership in a possible international commission of the Straits, "with the resulting involvement of the country would be given the necessary approval by the United States." On the other hand, the United States did not object to control of the Straits by others, if it were not discriminatory. Since the United States could not "be represented on a board of control,"

Richard Washburn Child, *A Diplomat Looks at Europe* (New York: Duffield, 1925), chap. 4; Howard, *The Partition of Turkey*, pp. 285–97.
    [50]*USFR* (1923), 2: 910–11.
    [51]Ibid., pp. 912–13.

however, it would have to be contented "with proper treaty assurances." There was evidently no inclination to fall in line with the recommendations of the General Board of the Navy on November 10.

Ismet Paşa the chief Turkish delegate opened the discussion of the problem of the Straits on December 4, citing the Turkish National Pact as to the security of Istanbul and freedom of commerce in the Straits. Chicherin, the chief Soviet delegate, followed with a statement calling for freedom of commerce, but insisting on complete closure of the Straits to warships, in peace and war, and on the complete restoration of Turkish sovereignty over the region of the Straits. Surprised at this "reversal" of established Russian policy, Lord Curzon declared that the Allies desired freedom of the Straits, demilitarization of the shorelines, and sought "no special advantage." They desired to secure the Black Sea states from danger, treat the Straits as a great international waterway, and secure the existence of the Turkish capital at Istanbul. To insure execution of the Allied scheme, it was proposed that an international commission be established, composed of one member each from France, Great Britain, Japan, the United States, Italy, Soviet Russia, Turkey, Greece, Rumania, and Bulgaria, and that the Turkish representative serve as president.[52]

It was now time for Ambassador Child to speak, having worked with Grew and Bristol through the night on a statement, and then gone "through it with a fine-toothed comb" until it met their "combined views,"[53] He delivered his masterpiece on December 6, following talks with Ismet Paşa and Lord Curzon, both of whom agreed that there was some danger that the Turks might have to accept the "Soviet proposal that the Straits be closed to all warships and that Turkey be allowed to fortify the Staits." The Turks seemed already to feel that cooperation with Soviet Russia had gone far enough and were fearful lest it "prove a menace to Turkey." According to Child,

[52]See, especially, Cmd. 1814, pp. 127–42, 151–54. See also Ali Fuad, La Question des Détroits (Paris, 1928), pp. 138–40; Louis Fischer, The Soviets in World Affairs, 1: 406–08. Ambassador Child had an appreciation of Ismet Paşa's qualities, as did Grew. The former noted that, in contrast to the scintillating Chicherin, Ismet avoided attacking the main enemy citadel. "He camps outside, saying little, doing nothing, estimating comparative realities of force. His policy is one of exhausting, of laying siege, of attrition. He entrenches himself also and waits, giving no sign, blowing no bugles, flying no banners. As an opponent I would choose the brilliant Russian; he would be easier to defeat." Child, A Diplomat Looks at Europe, p. 99.

[53]USRF (1923), 2: 916–17; Cmd. 1814, pp. 145–48; Grew, Turbulent Years, 2: 506–08. Child was much impressed with his contribution concerning the Straits and considered himself, somewhat mistakenly, as the inventor of the phrase, "the freedom of the Black Sea." See Child, A Diplomat Looks at Europe, p. 101; Anchieri, Constantinopli e gli Stretti, pp. 225–45.

the United States stood for complete freedom of commerce the world over. The discussions involved "the freedom of all nations which border on the Black Sea, and of all those nations outside the Straits who desire to reach them on their friendly errands." The United States could not accept the proposition that the future of commerce in the Black Sea was "the exclusive affair" of the riverain states. It was the concern of all nations. "The unlimited control of the Straits and the Black Sea by any one nation" was "against the policy of the world." Child considered disarmament of the Black Sea as the guarantor of freedom in that sea, while armament to "keep the Straits open" was in fact a danger to its freedom. He could not agree with the Soviet Delegation in proposing the exclusion of warships from the Black Sea. No nation had gone further, he said, than the United States in the direction of naval disarmament, and he added: "Ships of war are not necessarily agents of destruction; on the contrary, they may be agents of preservation and serve good and peaceful ends in the prevention of disorder and the maintenance of peace. We, I believe in common with every commercial nation, wish access to every free body of water in the world, and we will not be satisfied if our ships of war may not pursue their peaceful errands wherever our citizens and ships may go."

Hughes advised the American Mission at this time that the United States desired simply to assure freedom of passage for commercial and war vessels "by proper treaty provisions without an international board of control," to which he had basic objections:

> An international board of this nature would provide an opportunity for busybodies and be a constant source of irritation. It would also be easier to secure the desired assurances for freedom of passage of the Straits if no demand were made for a board of control. It would accord with the prevailing sentiment to allow such freedom of passage, and to assure it by treaty would not give any proper basis for objection as infringing upon sovereignty. With the restoration of peace, with the ordinary opportunities for diplomatic action, and with the unity of sentiment which any evasion of treaty obligations would arise, the Department believes that a treaty assurance would be ample protection because breach of such guarantee would be so serious a matter and so easily detected.[54]

In a talk with Sir Auckland Geddes, Hughes hoped that the Allies would be "satisfied with treaty assurances" and would "not create a situation leading to our abstention from participation on a board of control claimed by others to be necessary." Naturally, the United

---

[54]*USFR* (1923), 2: 916-17. The mission advised Hughes on December 11 that it was "making discreet suggestions that there be no board of control and that reliance be placed on treaty rights." Ibid., p. 920.

States could not be a member of such a board, with all the "entangle-ments" involved, although it was concerned with the protection of fundamental American interests.

Child reported on December 6[55] that the British, French, and Turkish delegations had privately expressed their satisfaction with his state-ment, and the Japanese had openly adhered to it. He felt that "the Soviet influence for closing the Black Sea to all war vessels and forti-fying the Straits" had been "almost lost upon the Turks." Moreover:

The drift is now all toward strict limitation of both military and naval armaments in the Black Sea, water passages, the sea of Marmora, and the islands in the vicinity of the Straits. In our opinion the stability of peace in the Near East will be greatly aided by this arrangement. It does not appear probable just now that we will be asked to enter into any entanglements at all on this subject. In order to secure ratification and the future of naval limitation programs we consider it very important that the Soviet delegates should be induced to enter into and sign a separate protocol on the Straits and to give pledges not to maintain large naval forces in the Black Sea. If not otherwise instructed, we will receive the Soviet delegates who may seek a conference with us and discreetly use our good offices, without making any commitments.

Hughes did not object to an informal meeting with the Soviet dele-gates, but fearing that they might make political capital out of the meeting, he asked for a report on the proposal for a separate agree-ment on the Straits as soon as possible, whether or not *de jure* recognition of Soviet Russia were contemplated thereby.

THE ALLIED PROPOSALS CONCERNING THE STRAITS

Ismet Pasa accepted the Allied proposals on December 8, with a reservation as to the security of Istanbul against a possible surprise attack, and, in time of war, Turkey being a belligerent, indispensable technical control of the Straits. In addition, he urged Turkish control over the islands of Tenedos, Imbros, and Samothrace, an autonomous regime in Lemnos, and a means of defense at Gallipoli (Gelibolu).[56] But Chicherin was completely opposed to the Allied plan for interna-tionalization of the Straits, and adverted to both the Panama and Suez canals in order to demonstrate the contrary of the British—and perhaps the American—position. Soviet Russia, he insisted, was asking for Turkey only what the United States and Great Britain already possessed at Panama and Suez, both of which had full right to fortify and protect their respective waterways, while the United States was even contemplating, for additional security, a second interoceanic canal in Nicaragua. The ideal solution, in his view,

---

[55]Ibid., pp. 917–18.   [56]For discussion, see Cmd. 1814, pp. 156–69.

would be naval disarmament on every sea; the only possible compromise was Turkish sovereignty and control over the Straits. The
proposed regime would deprive Turkey of its independence and serve
as a means for attack on Soviet Russia in the Black Sea. On the other
hand, Lord Curzon was happy to note the Turkish acceptance, with
reservations, and thought the question of political guarantee worthy
of examination. When Chicherin submitted a plan to Ismet Paşa
restricting the passage of warships to one-third of the Soviet Black
Sea fleet, Ismet demurred that concessions had to be made toward
the Allied Powers.

Despite the American objections, the Allies presented a new
scheme for the Straits on December 18, establishing an international
commission of the Straits and providing for an international
guarantee.[57] The new project, which became the basis for Article 18 of
the Lausanne Convention, proposed to give security to the region
of the Straits through an individual or collective appeal to the Council
of the League of Nations as to measures to be taken in the event of a
threat to the freedom of the Straits or of the demilitarized zones.
Should unanimity fail in the Council, the powers agreed to take such
measures as two-thirds of the Council might approve. This was not,
however, the complete individual and collective guarantee which
the Turkish Delegation desired or considered necessary. In contrast,
the Turkish draft admitted the principle of freedom of navigation,
with reservations and limitations as to warships, and accepted
demilitarization, with guarantees for Turkish security. In addition,
Turkey did not want an international commission with control
over the Straits, and did desire an individual and collective guarantee
to respect the inviolability of the region of the Straits.

Child indicated that if the Allied scheme were adopted the United
States might use it as an excuse for not participating. On December
20,[58] the mission advised Washington that it might be wise to suggest
that Turkey declare itself trustee of the region of the Straits for all
the world, for the purpose of securing passage of commercial vessels in

[57]*USFR* (1923), 2: 919 ff.; Cmd. 1814, pp. 236–38, 243–50, 250–53, 253–61, 275–76.
See also Ali Fuad, *La Question des Détroits,* pp. 138–42. Both the Soviet and Turkish
counterdrafts were presented on December 18, the Soviet proposal providing for complete Turkish sovereignty over the Straits and recognizing the Black Sea as a *mare
clausum.*

[58]*USFR* (1923): 2: 929–30. Child said he received the British proposal only a few
minutes before the December 18 meeting, and was incensed at the suggestion of an
International Commission, although that had been part of the scheme all along, and
particularly at the proposal as to American membership. He told Lord Curzon "that
an international commission would be no more than a log-rolling set of busy-bodies."
But Child took considerable credit for getting the Turks to accept the new Straits
regime. Child, *A Diplomat Looks at Europe,* pp. 110–11, 117–18.

peace and war, for limited passage of warships, and for control of the port and passage. Nations enjoying the privileges under such trusteeship were to pledge themselves to and through Turkey to all other beneficiaries not to violate the neutrality of the zone of the Straits. The American plan appeared to meet the Turkish position, avoided "involvement" on international boards, and would put pressure on Soviet Russia to join a "general accord." Moreover, it might be considered the best method of crystallizing the moral forces of the world "as opposed to armed force and fake internationalization." But was the plan a substitute for "genuine" as opposed to "fake" internationalization? Or, was it an attempt on the part of the United States to dodge any international obligation, such as had already been suggested by the General Board of the Navy on November 10? Hughes cabled his opposition to "guaranteeing the freedom of the Straits by means of the trusteeship of Turkey" and his reluctance to take the lead in offering such a proposal. Emphasis should be placed, it was said, on the binding treaty obligations assumed by Turkey. Since the mission knew the objections to a "board of control," this need not be pressed any further if the Allies and Turkey reached a substantial agreement, as the policy was not to hinder a settlement, once the freedom of the Straits were satisfactorily assured. On behalf of the Allies Lord Curzon rejected the Soviet proposal out of hand on December 19, and he was not prepared for further concessions to the Turkish Delegation. The Turkish Delegation itself, however, conceded on the afternoon of December 20, consenting to demilitarization of the Straits, freedom of passage, and the establishment of an international commission. But Turkey did not receive the satisfaction of a political guarantee, a point which would become of much interest in the years to come, especially after the advent of Hitler to power in Germany.[59]

By December 22 it was evident that an agreement on the Straits would soon be realized, and a draft convention was ready by January 31. Ismet Paşa accepted it on February 1, despite Soviet objections.[60] Chicherin positively refused to sign the convention because, he asserted, the new regime threatened the security of Soviet Russia, made a stable and peaceful settlement of the Middle East impossible, violated the Soviet–Turkish treaties of 1921, infringed the sovereign independence of Turkey, and threatened the security of Istanbul. The Straits question remained open and would continue to remain open.[61] While the United States favored the regime of com-

[59]Cmd. 1814, pp. 262-77, 280-88.
[60]*USFR* (1923), 2: 931-33; Cmd. 1814, pp. 449-50; London *Times*, January 9, 1923.
[61]Cmd. 1814, pp. 451-57.

mercial freedom which the draft convention guaranteed and was not opposed to the restrictions on warships, it was not prepared to sign the convention, or to accept membership on the projected international commission of the Straits.[62]

After a number of crises the first period of the Lausanne Conference, despite the agreement on the problem of the Straits, came to an end on February 4, 1923, when the Turkish Delegation refused to sign the draft treaty presented on January 31. The impasse had come because the new Turkish government rejected the capitulations or a substitute therefor, which provided international guarantees for a juridical regime of similar import under another name. Neither would Turkey cede the Mosul district to the British mandated territory of Iraq, as had been demanded, although it had conceded in Thrace, in Gelibolu, and in the matter of internationalization of the Straits. It seemed that failure to reach agreement was "due to a lack of unanimity among the Allies, to Curzon's disregard of Turkish nationalism, and the perserverance of the Turks."[63]

The Lausanne Conference: The Second Phase
April–July 1923

THE STRANGE INTERLUDE

Ismet Paşa explained the Turkish position to Admiral Bristol on the Orient Express out of Venice on February 6.[64] He made it clear that he wanted a settlement, but only on the basis of the Turkish National Pact. While he stood by the partial settlements which had been reached, he would not yield on the financial and economic stipulations. When he inquired about a treaty with the United States, he was told that the United States preferred to defer action until the definitive peace had been signed.

---

[62]*USFR* (1923), 2: 931-33, 935-36, 936-38. The mission advised Secretary Hughes on December 26 that the Turks were less conciliatory, and Curzon was convinced that the French, angry at him, had abandoned the plan for an international board, supporting a scheme for control by diplomatic missions in Turkey. Hughes warned on December 29 that the United States had a substantial "interest in cooperating with the Allies to obtain a satisfactory settlement of such matters as freedom of the Straits, the protection of minorities, and capitulations."

[63]Ibid., pp. 966-67. Following the break on February 4, Curzon complained to the Americans: "We have been sitting here for four mortal hours, and Ismet has replied to everything we have said by the same old banalities—independence and sovereignty" (Grew, *Turbulent Years*, 1: 531). See also Davison, "Middle East Nationalism," pp. 324-48.

[64]*USFR* (1923), 2: 969-70.

Naturally, there was much feeling against Great Britain in Ankara, since Lord Curzon was blamed for the rupture at Lausanne. There was also antagonism against the United States, although "our open door policy, our moderate attitude toward the subject of capitulations and our stand for the settlement of the Straits Question by treaty, rather than by a Straits Commission," placed the United States in a better light.[65] Between the session of February 4 and the reopening of the conference on April 23, many things happened.[66] The Grand National Assembly of Turkey rejected the Lausanne proposals on March 6, because of their conflict with the National Pact, although it decided to reopen negotiations. A new treaty, it was proposed, was to be based on the complete abolition of the hated capitulations, postponement of the Mosul settlement and the economic clauses, acceptance of the provisions as to Karagaç, but abandonment of the Turkish claim to the 1913 Thracian boundary in the Maritza delta, insistence on Greek reparations, acceptance of all other points, and immediate evacuation of occupied territories by the Allies after signature of the treaty. While the Allies were surprised at some of the points which they had considered settled, they notified the Ankara government that they were willing once more to confer with a view to making peace. Meanwhile, the American government was entering the Turkish drama somewhat more actively, it would appear, in connection with the vast Chester concession, which Hughes had rather vigorously contested in 1921, and the Grand National Assembly approved the project on April 9, no doubt with a view to obtaining more affirmative support when the Lausanne Conference reconvened.[67]

THE BASIC AMERICAN POSITION

Meanwhile, on the eve of the reopening of the conference in April 1923, the question arose as to whether the United States should be represented. Allen W. Dulles, chief of the Division of Near Eastern Affairs in the Department of State, advised Hughes that the Allies had not taken the United States into their confidence. He was also anxious about the conflict of economic interests and the Franco-Turkish agreement of October 1921. He explained:

[65]Ibid., pp. 970-71; Leland Gordon, *American Relations with Turkey, 1830-1930: An Economic Interpretation* (Philadelphia, University of Pennsylvania Press, 1932), chap. 15.

[66]*USFR* (1923), 2: 972-74.

[67]On the Chester concession, see, especially, John A. DeNovo, *American Interests and Policies in the Middle East, 1900-1939* (Minneapolis: University of Minnesota Press, 1963), chaps. 3, 5-7; *USFR* (1923), 2: 1172-252.

I cannot escape the impression that the Allied Powers are loath to abandon their projects which date back as far as 1916 in the Sykes-Picot Agreement and which were carried on under the Tripartite Agreement of 1920. Under these various arrangements France endeavored to consolidate a position of economic predominance in Northern and Eastern Anatolia, Italy in South-western Anatolia, and England to secure a free hand in Mesopotamia, together with a predominant position in Constantinople and the Straits. . . .
    Certain of the questions in which this Government expressed an interest . . . have been settled. The most important of these subjects are: (1) Freedom of the Straits; (2) Protection of minorities. . . . The most important questions left for reconsideration at Lausanne will be the Economic and Financial clauses and the annexes to the Lausanne Treaty which relate (1) to the regime applicable to foreigners in Turkey and (2) to the commercial regime in Turkey.[68]

Dulles thought the United States should participate in making decisions. Hughes instructed Grew to proceed to Lausanne on April 19, and gave him long instructions, supplementing those of November 17, 1922. If Grew were asked whether the United States would accede to the draft convention on the Straits, he was to give no pledges. If the capitulations were to go, some other regime would have to be substituted. The Department of State did not want to close the door to a possible American adviser in the Turkish legal service. Admiral Bristol, meanwhile, was having a number of talks with Ismet Paşa, who was on his way back to Lausanne, somewhat puzzled by the way in which the conference was being resumed. Ismet told the American Mission that "the Chester Concession" might be regarded "as the initiation of economic relations with the United States," which, he hoped "would become more intimate."[69]

THE ACHIEVEMENTS AT LAUSANNE: THE
STRAITS CONVENTION

    While economic and financial questions dominated the scene at the second phase of the Lausanne Conference, in the end a treaty was signed on July 24, 1923.[70] The conference marked a definitive end to the process of the dissolution of the Ottoman Empire, the beginnings of which were symbolized in the Treaty of Karlowitz in 1699. The Treaty of Lausanne, in reality, was the last of the great post-World War I treaties following those of 1919–20 negotiated at Paris. It confirmed the mandate system by which Great Britain and France received their shares of the Ottoman estate in Syria, Iraq,

[68]Dulles to Hughes, April 4, 1933; ibid., pp. 974–80.
[69]Ibid., pp. 981–87.
[70]See Howard, *The Partition of Turkey*, pp. 313–14; *USFR* (1923), 2: 1029 ff.; See also Psomiades, *The Eastern Question: The Last Phase*, passim.

and Palestine. It recognized the British protectorate in Egypt and the annexation of Cyprus, as well as the Italian position in the Dodecanese Islands. The problem of Mosul remained to be settled in 1926, when the British finally retained that important oil-rich vilayet for the mandate of Iraq. Istanbul and Eastern Thrace, with Adrianople (Edirné), went to the Turkish republic, as it rejoined the European Powers as an independent nation. The capitulations were abolished, and a new legal system was to be developed. A new convention of the Straits was written, placing those strategic waters under an international commission, while preserving, necessarily, the reality of British sea power in the Eastern Mediterranean. On the other hand, Armenia was forgotten, and the Bulgarians were to claim inadequate access to the Aegean Sea. In the end, an independent Turkish nation had triumphed.

The Lausanne Convention of the Straits, signed on July 24, 1923, did not differ essentially from the draft of January 31, with the exception that Turkey had obtained a right to a garrison at Istanbul and on the Gallipoli peninsula.[71] It was composed of twenty articles, with an Annex to Article 2, which laid down the rules concerning passage of commercial and war vessels and aircraft throughout the region of the Straits. Article 1 stated: "The High Contracting Parties agree to recognize and declare the principle of freedom of transit and of navigation by sea and air in the Straits of the Dardanelles, the Sea of Marmora and the Bosphorus, hereinafter comprised under the general term of the 'Straits'."

The first section of the Annex dealt with merchant ships, including hospital ships, yachts and fishing vessels, and nonmilitary aircraft. In time of peace, there was to be "complete freedom of navigation and passage by day and by night under any flag and with any kind of cargo." In time of war, Turkey being neutral, there was also to be "complete freedom," and the rights and duties of a neutral did not allow Turkey to take any measures which might interfere either with navigation through the Straits or the air above. In time of war, Turkey being a belligerent, there was to be freedom of navigation for neutral vessels and nonmilitary aircraft, if they did not in any way assist the enemy. But, while Turkey had "full power to take such

[71]For text, see United Kingdom, Foreign Office, Treaty Series No. 16 (1923), *Treaty of Peace with Turkey and other Instruments Signed at Lausanne on July 24, 1923, together with Agreements between Greece and Turkey signed on January 30, 1923 and Subsidiary Documents forming part of the Turkish Peace Settlement* (with map), Cmd. 1929, pp. 109-29; League of Nations *Treaty Series* 23 (1923): 115 ff.; Howard, *The Problem of the Turkish Straits*, pp. 21-24. See also the brief analysis in Feridun Cemal Erkin, *Les Relations Turco-Soviétiques et la Question des Détroits* (Ankara: Basnur Matbaasi, 1968), pp. 58-69.

measures" as it might consider "necessary to prevent enemy vessels from using the Straits," they were not to be of such a character "as to prevent the free passage of neutral vessels."

The second section dealt with warships, including fleet auxiliaries, troopships, aircraft carriers, and military aircraft. In time of peace, warships were given "complete freedom," but the maximum force which any one Power might send through the Straits was not to exceed that of the most powerful of the Black Sea states—the Soviet Union. However, the Powers reserved to themselves "the right to send into the Black Sea" at all times and under all circumstances, a force of not more than three ships, of which none was to exceed 10,000 tons. Turkey had no responsibility for the number of warships passing through the Straits, although the International Commission of the Straits was to keep a record of such passage and to keep account of the naval forces in the Black Sea in order to carry out the above provisions.

In time of war, Turkey being neutral, there was to be complete freedom for warships, although this was not to be applicable "to any belligerent Power to the prejudice of its belligerent rights in the Black Sea." Whatever rights or duties a neutral Turkey had, it was not "to take any measures liable to interfere with navigation through the Straits," whose waters as well as the air overhead were to "remain entirely free in time of war, Turkey being neutral, just as in time of peace." But warships and aircraft of belligerents were to undertake no hostile acts within the Straits. In time of war, Turkey being a belligerent, neutral warships were to enjoy "complete freedom." Nor were any measures which Turkey might take to prejudice the free passage of neutral vessels of war or aircraft. Submarines were to pass only on the surface, and strict rules were laid down for military aircraft. Warships in transit were not to remain longer than the time necessary for passage.

Special provisions covered sanitary measures. Warships which had had cases of cholera, plague, or typhus during the prior seven days or which had left an infected port in less than five days had to go through quarantine. A similar provision also applied to merchant vessels. Warships and commercial vessels calling at a port in the zone of the Straits were subject to the international sanitary regulations. Even these seemingly innocent regulations, however, had their political implications relative to passage of the Straits and were to bring on a controversy between the Turkish government and the International Commission of the Straits in 1924.

The demilitarized zones of the Straits included the Gallipoli peninsula, the Asiatic and European shores of the Dardanelles, the

Bosphorus, and the Sea of Marmara, running about seventy-five miles along the shores of the Dardanelles and the Sea of Marmara, to a depth of some fifteen miles. Along the Bosphorus, the zones ran the entire length at a depth of more than nine miles. In the Aegean Sea, the Rabbit Islands, Imbros (Imroz) and Tenedos (Bozcaada), which belonged to Turkey, and the Greek islands of Lemnos (Limnos), Samothrace, Chios, Mitylene, Nikaria, and Samos, were demilitarized. But, with the exception of Lemnos and Samothrace, Greece could keep a limited military force in the islands, and Turkey could transport troops through both the demilitarized zones and islands, while both Powers, in case of war and in pursuance of belligerent rights, could modify the provisions for demilitarization. No permanent fortifications, artillery organization, submarine engine of war, military air base, or naval base was to be permitted in the demilitarized zones, subject to the exception that a garrison of 12,000 could be maintained at Istanbul and a naval base and arsenal could be constructed there.

To implement the principle of freedom of the Straits, an International Commission of the Straits was established at Istanbul, composed of one representative each of Turkey (president), France, Great Britain, Italy, Japan, Bulgaria, Rumania, Soviet Russia, and Yugoslavia. The United States was to be entitled to representation on accession. The commission was to render an annual report to the League of Nations, to implement the provisions relative to warships and military aircraft, and "to prescribe such regulations" as might "be necessary for the accomplishment of its task." But the convention was not "to infringe the right of Turkey to move her fleet freely in Turkish waters."

Turkey had desired an individual and collective guarantee for the zone of the Straits, a proposal which the Allies rejected. Instead, in order to assure the demilitarization of the region without danger to Turkey or to the freedom of the Straits, the Powers provided in Article 18: "Should the freedom of navigation of the Straits or the security of the demilitarized zones be imperilled by a violation of the provisions relating to freedom of passage, or by a surprise attack or some act of war or threat of war, the high contracting parties, and in any case, France, Great Britain, Italy and Japan, acting in conjunction, will meet such violation, attack or other act of war or threat of war, by all the means that the Council of the League of Nations may decide for this purpose."

Such, in essence was the Lausanne Convention of the Straits which the Turkish government, despite its misgivings as to security, accepted. While the Soviet government had denounced the new convention, ultimately, on August 14, 1923, the Soviet signature was affixed to the convention at Rome.[72] The convention was to endure until replaced, on July 20, 1936, by the Montreux Convention of the Straits.

Turkish-American Relations, 1923-1933

THE TURKISH-AMERICAN TREATY OF LAUSANNE, AUGUST 6, 1923

Although it did not sign the general treaty of Lausanne or adhere to the convention of the Straits, the United States Delegation concluded a treaty with Turkey shortly after the formal closing of the Lausanne Conference.[73] One of the reasons for having a delegation at Lausanne was to negotiate a Turkish-American treaty, although, for obvious reasons, it was agreed that a separate instrument should not be signed until the general conference had reached a successful conclusion. By January 18, 1923, Secretary Hughes indicated that the Turkish-American treaty should conform to similar agreements, providing for protection of philanthropic and religious enterprises, a substitute for the capitulatory regime, "free navigation of Dardanelles and Bosphorus," adjustment of claims, safeguarding of minorities, regulation of naturalization, and archeological research, When the Lausanne Conference resumed, in April 1923, the American negotiations took on more form and substance. The question of the capitulations continued serious, although there was some recognition that they were gone forever, in view of the Turkish position. An American draft, forwarded to Washington on June 2, provided for resumption

---

[72]The Soviet government was not satisfied with the Lausanne Convention. When Chicherin was invited to send a delegation to the Rome Naval Conference, called by the League of Nations in February 1924 to apply the principles of the Washington Conference (1921-22) to nonsignatories, he stated that at Lausanne the USSR had "defended the principle of closing the Straits for warships, the result of which would have been a diminution of the chances of armed conflicts and the reduction of naval conflicts." In a note of February 21, 1924, the Soviet naval delegation indicated that the safety of a state lay either in armaments. or in conventions of disarmaments and guarantees, such as those provided at Washington. The Soviet Union would be "satisfied with a total tonnage of 280,000 tons," under certain conditions, among which was the provision that the Straits be closed, "in accordance with the proposal which we made at the Lausanne Conference." Subsequently, the USSR entered into a nonaggression agreement with Turkey on December 17, 1925. See Henri Barbusse, ed., *The Soviet Union and Peace* (New York: International Publishers, 1930), pp. 78-81, 126-28; League of Nations, *Official Journal* 5, no. 4 (April 1924): 707-09; Annex 622a, C.76.1924.IX.

[73]*USFR* (1923), 2: 1040-52. See also Grew, *Turbulent Years*, II: chap. 21; E. W. Turlington, "The American Treaty of Lausanne," *World Peace Foundation* 12, no. 19 (1924): 564-602; Howard, *The King-Crane Commission*, pp. 308-10.

of diplomatic and consular relations, the adjustment of disputes, and included a longer treaty which Secretary Hughes favored, stipulation of "freedom of commerce and navigation" between the parties, together with most-favored-nation treatment. There were no irreconcilable differences, despite difficulties concerning the protection of Christian minorities, American educational institutions, and freedom of economic opportunity for Americans.[74]

The treaty was finally signed on August 6, 1923, with letters covering schools, and declarations with regard to judicial and sanitary problems. The capitulations were abolished. Grew explained that "the ships and aircraft of the United States would not be obliged to conform to the rules established by the Straits Convention" except when they were in force "at any given moment." Although the treaty was far from what Grew had really desired, more favorable terms were impossible, and the mission felt that "the Turks were essentially honest." Normal relations could now be resumed between the United States and Turkey. Article X declared: "The commercial vessels and aircraft and the war vessels and aircraft of the United States of America shall enjoy complete liberty of navigation and passage in the Straits of the Dardanelles, the Sea of Marmora, and the Bosphorus, on a basis of equality with similar vessels and aircraft of the most-favored-nation upon conforming to the rules relative to such navigation and passage established by the Convention signed at Lausanne, July 24, 1923."[75] But the resumption of diplomatic relations under the new treaty required American action and the question of Senate approval and presidential ratification became a political issue in the years ahead.

AMERICAN-TURKISH RELATIONS

There were now serious difficulties relative to ratification, primarily because it became a football of American politics, centering around the so-called Armenian issue, but also involving other matters, such as missionary-educational and business activities in Turkey. Secretary Hughes, on January 23, 1924, delivered an address before the Council on Foreign Relations in New York, in which he touched, among other things, on the problem of the Turkish Straits.[76] Hughes spoke of the new nationalism and the "desire for freedom from out-

[74]*USFR* (1923), 2: 1049-88, 1105-16.

[75]Ibid., pp. 1121, 1138-42, 1148-51, 1151-71.

[76]*USFR* (1924), 2: 709-15. Turkish relations with the Allied Powers were soon regularized, Istanbul being evacuated on August 23, 1923, and formally occupied by Turkish authorities on October 6, 1923. See also Trask, *The United States Response to Turkish Nationalism and Reform*, pp. 37-64.

side control" which had "made itself felt in the Near East." "No-
where," he remarked, "had the evangel of self-determination found
a more eager response," and "the nationalistic movement was particularly significant in Turkey." Hughes traced something of the historical developments which had taken place prior to the Lausanne
Conference: "The Allies frankly recognized that the situation of 1918
no longer existed and that after the stubborn resistance of the Turks,
culminating in their recapture of Smyrna, it was impossible to dictate
the terms of peace. A treaty was therefore negotiated in which the
Turks ceded very considerable territories and for the first time in their
history agreed to open the Straits not only to merchant ships but to
foreign warships, but in which the Allies, on the other hand, agreed
to renounce their historic capitulatory rights in Turkey." An American–Turkish treaty was negotiated which followed the outlines of the
general treaty, but "without its territorial, political and financial
features." But the United States had "gained the same general rights
and privileges as the Allies, including the freedom of the Straits, and
like the Allies consented to the abrogation of the capitulations, that
is, of the exercise of ex-territorial rights in Turkey which the Turks
regarded as in derogation of their sovereignty."

Despite the importance of the treaty and the fact that approval
was urged by American business and missionary interests in Turkey,
there were delays and complications in the United States Senate. In a
letter to Hughes on December 29, 1924, Secretary of Commerce
Herbert Hoover emphasized the importance of early action, noting
the most-favored-nation aspects of the treaty and stressing that there
were no "new specific obligations" on the part of the United States.
There was "involved in this situation not only the trade with Turkey,
but with all the areas surrounding the Black Sea, for one of the important provisions embodied in the original treaty, which is extended
freely and without obligation to the United States by our treaty, is the
assurance to ships of treaty nations of the freedom of the Straits,
through which vessels for Black Sea ports must pass. The interests of
our shipping as well as our trade, therefore, make desirable the early
ratifcation of the treaty with Turkey in the form essentially as concluded."[77]

Whatever the argument, and whatever the significance of the treaty,
the Senate was unmoved. Ultimately, diplomatic relations between
Turkey and the United States were renewed, not on the basis of a
treaty, but of a *modus vivendi*, and Joseph C. Grew went out to Turkey as ambassador in 1927, while Muhtar Bey served as the Turkish

[77]*USFR* (1924), 2: 729.

ambassador in Washington.[78] Problems were not insurmountable. On the occasion of the renewal of the Turkish-Soviet agreement of December 17, 1925, in 1929, Under Secretary Numan Menemencioglu advised Grew that the negotiations were limited to Turkish-Soviet relations, which in no way involved the United States.[79] Grew indicated on December 20 that while the new agreement undoubtedly tightened Turkish-Soviet relations, it could not be regarded "in any way as an alliance." The current rumor in Istanbul was "that the Russian Government was disquieted by the recent visit of the British Fleet to Constantinople and by the unusually cordial reception which it received and that the Soviet Government proposed the present protocol out of fear lest Turkey should drift into a political alliance with Great Britain or some other European Power. There are however no official indications to support this theory. In fact the same apprehension might equally well exist in the mind of the Turkish Government as regards Soviet Russia." The major problem in Turkish-American relations during 1930 was that of the negotiation of a treaty of establishment and sojourn, which did not involve the question of the Straits. Signed on October 28, 1931,[80] with Senatorial consent on May 3, 1932, ratifications were finally exchanged on February 15, 1933.

Despite the difficulties in American-Turkish relations following the end of World War I, there was a gradual readjustment, based on mutual respect, within the decade following the Lausanne Conference. Political relations developed along friendly lines, and there were some significant developments in commercial relations which placed the United States in second place as a purchaser of Turkish goods, and seventh as an exporter to Turkey, with capital goods constituting 50 percent of American exports by 1928.[81] American merchant ships appeared in the Straits in modest numbers. But the United States maintained its traditional interest in the principle of freedom of transit and navigation. By 1939 the significant strategic interest was to become all too evident, and on the eve of the American entry into World War II the defense of Turkey was declared vital to that of the United States.

[78]Ibid. (1927): 803-04; Grew, Turbulent Years, 2: chaps. 25-29; Roger R. Trask, "Joseph C. Grew and Turco-American Rapprochement, 1927-1932," Studies on Asia, 1967, pp. 139-70.
[79]USFR (1930), 2: 842-44.
[80]USFR (1930), 2: 852-72; (1931), 2: 1037-44; DeNovo, American Interests and Policies in the Middle East, pp. 236-49.
[81]Gordon, American Relations with Turkey, chap. 19; DeNovo, American Interests and Policies in the Middle East, chap. 8. On March 8, 1931, a Turkish-Soviet agreement was signed, providing that neither party was to increase its Black Sea fleet without six months' notice to the other party.

Chapter V

The United States and The Montreux Convention of the Straits (1933-1939)

Toward Revision of the Lausanne Convention of the Straits

TURKEY AS A STABLE ELEMENT AT THE INTERCONTINENTAL CROSSROADS

While the Turkish government had gained a very substantial victory at Lausanne, it was none too happy with the international regime of the Straits, especially with the provisions concerning the international zone of the Straits and its security. Turkey's protests against the Lausanne Convention, however, did not become very audible until the breakdown of confidence in collective security under the League of Nations after 1931, the aggressive expansion of Japan on the continent of Asia, and the advent of Adolf Hitler to power in Germany.

Meanwhile, Turkey had become a stabilizing element in the Eastern Mediterranean and the Middle East. Its friendship with the USSR dated from 1921 and 1925. On July 18, 1932, Turkey became a member of the League of Nations and helped to pave the way for Soviet membership on September 18, 1934.[1] Turkey and Greece had signed an important treaty on October 30, 1930, had solidified their friendship on September 14, 1933, and the two countries, which had taken the leading role in the Balkan conferences since 1930, joined with Yugoslavia and Rumania to establish the Balkan Entente on February 9, 1934. Like many other states in the immediate neighborhood of the Soviet Union, on July 3, 1933, Turkey signed a non-

---

[1]League of Nations, *Official Journal. Special Supplement No. 12. Records of the Special Session of the Assembly*, II, July 1932 (Geneva, 1933): 17, 21-23.

aggression agreement with the USSR.[2] Meanwhile, on March 7, 1931, Turkey and the Soviet Union added a naval supplement to the agreement of 1925 (renewed on December 17, 1929),[3] which provided that neither would lay down "any naval fighting unit whatsoever for the purpose of strengthening its fleet in the Black Sea or in neighbouring seas, or . . . place orders for any such unit in foreign shipyards, or . . . take any other measure the effect of which would be to increase the present strength of its war fleet in the above-mentioned seas, without having notified the second Contracting Party six months previously." This agreement was renewed subsequently down to November 7, 1945.

Relations with the Western Powers were now also placed on an evidently sound basis, despite the gravely critical years immediately ahead, and Turkey seemed in a good position to work for the revision of the Convention of the Straits at an appropriate moment. The United States had a certain interest in all these developments, in the light of the principles which it had enunciated concerning the problem of the Straits as early as 1830 and as recently as the Conference of Lausanne.

THE PROBLEM OF REVISION OF THE STRAITS
CONVENTION

Dr. Tewfik Rüştü Aras, the Turkish foreign minister, first broached the problem of revision at the League of Nations Conference on Reduction and Limitation of Armaments in 1932, referring to the Straits Convention and the Turkish interest in international peace and security, as demonstrated by Turkey's nonaggression agreements with the USSR and the treaties with Iran, Italy, Greece, Bulgaria, Hungary, France, and Spain. Dr. Aras was much disturbed by the question of world rearmament.[4] But the question was not officially raised until early in 1933, when, on March 16, the United Kingdom Delegation presented a draft convention, article 96 of which was to replace the provisions concerning limitation of arms and armed forces of Germany, Austria, Hungary, and Bulgaria in the

[2]See, especially, Robert J. Kerner and Harry N. Howard, *The Balkan Conferences and the Balkan Entente, 1930-1936* (Berkeley: University of California Press, 1936), chap. 6; Dimitrios G. Kousoulas, *The Price of Freedom: Greece in World Affairs, 1939-1953* (Syracuse: Syracuse University Press, 1953), chaps. 2 and 3.

[3]Helen Miller Davis, *Constitutions, Electoral Laws, Treaties of States in the Near and Middle East* (Durham, N.C.: Duke University Press, 1947), pp. 375-77.

[4]League of Nations, *Conference for the Reduction and Limitation of Armaments. Conference Documents*, 2: 476. See Department of State, *The Foreign Relations of the United States, 1934* (Washington, D.C.: USGPO, 1950-52), 2: 976-79. Hereafter referred to as *USFR.* See also Feridun Cemal Erkin, *Les Rélations Turco-Soviétiques à la Question des Détroits* (Ankara: Basnur Matbaasi, 1968), pp. 70-77.

peace treaties of 1919–20. On March 20, Cemal Hüsni Bey, the Turkish representative, noted that the Treaty of Lausanne had been omitted, although it "contained military provisions relating to the Straits and certain parts of the European continental territory of Turkey," which "must undergo the same fate." He wanted to ensure "freedom of the Straits and Turkey's obligation to keep them open." In the Turkish view, Articles 3–9 of the Lausanne Convention "constituted a hindrance to that liberty and to the exercise of the obligation assumed by Turkey"; they "had now fallen into disuse, not only in anticipation of an effective disarmament Convention, but because they had lost all real and practical meaning."

Sir John Simon, of the United Kingdom, on March 27, denied that the Treaty of Lausanne contained similar clauses, since the arms and armed forces of Turkey were not restricted by treaty. After private discussion with Simon on May 23, Aras proposed the establishment of a special committee, "composed of Mediterranean and Black Sea riparian States, together with representatives of the United States of America and Japan to consider the situation of the Straits."[5] Although not necessarily unsympathetic with the Turkish position, the United Kingdom Delegation thought consideration of the problem should be deferred. Nevertheless, on June 1, the Turkish Delegation submitted an amendment to Article 96 of the British draft, including a reference to the Lausanne Treaty and also to the convention in regard to the frontier, obviously to meet the Turkish desire for the remilitarization of the zone of the Straits. Indeed, the Turkish Representative remarked that, in addition to the problem of the Straits, there was also the question of "the military clauses relating to the frontiers." Both Eden of the United Kingdom and Paul-Boncour of France, however, preferred to postpone these specific issues, because of the conference's preoccupation with the more general issue of armaments. While Aras appreciated these considerations, he thought that the Turkish Delegation "could certainly not be accused of intransigence," if it urged attention to all possible solutions which "were calculated to enhance both the security of the Turkish coasts and the guarantee of the freedom of the Straits."

While the Turkish government did not formally raise the problem of revision in 1934, it took numerous informal soundings on the subject. Fearful of possible designs of Fascist Italy in the Eastern Mediterranean, the Turkish government informally communicated its desire

---

[5]League of Nations, *Conference for the Reduction and Limitation of Armaments, Geneva: Records of the Conference. Series B. Minutes of the General Commission,* 2: 366, 400, 486–87, 488.

to refortify the zone of the Straits to the members of the Balkan Entente.[6] There were private discussions on the subject on May 31, 1934, when the British and Turkish delegations at Geneva talked over the question. Moreover, on June 1, Aras submitted a resolution asking the conference "to enter without delay upon an exhaustive study of the problem of security," for the purpose of arriving at solutions, based on principles embodied in the Locarno Agreements and the Balkan Entente, which might make possible agreements for the reduction and limitation of armaments.[7]

THE INTEREST OF THE UNITED STATES

Some days later, on June 12,[8] Ambassador Robert P. Skinner informed the Department of State that Aras had returned from Geneva, that "no formal steps of any kind" appeared "to have been taken with regard to the Dardanelles," and that Aras had not raised the issue because Turkey was "in a position to defend the Straits." Turkey did not require the approval of "anybody" to do it under the Lausanne Convention. Ambassador Skinner felt this to be correct, since, under Article 4 of the Convention, Turkey had the right to send armed forces through the demilitarized zones, the Turkish fleet had a right to anchor in territorial waters, and long-range guns, outside the demilitarized zones, could be effective. Nevertheless, in view of rumors and of an article in *The New York Times*, on June 17, the embassies in the United Kingdom, Turkey, Japan, Italy, and France, and the consulate in Geneva were instructed to inquire discreetly concerning possible Turkish moves for revision of the Straits Convention. In addition, Skinner's views were requested as to a possible American–Turkish agreement, perhaps prior to the conclusion of a consular convention with Turkey, covering American rights in the navigation of the Straits, substantially as follows: "The commercial vessels and aircraft and war vessels and aircraft of the United States of America shall enjoy complete liberty of navigation and passage in the Straits of the Dardanelles, the Sea of Marmora, and the

[6]Tevfik Rüştü Aras, *10 Ans sur les Traces de Lausanne* (Istanbul: Aksam Matbaasi, 1935), pp. 245-53; Kerner and Howard, *The Balkan Conferences*, p. 141; Arnold J. Toynbee, *Survey of International Affairs* (London: Oxford University Press for the Royal Institute of International Affairs, 1934), p. 518; (1936), p. 601.

[7]The London *Times*, June 2, 26, 1934; *L'Esprit International*, no. 31 (July 1934): 463-64; no. 32 (October 1934): 586-89.

[8]*USFR* (1934), 2: 962-65, 971-72. Ambassador Skinner reported on June 1 as to Turkish anxiety concerning Italian ambitions, and the Turkish "desire to enjoy greater liberty with respect to the Dardanelles and to be permitted to create a system of land defenses inasmuch as mines cannot be laid in the narrow waters without preventing the passage of merchant vessels." See also Charles H. Sherrill, *A Year's Embassy to Mustafa Kemal* (New York: Scribner's, 1934), passim.

Bosphorus, on a basis of equality with similar vessels and aircraft of the most favored nation."[9]

The replies were soon forthcoming. On July 10, 1934, it was learned that France "was opposed to any revision of the Straits Convention and had so informed the Turkish Minister for Foreign Affairs."[10] The Italian government was unaware of any Turkish overtures, but, in any event, in view of the Turkish accumulation of war supplies outside the zone of the Straits, it was felt that Turkey "would be merely asking for the approval of a situation which might be regarded as already practically existing."[11] The Consulate in Geneva observed that the problem had arisen unofficially at the Arms Conference and noted stories repeated in London that "the Soviets met with a signal defeat behind the scenes at the recent Geneva meeting with regard to the fortification of the Straits. They attempted to use the Turks to force the English into the corner of having to choose between the militarization of the Straits and the closing of them in time of war and English participation in a Mediterranean Locarno. The British, to meet this attack, explained the situation to Tewfik Rushdi Bey at Geneva and brought this pressure at Ankara with the result that the Turks decided not to press this issue and left the Soviets high and dry."

The question had not come before the League of Nations and it appeared that the Turkish government had "no present intention of pressing this question." The Foreign Office advised Ambassador Robert W. Bingham by July 13[12] that aside from the steps at the Geneva Conference in 1933 the Turkish government had taken no formal steps concerning the Straits, although on various occasions Turkish statesmen had alluded to the subject, as Simon had indicated in the House of Commons on June 19. Moreover, at the end of May, he had mentioned the matter to Aras in Geneva and was assured that Turkey did "not desire to press the matter." The British view had been "that Turkey had earned an excellent reputation for abiding by her treaties, and it would be most unfortunate should she take any action which would alter this. The plea of the Turks that they had as much right as Germany to a revision of the treaties was countered with the argument that there was no analogy since in the case of

[9]*USFR* (1934), 2: 973-74.
[10]Ibid., pp. 974-75. Ambassador Grew reported on August 24 that Japan had not been approached and was not in a position to state its attitude because of a possible change in circumstances (ibid., p. 982).
[11]Ibid., pp. 975-76, 981-82.
[12]Ibid., pp. 979-80. See also United Kingdom, *Parliamentary Debates, House of Commons* 290, col. 1324.

Germany the Treaty was imposed, while in the case of Turkey the treaties and conventions were negotiated by the Allies in conference with Turkey." The Turkish argument at Geneva in 1933 had been based on the MacDonald Plan for eliminating heavy artillery and, in that case, Turkey had insisted that it would be left at a great disadvantage in protecting the Straits. But this plan had failed and the point was now "purely academic." The Foreign Office was pleased that Aras had agreed "to drop the question" and felt that "the less said about it the better."

On July 20, Skinner confirmed that the Turkish government had no present intention of raising the question officially.[13] Even if authority were obtained for the construction of permanent fortifications in the zone of the Straits, the enormous cost would probably "prevent their realization without long delay." Nevertheless, the Turkish government was improving the highways to Gallipoli (Gelibolu) and Çanak and was reorganizing its forces near the Straits. As to the desirability of a Turkish–American agreement, Skinner noted that the United States already enjoyed "complete liberty of navigation and passage" in the Straits, although it was not a signatory of the Lausanne Convention and would gain nothing through a new agreement.

Before discussing the problem with the Turkish authorities, however, the Department of State wanted Ambassador Skinner's views as to whether the Turkish government would be "willing to negotiate such an agreement at a time when" it was "presumably giving consideration to the abrogation of the Straits Convention." Would it be willing at this time "to confirm and renew the pertinent provisions" of the Lausanne Convention? The United States was hesitant to suggest the negotiation of a consular convention with Turkey until it had cleared up "the still unsettled matter of the rights of American vessels and aircraft in the navigation and passage of the Straits," and the Turkish government itself might be somewhat hesitant. Since it evidently was intent on bringing the Lausanne Convention appropriately to an end, the Turkish government might hesitate "to reaffirm the essential provisions of that Convention in a new treaty with us." On the other hand, it might be willing to give the desired assurances in an exchange of letters. Once the issue of freedom of passage were resolved, the United States could go ahead with the negotiation of other treaties.[14] When Skinner conferred with Aras on

[13]*USFR* (1934), 2: 980-81.
[14]Ibid., pp. 983-84. See, especially, Phillips to Skinner, September 10, 1934, and Wallace Murray to Howland Shaw, October 23, 1934. A treaty of establishment and sojourn, effective for three years, was signed on October 28, 1931 (*USFR* [1931], 2: 1042-45).

October 29,[15] among other things, the differences in the administration of the Panama and Suez canals came up. Aras remarked that Turkey would be "delighted to negotiate a separate Straits Convention with the United States, provided the United States would assume the same responsibilities for the defense of the Straits as the Powers signatory of the Straits Convention." But Skinner thought that would hardly work in the case of the United States, since Article 18 of the Convention left it to the League of Nations Council to determine "how and when attacks or other acts of war or threats of war involving the freedom of navigation of the Straits should be met." He also pointed out that under the Panama Canal Treaty (1901) and the Suez Canal Convention (1888), "freedom of navigation was assured to all nations observing the rules on terms of entire equality and without any obligation to engage in the defense of either passage." After dealing with it casually, the subject was dropped, and the Ambassador doubted the wisdom of proceeding with the problem, since "a special agreement of our own with Turkey would give us nothing we do not already possess."

THE EVOLUTION OF THE TURKISH POSITION

It was in the critical years of 1935-36 that the drive toward revision of the Lausanne Convention was really undertaken, particularly as Italy moved toward invasion and conquest in Ethiopia and Germany toward refortification of the Rhineland. Aras reopened the subject of the Straits in the League of Nations Council on April 17, 1935, declaring that, "should there be changes in the situation fixed by the existing treaties," Turkey would be obliged "to make them dependent upon consequent modifications in the military regime of the Straits."[16] While the USSR placed no obstacles in the way of the Turks, the representatives of the United Kingdom and France reserved their rights, and the Italian Representative declared that his government would not consider the question formally to have been raised. Since Turkey had supported the French position relative to German rearmament, it was disappointed with the French attitude and, as Skinner reported on April 30, it particularly disliked the International Commission of the Straits because it was a reminder of "a sort of foreign tutelage." The Ambassador thought that Turkey would keep the problem of revi-

[15]USFR (1934), 2: 984-85. See also the Gilbert dispatch of December 4, 1934, analyzing the relations between the Straits Commission and the League of Nations.
[16]League of Nations, Council, *Official Journal, XVI, Minutes of the 85th (Extraordinary) Session*, pp. 562-63; see also Gilbert's report from Geneva, April 17, 1935; *USFR* (1935), 1: 1026-27; Maria Papouktchieva, *La Politique de la Russie a l'Égard des Détroits* (Lausanne: Payot, 1944), pp. 158-63.

sion before the Powers until its proposals were definitely accepted. Turkish pride was involved, and he noted on May 18 that the Turkish government "regarded this as a favorable moment for pressing the demand."[17]

At its meeting of May 10–13, 1935, the Balkan Entente agreed to support the Turkish position. The Straits were "Turkey's most vulnerable point," and Skinner was informed that when Great Britain had recently opposed refortification of the Straits, Aras had replied that Turkey would willingly refrain, provided the United Kingdom would sign a treaty to protect the area! The American Ambassador felt that, with or without revision, Turkey was "already prepared to defend the Straits," and it was "open to doubt whether, questions of pride apart," Turkey had "much to gain from revision." There were mobile defenses and craft in readiness in the Marmara. Doubtless the Soviet Union was "urging Turkey to obtain now what Mr. Chitcherin could not get in 1923." Skinner pursued this theme further on May 29,[18] following a trip to Izmir, during which he observed the hard-surface highway between Çanakkale and ancient Troy, as well as a new military encampment at the Asiatic mouth of the Dardanelles. But he thought it unfair to assume that Turkey proposed to imitate Germany, although "it was clearly the case that the military authorities" were "taking the most active preparatory steps to the end in view." Indeed, Aras had advised Sir Percy Loraine, the British ambassador, that the Turkish proposals at Geneva were "not intended in any case as an ultimatum but merely as the raising of a question of interest to Turkey." Sir Percy felt that the Turkish government looked upon "the demilitarized zone as a blot upon Turkish domination." He also believed that the USSR was back of the Turkish position, and Ambassador Skinner wondered whether the Turkish leaders might not be "getting into deeper water with the Russians" than they knew, "or had any intention of getting." As Loraine remarked: "The Russians, after all, do not change. In the days of the Tsar, their eyes were constantly fixed upon Constantinople. The new Tsar, Stalin, works in a different way. He makes a military alliance with Turkey; he becomes indispensable to Turkey, or so he believes; he encourages the fortification of the Straits; he endows Turkey with certain industries; he obtains a privileged position, generally, in this country. How far will this movement proceed, and what would happen if the strong and able leader of Turkey today should disappear as some time he must, leaving the Government in hands of men of untested ability who might or might not agree among themselves? In such circumstances

[17]*USFR* (1935), 1: 1027, 1028.   [18]Ibid., pp. 1029–30.

would not Russia command the situation?" It would be "extremely
interesting to return to this country 25 years hence and institute
comparisons!"

Aras had high hopes of Anglo-French support, and "the most
definite support" of Greece, Yugoslavia, and Rumania in the Balkan
Entente.[19] The problem had been discussed in the Balkan Entente, with
agreement on the following Turkish demands:

1. The right to install a certain number of mobile coast batteries;
2. The militarization of Turkish territory in Europe through protection of
   routes leading to the Straits by means of mobile guns;
3. The right to plant submarine mine carriers on the coast;
4. The right to maintain at Çanakkale two bases for submarines each with
   a given number of those vessels;
5. The right to maintain a base for hydroplanes and another for airplanes.

These were "definitely the complete Turkish desires respecting the rearmament of the Straits." Aras was concerned with Italian ambitions
in Ethiopia, developments in the Balkans, and the attempt at insurrec-
tion in Greece on the part of the elder Venizelos, as well as with
Turkish–Soviet relations: "The Turks were getting a good deal of
material assistance from Russia and Russia was getting invaluable
support from Turkey, so accounts were even. There was no likelihood,
and in fact, no possibility, that the Sovietic principles of government
would ever be adopted in Turkey, which was absolutely opposed to
them and looked upon Russia as a foreign government, just as she
looked upon Germany and Italy as foreign governments, domestic
systems not being matters with respect to which Turkey felt she had
any concern whatever."

According to Ambassador Skinner the movement toward rearmament had made a profound impression in Ankara, and the government
was worried about defense, particularly against Italian aggression,
and against any threats which might arise in connection with a general European war. Turkey was not convinced that the League of
Nations or the Lausanne Convention provided security, in the light of
events in China, Ethiopia, and elsewhere. While the Lausanne Convention did not prevent Turkey from defending the Straits, there were
problems of defense. There were some 16,000 troops in the Dardanelles area, and Turkey was in a position to place some 13,000 men
on the Çanak side of the Straits within a few hours. Some 20,000 men
were at Istanbul and 32,000 in Thrace, and two-thirds of the army
were at points west of Ankara. Turkey felt that it had "nothing to
fear from the Soviets." But the Turkish Navy was not an efficient

[19]Ibid., pp. 1030–34. The Skinner communication of June 25, 1935.

fighting force. Unless some Power were willing to assume responsibility for defense of the Straits in the event of attack, it was not clear what Turkey would secure under a new convention. But there was reason to believe that "if Turkey should work out some kind of Mediterranean pact," the British government "would be prepared to approve it quickly and thus give it a certain amount of moral support," since it was "sensitive to anything affecting the Straits."[20]

While the Western European Powers were cautious about establishing a precedent for treaty revision, and "old sore points and new diplomatic combinations" were very much affected, Skinner believed that the United States was not directly concerned with these matters, although it could not but deplore rearming of the Straits as a phase of general rearmament. But it was hard to see that the United States could

> do anything effective about it since Turkey can be influenced only by Powers willing to give some sort of undertaking to take military measures or at least to bring effective political pressure to bear. Our more tangible interest is in the freedom of navigation of the Straits. For the past eleven years even without any provision specifically applying to us the benefits of the Straits Convention, our shipping has received precisely as favorable treatment as that of any other country. Should the demilitarized zones be abolished and Turkey take over unrestricted control of the Straits, I do not believe that freedom of navigation would in any way be affected in time of peace. In this respect at least, it would clearly not be in Turkey's interest to establish any regime less generous than that provided in the Straits Convention. In time of war, whether Turkey should be a neutral or a belligerent, we are perhaps justified in believing that a Turkey in unrestricted control of the Straits might not accord the same degree of liberty of navigation as that which is set forth in the Convention.

In any event, no sudden action was about to be taken. But if Turkey persisted, it seemed clear that the obvious course "would be to endeavor to draw as sharp a distinction as possible between the provisions of the Straits Convention having to do with demilitarization and those which deal with freedom of navigation," and a serious effort should be made "to induce the Turks to incorporate these later provisions in a new multi-lateral treaty." Turkey might prove receptive to such ideas, as Aras had intimated in April 1935. The question before the United States was: Were the demilitarized zones and the International Commission "essential to freedom of the Straits," or could "the principle be satisfactorily safeguarded in other ways?"

[20]Ambassador Skinner's dispatch of July 3, 1935; ibid., pp. 1034–40. Skinner recalled that Marshals Voroshilov and Budeny and other Soviet staff officers had visited Turkey in October–November 1933 and, under the guidance of Turkish military authorities, had visited Izmir, Balikesir, and the Straits region generally. Shortly thereafter "the first Soviet mines began to arrive in Turkey."

The Navy Department had already reached the conclusion that a Turkish-American treaty embodying a provision similar to Article I of the Straits Convention or Article X of the Turkish-American treaty of August 6, 1923, providing for "most favored nation" treatment, would be satisfactory. It also urged that provision be made "for the right of vessels and aircraft, public and private, of the United States of America to navigate the Straits of the Dardanelles, the Sea of Marmora, and the Bosphorus on a basis of equality with similar vessels and aircraft of the most favored nation; that the United States should not by any act or undertaking assist to perpetuate the Straits Commission; that if such a Commission is continued the United States should not have a representative on this Commission; and that we should insist upon our right to deal directly with the Turkish Government regarding the rules of navigation of the Straits." These views were forwarded to the Embassy in Ankara on September 11, although the Department of State was uncertain that the Turkish government would be willing to conclude a new agreement, unless the United States were ready to assume certain responsibilities "for the defense of the Straits," a condition which was "obviously impossible."[21] In other words, the United States was concerned only with the maintenance of the principle of commercial freedom in the Straits, and it saw no reason for becoming involved directly in other aspects of the problem. Only with the end of World War II did its basic views change.

Aras raised the question of the demilitarized zones again in the League of Nations Assembly on September 14, 1935, but it was not until the invasion of Ethiopia on October 3 that final steps toward revision were to be taken.[22] He told Skinner on November 1 that the problem was still much on the Turkish mind and that official discussions might become active soon. Skinner "slipped in a question" about the Turkish attitude if the United States felt inclined to propose a separate treaty on the subject. Aras indicated that the United States "would not be likely to have special difficulties," if its desires "were limited to free transit for our vessels in time of peace and war, on the same terms as those granted to other nations." The Ambassador thought that nothing should be attempted for the moment, and that the problem be dealt with practically when it became evident that the Straits Convention was to be modified.[23]

[21]Ibid., pp. 1040-42. The Skinner dispatch of July 3 had been forwarded to the Navy Department which, on August 17, confirmed views which had been reached as early as July 13, 1931.

[22]League of Nations, Assembly, *Verbatim Records of the 16th Ordinary Session of the Assembly* (1935): 2.

[23]*USFR* (1935), 1: 1042.

With the Italian invasion of Ethiopia, Turkey, considering itself threatened at least by implication, followed the British lead in applying economic sanctions against Italy and in supporting the League of Nations system of collective security. In the fall of 1935, Great Britain asked the several Balkan states if they would be willing, in the event of military measures being aimed by Italy against Great Britain, to collaborate in resistance to such measures. On January 22, 1936, Turkey—along with Greece, Rumania, and Yugoslavia—replied that it would be willing to fulfill its obligations under the Covenant. In turn, the Turkish government asked "reciprocal assurances" from the United Kingdom, and they were duly conveyed, similar assurances being given to the other states.[24]

THE DRIVE TOWARD REVISION

On April 10, 1936, following German remilitarization of the Rhineland on March 7, the Turkish government presented a formal note to the Lausanne signatories requesting revision of the Straits Convention.[25] The next day, Ambassador Mehmet Munir Ertegun presented a copy to Secretary of State Cordell Hull, who stated that, while the United States "was not a party to the Lausanne Treaty," it was "naturally interested in all important phases of world affairs, including the Ambassador's part of the world."[26] The Turkish note pointed to the changed situation in the world since 1923, outlined the movement toward world rearmament, and indicated that the security of the Straits had now disappeared, and that Turkey "at her most vulnerable point," found "herself exposed to the worst dangers without any counterpoise to that disquieting insecurity." While Article 18 of the Lausanne Convention contained security provisions, they were decidedly inadequate in the very troubled world of 1936. It could hardly be affirmed that the security of the Straits was "certainly assured by a real guarantee" and Turkey could not be indifferent to the possibilities of a dangerous default. Circumstances beyond the control of the Lausanne signatories had rendered inoperative clauses drafted in good faith, and since the stake was "the existence of Turkey and the security of all her territory," Turkey had to adopt new measures and had advised the signatories that it was ready to initiate negotiations looking toward new agreements "to regulate the regime

[24]United Kingdom, Foreign Office, Ethiopia No. 2 (1936), *Dispute between Ethiopia and Italy. Correspondence in connexion with the application of Article 16 of the Covenant of the League of Nations,* January 1936, Cmd. 5072.
[25]Stephen Heald and J. W. Wheeler-Bennett, *Documents on International Affairs* (London: Oxford, 1937), pp. 645-46. See also Erkin, *Les Rélations Turco-Soviétiques et la Question des Détroits,* pp. 70-77.
[26]*USFR* (1936), 3: 503.

of the Straits," under conditions of security indispensable "to the inviolability of Turkish territory, and in the most liberal spirit towards the constant commercial navigation between the Mediterranean and the Black Sea."

Meanwhile, Aras gave a copy of the note to G. Howland Shaw, counselor in the American Embassy, on April 10,[27] since he wanted to keep the United States informed. Shaw was pleased that Turkey was prepared to negotiate and not to confront the world with a *fait accompli*. In the long discussion, Aras was "most emphatic that Turkey stood squarely not only for the facilities set up under the Lausanne Convention, but for any extension and liberalizing of those facilities that could be worked up. He pointed out that Turkey had always considered the Lausanne Convention as applying not only to the commercial vessels of the signatory countries but to all commercial vessels and that they would not depart from this view in the future." Aras was ready to propose the pertinent parts of the Lausanne Convention as to commercial passage, and went so far as to state that Turkey "would have no objection to the continuance of some kind of international Straits commission." Nor did Turkey intend to raise any question concerning the demilitarized zone between Turkey and Bulgaria, unless Bulgaria rearmed, in which case Turkey would insist on fortification of Edirné. But the note clearly pointed, of course, toward remilitarization of the region of the Straits. The Embassy felt that Turkey seemed

to have taken advantage very adroitly of the conjuncture of European affairs consequent upon the German remilitarization of the Rhineland and (incidentally, though not negligibly, from the view point of the Near East) upon the Austrian reestablishment of conscription. Not only is the moment one at which Turkey might expect to find a minimum of effective opposition, because of the preoccupation of the principally interested Powers with far graver "revisionist" threats to their interests and to their actual security; but the course of the discussions that have thus far taken place between Germany and the other Locarno Powers—discussions in which the latter have in effect taken the position that they would consent to the revision of the Versailles Treaty and the reconsideration of the Locarno Treaty if only Germany would pay at least symbolic deference to the sanctity of those instruments—would seem to have stopped Great Britain and France and Italy from taking any strong stand against the less vital revision of military restrictions which Turkey now proposes to effect by negotiation and mutual accord. It would thus seem that Turkey is likely not only to achieve her present pur-

[27]Ambassador J. V. A. MacMurray to the Secretary of State, April 14, 1936; ibid., pp. 506-10. For German views, see Department of State, *Documents on German Foreign Policy, 1918-1945*, series C (1933-1937), (Washington, D.C.: USGPO, 1949 ff.), 5: 430-31. Cited hereafter as *German Documents*.

pose, but to acquire, in doing so, the *kudos* of having set an example of correctness and good-will in her international relationships.

There was a possibility, indeed, that Sir Percy Loraine, who had done so much to restore Anglo-Turkish relations to their old friendship, had played a role in the "wise moderation" of the Turkish government. The Embassy thought that Italy might raise objections, and that France and Great Britain might be embarrassed in dealing with the Turkish proposals until the question of the remilitarization of the Rhineland had been worked out.

The problem was now formally presented, and Consul Prentiss B. Gilbert, in Geneva, thought it might come before the May session of the League of Nations Council.[28] The Secretariat considered the Turkish move "salutary," in contrast to the recent series of unilateral denunciations of treaties, and thought that it might "presage action under Article 19 of the Covenant which would bring the League usefully into play and increase its prestige." Gilbert had found a favorable attitude toward the Turkish position among members of the Balkan Entente (Greece, Rumania, Turkey, and Yugoslavia), running "counter in the same field of their basic policy of anti-revisionism." In response to Secretary Hull's inquiry, the Embassy in Ankara, on April 21, doubted that Turkish troops had already entered the demilitarized zone, and thought it highly unlikely in view of the nature of the Turkish démarche and its reception. While the British Foreign Office would have preferred action under Article 19 of the League of Nations Covenant, it was realized that this would have afforded representatives of the antirevisionist governments in the League an "excellent opportunity to block Turkey's aspirations." The Foreign Office considered the Turkish proposal "straight-forward" and "quite proper," and the timing an evidence of good judgment. While Fascist Italy would oppose refortification of the Straits, the Foreign Office was interested in seeing what kind of case Italy, "a revisionist country and an outstanding treaty-breaker, could make against Turkey." With the possible exception of France, the Foreign Office doubted that there would be much opposition to the Turkish move. Rumania, like Greece, a member of the Balkan Entente, appeared well disposed, and Bulgaria seemed agreeable. The Soviet Union had been friendly with Turkey at least since December 17, 1925, had never ratified the Lausanne Convention, and had already assumed a very favorable attitude, as had the United Kingdom. In any event, from a purely military standpoint, Turkey could block the

[28]*USFR* (1936), 3: 510, 511–12, for communications of Gilbert (April 15), Hull (April 20), Bingham (April 30), and MacMurray (April 21).

Straits within a few hours, even under the Lausanne Convention, but because of the great advances in the air, such action alone could not afford protection to Istanbul. The question of refortification was, therefore, largely academic. In discussing the problem with the Foreign Office, the American Embassy in London was struck with the change which had occurred in British thinking since 1934.

AN EXPOSITION OF THE TURKISH VIEW

Aras told Ambassador John V. A. MacMurray on April 22 that he did not believe war imminent, despite the troubled state of Europe, although he did not expect the problems vexing European statesmen to be solved, with the possible exception of the question of the Straits.[29] For fifteen years the Turkish foreign minister had sought understanding among the Balkan states and, while he had not received formal replies from all interested governments, he counted on favorable responses. Great Britain had already consented to negotiate, France would probably do so shortly, and Italy might be expected to make a reservation similar to those it had hitherto made as to entering into agreements with states applying sanctions against Italy. Japan would only stipulate that the negotiations take place outside the League of Nations. No difficulties were expected from members of the Balkan Entente, or from Bulgaria. Aras expected to discuss procedural problems in Geneva, and he believed that the interested governments would want to consider the Straits question at a special conference, rather than at the League of Nations. But he was uncertain as to what form the revision of the Lausanne Convention should take. While there would probably be a multilateral convention, it might also prove necessary to conclude one or more bilateral conventions dealing with the particular interests of the Black Sea states, and more particularly of the Soviet Union. The revision would deal with (1) the commercial navigation of the Straits; (2) the remilitarization of the zones; and (3) the passage of naval vessels. But the first two subjects, which presented "no issue at all," could be "disposed of in half an hour."

Turkey was prepared to agree out-of-hand to continuation of the Lausanne regime of free commercial navigation, "and to consider any improvements" which might be proposed "for the impartial benefit of all nations." Aras believed that the interested Powers were prepared to recognize the abolition of the demilitarized zone of the Straits. The only question likely to involve difficulties was that pertaining to the passage of warships and aircraft. While the USSR might insist

[29]Ibid., pp. 512-18.

upon maximum restrictions on the movement of warships or aircraft, Great Britain and Italy would probably insist upon minimum restrictions. The Turkish government considered it possible to find "a technically sound system of controlling the transit of such craft through the Straits so as to obviate dangers and surprises, either to Turkey herself or to other Powers in the Black Sea or in the Mediterranean." In the interest of Turkish security, Aras thought it might be provided that such craft could pass through the Straits only one by one, and there might be provision for advance notification to the Turkish government, which would thereupon notify all other governments concerned. If there were any great delay as to remilitarization, "Turkey would request the approval of the signatory Powers for her taking necessary provisional measures, subject to eventual agreement on a permanent basis." Aras pointed out that there was a theoretical danger of Turkey's becoming involved in hostilities, both in view of the general European situation and of the situation in the Mediterranean. Turkey was applying sanctions against Italy under the League of Nations, and there was a danger that Italy's animosity against Great Britain might lead to war, with Italy and Germany on one side and Great Britain, France and the USSR on the other, "a situation in which either group, while having no intrinsic quarrel with Turkey, might feel impelled for military reasons to attempt control of the Straits." Turkey could not, therefore, afford to "ignore possibilities so vitally endangering her security, and would feel justified even under the terms of the existing Convention, in taking necessary measures of precaution." But she preferred to act with the acquiescence of the other signatories rather "than to proceed solely upon her own construction of her obligations." Dr. Aras was confident that the Lausanne Convention could be completely abrogated and the following substituted therefor:

1) A declaration, *ex proprio motu*, assuring equally to all nations unimpeded commercial navigation of the Straits, in terms substantially identical with those set up by the Convention, although perhaps taking account of ameliorative suggestions from the maritime nations; and
2) A treaty or convention, among those Powers having naval interests in the Mediterranean and the Black Sea, establishing some system of control over the transit through Turkish territory of warships and aircraft—this multilateral treaty possibly being supplemented by bilateral agreements between Turkey and certain of the Powers more particularly concerned.

Ambassador MacMurray considered that the United States had "no treaty right, direct or indirect, with respect to the Straits Convention" or any concern with the military and political aspects of the Convention. The sole American interest lay in "the maintenance (or perhaps amelioration) of the regime of freedom of commercial navigation through the Straits." There was even reason to believe in the Turkish intent to maintain that regime and no need for anxiety about the rights of American shipping. Since the interests of the United States were strictly confined to matters in which it could "expect the most favorable treatment of our shipping," MacMurray saw no reason to send observers to the forthcoming conference, and he thought he should be authorized to tell the Turkish authorities as much.

SOME VIEWS OF THE POWERS ON REVISION
OF THE LAUSANNE CONVENTION

The Turkish overture was generally well received. On April 14 the British government accepted the demand for a conference and assured the Turkish government of its favorable attitude. The USSR announced its complete accord on April 16, noting that it had always believed that the zone of the Straits should be under Turkish sovereignty, a position which it had taken at Lausanne:

> Since that time the view of the Soviet Government had not changed. . . .
> The Soviet Government considers quite well-founded the Turkish Government's apprehension of the dangers to general peace at the present moment and the serious menace of war. . . . Thus it believes that under the present circumstances the Turkish Republic's intention to guarantee the safety of its territory by a change in the regime of the Straits is quite natural. In view of the above, the Union of Soviet Socialist Republics expresses its readiness to accept the offer of the Government of the Turkish Republic to take part in negotiations for altering the regime of the Straits in the interests of Turkey's safety and to guarantee peace and tranquillity in this zone.[30]

Ambassador Bullitt reported Moscow rumors that Turkish–Soviet relations were not, however, as intimate as they had previously seemed, and there was a feeling that the increasing Anglo-Italian antagonism would lead Great Britain into closer friendship with Turkey, in which case Turkey would become less dependent on the USSR. Soviet–Turkish friendship had been a "mariage de convenance," and there was no reason to suppose that it would "long outlive the practical advantages," even if it were still "mutually advantageous." Ambassador Joseph C. Grew reported on April 27 that the Japanese government was willing to discuss the problem of militarizing the Straits, but was expected to make reservations con-

[30]See Ambassador William C. Bullitt's dispatch of April 24, 1936; ibid., p. 518; *Izvestiya*, April 18, 1936; Great Britain, Foreign Office, Turkey, no. 1 (1923), *The Lausanne Conference on Near Eastern Affairs, 1922-1923*, Cmd. 1814, pp. 129, 160, 236-40, 252, for Soviet position at Lausanne.

cerning any change in the status of the Straits which might "free the Soviet Black Sea fleet."[31] The Balkan states were now ready to act by the end of April. During the meeting of the Council of the Balkan Entente in Belgrade, May 4-6, all problems were dealt with in a friendly spirit and solutions reached, although Rumania was concerned with the problem of free passage through the Straits, its sole exit to the sea, and Greece took note of the question of the refortification of its Aegean Islands. The Council of the Little Entente (Czechoslovakia, Rumania, Yugoslavia), which met in Belgrade during May 6-7, adopted a similar point of view.[32]

The British government officially announced acceptance of the Turkish invitation to attend a conference at Montreux on June 5. But there was little evidence as to French policy, although it was assumed that France would follow the British lead, while Fascist Italy refused to be represented. The United States, which was not a Lausanne signatory, and was essentially interested only in "safeguarding American rights in the navigation of the Straits," indicated that it did not intend even to send an observer to the forthcoming conference, although it desired to be kept informed of the proceedings.[33]

The Montreux Conference, June 22–July 20, 1936

The conference for the revision of the Lausanne Convention of the Straits met at Montreux, Switzerland, during June 22–July 20, 1936.[34]

---

[31] *USFR* (1936), 3: 519.

[32] Ibid., pp. 519-20; *Les Balkans* 8, nos. 1-8 (September 1936): 91-92; Secretariat du Conseil Permanent de la Petite Entente, *Communiqué des Conférences des Ministres des Affaires Etrangères des Etats de la Petite Entente et des Sessions du Conseil Permanent*, Belgrade, July 1936, p. 75.

[33] *USFR* (1936), 3: 520-23. Count Ciano told the Turkish Ambassador on June 15 that Italy's absence was due to the application of sanctions against it. Malcolm Muggeridge, *Ciano's Diplomatic Papers* (London: Oldhams, 1948), p. 490; *German Documents* (C), 5: 668.

[34] For minutes, see *Actes de la Conférence de Montreux concernant le régime des Détroits. 22 juin-20 juillet 1936. Compte-rendus des séances plenières at de proces-verbal des débats du comité technique* (Liege, Belgium, 1936). See also M. C. Djonker, *Le Bosphore et les Dardanelles: Les Conventions des Détroits de Lausanne (1923) et Montreux (1936)* (Lausanne: Held, 1938); Erkin, *Les Rélations Turco-Soviétiques et la Question des Détroits*, chaps. 2 and 3; Fernand de Visscher, "La nouvelle Convention des Détroits," *Revue de Droit International et de Legislation Comparée* 17 (3rd ser.) (1936): 669 ff.; G. D. Warsamy, *La Convention des Détroits* (Montreux, 1936) (Paris: Pedone, 1937); Juliette Abrevaya, *La Conférence de Montreux et le Régime des Détroits* (Paris: Editions Internationales, 1937); Joachim Suche, *Der Meerengenvertrag von Montreux* (Munich, 1936); André Blondel, *La Conférence de Montreux et le Nouveau Régime des Détroits* (Paris, 1938); Pierre Mamopoulos, "La Convention de Montreux," *Les Balkans* 8, nos. 1-8 (September 1936): 2-28.

It was understood from the outset that there would be a new convention, that commercial freedom would be guaranteed, and that Turkey would have the right to remilitarize the Straits. But there was basic disagreement, particularly because Great Britain and the continental European Powers differed concerning the Turkish right to close the Straits to warships. When the conference began, Aras, who headed the Turkish Delegation, presented a draft convention which abolished the International Commission of the Straits and placed the zone under complete Turkish sovereignty, with the right of closure. The project guaranteed freedom of commerce, but remilitarized the Straits. Nonriverain Powers were to be limited, at any given time to 14,000 tons of warships in the straits and 28,000 in the Black Sea. Submarines and civil and military aircraft were completely excluded from the zone of the Straits.

Other delegations challenged the Turkish project, although they agreed in principle that a change was necessary. The Soviet Delegation contested those features which would have limited the right of Soviet warships to pass to and from the Mediterranean, Moscow's aim being to make the Black Sea a *mare clausum* to all except the fleets of the Black Sea Powers, and essentially to the Red fleet itself. The British Delegation which, of course, favored commercial freedom, as in the past, opposed complete closure to warships, either of the Straits, or of the Black Sea. On the second day of the conference, June 23, Maxim Litvinov, who headed the Soviet Delegation, made the Soviet position very clear:

> We all know that these Straits—in particular the Straits of the Dardanelles and the Bosphorus—have a special character and are not comparable with certain international canals and other Straits, since they lead only into the Black Sea, which is a closed sea; they cannot be utilized for transit to a destination of other countries. It is in taking into consideration these circumstances that numerous European statesmen, including, for example, Lord Palmerston, the Duke of Wellington, pronounced themselves on numerous occasions in favor of closure of the Straits.
>
> Closure of these Straits is of very great importance, for the security, not only of Turkey, but of all the States of the Black Sea. Doubtless the best way to guarantee security would be to close the Straits completely to warships of nonriverain States. Nevertheless, my Government does not insist on closure and is ready to support the Turkish proposition tending to keep the Straits open for certain ends and under certain limitations to the warships of all nations, with full freedom of passage for commercial vessels.[35]

The next day, Litvinov stressed that there was no other sea in the same geographical situation, and observed that if the Baltic and

[35]*Actes de la Conférence de Montreux*, pp. 33-34.

Mediterranean seas were similarly situated, he would not oppose equality of rights in the Black Sea: "The Mediterranean is not a closed sea—you can penetrate it through its two extremities and that is also the case of other seas. If, to the contrary, you wish to penetrate the Black Sea, it is for a definite end. This may be either to pay a visit or to offer your assistance to a state in difficulty in application of a decision of the League of Nations. For my part, I cannot imagine another legitimate aim for which foreign vessels would enter the Black Sea. The situation is entirely different when it is a question of seas which have to be crossed to reach further regions."[36]

THE AMERICAN INTEREST IN COMMERCIAL NAVIGATION

Meanwhile, Aras had assured the Polish and American governments as to continued commercial freedom in the Straits, although Gilbert observed on June 23 that the Turkish draft convention did not mention continuation of the International Commission of the Straits, a matter which was causing some difficulties at Montreux, along with the question of warships. Indeed, Gilbert thought that the real question would be that of the passage of warships, and particularly the "adjustment of the British and Russian positions." The United States was concerned almost exclusively with commercial freedom in the Straits, and on June 26, the Embassy in Ankara confirmed that the Aras statements on April 22 were "official declarations of the Turkish government's policy with respect to commercial navigation of the Straits and were deliberately given as such." Navigation in the Straits was "to be at least as free as under Lausanne Convention and vessels of all countries whether or not signatory to the new Convention" would "benefit without any discrimination whatsoever." The text of the Turkish proposal at Montreux bore out this view, and the statements concerning commercial navigation were essentially similar to those of Aras and other officials of the Turkish Foreign Ministry. Indeed, from the very outset, the Turkish government had "spared no efforts" to make its "position on this point perfectly clear to everybody."[37]

CONFLICTS OF INTEREST AT MONTREUX

Gilbert summarized the various positions at Montreux as early as June 26. He pointed out that Great Britain, Bulgaria, and Rumania all held that commercial shipping interests should be safeguarded

---

[36]Ibid., p. 44.
[37]USFR (1936), 3: 522-23. For the Turkish draft, see Actes de la Conférence de Montreux, pp. 285-87.

through some form of international control or regulation, while the Soviet Union desired free egress and ingress for the warships of the Black Sea Powers, but opposed equality of rights for non-Black Sea Powers. Except for courtesy visits of small naval units, unless in implementation of decisions of the League of Nations or of a regional security pact, the Black Sea should be closed to the warships of non-Black Sea Powers. During wartime, the warships of nonriparian Powers could not enter the Black Sea. On the other hand, Bulgaria and Rumania were opposed to these provisions concerning warships, but generally favorable to mutual assistance arrangements. Broadly speaking, the French position, except insofar as to support the Soviet position on mutual assistance, had not yet been disclosed. The Italian representative at Geneva, who had made a "personal but official visit" to Montreux, had entered a general reservation concerning remilitarization and transit of warships. In the Italian view, Turkey should be permitted to remilitarize, but not fortify the Straits. Italy was also opposed to any discrimination in behalf of the Black Sea Powers concerning the transit of warships. Turkey, on the other hand, wanted to prohibit passage of warships through the Straits in sufficient strength at any one time which might threaten Istanbul, with the exception that riparian states should have unrestricted right of passage, others being limited to courtesy visits. If ratification of a general convention failed, Turkey desired to have the right to fortify the Straits immediately upon signature or under the terms of a special separate protocol, as well as the right to close the Straits to nonriparian warships in case of threat of war. Japan believed that the warships of nonriparian Powers should have the right of ingress into the Straits upon equal terms with those of the Black Sea Powers. It opposed any reference to the League of Nations and declined to give any commitments to defend the Straits. Great Britain, it was thought, was awaiting Italy's entry into the conference, when Great Britain, Italy, and Japan would "concert their tactics to achieve a bottling up of Russia in the Black Sea." But it was not known to what extent the United Kingdom would support Italy on a possible Italo-Balkan issue, or maneuver for a middle position. On June 29, it appeared that British policy had taken a "definite turning toward an acceptance of the Turkish demands and also of the Russian," with some "escalator" provision in respect of the Soviet Union, "to the effect that an increase beyond a certain point in the Russian Black Sea fleet" would permit a proportionately larger ingress of naval units of non-Black Sea Powers. But there was a lack of fixity in British policy, in part because of the possible attitudes of Italy and Japan, and some apprehension that the Japanese attitudes might disrupt the conference. Nicholas Politis, the Greek representative, had indicated that the Balkan Entente unanimously supported Turkey, but doubted that Italy would be officially represented at Montreux.[38]

The essentially accurate estimate of the British position was reflected in the British counterproposal of July 6,[39] which raised the tonnage limitations for warships in the Straits and the Black Sea (the latter to 45,000 tons for nonriverain states), and provided that in wartime belligerents could pursue their enemies through the Straits into the Black Sea—an obvious threat both to Turkey and the USSR. Moreover, the Turkish right to close the Straits was to be decided by a two-thirds vote of the League of Nations Council. The British proposal also provided for an International Commission of the Straits. Naturally, the British draft aroused the opposition of the Turkish and Soviet delegations, to say nothing of the Balkan Entente, and some felt that the United Kingdom had been instigated into taking its position by the German government which, for obvious reasons, desired to handicap the Soviet Union. So incensed was the Soviet Delegation that it appeared ready to leave the conference. Rumania now came out strongly against the British position, and Nicholas Titulesco, the Rumanian foreign minister, actually accused the British Delegation of outright duplicity in supporting collective and regional security at Geneva and then sabotaging it at Montreux.[40] But by July 15 Great Britain changed its position. The announcement of the Austro-German accord of July 11, under Italian auspices, may have had something to do with the change of course. Throughout this phase of the conference, Josef Paul-Boncour of France acted as the mediator between the British and Soviet and Turkish positions. The result was the Montreux Convention of July 20, 1936.

THE MONTREUX CONVENTION OF THE STRAITS, JULY 20, 1936

As a result of the Montreux conference, Turkish sovereignty over the region of the Straits was reestablished, with the right to remilitarize the zone. The International Commission was to cease func-

---

[38]*USFR* (1936), 3: 524-25.

[39]*Actes de la Conférence de Montreux*, pp. 287-298, submitted as amendments to the Turkish draft.

[40]See especially the discussion on July 9; ibid., pp. 107-19. It will be recalled that there were several interlocking regional pacts which might be involved: (1) the Little Entente (Czechoslovakia, Yugoslavia, and Rumania), 1920-21; (2) the Balkan Entente (Greece, Turkey, Yugoslavia, and Rumania), February 9, 1934; (3) the Franco-Polish Alliance, February 19, 1921; (4) the Franco-Czechoslovak Alliance, January 25, 1924; (5) the Franco-Rumanian Alliance, June 10, 1926; (6) the Franco-Yugoslav Alliance, November 11, 1927; (7) the Franco-Soviet Alliance, May 2, 1935; (8) the Czechoslovak-Soviet Alliance, May 16, 1935. The Turkish-Soviet agreement of December 17, 1925 was not an alliance, but an agreement of friendship and non-aggression.

tioning after October 1, 1936. Like the Lausanne Convention, the Montreux Convention recognized and affirmed "the principle of freedom of transit and navigation by sea in the Straits," which was to "continue without limit of time."[41] In time of peace, merchant ships were to enjoy complete freedom, although they were subject to sanitary regulations. In wartime, Turkey being nonbelligerent, merchant ships under any flag or with any cargo were also to enjoy complete freedom of transit and navigation in the Straits. If Turkey were a belligerent, merchant ships of friendly Powers were to enjoy freedom of transit and navigation in the Straits provided they did not assist the enemy. Moreover, such vessels were to enter the Straits by day and to travel a route indicated by the Turkish authorities. Similar provisions were to apply if Turkey considered itself in imminent danger of war.

In time of peace, light surface vessels, small warships and auxiliaries, whether under the flag of a Black Sea Power or of a nonriparian Power, were to enjoy freedom of transit through the Straits, although passage was to be made by day. The maximum naval tonnage which foreign Powers might send through the Straits at any one time was not to exceed 15,000 tons, although Black Sea Powers might exceed that tonnage on condition that their vessels passed through singly, escorted by not more than two destroyers. Notice of intention to pass warships through the Straits was to be given in all cases. In no event were warships to use any aircraft which they might be carrying.

Under ordinary circumstances the aggregate tonnage which non-Black Sea Powers could have in the Black Sea was not to exceed 30,000 tons. However, if the strongest fleet in the Black Sea (the Soviet fleet) should exceed by 10,000 tons the tonnage of the strongest fleet in the Black Sea at the date of the signature of the Montreux Convention, the nonriverain tonnage could be increased by 10,000 tons to a maximum of 45,000 tons. But, whatever the mission, vessels of nonriverain Powers were not to remain in the Black Sea longer than twenty-one days.

In wartime, Turkey being neutral, warships were to enjoy complete freedom of transit and navigation through the Straits under the same

[41]Ibid., pp. 301–10; United Kingdom, Foreign Office, Turkey No. 1 (1936), *Convention Regarding the Regime of the Straits with Correspondence Relating Thereto*, Montreux, July 20, 1936, Cmd. 5249; League of Nations *Treaty Series*, 173: 213; Harry N. Howard, *The Problem of the Turkish Straits*, Department of State Publication 2752, New Eastern Series 5 (Washington, D.C., USGPO, 1947), pp. 1–12, 25–28; J. C. Hurewitz, *Diplomacy in the Near and Middle East* (Princeton, N.J.: D. Van Nostrand, 1956), 2: 197–203.

conditions as those outlined above, embodied in Articles X to XVIII. Belligerent warships, however, were not to pass through the Straits, "except in cases arising out of the application of Article XXV," which provided that nothing in the convention should prejudice the "rights and obligations of Turkey, or of any of the other High Contracting Parties members of the League of Nations, arising out of the Covenant of the League of Nations." Another exception would arise "in cases of assistance rendered to a State victim of aggression in virtue of a treaty of mutual assistance binding Turkey, concluded within the framework of the Covenant of the League of Nations, and registered and published in accordance with the provisions of Article XVIII of the Covenant." Belligerent warships, however, were not to make any capture or carry out any other hostile acts within the Straits.

Article XX provided that in wartime, Turkey being belligerent, the provisions of Articles X to XVIII should not be applicable, and the passage of warships must be left exclusively to the discretion and judgment of the Turkish government. Moreover, if Turkey considered itself in danger of imminent war, the provisions of Article XX were to apply. In such instance, however, Turkish actions were to be subject to a vote of the League of Nations Council and, if disapproved by a two-thirds vote, to be disallowed.

To assure passage of civil aircraft between the Mediterranean and the Black Sea, the Turkish government was to indicate the routes to be traveled, "outside the forbidden zones" which might "be established in the Straits." The functions of the International Commission of the Straits were to be transferred to the Turkish government, which was to collect and maintain shipping data concerning traffic in the Straits.[42] Likewise, it was to supervise the execution of all provisions relative to the passage of warships through the Straits. An annual report was to be made to the secretary-general of the League of Nations.

The Montreux Convention was to be ratified and to remain in force for twenty years, but "the principle of freedom of transit and navigation affirmed in Article I" was to continue "without limit of time." If no notice of denunciation, however, was given two years prior to the expiry of the convention, it was to remain in force "until two years after such notice shall have been given."[43] But in the event of denun-

---

[42]For these annual reports, see Republique Turque, Ministère des Affaires Etrangères, *Rapport Annuel sur le Mouvement des Navires à Travers les Détroits*, 1936 ff.

[43]As will be noted later, the convention entered into force on November 9, 1936. Had it been denounced by any signatory on November 9, 1954, it would have expired on November 9, 1956. But under Article 28 it now remains in force for a period of two

ciation, the contracting parties agreed to call a conference for the purpose of concluding a new convention of the Straits. However, under Article XXIX, at the end of each five-year period the signatories might make proposals for revision of the convention, although to be valid such proposals had to be seconded by another signatory, where the passage of warships through the Straits was concerned, or by two signatories in the case of any other proposed modification. Any request for revision was to be notified to all signatories three months prior to the expiry of the current five-year period.

There was much satisfaction with the new convention. Aras observed at the closing session on July 20 that, when people were animated with a spirit of good will and conciliation the most difficult problems could be resolved.[44] Lord Stanhope felt that the conference had done its best, not only to safeguard Turkish security, but to write an enduring convention based on sound foundations. The French and other representatives reechoed these sentiments. But the remarks of Litvinov are of special interest, for they not only bespeak the achievement but note the problems which lay ahead. Litvinov declared:

The Montreux Conference, called to revise an international Convention to adapt it to changing conditions, has fulfilled its task worthily. It has taken note of all the conditions which had developed. It has recognized that the guarantee of the security of the Straits, as envisaged by the Lausanne Conference, could not inspire a sentiment of true security in Turkey, and it has drawn appropriate conclusions.

The Conference has done even more. It has revised some outmoded opinions, according to which the problem of the Straits involved an ancient conflict between certain Powers, because of which the Conference could only fail. To avoid failure, the Conference has had to understand that in place of the decrepit Ottoman Empire, which was only a pawn on the diplomatic chessboard of imperialist governments, there was now the young Turkish Republic, full of hope and energy, which has made such great progress under the leadership of its creator and its great reformer, Atatürk, and which plays an ever greater and more independent role in the organization of peace in Europe. The Conference has also had to understand that in the place of Imperial Russia, which attempted to use the Black Sea as a base for its participation in the imperialist struggles of the Great Powers, and for the realization of new territorial conquests, there is today a new Soviet Socialist State, which occupies the greater part of the Black Sea, one of whose first acts was to renounce completely all imperialist ambitions, and which since, invariably and systematically, has pursued a policy of peace, jealous alike of its own security and that of all other states, near and far.

---

years after any date on which it may be denounced. It is not merely a matter of the Powers honoring an "expired" Convention as George Lenczowski suggests (*Soviet Advances in the Middle East* [Washington, D.C.: American Enterprise Institute, 1971], pp. 155–56), but of a legally valid instrument.

[44]*Actes de la Conférence de Montreux*, pp. 179–80, 180–81, 181–85.

This Conference has also recognized that the close friendship which for fifteen years has united these two regenerated States—the Soviet Union and Turkey—is indissoluble and constitutes no ephemeral combination. *The Conference has recognized, although in an insufficient way, the special rights of the riverain states of the Black Sea in the Black Sea in connection with the passage of the Straits, as well as the special geographical situation of the Black Sea, in which the general conceptions of the absolute freedom of the seas could not be entirely applied.*[45]

According to Litvinov, the Soviet Union was not opposed "for a single instant" to unlimited freedom of commercial navigation or to the safeguarding of communications between the Black Sea and other ports. It had tried to limit freedom of navigation only for the warships of nonriverain powers in time of peace, and especially in wartime, and to protect the region of the Black Sea from the horrors of war. Finally, it had attempted to establish a direct connection between the new convention and the Covenant of the League of Nations and pacts of mutual assistance. The USSR noted "with an immense satisfaction" that it had "attained these aims in great part if not completely," and Litvinov thanked all his colleagues for having collaborated so well "in creating this atmosphere of understanding and mutual conciliation" which had marked "especially the latter days of the Conference." Moreover, the conference had been a landmark in demonstrating that with good will difficult problems could be solved. Its results indicated that international life was definitely emerging from "sterile discussions and controversies," moving into the "great ocean of true international collaboration," and finally would reach the harbor over the entry of which were inscribed the words: "General Peace and Security for all Peoples."[46]

ENTRY INTO FORCE OF THE MONTREUX CONVENTION

In a separate protocol the signatories agreed that Turkey might "immediately remilitarize the zone of the Straits" and that as from August 15 the Turkish government provisionally could apply the new regime.[47] On July 22 Turkish troops occupied the upper Bosphorus and

[45]Ibid., pp. 181–82 (italics supplied). See also Papouktchieva, *La Politique de la Russie a l'Égard des Détroits*, pp. 163–82; Erkin, *Les Rélations Turco-Soviétiques et la Question des Détroits*, pp. 129–37.

[46]For an authoritative Soviet view, see V. P. Potemkin, *Istoria Diplomatii* (3 vols.; Moscow, 1941–45), French translation, *Histoire de la Diplomatie* (3 vols.; Paris: Librairie de Medicis, 1945, 1947). It is noteworthy that in 1945 this history should declare that "despite certain faults in this convention, its adoption had a great positive importance and constituted a great victory of Soviet diplomacy" (3: 586). See also Kazimierz Grzybowski, "The Soviet Doctrine of *mare clausum* and Policies in the Black and Baltic Seas," *Journal of Central European Affairs* 14, no. 4 (January 1955): 339–53.

[47]*Actes de la Conférence de Montreux*, p. 310; Cmd. 5249, p. 39.

Dardanelles demilitarized zones, along with the islands of Imbros (Imroz) and Tenedos (Bozcaada), at the entrance of the Dardanelles.[48]

Aras returned triumphantly to Istanbul on July 24, and gave much of the credit for his successes at Montreux to British support. He held Franco-Soviet insistence on keeping the Straits open for the uses "of the Franco-Soviet combination while closing them to the naval forces of other Powers" responsible for some of his difficulties. This was an obvious reference to Article XIX of the new convention, but Aras told Ambassador MacMurray on July 25 that Turkey

could never have accepted such a situation, in which she would have been compelled to compromise her neutrality as guardian of the Straits. Happily, a way out of the impasse had been found by the formula that Turkey should allow the passage of naval forces acting either under the mandate of the League or under the terms of a mutual assistance treaty to which Turkey herself might be a party. The latter alternative was altogether out of the question, as Turkey has no present or imaginable intention to become a party to such a treaty; so the promise was based upon a condition contrary to the fact and therefore meaningless save as it was acceptable to the French and Soviet Governments because enabling them to make it appear to their home constituencies that the Conference had given them some additional elements of security.[49]

The Foreign Minister reiterated that the Montreux Convention "fully and impartially" preserved "the free commercial navigation of the Straits" and, indeed, further facilitated it "by a slight alleviation of the existing charges for certain services to navigation." MacMurray considered the Aras statement about the British position at Montreux significant, because of its indication of the intention of the Turkish government "to manifest an attitude of complete satisfaction, and indeed of solidarity, with that of Great Britain. It is not yet fully apparent whether this is due to the favorable results finally attained at Montreux, or to what extent it may be induced by a feeling of common cause with Great Britain with relation to the apprehended pretensions of Italy in the Eastern Mediterranean."

When Aras submitted the new convention to the Grand National Assembly on July 31, he observed that one of its essential characteristics was that it restored "full and complete sovereignty" over the Straits and recognized the Turkish "right to fortify the Straits," which the defense of the republic clearly demanded.[50] Some months later, on November 12, the necessary instruments of ratification having been deposited, MacMurray was notified that the Montreux

[48]*USFR* (1936), 3: 526.
[49]Ibid., pp. 526-28. See also the Atatürk statement in *Cumhuriyet*, July 10, 1936.
[50]See also Carnegie Endowment for International Peace, *Turkey and the United Nations* (New York: Manhattan, 1961), p. 45.

Convention had entered into force on November 9, and Aras volunteered to make a formal communication as to Turkey's intentions relative to American participation in the benefits of the convention. Indeed, he had already gone further than merely giving such assurances, for in reporting to the Grand National Assembly, he had explained that the convention embodied "a recognition of the principle of free commercial navigation of the Straits" and that such recognition was "therefore implicit in the Turkish ratification."[51]

The Development of the Turkish Position, 1936–1939

The years between the signature of the Montreux Convention and the beginning of 1939 witnessed some momentous developments in the position and policy of Turkey and in Turkish relations with the other states of Europe and the world. As already observed, the new Convention of the Straits was very well received, especially in the Soviet Union. Nevertheless, toward the end of 1936, Litvinov proposed a bilateral Soviet-Turkish pact for joint defense of the Straits in line with an enduring Soviet policy, and reminiscent of Hünkar Iskelesi (1833). The Turkish government declined and, much to the annoyance of the Soviet government, informed the British government of the Soviet move.[52]

Nazi Germany, which had not been a signatory of the Lausanne Convention, and Italy, which had refused participation at Montreux, however, were much displeased with the new regime of the Straits and neither looked favorably upon the possibility of Soviet naval forces in the Mediterranean. Germany was also disturbed by the ever-growing Anglo-French influence at Ankara, which might prove a limiting factor with respect to Nazi ambitions both in Southeastern Europe and in the Middle East. Fascist Italy, of course, had definite ambitions in the Eastern Mediterranean which, as has been observed, had been one of the dominant factors leading the Turkish government to demand revision of the Lausanne Convention.[53] On the other hand, Great Britain had now moved to the fore in the development of Anglo-Turkish relations, based in part on British adjustments at Montreux. Anglo-Turkish relations were now much strengthened, and the new friendship served to counterbalance both the Italian

[51]*USFR* (1936), 3: 528–29.
[52]Cevat Açikalin, "Turkey's International Relations," *International Affairs*, 23 (October 1947): 479; Erkin, *Les Rélations Turco-Soviétiques et la Question des Détroits*, chap. 4.
[53]Altemur Kiliç, *Turkey and the World* (Washington, D.C.: Public Affairs Press, 1959), pp. 65–69.

fortifications in the Dodecanese Islands and Italian advances in East Africa. France appeared at the time not too averse to the strengthening of the Soviet position in the Mediterranean, in view of the Franco-Soviet alliance of May 2, 1938 and the ever-increasing Nazi-Fascist menace. While the Moscow government was pleased with the Montreux Convention, the new westward orientation of the Turkish government and the renewed Anglo-Turkish cordiality brought about a corresponding coolness between Moscow and Ankara.[54]

Meanwhile, just two days before the signing of the Montreux Convention, namely, on July 18, the Spanish civil war broke out, with the Fascist forces of Generalissimo Franco encouraged and abetted by Germany and Italy. On October 25, the Rome-Berlin axis was formed, with Japan added on November 17, 1936. Great Britain and Italy signed a "gentleman's agreement" on January 2, 1937, affirming the independence and integrity of Spain and freedom of passage through the Mediterranean. In the long run, however, the new Anglo-Italian agreement did not dispel the suspicions aroused by Italian activities in the Mediterranean and the Middle East. All these moves were followed by increasing Nazi-Fascist pressures, political and economic, in Southeastern Europe. Thus, on January 24, 1937, Bulgaria and Yugoslavia signed a pact of "eternal friendship," which was really a blow against the Balkan Entente, and this was followed by the Italo-Yugoslav nonaggression agreement of March 25, guaranteeing existing frontiers and the maintenance of the status quo in the Adriatic. But this was a blow both to the Balkan and the Little entente and to French influence in the area as well. While the Pact of Sa'dabad, July 9, 1937, among Turkey, Afghanistan, Iran, and Iraq, a nonaggression and consultative pact, was a stabilizing influence, it carried little weight in the balance of forces. Toward the end of 1937 the way was prepared for the development of a totalitarian structure in Rumania, a grand design which King Carol carried into execution in 1938.

The Turkish government viewed all these developments with a very cautious eye, but did not appear especially disturbed by the German and Italian attitudes toward the Montreux Convention. While there had been earlier consideration of the problem,[55] it was not until after

---

[54]Among other things, see Potemkin, *Istoria Diplomatii* 3: 582-86; Max Beloff, *The Foreign Policy of Soviet Russia, 1929-1941* (New York: Oxford University Press, 1949), 2: chap. 3; Kiliç, *Turkey and the World*, pp. 58-65; Muggeridge, *Ciano's Diplomatic Papers*, pp. 121-22. For German comment and analysis, see *German Documents* (C), 5: 675-76, 745-46, 795, 799, 830, 835-39.

[55]The Turkish-German discussions may be followed in *German Documents*, series D (1937-45), 5, *Poland; The Balkans; Latin America; The Smaller Powers, June 1937-March 1939* (Washington, D.C.: USGPO, 1953), especially pp. 706-07, 707-12.

the signature of the supplementary Anglo–German naval agreement on July 17, 1937 that the German Foreign Ministry opened negotiations relative to the Montreux Convention and the question of German adherence. These negotiations continued at various intervals during 1937–39, with the Turkish government pursuing a very cautious course, explaining that Germany had not been represented at Montreux since it was not a Lausanne signatory, that it was not the "proprietor" of the convention and that other signatories were interested parties to be consulted, and that, in any event, all states, signatories or not, had the same rights under the Montreux Convention. While Italy finally adhered to the convention on May 2, 1938, Nazi Germany never did so, and it complained in August 1938 that while German–Turkish relations remained "unchanged," Turkey still hesitated to give those relations a "new and more intimate form, at least at the present time."[56]

The Munich crisis in September 1938, followed by concerted German moves toward outright domination of Southeastern Europe and the conversion of this great area from the North to the Black Sea into a German *Grossraumwirtschaft*, made its inevitable impression on Turkey. During the negotiations for a German–Turkish credit agreement, which was signed on January 16, 1939, there was a draft proposal in which Turkey affirmed that the Montreux Convention applied to all foreign Powers equally and that Turkey was willing to give Germany equality with the other signatories with reference to passage of the Straits both by merchantmen and warships.[57] By now, however, momentous events were taking place in Central and Southeastern Europe and the clouds of war were gathering ominously. The independence of Czechoslovakia was destroyed between March 10 and 17, 1939, and Fascist Italy, not to be outdone, seized Albania on April 7. Anglo–French statesmen sought to counterbalance these moves by actions of their own, both in Eastern Europe and the Eastern Mediterranean, although the hour was, indeed, much later than they thought.[58]

[56]Ibid., pp. 735–36. During January–February 1939, the German Foreign Ministry considered that Turkish anxiety relative to the Soviet Union was a factor in the situation, observed that Turkey had been unable to reach an agreement with Germany, and indicated that it could "by no means understand the legal subtleties which the Turks had brought up" (ibid., p. 743). For rumors concerning a Soviet proposal for collective defense in the region of the Black Sea and the Straits, see D. J. Dallin, *Soviet Russia's Foreign Policy, 1939–1942* (New Haven: Yale University Press, 1942), pp. 109–11; *New York Times*, February 8, 1939.

[57]See, especially, *German Documents* (D), 5: 738–44.

[58]On April 21, 1939, an Anglo–Turkish agreement for the construction of a naval base at Gelcuk was signed. An April 1 (effective November 30, 1939) the United States and Turkey signed a reciprocal trade agreement which provided for "unconditional most-favored-nation treatment" (Executive Agreement Series 163 [1939]).

The United States, concerned only with maintenance of the principle of freedom of transit and navigation for commerce in the Turkish Straits, without direct or enduring politico-strategic interests in the area, was eminently pleased with the Montreux Convention. Its immediate objectives had been achieved without direct involvement and the principle had been enshrined in the new convention "without limit of time." Within a period of ten years, however, the United States was to discover that it was still concerned with developments in the Eastern Mediterranean and that its basic and enduring interests in the Turkish Straits extended well beyond those of commerce.

Chapter VI

The Entry of Turkey into World War II

As was natural in view of its position at the intercontinental cross-roads, the Turkish republic was of great interest both to the Axis Powers and to their enemies during World War II, including the United States.[1] Turkey was especially concerned with developments early in 1939 which pointed toward possible Axis domination over Southeastern Europe down to the very borders of Turkey. As early as February 1939, the Soviet Union proposed a Black Sea pact with Turkey to protect the southern approaches to the USSR.[2] The Italian invasion of Albania on April 7 caused much concern in Turkish official circles despite the reassurances from Il Duce. The Turkish govern-ment was, therefore, somewhat receptive when the British and French governments began overtures in its direction, especially after April 13. On May 12, 1939, heads of agreement were signed

[1]Recent documentary publications which throw much light on the Turkish problem include: Department of State, *Foreign Relations of the United States. Diplomatic Papers 1939–1945* (Washington, D.C.: USGPO), hereafter cited as *USFR*; Department of State, *Documents on German Foreign Policy, 1918–1945* (Washington, D.C.: USGPO, 1949 ff.), series D, vols. 1–13, hereafter cited as *German Documents*. United Kingdom, Foreign Office, *Documents on British Foreign Policy, 1919–1939* (London, HMSO, 1952 ff), third series, hereafter cited as *British Documents;* The Soviet Foreign Ministry, *Dokumenti Ministerstva Inostranikh Diel Germanii,* Vipusk II. *Germanskaia Politika v. Turtsii. Documents (1941–1943).* OGIZ-Gospolitizdat, 1946 (French translation: *La Politique Allemande. Documents Secrets du Ministère des Affaires Etrangéres d'Allemagne* (Paris, 1946), hereafter cited as *GPT.* The Nurnberg documents are: Office of the U.S. Chief of Counsel for Prosecution of Axis Criminality, *Nazi Conspiracy and Aggression* (8 vols.; Washington: USGPO, 1946–48); and Supplements A and B, hereafter cited as *NCA.*

[2]See David Dallin, *Soviet Russia's Foreign Policy, 1939–1942* (New Haven: Yale University Press, 1942), pp. 109–11; *New York Times,* February 8, 1939. See also Winston Churchill, *The Second World War* (Boston: Houghton Mifflin, 1948), 1: chaps. 19–20; A. N. Kochetkov and X. I. Muratov, *Borba Rossii za Vikhod k Chernemu Mariu* (Moscow, 1951). For a recent study see Edward Weisband, *Turkish Foreign Policy, 1943–1945: Small State Diplomacy and Great Power Politics* (Princeton, N.J.: Princeton University Press, 1973), chaps. 1–13.

with Great Britain, followed by a similar agreement with France on June 23.[3]

At the same time Turkey sought to consolidate its relations with the Balkan states, partly with Soviet encouragement, although the situation changed fundamentally with the signature of the Nazi-Soviet agreement of August 23, 1939, a bare week before the outbreak of World War II. It may be observed that, during this period, partly in a seductive effort to offset possible Soviet apprehensions, the Nazi government renounced any political interests, either in the Balkan area or in the Turkish Straits.[4] With the coming of the war, Turkey moved toward formalizing the alliance with Great Britain and France, although this time without the blessing and basically against the wishes of the USSR, which collaborated with the Nazi government, first in an attempt to block the achievement of the alliance and then in an attempt, in any event, to water down the agreement. Foreign Minister Şükrü Saracoglu journeyed to Moscow during September 25-October 17, 1939, for discussions of the draft agreement, when Stalin pressed for changes in the draft to obviate any obligation on the part of Turkey to oppose the USSR and sought modifications in the Montreux Convention to bring the Straits under effective Soviet control. But the Soviet tactics, even when flavored with vodka, caviar, and the Bolshoi ballet, were so obvious that, finally, the Turkish delegation left Moscow on October 17, and two days later the Anglo-Franco-Turkish Alliance was signed. The new alliance pledged assistance on the part of the signatories, "in the event of an act of aggression by a European Power leading to war in the Mediterranean area," although it was specifically stated that Turkey's obligations could not compel Turkey to take action which might involve entry into armed conflict with the USSR. Turkey's adherence was roundly condemned by Foreign Minister V. M. Molotov, who warned the Turkish government on October 31 of possible dire consequences.[5]

---

[3]See, especially, *British Documents, 1919-1939*, third series, 5: chaps. 4-6, for detailed negotiations which ultimately led to the alliance of October 19, 1939 (ibid., chaps. 6 and 7).

[4]See, especially, *German Documents* (D), 7: 142-51, 156-57, 161, 167-69, 187, 188-90, 225-29, 245-47; 10: 10-11; Raymond James Sontag and Steuart Beddie, eds., *Nazi-Soviet Relations 1939-1941. Documents from the Archives of the German Foreign Office* (Washington, D.C.: USGPO, 1948), pp. 1-50, 76-78, 157-58. Hereafter cited as *NSR*.

[5]*German Documents* (D), 7: 522; 8: 5, 66-68, 72, 80, 105-06, 111, 116, 124-25, 164-68, 173-74, 183, 200, 236, 244, 306-07, 329; *USFR* (1939), 1: 44, 446-47, 449, 455-56, 456-57, 489-90, 501-03; (1940), 1: 444-51; Feridun Cemal Erkin, *Les Rélations Turco-Soviétiques et la Question des Détroits* (Ankara: Basnur Matbaasi, 1968), chap. 5; Nihat Erim Kocaeli, "The Development of the Anglo-Turkish Alliance,"

Turkey remained a nonbelligerent ally of Great Britain and France, based on the preliminary agreements of May-June and the treaty of October 19, 1939. As the war moved down through the Balkan peninsula during 1940-41, there was much concern with the attitude and position of Turkey, particularly after the Italian entry into the struggle in June 1940, the attack on Greece on October 28, 1940, and the German advance into Rumania and Bulgaria, with the ultimate Nazi aggression against Yugoslavia and Greece on April 5-6, 1941. During January-February 1941, President Roosevelt sent Colonel William J. Donovan to this troubled region to stimulate resistance, and Turkey and the United States seemed in basic agreement on the outlook toward the war.[6] But the alliance was never formally invoked. Turkey remained a nonbelligerent substantially until the end of the war, although American entry into the conflict on December 7, 1941, without doubt, had a very positive influence in Ankara, and the defense of Turkey was declared vital to that of the United States under the Lend-Lease Act.

There was little difficulty, as such, with the problem of the Turkish Straits during the war, despite objections raised from time to time concerning the passage of German naval vessels. During the Hitler-Ribbentrop-Molotov conversations of November 12-13, 1940, the Soviet government made clear its desires as to revision of the Montreux Convention and delineated the "center of gravity" of Soviet policy and interest south of Baku and Batum in the general direction of the Persian Gulf. There were hints that, if the Soviet demands were met, the USSR might join the Axis—into which Turkey might be pushed, willingly or otherwise.[7] There was considerable trouble about the problem of Lend-Lease supplies and the Turkish shipment of chrome to Germany, much misunderstanding of the Turkish situation generally, and especially in Washington, great concern over the Turkish-German agreement of June 18, 1941, just four days prior to the Nazi attack on the USSR on June 22, 1941. Shortly thereafter, on August 10, 1941, however, Great Britain

---

Asiatic Review, N.S. 42 (October 1946): 347-51; Gregoire Gafenco, *Préliminaires de la Guerre à l'Est* (Paris: Egloff, 1944), pp. 303-10; Sir Hughe Knatchbull-Hugessen, *Diplomat in Peace and War* (London: John Murray, 1949), chap. 12; United Kingdom, Foreign Office, Turkey No. 4 (1940), *Treaty of Mutual Assistance between His Majesty in Respect of the United Kingdom, the President of the French Republic and the President of the Turkish Republic* (Angora, October 19, 1939), Cmd. 6165. See also *USFR, The Soviet Union 1933-1939*, pp. 786-90; London *Times*, October 18, 1939; *New York Times*, November 1, 1939; *Izvestiya*, October 20, 22, 1939. See also Molotov's official statement of October 31, 1939.

[6]*USFR* (1940), 1: 444-51, for MacMurray's dispatch of November 9, 1939.

[7]See especially *NSR*, pp. 217-25, 226-34, 234-47, 247-54, 257-58; *German Documents* (D), 11: 334 ff. and passim; *USFR* (1940), 1: 573-74, 575-79, 581-82, 583-88.

and the Soviet Union formally confirmed their fidelity to the
Montreux Convention, announced that they had no aggressive intentions or claims regarding the Straits, and declared that they were
prepared not only "scrupulously to observe the territorial integrity of
the Turkish Republic," but, in the event of an attack by a European
Power, to render assistance.[8]

While certain pressures were brought, particularly after the
Moscow and Tehran conferences, and during 1944, concerning active
Turkish belligerency, it now seems clear that in the last analysis
neither the United States nor the United Kingdom, nor even the
Soviet Union, actually desired Turkish entry into the shooting war
or had any well-developed plans therefor. On the other hand, the
Turkish government, in the event of actual hostilities, was anxious
about sufficient supplies and equipment and had no desire either to
undergo possible Nazi conquest or subsequent Soviet "liberation."
Stalin showed little interest in the matter at Tehran in November
1943, although there had been some discussion of it at the earlier
Moscow meeting in October. At the Cairo Conference in December
1943, President Roosevelt was little interested, did not blame the
Turkish leaders for not wanting to get caught "with their pants
down," and General Marshall feared that supplies for Operation
Overlord would be diverted and that the Turks would "burn up all our
logistics." When President Roosevelt put the problem of Turkish
entry to the Joint Chiefs of Staff in July 1944, General Marshall's
reply was essentially in the negative although expressed in affirmative language. Turkey broke with Germany in August 1944 and formally declared war on February 23, 1945, some days after the conclusion of the Yalta Conference.

The Entry of the United States into the War

Thanks to the Japanese attack on Pearl Harbor on December 7, 1941,
the United States entered the lists against Japan and a few days
later was formally at war with Germany and Italy. Immediately
prior to the attack, on December 3, the United States had publicly declared the defense of Turkey essential to that of the United States
and formally extended Lend-Lease assistance to the Turkish republic.[9] During this period there was much German discussion as to the
position of Turkey and as to the possible impact of the American entry
into the war. The Germans well knew that Turkey desired to avoid
open hostilities, but pointed out that while Great Britain could offer

[8]*USFR* (1941), 3: 891–92.   [9]Ibid., pp. 814 ff.

nothing to Turkey, Germany held in its hands the Greek islands at the entrance to the Dardanelles, which were of vital importance to Turkey. In the event of success against the Soviet Union, Turkey must become "more and more friendly," although since the era of the great Atatürk, Turkey had been pursuing a policy of national consolidation and domestic reconstruction and had expressed no desire at all "to obtain territorial gain." Nevertheless, it was thought, it might be induced to "enlarge its benevolent neutrality and to facilitate access to the Arab territories and the Suez Canal for the German High Command."[10]

Prime Minister Churchill came to Washington for talks with President Roosevelt, arriving on December 22, and in a memorandum of December 18, he discussed the Turkish problem, noting the cautious Turkish policy and the improbability of a German southward thrust.[11] While the Washington discussions were going on, Foreign Secretary Anthony Eden was in Moscow considering war problems with the Soviet authorities, and in a talk with Marshal Stalin on December 16 Stalin outlined in some detail Soviet proposals concerning postwar settlements, especially as to Eastern and Southeastern Europe and Turkey. Stalin, it may be observed, thought Turkey should receive the Dodecanese Islands, with possible adjustments in favor of Greece in the Aegean Islands, while Turkey might also receive certain districts in Bulgaria and possibly also in Northern Syria. There was evidently "no uneasiness with regard to Turkey."[12] But, in view of prior undertakings with the United States, Eden explained that it was "quite impossible" for Great Britain to commit itself to any postwar frontiers. The Foreign Secretary reaffirmed the Anglo-Soviet position concerning Turkey before the House of Commons on January 8, 1942, noting that "the references to Turkey were in all respects friendly, and such as the Turkish Government themselves would have been glad to hear." Turkey had nothing to fear from an Allied victory, its territorial integrity was in no way threatened by either Great Britain or the USSR, and "the Anglo-Soviet pledges that we gave to Turkey last autumn" would be "fully honoured." Both the Soviet Union and Great Britain wished "to see Turkey strong and prosperous."[13]

---

[10]*GPT*, pp. 10–17.
[11]Churchill, *The Second World War*, 3: 647–48, 651.
[12]Ibid., pp. 628–29; *USFR* (1941), 1: 196–205.
[13]*Parliamentary Debates, House of Commons*, 377, col. 373. This position was reaffirmed by the British and American press representatives in Ankara on January 13, 1942, and by Sir Hughe Knatchbull-Hugessen, the British ambassador, who had been in Moscow with Foreign Secretary Eden (Knatchbull-Hugessen, *Diplomat in Peace and War*, pp. 173–79).

The German ambassador in Ankara, Baron Franz von Papen, advised Berlin on January 6, 1942, that American entry into the war had produced a "sentiment of profound deception in Turkey" and, as a result, he was certain that Turkey would "reiterate and emphasize" its desire to avoid hostilities and would not become engaged in a struggle for "interests which did not involve Turkey."[14] The fact that Great Britain had decided to establish "a new order in Europe," with Soviet assistance, had disturbed Turkey. While the United States seemed invincible to the Turks, the Axis could turn the issue of the war to its advantage by inflicting a defeat on the British Empire, although Turkey preferred a balance of power in the Mediterranean, not Italian predominance. Another possible outcome would be the complete victory of the Anglo–American bloc, with Soviet assistance which, in the Turkish view, would mean that Europe would fall under Soviet domination. Thus, in von Papen's view, Turkey would attempt "to find the possibility of a compromise." Two possibilities might animate Turkey to abandon the principle of neutrality in favor of one side or the other. One was a decisive German victory over the Soviet Union in the spring of 1942 and, especially, an advance toward the Caucasus and a threat to the British oil region in the Persian Gulf, although any German attempt to "push Turkey prematurely" would "inevitably lead Turkey to take the other side." Some days before, von Papen had urged on President Ismet İnönü the Turkish interest in the destruction of the USSR, only to find that the Turkish president emphasized the neutrality of Turkey which, he said, was more advantageous to the Axis than to Great Britain. If Turkey were effectively on the side of Great Britain, "the British Fleet would support the Russian flank in the Black Sea and a convenient way for the defense of the Caucasus would be found." As a result of discussions with Saracoglu and Menemencioglu, von Papen felt that the confidence of the Turkish government in German promises not to do anything which might prejudice its "morally delicate position with regard to the British ally," would not be shaken, although he considered Turkish faith in German victory unbroken. Nevertheless, von Papen concluded that any "modification of Turkish foreign policy to the advantage of either side" would be "the consequence of the later development of the military situation." On February 16, von Papen noted that, until the summer of 1941, Turkey had feared "above all a complete victory of the Axis States and the domination of Italy over the eastern Mediterranean region." But the war against the Soviet Union had "totally modified this aspect of things," and now the fear

[14]Franz von Papen, *Memoirs* (London: Deutsch, 1952), pp. 485–89.

was that with the aid of Anglo–American forces the Soviet Union would rise again and "dictate the laws of the new order in Europe."[15]

The German Ambassador flew to Berlin again in mid-March to obtain further guarantees for Turkey from the Führer.[16] While the immediate Soviet threat to Turkey had been lessened, he thought, British pressure to bring Turkey into the war would increase as soon as there was a new German setback in North Africa. To keep Turkey independent of the United Kingdom, von Papen's idea was to supply it with arms for one or two divisions. If Hitler approved, matters could be kept in better balance and, as a matter of fact, Minister Carl Clodius visited Ankara in the summer of 1942, a new commercial agreement was signed, and a 100,000,000 RM loan was granted to Turkey. While von Papen seemed to have lost confidence in German victory, he also arranged for Turkish military missions to visit both the eastern and western fronts to see German troops in action.

On the other hand, the American ambassador, Laurence A. Steinhardt, who had moved from Moscow to Ankara, was convinced that the Turkish people would certainly fight if they were attacked. He advised Harry Hopkins in March 1942[17] that new Lend-Lease shipments had made a marked impression, while Germany had not fulfilled promises of armaments, with the result that the Turks feared the Germans and ardently hoped for an Anglo-American victory, despite all their skepticism concerning Soviet policies relative to the Turkish Straits. Steinhardt found little evidence that Germany planned to attack Turkey in the immediate future. While Germany had prepared bases in the Balkans, there were insufficient troops in Bulgaria and Greece for such an attack. The Ambassador thought the critical moment for the Turks would come "when the coming German offensive in southern Russia either stalls or goes through to the Caucasus," and the Germans would then have to decide "whether to try and go through the difficult terrain in Turkey or keep hammering at the Russians." But it was unlikely that either of these two considerations would exist before July or August 1942.[18]

[15]*GPT*, no. 18, See also H. R. Trevor-Roper (Intro.), *Hitler's Secret Conversations, 1941-1944* (New York: Farrar, Straus and Young, 1963), p. 265, for Hitler's similar views after Japan's attack on Pearl Harbor, in which he indicated that it was "enough for us to inform Turkey that we are renewing the Montreux Convention, and that we are enabling her to fortify the Straits," thus avoiding maintaining "an important fleet in the Black Sea, which is merely a frog-pond." Hitler thought the Turkish attitude toward Great Britain was "blowing cold."

[16]Von Papen, *Memoirs*, pp. 487-89; USFR (1942), 4: passim.

[17]Robert E. Sherwood, *Roosevelt and Hopkins: An Intimate History* (New York: Harper, 1948), pp. 552-53; USFR (1942), 4: 680-85.

[18]But see Count Ciano, *The Ciano Diaries, 1939-1943* (New York: Doubleday, 1946), pp. 76-77; *The von Hassell Diaries, 1938-1944. The Story of the Forces Against Hitler*

Such were the views during the early part of 1942, although the Turkish situation had changed somewhat with the new American position as an active belligerent. Near Eastern questions in general, and the problem of Turkey, in particular, figured largely in the Hitler-Mussolini conversation at Salzburg on April 29,[19] when Hitler declared that "Turkey was moving slowly but surely over to the Axis," the Turkish "hatred of the Russians" being "especially favorable" to this development. In Hitler's view, Turkey would "never be an enemy of the Axis" and, at most, "would remain neutral to the end of the war." The Führer also believed that the Turkish desire for an increase in territory would prove an influential factor. To a question of Il Duce, Hitler indicated that he had obtained, through unofficial channels, information that Turkish territorial desires centered around frontier adjustments in the neighborhood of Edirné and along the Baghdad railway, and stated that Schulenberg's telegram of November 26, 1940,[20] which had been brought to Turkish attention, had proved very enlightening to the Turkish Foreign Ministry, since it outlined Soviet ambitions in some detail, especially as to the Straits. Mussolini declared that he had advised the Turks that Italy had no designs on Turkish territory and was prepared to cede Castellorizzo, which was within Turkish waters. The matter of an Axis declaration regarding India and Arabia was then taken up, but it was agreed that this could wait, and Hitler took the position that such a declaration would only be practical "when the Axis troops stood south of the Caucasus."

The German pressure on Turkey continued as the weeks passed. There were many discussions with Ambassador H. Husrev Gerede in Berlin,[21] whom Hitler considered a very able diplomat. Constant stress was laid on the Soviet threat to Turkey, the German victories, pan-Turanism, and the American "bluff" in the war. Von Papen had his first interview with Numan Menemencioglu as foreign minister on August 26,[22] and quoted him as reflecting the Turkish interest in

Inside Germany, as Recorded by Ambassador Ulrich von Hassell, a Leader of the Movement (New York: Doubleday, 1947), p. 249.

[19] For text, see Department of State *Bulletin* 15, no. 367 (July 14, 1946): 57-64; Ciano, *The Ciano Diaries*, p. 472.

[20] See *German Documents* (D), 4: 533-49, 550-70, 714-15. When Molotov visited Washington in May 1942, President Roosevelt touched briefly on the difficulties between the Russians, on the one hand, and the Iranians and the Turks, on the other, but Molotov was not much impressed and, as Hopkins surmised, felt that the Russians "knew a good deal more about their relations with Iran and Turkey than we did" (Sherwood, *Roosevelt and Hopkins*, p. 559).

[21] *Hitler's Secret Conversations*, p. 443; *GPT*, no. 23.

[22] *GPT*, no. 26. Prime Minister Saydam died on July 8 and Saracoglu succeeded him as prime minister. Menemencioglu became foreign minister on August 13, 1942.

"the most complete defeat of Bolshevik Russia," and indicating that Turkey had never entered into any *pourparlers* with the USSR, with the exception of the declaration of March 24, 1941, under British pressure, reaffirming the friendship agreement of December 17, 1925. While von Papen was grateful for these assurances, he did not hide the German impression that Turkey had been listening altogether too much to the British and the Americans to the effect that Germany might be more dangerous in the future in the Black Sea than the Soviet Union, now seriously weakened. Menemencioglu, in any event, indicated that Turkish collaboration would be limited, to a certain extent, by the necessity of preserving neutrality.

Von Papen had a long talk the next day with the new prime minister, Şükrü Saracoglu, on the question of the Turkish-Mongol minorities and the future of the USSR.[23] According to von Papen, Saracoglu desired "passionately the destruction of Russia," which was an "exploit" of the Führer, to be accomplished only once in a century. While the Führer had assured President Inönü of a place for Turkey in the new order, as a power advance post in the southeast, the Prime Minister believed it "indispensable to preserve the absolute neutrality" of Turkey, equally in order not to compromise the position of Turkey for, in his view, the defeat of the USSR was near, and the British would be led to conclude peace. The questions of possible Turkish collaboration and Turkish interests in the administration of conquered Soviet areas would have to be the subject of confidential talks.

Meanwhile, a new trade agreement with Germany was signed on June 2, 1942, and it was announced on September 29 that Turkey had contracted to send some 45,000 tons of chrome, or approximately one-half of the annual production, to the Krupp munitions plant in exchange for German arms. Despite Anglo-American pressure, there seemed little doubt at the time as to the execution of the agreement.[24] While Great Britain and the United States had their objections to the new commercial agreement, especially as to chrome, Great Britain apparently did not want more active Turkish participation in the war until after the great British desert victory at El Alamein in October 1942. From that time on some pressure was

[23]*GPT*, no. 27. On Pan-Turanism, see Sir Olaf Caroe, *Soviet Empire: The Turks of Central Asia and Stalinism* (London: Macmillian, 1953); Charles W. Hostler, *Turkism and the Soviets* (London: Allen and Unwin, 1957); Serge A. Zenkovsky, *Pan-Turkism and Islam in Russia* (Cambridge: Harvard University Press, 1960); Ivar Spector, *The Soviet Union and the Muslim World* (Seattle: University of Washington Press, 1959).

[24]*USFR* (1942), 4: 742-88, 805-11, especially for American representations, September–December 1942, as to passage of certain Axis vessels through the Straits.

brought to bear to bring about more active participation, although there were differences between the British and American positions in this matter.[25]

On November 8 began the Anglo-American invasion of North Africa, with General Dwight D. Eisenhower in command of the American forces. Meanwhile, German forces had held the Balkan region, including Greece, firmly in their hands since the spring of 1941, and had continued their advance into the western and southwestern portions of the USSR, although the Russians not only held firm at Stalingrad but, on February 2, 1943, liberated the beleaguered city. It was during this uncertain period, with the German advance into the Caucasus and in anticipation of the fall of Stalingrad, that the anti-Soviet propaganda campaign in Turkey reached new heights. But events themselves altered the picture, and the cautious Turkish government veered gradually in the other direction.

In a conversation with Ambassador John G. Winant, General W. B. Smith, and Foreign Secretary Eden on November 9, 1942, Prime Minister Churchill indicated that he was turning to the idea of bringing Turkey into the war, with its forty-five divisions, armed and equipped by the Allies for an invasion of the Balkan peninsula, and he wanted Harry Hopkins, General Marshall, and Admiral King to return to London for further discussion of future plans.[26] Churchill, indeed, surveyed the problem on November 18, in a note to the British Chiefs of Staff, stressing that "a supreme and prolonged effort be made to bring Turkey into the war in the spring," although he expected naval forces would be fully engaged in the central Mediterranean and that only minor amphibious facilities would be available in the eastern Mediterranean. Moreover, access to Turkey could be obtained by rail through Syria, by coastal shipping, and a gradual buildup of air protection. The Dardanelles might become open to supplies for Turkey.[27] If proper means were taken, in the Churchill view, Turkey

---

[25]See *New York Times*, December 20, 1942; Knatchbull-Hugessen, *Diplomat in Peace and War*, pp. 185–88. See also *The Memoirs of Field-Marshal The Viscount Montgomery of Alamein, K.G.* (New York: Signet, 1958), chap. 8; George F. Howe, *United States Army in World War II. The Mediterranean Theater of Operations. Northwest Africa: Seizing the Initiative in the West* (Washington: Department of the Army, 1957), pp. 72 ff.; George Kirk, *The Middle East in the War, 1939–1945* (London: Oxford University Press [RIIA], 1950), pp. 455–56; Alan Moorehead, *The March to Tunis: The North African War, 1940–1943* (New York: Dell, 1968).

[26]Sherwood, *Roosevelt and Hopkins*, pp. 656–57. Churchill wrote Stalin on November 13, 1942, concerning the passage of military traffic through the Mediterranean to Turkey [*USSR. Committee on Publication of Diplomatic Correspondence with Churchill, Atlee, Roosevelt and Truman, 1941–1945* (New York: Dutton, 1958), 1: 75–76. Hereafter cited as *Stalin's Correspondence*].

[27]Churchill, *The Second World War*, 4: 697–98.

could be won, since it was an ally and would want to sit at the peace conference at the end of the war. Moreover, Turkey desired to be well armed, and its army was in good condition except for certain modern weapons. Hitherto, Turkey had been restrained from fulfilling its obligations, and an indulgent view had been taken of this situation because of British inability to help. But the situation had now changed, and with the destruction of Rommel's forces, large forces might "presently become available from Egypt and Cyrenaica." On the assumption of the Soviet Union maintaining its position in the Caucasus and holding the Caspian Sea, Churchill considered it possible "to build up a powerful British land and air force to assist the Turks," and felt the target date for the concentration should be April or May 1943. Turkey should be offered an Anglo-American–Soviet guarantee of territorial integrity and status quo, with which the Russians had agreed, followed by the dispatch of a strong Anglo-American military mission to Turkey. Through the winter, Mr. Churchill proposed equipment of Turkey from Egypt and the United States with antitank and antiaircraft guns and active construction of airfields. If operations were successful, the ultimate result would be "the opening of the Dardanelles, under heavy air protection, the passage of supplies to Russian Black Sea ports, and to any naval assistance the Russians might require in the Black Sea."[28]

Churchill advised Stalin on November 24 that Roosevelt was in substantial agreement and thought a new effort to bring Turkey into the war was in order, noting his desire to have the United States join in an Anglo-Soviet guarantee of Turkey's territorial integrity and status. He also indicated that a considerable consignment of munitions, including 200 tanks, would be going to Turkey and that by the spring he hoped to assemble a sizable force in Syria. If Turkey were to enter the conflict, the Allies could attempt to open the shipping route to the Black Sea and bomb the Rumanian oil fields. Stalin agreed on November 28, remarking that entry of Turkey in the war by the spring would be "of great importance in order to accelerate the defeat of Hitler and his accomplices."[29]

Whatever the presumed consensus between Churchill and Roosevelt, however, there was much difference of view in the United States as to the possible entry of Turkey into the war.[30] On November 25, 1942, at any rate, Roosevelt and General Marshall discussed future operations, including action in Turkey, and "it was agreed that there were many diplomatic questions involved," and

[28]Ibid., pp. 698–99; *Stalin's Correspondence*, 1: 78–79.   [29]Churchill, 4: 696.
[30]Sherwood, *Roosevelt and Hopkins*, pp. 653–59.

that Turkey was unlikely to enter until it had received "considerable armament and other munitions of war." Marshall was dubious about sending heavier weapons to Turkey. While the Turkish government was fully aware of the efforts to bring about a Turkish–Soviet rapprochement, the Turkish press was suspicious lest the United States and Great Britain concede Soviet claims relative to Turkey, and the press took Eden to task for declaring in the House of Commons on December 2 that postwar peace depended on continuing the cooperation of the Great Powers, despite the Eden disclaimer of any Great Power dictatorship.[31] When Sir Hughe Knatchbull-Hugessen visited London in December, he conferred with Churchill, Eden, and the Chiefs of Staff and explained the Turkish position. While the desirability of persuading Turkey to enter the war was assumed, in principle, there was a realization of the "many attendant problems and qualifications" which continued to engage Great Britain for months to come. Sir Hughe returned to Ankara with a message from Eden to Saracoglu, taking note of the continuity in Turkish good will and declaring that Turkey "could count on the friendly sympathy and understanding of her Allies as an important factor serving the common interests of the two countries."[32]

The Turkish Problem at Casablanca and Adana

Roosevelt and Churchill discussed the problem of Turkish entry into the war at their Casablanca meeting during January 17–27, 1943.[33] It was agreed that Churchill should "play the cards" in Turkey, both for the United Kingdom and the United States in military matters, with the result that the United States played a secondary role in Turkey, although Turkish problems occupied a "considerable corner" in American foreign policy planning. On January 20, Churchill advised Eden of his plans to fly to Cairo and urged that if Deputy Prime

[31]*Parliamentary Debates, House of Commons,* fifth series, 358, col. 1254; Kirk, *The Middle East in the War,* pp. 455–56; Arthur Bryant, *The Turn of the Tide, 1939–1943: A Study Based on the Diaries and Autobiographical Notes of Field Marshal The Viscount Alanbrooke, K.G., O.M.* (London: Collins, 1956), pp. 520–30.

[32]Knatchbull-Hugessen, *Diplomat in Peace and War,* pp. 185–86. Von Papen (*Memoirs,* p. 493), who talked with Menemencioglu on January 7, 1943, as the Stalingrad disaster approached, reported that Turkey was more than ever determined to keep out, although he felt that each new Allied success would make it more difficult for Turkey to withstand the pressure.

[33]See, especially, *USFR, Conferences at Washington, 1941–1942, and Casablanca, 1943,* pp. 487–849. For backgrounds, see Maurice Matloff . . . , *Strategic Planning for Coalition Warfare, 1943–1944* (Washington, D.C.: Department of the Army, 1959), pp. 64 ff.

Minister Attlee and Eden agreed, Eden should "make the proposal to the Turks without delay." After consultations with the war cabinet, however, Churchill was urged, on January 21, to return direct to London to give an account of the Casablanca meeting to Parliament, his colleagues being opposed to the trip on security grounds. But even "more strongly did they resist the Turkish proposal," since they were convinced "that the moment was not ripe for an approach" and did not want to court either " 'rebuff or a failure.' "[34]

The unhappy Prime Minister cabled Eden on January 21 that he thought a golden opportunity might well be lost, denied any intention to extort a pledge from Turkey, and declared that he was going only to explain how Turkey could be placed in a position of security by guarantees, substantial munitions, and reinforcements in the event of attack. After talking with Roosevelt, Churchill cabled Attlee and Eden, requesting a cabinet review and the dispatch of a cable to Ankara indicating his willingness to come "to a most secret rendezvous" with President İnönü and other Turkish leaders, and noting that he had been charged to speak both for Great Britain and the United States on equipment of the Turkish army and the general defensive security of Turkey. The war cabinet, however, maintained its position and felt that an approach at the summit would be premature. Churchill repeated his request on January 25, and on January 27 the Turkish government agreed to a meeting at Adana, which took place on January 30.[35]

On the way to Adana, Churchill prepared a "wooing letter containing an offer of a platonic marriage" both from himself and Roosevelt. He stressed Anglo-American agreement that Turkey should be closely associated with the two Western democracies not merely during the closing stages of the war, "but in the general work of rehabilitation" to follow.[36] He fully appreciated the Turkish position, but noted that the Anglo-Americans, immediately on Turkish entry, would send at least twenty-five air squadrons and special units. He also observed that the war "temperature" would rise in the summer of 1943, with possible operations in the Black Sea, and added that Stalin was "most anxious to see Turkey well armed and ready to defend herself against aggression." Both the United States and the United Kingdom, moreover, wanted Turkey as a "full partner in the

[34]*USFR* (1943), 4: 1058-60; Sherwood, *Roosevelt and Hopkins*, p. 683; Churchill, *The Second World War*, 4: 669-703; Cordell Hull, *The Memoirs of Cordell Hull* (New York: Macmillan, 1948), 2: 1365.
[35]Churchill, *The Second World War*, 4: 702-03: *Stalin's Correspondence*, 1: 88-89; Bryant, *The Turn of the Tide*, pp. 565 ff.
[36]Churchill, *The Second World War*, 4: 706-09.

Peace Conference," where all questions of changes in the status quo would have to be settled.

The purpose of the meeting on January 30 was to exchange views and impressions and to explore the possibilities of Turkey taking an active part in the war during the year, and the discussions turned largely on (1) the structure of the postwar world and (2) the arrangements for an international organization and the future of Soviet–Turkish relations.[37] While Churchill assured Turkey that the USSR would cooperate in the postwar years and concentrate on internal reconstruction, and that Communism had "already been modified," the Turkish leaders were skeptical.[38] When Saracoglu adverted to Soviet imperialism, Churchill pointed out that there would be an international organization after the war, and that if things turned out badly, "it was better that Turkey should be strong and closely associated with the United Kingdom and the United States." In the event of Soviet aggression, "the whole international organization . . . would be applied on behalf of Turkey," and Churchill "would not hesitate to say so to Stalin."

On the whole, the visit appeared to have been successful, and Churchill seemed convinced that from then on Turkish neutrality would be more "biased" in favor of the Allies, "somewhat similar to that of the Americans prior to their entry into the war."[39] On February 2, 1943, he cabled Roosevelt, now back in Washington, that the highest Turkish security in the postwar era would be found in Turkey taking its place as one of the Allies, and he surveyed the possibility of Turkey becoming an active belligerent, perhaps in Balkan operations. Before incurring additional risks, however, he felt it would be right for Turkey to seek precise guarantees. Great Britain would be glad to give these, or join in a treaty with the USSR. Churchill was certain that the President "would gladly associate himself with this treaty," which "would naturally fall within the gambit of the world organization to protect all countries from wrong-doing."[40] He advised

[37]The Churchill memorandum was given to Inönü at the first meeting on the Inönü train. Churchill was accompanied by Generals Sir Harold Alexander, Sir Henry Maitland Wilson, Sir Alan Brooke, and Sir Wilfred Lindsell, Air Marshal Drummond, Commodore Donas, and Sir Alexander Cadogan of the Foreign Office. Prime Minister Saracoglu, Foreign Minister Menemencioglu, and Marhsal Fevzi Çakmak accompanied Inönü. See Bryant, *The Turn of the Tide*, p. 570.
[38]Knatchbull-Hugessen, *Diplomat in Peace and War*, pp. 188–89. Von Papen, *Memoirs*, pp. 494–95, states that the Turks were more concerned with future Turkish–Soviet relations than with entry into the war.
[39]*USFR* (1943), 4: 1060–64, for Steinhardt's report; Bryant, *The Turn of the Tide*, p. 573; Kirk, *The Middle East in the War*, pp. 456–58.
[40]Hull, *Memoirs*, 2: 1369.

Stalin similarly of the Adana meeting, but the latter replied cooly on February 6,[41] declaring that the USSR had made many friendly gestures to Turkey and that the Turks "did not react to our steps," evidently because they were afraid "to incur the wrath of the Germans," and he was afraid of a similar reception to any new overture. But if Turkey wished "to make her relations with the USSR more friendly and intimate," the Turkish government could say so. The Soviet Union would be willing to meet Turkey half way, and Stalin did not object to Churchill's stating that he had been kept informed of the Adana meeting, although he could not "say that the information was very full." A few days later, on February 11, Churchill told the House of Commons of the meeting and declared the British wish to see Turkish territories, rights, and interests effectively preserved, and the desire to have "warm and friendly relations between Turkey and the Soviet Union."[42]

Some progress appeared to have been made, and on February 13 Menemencioglu told Ambassador Vinogradov that he wished to enter into negotiations for an improvement in Turkish–Soviet relations.[43] While events moved slowly, the Germans were somewhat concerned with what had taken place at Adana. On February 20 President Inönü confirmed that it was a matter of Turkey's own volition whether it entered actively into the war, although he stressed the "indestructible" bonds between Great Britain and Turkey. Moreover, on March 18 Saracoglu publicly referred in warm terms to the meeting with Churchill, stating that Anglo-Turkish friendship was "not only dictated by our mutual interests," but was "a necessity vital to the interests of the two countries."

Shortly after the Adana meeting, von Papen journeyed once more to Berlin, returning with an assurance that Turkey would not be attacked, and there were rumors that assurances had been given to Germany, based on the agreement of June 18, 1941, that Turkey would remain faithful to its written "engagements." Nevertheless, it appears that preference was given to the Anglo-Franco-Turkish treaty of October 19, 1939, for neither at Adana, nor later at Cairo, "never once were the terms of the German treaty quoted" to the British as "precluding action on our side."[44] Indeed, Churchill felt that

[41]Churchill, *The Second World War*, 4: 713-16; *Stalin's Correspondence*, 1: 90-91, 92-93, 386-87.

[42]*Parliamentary Debates, House of Commons*, fifth series, 386, cols. 1467-68; *Stalin's Correspondence*, 1: 96, for Churchill's note of February 17, 1943.

[43]Churchill, *The Second World War*, 4: 716; *Stalin's Correspondence*, 1: 97.

[44]Knatchbull-Hugessen, *Diplomat in Peace and War*, pp. 190-91; Von Papen, *Memoirs*, pp. 494-95; *Stalin's Correspondence*, 1: 99-102.

he could have had Turkey on the Allied side before the end of 1943, with no damage and much advantage both to Turkey and the Allied cause.[45]

The Turkish Problem at Moscow, October 19-30, 1943

The next great conference at which Turkish problems were to be discussed substantially was that at Moscow. But there were important developments, both on the battlefield and on the diplomatic chessboard in the intervening period. Germany was much concerned with the Turkish attitude, and on June 15, 1943, Turkey confirmed its friendly relations with the USSR. By the summer, new Lend-Lease material reached Turkey, although there was no indication of Turkey's active participation in the war.[46] The invasion of Italy and the downfall of Mussolini made a deep impression in Turkey, as elsewhere, as von Papen did not fail to note. There were also misunderstandings on the part of the United Kingdom as to the position of the United States regarding Turkey. Shortly after the Casablanca meeting and that at Adana, during the Eden visit to Washington in March 1943, Secretary of State Hull got the impression that the British government was interpreting the President's agreement as to Great Britain's "playing the cards" with Turkey in a military way, to signify that it would also "handle all our relations in the political and economic spheres as well." While the President had spoken in general terms, by July 1943, it was clarified that the agreement applied only in the military sphere.[47]

At the same time, Nazi Germany exerted strong pressure on Turkey during the spring and summer of 1943, and not merely through the several "peace" messages of the Führer, in which assurances were extended to Turkey. Ambassador von Papen hinted that if Turkey entered the war, or even increased its collaboration with the Allies, the German Luftwaffe would bomb Istanbul and other Turkish cities. While the Turkish press continued to stress neutrality, Saracoglu, who also reemphasized the Turkish position, continued close military collaboration with the British. Nevertheless, a group in

[45]Churchill, *The Second World War*, 4: 716, later wrote: "Now in these years after the war when we see the United States sustaining Turkey with her whole power all has been put right, except that we did not have the considerable advantages of Turkish aid and all that this implied in the Balkan situation in the early months of 1944."

[46]See *Stalin's Correspondence*, 2: 67-68, for Roosevelt's letter of June 4 on laying the groundwork for passive or active Turkish participation.

[47]See *USFR* (1943), 4: 1067-71; Hull, *Memoirs*, 2: 1367-68.

the Turkish government, perhaps headed by Menemencioglu and Field Marshal Fevsi Çakmak, opposed increased collaboration with the Allies, since the German summer campaign might be directed against Turkey and it would be "ill advised" to commit Turkey too far in the Allied direction. But even this group, it appeared, was prepared "for a radical change" in Turkey's status, provided there were more adequate preparation, equipment, and substantial guarantees for the postwar period.[48]

Churchill wrote to Roosevelt on July 26 that the collapse of Italy should fix the moment for the United Kingdom, the United States, and the Soviet Union to put "the strongest pressure on Turkey" to act in the spirit of the alliance.

Roosevelt and Churchill discussed the subject of Turkey once more at the Quebec Conference (August 17-24, 1943), when it was agreed that Turkey was to be asked to interpret the Montreux Convention strictly to keep German shipping of military value out of the Straits, to stop chrome shipments to Germany, and to improve rail communications, airfields, storage facilities, and the Turkish armed forces. On the other hand, the Turkish government was to be supplied with as much equipment as could be spared. But it is noteworthy that the President, the Prime Minister, and the Combined Chiefs of Staff decided that from the military point of view the time was "not right for Turkey to enter the war on our side." As already noted, Churchill was anxious to persuade Turkey either to come into the war or to make available to the Allies the Turkish airfields which the British had been developing. He hoped that the Allies might quickly dominate the Aegean and the Black Sea and establish a direct supply route to the USSR through the Straits. The American military advisers, however, maintained their strategy and opposed the assumption of new commitments in the Eastern Mediterranean.[49]

The Turkish government did not respond to the Churchill overtures, and its hesitance led to a severe propaganda attack upon Turkish neutrality in *War and the Working Class*, charging Turkey with failing

[48]Altemur Kiliç, *Turkey and the World* (Washington, D.C.: Public Affairs Press, 1959), pp. 103-05. See also Herbert Feis, *Churchill, Roosevelt, Stalin: The War They Waged and the Peace They Sought* (Princeton: Princeton University Press, 1957), pp. 151-53, 692.

[49]*USFR* (1943), 4: 1086-167; *USFR, Conferences at Washington and Quebec 1943*, pp. 391-1340; Hull, *Memoirs*, 2: 1368; Henry L. Stimson and McGeorge Bundy, *On Active Service in Peace and War* (New York: Harper, 1948), chap. 17; Dwight D. Eisenhower, *Crusade in Europe: A Personal Account of World War II* (New York: Doubleday, 1948), p. 194; Sherwood, *Roosevelt and Hopkins*, pp. 591, 746-47, 764-65; Churchill, *The Second World War*, 5: 133-137, 286-89. See also Matloff, *Strategic Planning*, pp. 229, 261-62; John Ehrman, *Grand Strategy* (London: HMSO, 1956), 5: 88-92. See also *USFR* (1943), 2: 332-35.

to assist Yugoslavia and Greece and signature of the Turkish–German agreement of June 18, 1941. All this was most interesting in the light of Soviet policy during the earlier stages of the war, of the policy regarding Turkey in particular, and of the fact that in the last analysis the USSR wanted no Turkish participation in the Balkan neighborhood and, in reality, demonstrated little interest in Turkey's entry into the war.

Not long after the Quebec meeting came the Italian surrender (September 3) and, during October 19–November 1, 1943, the Moscow Conference. Lord Ismay, who accompanied Eden to Moscow, noted that Churchill had foreseen that an Italian collapse would give a "wonderful chance of seizing Rhodes and the other islands in the Dodecanese." With the Aegean in Allied hands, the Prime Minister considered that Turkey "would probably come into the war," and "convoys could then be sent to Russia via the Dardanelles and the Black Sea, instead of through the hazardous Arctic Ocean."[50]

At Moscow the British Delegation set forth a twelve-point program which included "a common policy towards Turkey, a common policy in Persia."[51] Moreover, after the preliminaries on October 19, Molotov circulated a proposal "that the three Powers suggest to the Turkish Government that Turkey should immediately enter the war."[52] On October 20, the Prime Minister advised Eden to find out whether the Russians were really attracted to British action in the Aegean, getting Turkey into the war, opening the Straits into the Black Sea, and operations in the Balkans.[53] Churchill was convinced of the great significance of getting into Rhodes and the other islands and building up an effective air and naval superiority in the Aegean, but wondered whether the Russians viewed sympathetically the British effort to hold Leros and the desire to take Rhodes. He noted on October 23 that if Turkey were forced into the war, it would demand air support which could be provided only to the detriment of primary operations in Italy. If it entered on its own initiative, through non-

---

[50]Churchill, *The Second World War*, 5: 218-19, Lord Ismay, *The Memoirs of General the Lord Ismay* (London: Heinemann, 1960), p. 322. Ismay notes that the Churchill objective was similar to that which had inspired the Dardanelles campaign in 1915, but that there was much opposition in Washington and some in Whitehall. If only Alan Moorehead's *Gallipoli* (New York: Ballantine, 1956) had been available to the military planners!

[51]See *USFR* (1943), 1: 513-800, for the American documentation. Through "Operation Cicero," von Papen learned the details of the Moscow, Tehran, and Cairo meetings. See L. C. Moyzisch, *Operation Cicero* (New York: Bantam, 1952); Elyesa Bazna, *I was Cicero* (New York: Dell, 1962); von Papen, *Memoirs*, pp. 499-505; Ehrman, *Grand Strategy*, 5: 100-01.

[52]Churchill, *The Second World War*, 5: 284-85.   [53]Ibid., pp. 286-87.

belligerency, there would not be the same obligation, but a great advantage might be achieved. "The prize would be to get into the Black Sea with supplies for Russia, warships, and other forces," and Mr. Churchill did not consider such a Turkish move impossible, particularly if the Germans began to cut their losses in the Balkans.[54] Molotov had, indeed, raised the question both of Turkish and Swedish participation on October 20, and Eden not only noted the difficulties of equipment, but stated that "under present conditions Turkey, whose military preparedness is still very backward, would, as our partner in the offensive, probably be more of a liability than an asset."[55] Hull, who could add nothing to the Eden comment, preferred not to speak on military matters. On October 28 Churchill cabled Eden confirming his own view that "we should not discourage the Russian desire that Turkey and Sweden should of their own volition become belligerents or actual allies." The United Kingdom should agree in principle, "and let the difficulties manifest themselves, as they will certainly do, in the discussion of ways and means."[56]

Molotov told Hull on October 25 that the three Powers should "suggest peremptorily," in other words "command," that Turkey enter the war. Hull repeated that this was a "purely military matter" which came within the province of the President and the Chiefs of Staff. The President communicated the view of the Joint Chiefs of Staff on October 26: "It would not be deemed advisable to push Turkey at this moment into a declaration of war on the side of the Allies since the necessary compensation to the Turks in war material and war supplies including armed forces and ships would divert too much from the Italian front and the proposed OVERLORD operation. However, inquiries could be started on basis of lease by Turkey as a neutral of air bases and transportation facilities."[57] Hull communicated Roosevelt's views to the conference on October 28, when Molotov brought up the subject of Turkish entry once more. It was now agreed that the USSR, the United Kingdom, and the United States should study the problem and Stalin expressed his "disappointment" when he conferred with Eden the next evening.[58]

---

[54]Ibid., p. 289; *USFR* (1943), 1: 621-22.

[55]Ibid., pp. 583-88, for general discussion.   [56]Hull, *Memoirs*, 2: 1297.

[57]*USFR, The Conferences at Cairo and Tehran 1943*, pp. 117, 121. Molotov saw no point in supplying arms to Turkey "without getting some fighting out of her." See also ibid., pp. 43, 86, for Roosevelt's letter of October 26, 1943, expressing his hope for a talk, and Inönü's agreement (November 14, 1943).

[58]Churchill, *The Second World War*, 5: 291-94. Eden conferred twice with Hull on the problem of Turkish air bases. Molotov objected to the "mild move" concerning bases, and ultimately it was agreed that Eden "would make a request of Turkey for

On November 1, an Anglo-Soviet agreement that Eden see the
Turkish leaders on his return to London was signed.[59] While Hull was
on his way home, Roosevelt advised Churchill of his agreement that
the United States would join "in making immediate demand on
Turkey for use of air bases and later pressing Turkey to enter the
war before the end of the year," subject to the condition that no
British or American resources were to be committed to the Eastern
Mediterranean area which were necessary for OVERLORD or for
operations in Italy.[60]

The decision to invite Turkey to enter the war was "an abrupt departure" from the Anglo-American position, and the "most difficult
period" in relations with Turkey was now in the offing. Eden went
to Cairo for three days of discussion with Menemencioglu (November 4-6),[61] during which he pointed out the urgent need of air bases
in southwest Anatolia and explained the precarious British position
at Leros and Samos. He also stressed the advantages to be derived
from Turkey's entry into the war, stressing possibilities in the
Balkans, the cutting off of Turkish chrome to Germany, and the
Turkish contribution to Germany's defeat. The Turkish delegation,
however, was unmoved by these arguments, since it was fearful
of German air attacks, and Menemencioglu was upset by Eden's
"threatening tone." Indeed, the Turkish Foreign Minister contended that "to give the Allies the free use of Turkish air bases,"
almost certainly would involve Turkey in war and could not be discussed as an isolated issue. It was also distasteful to enter the war
at the eleventh hour and play the unheroic Italian role. Turkey, he
said, "must have a definite task," and there were political and military points to be clarified. In view of this position, it was decided that
Menemencioglu should return to Ankara, and that a final answer
should be given as soon as possible as to whether, in principle, Turkey

---

the immediate use of air bases, while Great Britain would join with the USSR at a
later date in requesting Turkey's entry into the war before the end of the year."
Hull, *Memoirs*, 2: 1312.

[59]*USFR, The Conferences at Tehran and Cairo 1943*, pp. 134-36.

[60]Ibid., pp. 151-55. See also Anthony Eden, Earl of Avon, *The Memoirs of Anthony
Eden, Earl of Avon. The Reckoning* (Boston: Houghton Mifflin, 1965), pp. 477, 483-
84. Eden agreed that Turkish entry was desirable, but notes that, on balance, "Turkey
as an active ally might be more of a liability than an asset"—a view shared by many
Americans—because of its unpreparedness.

[61]*USFR, The Conferences at Cairo and Tehran 1943*, pp. 161-67, 174-75, 180-82,
190-92; Churchill, *The Second World War*, 5: 334-35; Hull, *Memoirs*, 2: 1369;
Knatchbull-Hugessen, *Diplomat in Peace and War*, pp. 196-97; Ehrman, *Grand
Strategy*, 5: 102; Erkin, *Les Relations Turco-Soviétiques et la Question des Détroits*,
pp. 245-49. Lord Ismay notes that the advantages to Turkey of entry into the war
"were not so obvious" as the advantages to the British (*Memoirs*, pp. 330-31).

was ready to act. Further discussions would follow an affirmative reply. Otherwise, it seemed clear that relations with Turkey "could hardly fail to be affected by such a disappointment."

There were prolonged discussions in the Turkish cabinet as well as all-night sessions of the People's party in Ankara, and further discussions among the American, British, and Soviet leaders after the Eden-Menemencioglu meetings. It was now clear that the problem would come up at Tehran.[62] Menemencioglu advised von Papen on November 13 that Eden had requested Turkish entry into the war, but he evaded any question as to Turkish bases. The Foreign Minister told Ambassador Steinhardt that if the Turkish government could be satisfied that the Russians harbored no Balkan ambitions, the former "cordial and intimate friendship" could be restored. But Soviet officials professed to know nothing of Turkish fears, while considering that Turkish entry into the war would prove valuable. These, too, were matters which could be discussed at Tehran, along with the problem of the Straits.[63] On November 18, the American Joint Chiefs of Staff agreed that it was desirable to bring Turkey into the war, but once more declared that it would have to be done "without diversion of resources that would prejudice the success of our commitments elsewhere." It was also noted that Turkey's fear of Soviet domination in the Balkans or the Dardanelles would probably lead to Turkey's entry in order to obtain a voice in the peace.[64]

The Turkish reply of November 22 announced the decision "in principle to enter the war," but it was accompanied by an equally clear statement that action was impossible unless Turkey received adequate defense against a German attack. The government believed it should take an effective part in the war on the Allied side, but laid great stress on the inadequacies of Turkish defenses. On the whole, the reply was encouraging, and one with which the British Ambassador was in essential agreement.[65] Churchill felt that "con-

---

[62]*USFR, The Conferences at Cairo and Tehran 1943*, pp. 71, 74-75.

[63]Ibid., pp. 193-94, 199-200, 201-03.

[64]Ibid., pp. 210-16. At a meeting of the Joint Chiefs of Staff with the President on the USS *Iowa* on November 19, Admiral King pointed out "that if Turkey entered the war it would result in drawing away supplies and troops from other operations" (ibid., p. 260). Ambassador Harriman noted on November 21 that the USSR might be satisfied if Turkey came into the war "this winter" and thought pressures should be "intensified" (ibid., pp. 265-66).

[65]Ibid., pp. 374-76; Knatchbull-Hugessen, *Diplomat in Peace and War*, pp. 196-97. Ehrman, *Grand Strategy*, 5: 103, indicates that by the third week in November the Turkish government was sympathetic, but clearly "unwilling to enter the war without complete military, and possibly diplomatic, security; the Aegean was again in German hands; and the Americans had shown themselves opposed to any diversion of forces to the area."

sidering what had been happening under their eyes in the Aegean," the Turkish leaders could "hardly be blamed for their caution." In any event, arrangements had been made, late in November, for a meeting of Inönü, Roosevelt, and Churchill, together with a Soviet representative, in Cairo, following the Tehran Conference. The Turkish President was willing to come provided he were not merely to be told of decisions already reached affecting Turkey, "but was being asked to participate in a free discussion between equals."[66]

At the same time, German military estimates of the Turkish position in late 1943 are of much interest.[67] Estimates in November 1943 by the Armed Forces Operations Staff indicated that while Turkey had maintained a policy of clear neutrality, the closer the Soviet armies came to the Balkans the more difficult Turkey's position would be, although no surprise attack on the Axis was expected. Turkey's position, in the German military view, was dominated by the question of the Straits, but expansionist claims, even against Bulgaria, did not exist. Nevertheless, if Turkey did change its attitude, further possible enemy operations from the European bridgehead of Turkey and operations against the Bulgarian-Rumanian Black Sea coast would have to to be taken into account. The Germans were under the impression that Turkey was determined to remain a nonbelligerent, but was willing to make further concessions to the enemies of Germany.

The Tehran Conference, November 28–December 1, 1943

The road to the Tehran Conference was now well paved. On the way to the Iranian capital, Roosevelt and Churchill met at Cairo on November 22 and in addition to conferring with Generalissimo and Mme. Chiang-kai Shek about the Far East found time to discuss Turkish and other problems prior to their meeting with Stalin.[68] They considered Mediterranean operations on November 24. Roosevelt wondered concerning the effect of action in the Mediterranean, including the question of Turkey's entry into the war, on OVERLORD.[69] While Churchill felt that preparations for OVERLORD should move forward, he still believed that nothing was needed in

[66]Hull, *Memoirs*, 2: 1369; *USFR, The Conferences at Tehran and Cairo 1943*, pp. 43, 86, 100–01.
[67]*NCA*, pp. 949–52, 954–58.
[68]See *USFR, The Conferences at Cairo and Tehran 1943*, pp. 293–455 for records.
[69]Ibid., pp. 329–34; Churchill, *The Second World War*, 5: 328; Sherwood, *Roosevelt and Hopkins*, pp. 766–76; Matloff, *Strategic Planning*, pp. 352–56.

the Mediterranean which could be applied elsewhere, and if Rhodes were taken, "the whole Aegean could be dominated by our air forces and direct sea-contact established with Turkey." Moreover, if Turkey could be persuaded to enter the conflict, or to "strain neutrality," the Aegean could be dominated and the Rhodes operation would be unnecessary. Without taking men or equipment from the decisive battles elsewhere, the Black Sea could be dominated and a supply route to the USSR opened through the Straits.[70]

The American position became very clear at the outset of the Tehran Conference on November 28, when Roosevelt met with the Joint Chiefs of Staff.[71] While they had recommended a common policy concerning Turkey on November 26, to include the Soviet proposal to force Turkey into the war, there was to be "no diversion of forces or supplies for Turkey . . . to the prejudice of approved operations elsewhere." When Admiral King reviewed the British project for taking Rhodes, with the thought that the Turks would take all the other islands, he noted that the Allies would "have to give material, ships and supplies for opening up the Dardanelles." Roosevelt remarked that he did "not have the conscience to urge the Turks to go into the war."[72] In a preliminary review of the course of the war at the first plenary session on November 28, the President noted the possible points of operation in the Mediterranean, but stressed that "the large cross-channel operation should not be delayed by secondary operations." Stalin thought it would be helpful for Turkey to enter the war "and while with Turkish participation operations there would be useful, northern France was still the best."

Churchill also presented his views on November 28[73] and coming to the "biggest problem," namely, that of bringing Turkey into the war, he adverted to his persistent theme. But how was it to be done? Was Turkey to move into the Balkans? What would be the reactions in Southeastern Europe and what influence would be exerted on the Germans in Greece? What was the Soviet view? Would the USSR wish to go ahead, "even if it meant a delay of some two months from May 1 in launching 'OVERLORD'?" There was also the further project, as Roosevelt indicated, "of moving up to the Northern Adriatic and then northeast to the Danube," although his staff was not pleased

[70]Churchill, *The Second World War*, 5: 346
[71]*USFR, The Conferences at Cairo and Tehran 1943*, pp. 459-652.
[72]Ibid., pp. 426-27, 477-82; Omar N. Bradley, *Bradley: A Soldier's Story* (New York: Holt, 1951), p. 220.
[73]Churchill, *The Second World War*, 5: 350-53; Feis, *Churchill, Roosevelt, Stalin*, pp. 257-66; Matloff, *Strategic Planning*, pp. 352-56. Sherwood, *Roosevelt and Hopkins*, pp. 779-81, states that Churchill repeated his position as to Turkey "with a persistence that was both admirable and monotonous."

with this remark. Roosevelt, indeed, did not favor "any secondary operations which might tend to delay the cross-Channel invasion, OVERLORD," although he and Churchill had discussed possible future operations in Italy, the Adriatic and Aegean seas, and from Turkey as a base, in the event that the Turks might be induced to enter the war.

Stalin commented at length on the Churchill remarks, inquired about OVERLORD, and wondered how many divisions of Anglo-American troops would have to be allotted if Turkey entered the war. Told that some twenty air force squadrons and several antiaircraft regiments would have to be assigned to Turkey, Stalin thought it would be a mistake to divert forces to Turkey and Southern France, the "best course" being to make OVERLORD the basic operation in 1944. In any case, he did not expect Turkey to take action. Finally, Churchill inquired whether the Soviet government was "not very anxious to get Turkey into the war," and Stalin replied that he was "all in favor of trying again. . . . We ought to take them by the scruff of the neck if necessary." The President suggested that the timing of operations required careful thought, noting once more that any Mediterranean operation would probably postpone OVERLORD until June or July. While Churchill did not disagree in principle, he felt that his suggestions concerning Yugoslavia and Turkey did not conflict with the general conception, and he could not agree to sacrifice Meditterranean activities in order to keep the precise date of May 1 for OVERLORD, noting that if Turkey refused to come in, it could not be helped. Ultimately, Stalin agreed that the politico-military problem of Turkey should be discussed, and since Turkey was an ally of the United Kingdom and a friend of the United States, they should persuade Turkey to enter the war actively. When Churchill suggested that Turkey would be "mad" if it declined the Soviet invitation and lost British sympathy, Stalin declared that many people preferred to be "mad," and neutrals generally considered belligerents to be "fools." In turn, Roosevelt stated that should he meet President Inönü he would, of course, "do everything possible to persuade him to enter the war, but that if he were in the Turkish President's place he would demand such a price in planes, tanks and equipment that to grant the request would indefinitely postpone OVERLORD."[74]

[74]USFR, The Conferences at Cairo and Tehran, pp. 496, 508; Sherwood, Roosevelt and Hopkins, p. 781; Churchill, The Second World War, 5: 353–57; Matloff, Strategic Planning, pp. 356–69.

General Sir Alan Brooke substantially reiterated the Churchill position at a tripartite military staff meeting on November 29, while Marshall stressed the limitations and the importance of OVERLORD.[75] Churchill also adverted to the Turkish problem on the afternoon of November 29, when he questioned that Turkey's entry into the war would mean the diversion of more than two or three Allied divisions at the most. When he inquired what the Soviet Union would do if Bulgaria were to attack Turkey, Stalin replied that it would consider itself immediately at war with Bulgaria, if, as a result of Turkish entry, Bulgaria threatened Turkey, and he was willing so to inform the Turkish government. But he did not believe Turkey would come in and continued "that there was no difference of opinion as to the importance of helping the Partisans, but that he must say that from the Russian point of view the question of Turkey, the Partisans and even the occupation of Rome were really not important operations. He said that OVERLORD was the most important and nothing should be done to distract attention from that operation." Roosevelt was "most interested" in all these views, but repeated his opinions as to logistics, timing, and holding to the original date of OVERLORD.[76] As the discussion continued, Churchill declared that if the effort to bring Turkey into the war were unsuccessful, "that would be the end of the matter."

Churchill was ready to argue concerning the date of OVERLORD and suggested a technical military committee to discuss it, but there was no agreement as to Aegean operations when the Combined Chiefs met on the morning of November 30. When Hopkins, Eden, and Molotov met at lunch that day, however, there was much discussion of the Turkish problem, when Eden proposed a joint "summons" to Turkey, "making clear" the consequences if Turkey refused, "with all three of us backing the demand." If agreeable, an invitation could be extended to President Inönü to come to Cairo for a "summit" meeting. While Molotov favored bringing Turkey into the war immediately, he was less optimistic about it after the Eden–Menemencioglu talks in Cairo, and when Hopkins stated the Roosevelt understanding that this might delay operation OVERLORD, he stated that "Marshal Stalin would be against getting

[75]*USFR, The Conferences at Cairo and Tehran 1943*, pp. 514–28.
[76]Ibid., pp. 533–40, 540–52; Churchill, *The Second World War*, 5: 368; Sherwood, *Roosevelt and Hopkins*, p. 788. Eden, *The Reckoning*, pp. 496–97, notes that Stalin had changed his mind since the Moscow Conference in October, that the Combined Chiefs of Staff were "lukewarm," and that Stalin was now opposed to putting pressure on Turkey, although he thought "we should go on asking for air bases."

Turkey into the war now if this necessarily meant a delay in OVER-
LORD." Molotov also inquired what Churchill had meant when he
had suggested that if Turkey rejected the demands, "its post-war
rights in the Bosphorus and the Dardanelles would be affected." Eden
did not know, but supposed that "the whole basis of relationship with
Great Britain would be changed."[77]

The latter problem was somewhat clarified when Stalin and
Churchill lunched with Roosevelt on November 30.[78] Churchill declared
that such a "large land mass" as the USSR "deserved the access to
warm water ports," and that the question "would of course form part
of the peace settlement" and "could be settled agreeably as between
friends." Stalin thought the question could be raised "at the proper
time," inquired as to the regime of the Straits, and indicated that
since Great Britain no longer objected, "it would be well to relax that
regime." Churchill agreed, but questioned the advisability of doing
anything at the time, "as we were all trying to get Turkey into the
war." Stalin thought there was no "hurry," and was merely interested in discussing it "in general." Churchill saw no objection "to
this legitimate question," and hoped "to see Russian fleets, both
naval and merchant, on all the seas of the world." In a general
observation, Roosevelt declared that the Baltic should be free to
merchant vessels, with free zones in the ports, and that trustees
should be appointed for the Kiel Canal, "while the Dardanelles
ought to be free for the commerce of the world."

The Turkish problem was discussed again at the Roosevelt–
Churchill–Stalin luncheon on December 1.[79] Some consideration
was given to the proposed meeting with Inönü in Cairo and much
to the assistance to be given to Turkey if it entered the war. Churchill
reiterated his well-known position and stated that if the Turkish
President did not come to Cairo, he would see him subsequently in
Ankara "and present to him the ugly case which would result from the
failure of Turkey to accept the invitation to join in the war, and the
unappetizing picture of what help could be afforded her if she did."
On the military side, Hopkins pointed out again that the U.S. Chiefs
of Staff had not considered the detailed requirements of the Turkish
operation, the question of available landing craft, among other
things, being of crucial importance. Churchill persisted, however,

---

[77]USFR, The Conferences at Cairo and Tehran 1943, pp. 555–64; Churchill, The Second
World War, 5: 371–72; Sherwood, Roosevelt and Hopkins, p. 792.

[78]USFR, The Conferences at Cairo and Tehran 1943, pp. 565–68, 585–93.

[79]Ibid., pp. 585–93; Churchill, The Second World War, 5: 389–93; Sherwood, Roosevelt
and Hopkins, pp. 793–95. Hopkins, Eden, Clark-Kerr, and Harriman were also
present.

noting the "priceless opportunity" for Turkey to sit at the peace conference, and stressing the Soviet guarantee as to Bulgaria and the
advantages of association with the victorious Allies. Stalin thought
it possible that Turkey would not even have to fight, although bases
might be given. Eden explained that these facilities had been refused on the ground that Germany would react against Turkish
provocation, and Menemencioglu preferred to "come in by agreement," rather than be brought in indirectly as a result of such action.
Churchill considered this position largely an excuse, since the Turks
not only refused to "strain their neutrality" as to bases, but indicated
that they were "insufficiently armed" to become a belligerent. He
preferred to offer something substantial, and if it were refused,
"then they would wash their hands of Turkey, both now and at the
peace table." At this point, Molotov recalled the Churchill hint that a
Turkish rejection might adversely affect the Turkish position at the
Straits, but the Prime Minister indicated that he was far from his
cabinet, although he personally "favored a change in the regime of
the Straits if Turkey proved obdurate." Molotov had "merely meant
to indicate that the Black Sea countries were very much interested
in the regime of the Straits."[80] On the other hand, Roosevelt wanted
to see "the Dardanelles made free to the commerce of the world and
the fleets of the world, irrespective of whether Turkey entered the
war or not." In the end it was agreed that Inönü should be invited
to Cairo to meet with Churchill and Roosevelt, the Soviet Union
being represented by Vinogradov and Vyshinsky.

It was confirmed at Tehran on December 1, as foreshadowed at
Moscow, that from a military view "it was most desirable that
Turkey should come into the war on the side of the Allies before the
end of the year," and February 14, 1944 was set as the date on which
Turkey should be asked to enter the conflict as an active participant.
Moreover, note was taken of Stalin's statement that "if Turkey
found herself at war with Germany, and as a result Bulgaria declared
war on Turkey or attacked her," the USSR "would immediately be
at war with Bulgaria," a fact which "could be explicitly stated in the
forthcoming negotiations to bring Turkey into the war."[81] Churchill

[80]*USFR, The Conferences at Cairo and Tehran 1943*, p. 848. In a memorandum of
December 15, 1943, dealing with Soviet attitudes as expressed by Stalin at Tehran,
Charles E. Bohlen noted: "The Soviet Government would like to see the Montreux
Convention in regard to the Straits replaced by a regime affording freer navigation
to merchant and naval vessels both in war and peace. This question was not pursued
in any detail."

[81]Ibid., pp. 651-52. For disposition of Italian merchant and war ships, in which the
Russians were very much interested, see ibid., pp. 596-604, 622-23, 873-74, 876-77;
Churchill, *The Second World War*, 5: 392-93, 405.

was pleased that "strong efforts were to be renewed to bring Turkey into the war with all that might accompany this in the Aegean, and follow from it into the Black Sea."[82]

The Cairo Summit Conference, December 4–6, 1943

All arrangements were soon made for the gathering at Cairo, where the Turkish Delegation, headed by President İnönü, arrived on Saturday morning, December 4, for the "free and unprejudged discussion as to the best method by which Turkey could serve the common cause," on which the Turkish President had insisted.[83] The Turkish Delegation was to display a customary caution throughout the discussions, and someone remarked that the members "wore hearing devices so perfectly attuned to one another that they all went out of order at the same instant whenever mention was made of the possibility of Turkey's entering the war." But there was another side of the story. Although Churchill was "never discouraged," both Roosevelt and Hopkins were skeptical, and the American Chiefs of Staff "were actively alarmed that Turkey might come into the war and thereby, as General Marshall liked to put it, 'burn up our logistics right down the line.'"[84]

Prior to the meetings with the Turkish Delegation, the Anglo-American Combined Chiefs of Staff once more discussed the Turkish problem on December 3.[85] Sir Alan Brooke again declared that all necessary preparations were going forward in anticipation of Turkish action, and Admiral King raised a question as to requirements. The Combined Chiefs did not propose that Allied forces be concentrated in Thrace to cooperate with the Turks, who were to be "persuaded to stand on the defensive and to concentrate their forces for the protection of the Straits," while the Allies bombed Bulgaria. The opening of a supply route to the USSR through the Straits would

---

[82]Churchill, *The Second World War,* 5: 405.

[83]*USFR, The Conferences at Cairo and Tehran 1943,* pp. 662–67, 858–59; Knatchbull-Hugessen, *Diplomat in Peace and War,* pp. 197–98. İnönü evidently was authorized to go to war. Vyshinsky arrived only on December 7, when the President and Prime Minister were leaving.

[84]Sherwood, *Roosevelt and Hopkins,* pp. 799–800; Hull, *Memoirs,* 2: 1369. Robert Murphy, *Diplomat Among Warriors* (New York: Pyramid, 1965), pp. 237–38, 248, 390, 392, adds few details, but Erkin, *Les Rélations Turco-Soviétiques et la Question des Détroits,* pp. 249–70, does.

[85]*USFR, The Conferences at Cairo and Tehran 1943,* pp. 668–74, 675–83; Ehrman, *Grand Strategy,* 5: 184.

be useful, and bases would be asked for protection of convoys, and a "reasonable scale" of air defense for Turkish cities could be provided. Both Churchill and Roosevelt met with the Combined Chiefs on the morning of December 4. Churchill reiterated his position, and Roosevelt declared that nothing should be done to hinder OVERLORD or ANVIL (Southern France), adding that "we should scrape up sufficient landing craft to operate in the Eastern Mediterranean if Turkey came into the war." Eden thought the USSR would probably agree to postponing the date for Turkish action from December 31, 1943 to February 15, 1944.

When the President and Prime Minister met with Inönü on the afternoon of December 4,[86] they stressed Turkish entry into the struggle, although Churchill "would not invoke the alliance" or ask Turkey to enter "unless such action could be taken without unfair risk for Turkey." But the time had now come, and Churchill emphasized that the advantages for Turkey "would be permanent and lasting, more particularly from the point of view of Turkish relations with Russia." If the opportunity were missed, later Turkey might find itself alone, "not on the Bench, but wandering about in Court." The Soviet pledge as to Bulgaria was stressed, along with the great political consequences of Turkish action in the Balkans. Inönü, who was pleased with the invitation and "for the offer of study," reiterated Turkish fidelity to the alliance with Great Britain, but did not accept the thesis that there would be danger for Turkey in staying out of the war and noted its unpreparedness. If the Allies were prepared to meet the minimum essential requirements of Turkey, and Turkey could be useful, it would enter the war, although Inönü was convinced that "the Germans would react to the utmost of their ability." He did not believe that, thus far, preparations and supplies had been encouraging and could contemplate two things: (1) a plan of preparation involving supplies to Turkey and 2) a plan of collaboration. The Turkish President could not accept a background of suspicion "and a demand to come into the war blindly, with a statement that when Turkey had entered the war she would be told what her part was to be." At the close of the meeting, Churchill submitted a program embodying:

[86]USFR, *The Conferences at Cairo and Tehran 1943*, pp. 690–98. At dinner that evening, given by Roosevelt in honor of Inönü, Churchill did most of the talking. Later, Roosevelt told the Prime Minister that "if he, Roosevelt, were a Turk, he would require more assurance of aid than Britain had promised before abandoning neutrality and leading his nation into war" (Admiral William D. Leahy, *I Was There: The Personal Story of the Chief of Staff to Presidents Roosevelt and Truman* [New York: McGraw-Hill, 1950], p. 245).

1) A declaration after the present Conference that Turkish policy had not changed.
2) A period of approximately six weeks during which material, especially for anti-aircraft defence, would be pushed into Turkey.
3) Immediately thereafter, the placing of British and American combat squadrons on the prepared airfields.
4) German protests and Turkey's diplomatic reply, but steady continuation of reinforcements and preparation.
5) Reactions in the satellite countries—Bulgaria, Rumania and Hungary. These reactions would be very important, as they would dominate the attitude of Germany. Throughout this period Turkey would continue to send supplies including chrome (but only a little) to Germany. The Germans would be afraid to push things too far. They would be afraid of the Turkish advance towards belligerency having the effect on Bulgaria of making her change sides.[87]

The Churchill program was further discussed on the afternoon of December 5,[88] but Inönü once more insisted on "the practical side," and noted that if the Allies continued to insist on dates, "Turkey would be in the war in four or five weeks." Moreover, he regretted the Russian absence from the meetings, since it would have been "most useful" for the Russians to "realize that everybody was trying to help but that the method of fixed dates was impracticable." Roosevelt thought there was much in this and summarized the situation as being "that the Turks did not want to be caught with their pants down." The target date depended on the progress made. Finally, Inönü declared that "a general plan of preparation must be agreed among the experts" and that "both parties must play a part in reaching a decision as to what was a reasonable, practical plan." At the end, Churchill felt that the discussion "seemed to have got into a difficult circle."

Hopkins and Eden explored the problem in detail with Menemencioglu on December 5,[89] and the latter reiterated the Turkish view that the materials shipped to Turkey since the Adana meeting had been insufficient, a point which British officials contested. When General Wilson explained that the total force intended for Turkey would be 32,000, 11,600 of them air force, Menemencioglu indicated that the proposals for infiltration were acceptable in principle, but made a reservation as to precise numbers, pending consideration by the Turkish General Staff. But if the program of

[87]USFR, The Conferences at Cairo and Tehran 1943, pp. 705-11. Roosevelt and Churchill met with the Combined Chiefs of Staff on December 5, when Churchill repeated his project. Leahy declared that "as far as the United States Chiefs of Staff were concerned, they were quite right to leave the Turkish program to the British Chiefs of Staff to decide upon."
[88]Ibid., pp. 711-18.   [89]Ibid., pp. 726-33.

infiltration were accepted, Turkey would not take action leading to entry into war until sufficient supplies had been sent. In addition, Menemencioglu referred to the Soviet position relative to Bulgaria, a point which he wanted to discuss with the USSR. The Foreign Minister also indicated that "willing entry" was also the desire of the Turks, although they must, he repeated, have "a minimum of essential preparations," which, moreover was "a commitment to the Turkish people." All he asked was "comprehension" and it "lay in our hand to determine when Turkey could enter the war since this would be determined by the supply of the necessary material." But infiltration of personnel could go ahead while the discussion of supply and equipment was under way.

Inönü repeated the Turkish thesis at dinner with Roosevelt and Churchill on December 5. As Leahy observed, Churchill "pleaded, cajoled, and almost threatened the soldier President of the once powerful Ottoman Empire in an effort to commit him to taking his people into the war." Once more Churchill told him he would have to come in to have a seat at the peace-making. But "the Americans did not urge the Turks as vehemently as did the British."[90] The three leaders substantially repeated their performance on the evening of December 6.[91] Churchill repeated his plan of action, Inönü stressed the period for material preparation, and Roosevelt emphasized the cardinal point that such a period had not been envisaged, but rather a mixed period, in which Turkey would commit only neutral acts and receive equipment and material. Inönü noted that Turkey had not contemplated facing the German army alone for months, but had thought that "when the Germans declared war the Turks would be in touch with some Anglo-American forces." Neither Roosevelt nor Churchill, however, considered the possibility of German invasion as very great, although they thought there was a possibility of air attack, an eventuality for which Turkey would be prepared. Both thought the Turkish army, especially the infantry, "very good," since it had been mobilized for four years. Finally, Inönü, who was unwilling to come to a definite decision, indicated that he would be ready to reply within three or four days and would see what could be

[90]Leahy, *I Was There*, p. 214.
[91]*USFR, The Conferences at Cairo and Tehran 1943*, pp. 740–47, 811, 817. During the latter part of the evening, Hopkins slipped a handwritten note to the President saying: "Couldn't you see the President [Inönü] *alone* for five minutes to say goodbye— *and ask him to be ready to go to war February 15.*" The Combined Chiefs reported on December 6 that the Allies should "undertake such action to exploit the entry of Turkey into the war as is considered most likely to facilitate or accelerate the attainment of the overall objectives."

provided within two months. The Turkish staff would offer its observations. Inönü was "forcing himself to try to find a possible position in the Allied program." A preparatory two-month period was now offered. The Allies had the material and the transport, but he did not know how much was to be available, although the primary effort was to be concentrated on aviation material and personnel and, as he saw it, "it was contemplated that Turkey would enter the war with anti-aircraft preparation alone."

When Roosevelt left for home early on December 7, Churchill conferred for the last time with Inönü.[92] At the very outset he put the proposal that "by February 15th all measures should be taken to render possible the flying of the 20 Allied squadrons," by which time the situation might have evolved, although Churchill could not foresee enemy action between December and February 15, 1944. If Inönü, after February 15, would not receive the Allied squadrons, and wished to prolong the discussions, Churchill would have to think of other plans, the squadrons would have to be used elsewhere, the question could not be reopened with Turkey, and the Allies would be told that "our policy with Turkey had failed." To the Turks this was a repetition of previous conversations, and Inönü proposed to respond in three or four days. Churchill indicated that if the President envisaged a long program of re-equipment, this would be equivalent to saying that the "negotiations were ended." Inönü responded that the best answer Churchill could require would be simple acceptance of his proposal; or, if accepted, preparations could continue and a mutually acceptable plan be elaborated; if not, Churchill "would have the right to change his plans." Churchill thought this would mean a complete change of policy; the war would move west, and "Turkey would lose the chance of coming in and reaping the advantages which entry into the war would promise her." The alliance would cease to have any value for war purposes, although friendship would remain. Inönü thought it not impossible to find a solution, and in the end it was agreed that British experts should go to Ankara for military conversations.

So much for the Cairo discussions. Precisely what was Turkey's position? Inönü agreed "in principle" to enter the war, subject essentially to two conditions: (1) that there be a joint military plan of action; and (2) that Turkish deficiencies in equipment, supplies, and transport be made up so that Turkey could defend itself. Moreover, the Turkish leaders desired a "peep" into "the more distant

[92]Ibid., pp. 750–56.

political future." It was clear that the Turkish statesmen were much influenced by their suspicions that they were being pressed into the war as pawns on the global chessboard and that their acquiescence would be the occasion to use Turkish air and naval bases "without assigning any special role to the Turkish forces." In other words, Turkey was willing to fight only when it could be reasonably certain that it was strong enough to prevent the rapid destruction of the country or its principal centers. The strengthening would take time, but OVERLORD was now only six months away, and it was hardly possible to postpone this operation against the Germans in France.[93] The Cairo communiqué declared that the three leaders had examined the general situation, taken into account the "joint and several interests" of their countries, and indicated that "the closest unity" prevailed among them "in their attitude to the world situation," as well as with the Soviet Union.[94]

After the conference closed on December 6, Churchill told Ismay that the Turkish government would say that its policy was unchanged.[95] Preparation of the airfields would move forward and British squadrons would be ready to fly in within about six weeks. Churchill doubted that Bulgaria would attack Turkey, and he thought Turkey should continue to the last in relations with Germany and Bulgaria and should reply to any protest, while continuing preparations. Bulgaria might try to make a separate peace, and Churchill did not suggest that Turkey declare war at any stage, but continue its re-equipment "and await the enemy's actions." When the sea passage from Egypt to Turkey was cleared, every effort was to be made to get supplies into Izmir and through the Dardanelles, so that the further equipment of the Turkish Army and the feeding of Istanbul could proceed as fast as possible. On completion of the British fly-in, Churchill believed Turkey should facilitate the secret passage of six or eight submarines into the Black Sea.[96]

[93]Hull, *Memoirs*, 2: 1370; Knatchbull-Hugessen, *Diplomat in Peace and War*, pp. 198-200; Churchill, *The Second World War*, 5: 415-18. Von Papen, *Memoirs*, pp. 513-16, has a similar account of the Turkish position, but notes that the Turkish leaders were informed of the 1944 war plans, including Balkan operations, with the landing of Allied forces at Salonika. He adds that it was clear to Menemencioglu and the General Staff that the use of air bases would lead to "complete destruction" of Istanbul and Izmir, and certain by December 12 that preparations for a Salonika operation would not be complete.

[94]*USFR, The Conferences at Cairo and Tehran 1943*, pp. 831-32.

[95]Churchill, *The Second World War*, 5: 415-18.

[96]See Matloff, *Strategic Planning*, pp. 369-73; Ehrman, *Grand Strategy*, 5: 212-13, 221. When Churchill left on December 7, Inönü kissed him but Eden thought this was a poor result of fifteen hours of "hard argument" (Eden, *The Reckoning*, p. 497).

Menemencioglu told the Ankara press that the conference had been one of "the most important events in this phase of the war."[97] He was "extremely satisfied," noting that the comprehensive conversations had been "so intimate and searching" that he could say "that our relations with the United States and the Soviet Union" were "almost as cordial and strong as those with England." The problems had been studied "with a frankness which was sometimes brutal but with understanding." While Turkish policy had remained "unchanged," the delegation had left Cairo "in an atmosphere of complete cordiality."

While Churchill was grieved at the results of the conference, and the American Joint Chiefs of Staff were "sorry," they were also partly relieved because of logistical considerations.[98] The Russians were also evidently satisfied. Andrei Vyshinsky did not arrive in Cairo until December 7, but he indicated that he had not expected any Turkish commitment to enter the war by December 31 and was skeptical as to any irrevocable commitment on February 15. Steinhardt thought the Soviet government would be satisfied "if the Turks enter the war at any time in the spring as may fit in with the overall Allied plans." Moreover, he thought the Russians were permitting the British to take the lead in dealing with Turkey, subject only to the discussions concerning the Balkans and the position to be taken by the Soviet Union if Bulgaria should declare war on Turkey, aid Germany, or permit German troops to pass through Bulgaria.[99]

Near the end of 1943, Turkish cooperation with the Allies appeared at its peak, and the Allies were secretly using certain bases in the region of Izmir. Moreover, the American Office of Strategic Services and the British Intelligence Service worked actively in Turkey with the connivance of the Turkish government. Nevertheless, Turkey did not openly permit the use of airfields by the RAF when operations were launched against the Dodecanese Islands, although it did permit the shipment of supplies to the islands from the Turkish mainland. It also rendered assistance when the operations failed and Allied forces were compelled to evacuate.[100]

[97]*USFR, The Conferences at Cairo and Tehran, 1943*, pp. 838–40. Steinhardt thought the meeting had been "most helpful in drawing Turkey much closer to the Allies; although nothing definite was agreed upon for the time being" (ibid., p. 844).

[98]Feis, *Churchill, Roosevelt, Stalin*, p. 304.

[99]*USFR, The Conferences at Cairo and Tehran 1943*, pp. 858–59. Vinogradov told Selim Sarper, of the Turkish delegation, to pay no attention to the discussion as to Turkey's entry into the war, since the USSR did not consider it necessary. That evening, it was explained to Inönü that, since the Turkish principle was to do the opposite of whatever the USSR suggested, perhaps, the time had come for action.

[100]Kiliç, *Turkey and the World*, pp. 103–04. On December 27, Hitler advised a conference that "on February 15 the Allies want to put pressure on Turkey to enter the war.

Difficulties with Turkey

Von Papen conferred with Saracoglu and Menemencioglu immediately after the Cairo meeting, and he recalled both Soviet ambitions concerning Turkey and the Straits, as outlined in the Hitler-Molotov-Ribbentrop discussions of November 1940 and warned that war would follow if Turkish air and naval bases were made available to the Allies, a fact of which the Turkish leaders had long been aware.[101] Churchill considered the possibilities of a German invasion of Turkey "to be absolute rubbish."[102] He advised Roosevelt on December 18 that the commander-in-chief, Middle East, would also be in charge of Turkish operations. The British Chiefs of Staff suggested that, while negotiations with the Turks should continue, Aegean amphibious operations should be ruled out. Churchill told the President on January 4, 1944 that if discussions with Turkey developed favorably, certain Italian warships to be transferred to the USSR "would be ready to operate if desired in the Black Sea."[103]

Although not officially communicated, the Tehran decisions had become clear to Foreign Minister Menemencioglu during his November discussions with Eden. But there was little justification for the Turkish suspicion, although "a definite pact had been made, by which willy-nilly, Turkey would be in the war by January 1, 1944."[104] Meanwhile, work at the air bases was to be accelerated, a joint plan of campaign for Turkish participation was to be prepared, the political implications examined, and no blame was to attach to Turkey if the reply were negative. Even if the bases were made available, active Turkish participation was not necessarily expected. The Turkish government continued to hold that it could not rush use of the air bases unless its armed forces were equipped "beyond the possibility of disaster," and on this point progress proved impossible.

While Anglo-Turkish military staff discussions were carried on in January 1944, they broke down on February 3. At the outset, as the British government complained, the Turkish authorities considered

---

If there is a crisis in the Crimea then, it will make their propaganda for them." See Felix Gilbert, *Hitler Directs His War* (New York: Oxford University Press, 1950), p. 91.

[101]Von Papen, *Memoirs*, pp. 515–18.

[102]Churchill, *The Second World War*, 5: 422; Anthony Eden, *Freedom and Order* (Boston: Houghton Mifflin, 1948), pp. 226–39, for address of December 14, 1943.

[103]Churchill, *The Second World War*, 5: 424, 431–32, 457; Matloff, *Strategic Planning*, pp. 426–27; *Stalin's Correspondence*, 1: 186–87; 2: 115–18.

[104]Knatchbull-Hugessen, *Diplomat in Peace and War*, pp. 198–200. Nor was there any justification for the Turkish suspicion of a plan to partition the Balkans, under which Turkey would fall within the Russian sphere. On a Turkish view of difficulties, see Erkin, *Les Relations Turco-Soviétiques et la Question des Détroits*, pp. 270–85.

the United States less insistent on Turkey's entry into the war, and felt that the British alone were putting pressure on Turkey. While the British government wanted complete American support, Hull instructed Steinhardt on January 11 simply to tell the Turkish government, along with Great Britain, that the United States hoped that Turkey's decision would be "to join its forces with those of the United Nations for rapid victory." As the talks dragged on, the British felt that the Turks were deliberately demanding so much in war materials that they would remain neutral until the necessity for entry had passed. This was in line with Roosevelt's thinking! Hull advised the President of the stalemate on February 4 and proposed that the United States cooperate with the British by instructing Steinhardt to "cool off" in his relations with the Turkish government for the time being. Anglo-American arms shipments ceased early in February. The Anglo-Turkish gap could not be closed, but, as Knatchbull-Hugessen remarked, the British felt "that there was enough substance in the Turkish military point of view to justify" Turkey's "reluctance to enter the war till her genuine needs had been met."[105]

Although events now moved ineluctably toward a Turkish break with Germany, a period of difficulties ensued. There were Anglo-American discussions with Turkey as to the ways in which Turkish chrome shipments to Germany could be cut off, and at one time Roosevelt considered sending a personal message to Inönü on the problem,[106] and Turkish officials suggested bombing the Maritza bridge between Turkey and Bulgaria, over which 85 percent of the chrome reached Germany. When German negotiators reached Ankara to renew the Turkish-German commercial agreement, Ambassadors Steinhardt and Knatchbull-Hugessen, on April 14, warned that if arrangements were made to supply the Axis with strategic materials, the United States and the United Kingdom "would apply blockade measures similar to those we had applied to other neutrals during the war."[107] No doubt the Turkish government was also impressed with Anglo-American military successes and with Hull's vigorous address on April 9 regarding the neutrals.[108]

[105]USFR (1944), 5: 814–18; Hull, Memoirs, 2: 1370–71; Knatchbull-Hugessen, Diplomat in Peace and War, p. 200; Kirk, The Middle East in the War, p. 460.
[106]USFR (1944), 5: 820–36. See Stalin's Correspondence, 2: 131–32, for Roosevelt's message of March 18 to Stalin and Stalin's reply of March 20, in which he had little hope of "positive results."
[107]USFR (1944), 5: 825–31; Hull, Memoirs, 2: 1371–72. Steinhardt reported on April 14 that Menemencioglu had agreed to cut chrome shipments by 50 percent to some 4,200 tons monthly. Menemencioglu was very cooperative and von Papen protested almost daily.
[108]L. N. Goodrich and A. J. Carroll, Documents on American Foreign Relations (New York: Harpers, for the Council on Foreign Relations), 6: 25–35, for text.

On April 20 Turkey announced that chrome shipments were to stop immediately, as von Papen had been informed.[109] Menemencioglu had great difficulty in persuading the cabinet to suspend chrome shipments, which suspension became effective on April 21, causing consternation in German circles, which had no longer considered Turkey's entry into the war on the Allied side possible.[110] The step was so significant that both Steinhardt and Knatchbull-Hugessen thought a review of Anglo-American policy toward Turkey in order. They believed it advisable to seek global agreement with Turkey involving discontinuance of further shipments of all strategic materials to the Axis in return for agreement to supply Turkey with commodities essential to the maintenance of its economy. Second, both thought it desirable to be informed as to whether Turkey's active military participation in the war were envisaged or the objective were to be limited to "obtaining Turkey's full cooperation short of participation in the war." If active participation was the aim, immediate consideration should be given to preparations, since the Turkish government thought three to four months' preparation necessary. If not, but subsequent developments dictated later entry in the fall, without intervening preparations there would be an unfortunate repetition of the events of the fall of 1943. Steinhardt observed that Turkey would be prepared to participate actively if furnished the 180,000 tons of war material and the approximately 60,000 tons of gasoline previously requested and a plan of joint military operations were elaborated. If the United Kingdom and the United States were only interested in cooperation short of war, Steinhardt believed it could be obtained by advising the Turks definitely that this cooperation was the maximum desired and that "we are prepared to meet the country's essential economic requirements." Despite the obvious problems, the Department of State was in substantial agreement with Steinhardt.[111] It indicated that it would attempt to secure the views of the military authorities as to possible Turkish entry into the war, and recognized that agreement with the United Kingdom was necessary before definitive discussions with the Turkish government. It also observed that the basic bargaining position regarding Turkey was "extremely strong," since Turkey would need American supplies, and both the United States and the United Kingdom would be "on the giving rather than the receiving end."

Steinhardt and Knatchbull-Hugessen explained the situation to Menemencioglu on May 10 and protested a new Turkish–Hungarian

---

[109]Von Papen, *Memoirs*, pp. 524–25; Hull, *Memoirs*, 2: 1372.
[110]*USFR* (1944), 5: 831–34.   [111]Ibid., pp. 834–38.

agreement, only to meet the reply that the latter should not be taken "too seriously." While they wanted a complete stoppage, Menemencioglu was working for a 50 percent reduction and noted that Turkish economic life could not be entirely "strangled." The Foreign Minister was willing to consider a general agreement for (a) discontinuance of all chrome shipments to the Axis; (b) reduction of all other strategic shipments by 40 percent; and (c) agreement by the United States and the United Kingdom to furnish Turkey's essential shipments within their capacity to do so. But he had to refuse a demand for a complete cessation of all shipments involving a rupture with the Axis, a luxury which Turkey could not then afford. On May 13 the two ambassadors noted the difficulty in reconciling the Turkish–Hungarian agreement with Turkish assurances, but considered that the threat of an Anglo-American blockade would have adverse political repercussions and pointed out the Turkish willingness to enter into a general economic agreement with the United States and the United Kingdom. Time was of paramount importance they thought, (1) to make the Turks understand that the United States and Great Britain were in earnest, (2) to prevent a renewal of the Clodius and other Axis agreements, and (3) to stop the outflow of strategic commodities at the earliest possible moment. As a measure of good will, the Foreign Minister informed the two ambassadors on May 20 that he had directed Turkish authorities that exports of strategic materials to the Axis were to be reduced immediately by 55 percent.[112]

The Steinhardt proposals were approved on May 20 and he left an *aide memoire* with Menemencioglu on May 23 embodying them. The Foreign Minister considered them bases for agreement, which he was anxious speedily to conclude because of the pressure to which von Papen was subjecting him. But he had to deal with Parliament, wanted nothing in the proposals which might infringe Turkish sovereignty, and pointed out that premature publicity might cause the Germans to take action which could upset the negotiations. The Turkish government proposed a draft agreement on May 26 involving prohibition of chrome exports to the Axis, reduction in the export of other strategic materials by 50 percent, preferential orders from Allied sources, and mutual agreement as to the furnishing of supplies to Turkey. The British Embassy advised the Department of State on May 26 that as a result of the chrome decision and the generally favorable Turkish reorientation, once more the question had arisen, on the eve of operations in the West, whether the Allies

[112]Ibid., pp. 838–45.

"should not increase the threat to Germany's position in the South-east of Europe through Turkey by reestablishing military contacts with the Turks." But the United Kingdom was no longer willing "to pay any price for Turkey's entry into the war at this stage," although voluntary entry would be welcome, and it was thought that the best way to maintain the threat to Germany through Turkey was to con-centrate on the economic field until the launching of OVERLORD. The British government thought the effect on the Germans of the rupture of economic and diplomatic relations, coupled with the presence of a military mission might be "extremely satisfactory." Proceedings followed somewhat along these lines, and on June 1 the British government accepted the idea of an exchange of notes, and Steinhardt was authorized to sign, provided the Turkish govern-ment agreed to the reduction of Turkish shipments to the Axis and the Anglo-American supply of commodities.[113]

Meanwhile, the Turkish government approached the USSR on May 27, with a proposal for closer collaboration, including consulta-tion on Balkan problems, and on June 5 it was advised that the Soviet government was ready to talk if Turkey broke with Ger-many and entered the war as an evidence of its sincerity, in which event it could lay claim, both during the war and in the peace, "to a deserving place among the Allies."[114] In Ankara, Ambassador Vin-gogradov seemed relatively disinterested and considered these developments "a family affair between the British and the Turks," although he desired to be informed. But he indicated that the USSR had no direct interest in whether Turkey entered the war or not, since events had taken such a turn that a belligerent or nonbel-ligerent Turkey would affront the Soviet Union. In turn, the Turks felt that if they entered the war they would take their place among the victorious powers; but if they were subject to German invasion, they would have no alternative but to await liberation by another occupation, perhaps permanent and otherwise more terrifying. If Turkey remained aside, Anglo-Turkish harmony would be broken, Great Britain would no longer be interested, and the Soviet Union would have full freedom to discuss problems with Turkey at its leisure. Having calculated on these bases, the directors of Turkish policy evidently considered the second choice better than the first.

Despite the Turkish action as to chrome in April, Churchill told the House of Commons "bluntly" on May 24[115] that the war could be won without Turkey, that no pressures had been brought to bear, and that

[113]Ibid., pp. 845–53, 853–68.   [114]Ibid., pp. 863–65.
[115]*Parliamentary Debates, House of Commons,* fifth series, 400, cols. 762–86.

the course which Turkey had thus far taken would not "procure for the Turks the strong position which would attend their joining the Allies." However, the Prime Minister noted the suspension of chrome deliveries and looked toward the complete suspension of economic relations. Finally, he was confident that a still better day would dawn in Turkish–British relations and, indeed, "with all the great Allies." By June 10 came the Turkish decision immediately to reduce by 50 percent the export of other vital materials to the Axis and to consult with the Anglo-American representatives with a view to further reductions. By this time, however, there were other difficulties, especially in June, with respect to the passage of certain German warships through the Straits. The Foreign Office protested, and on June 14 Eden announced in the House of Commons that Great Britain "was profoundly disturbed" by the situation. Since Menemencioglu had been misled concerning the ships in question, which had passed from the Black Sea into the Aegean, he resigned on June 15, 1944.[116]

The Turkish Entry into the War

By this time, with Soviet forces pouring into Rumania in April 1944, the Balkan problem became an important subject of Allied diplomacy, in view of the question of whether the Soviet aim was liberation or the extension of Soviet power and control—a problem with which the Turkish government was much concerned.[117] The British government approached the United States on May 30 concerning approval of a possible Anglo-Soviet division of the Balkan area into spheres for military operations. Hull opposed the arrangement, but Roosevelt, on the urging of Churchill and without the

[116]*USFR* (1943), 4: 1086; (1944), 5: 859–60; *Parliamentary Debates, House of Commons,* fifth series, 400, cols. 1986–88; Harry N. Howard, *The Problem of the Turkish Straits,* Department of State Publication 2752, Near Eastern Series 5 (Washington, D.C.: USGPO, 1947), pp. 40–41, 50–68; Cemil Bilsel, "International Law in Turkey," *American Journal of International Law* 38, no. 4 (October 1944): 553–56; "The Turkish Straits in the Light of Recent Turkish–Russian Correspondence," ibid., 41, no. 4 (October 1947): 727–47; Ahmed Şükrü, "The Straits: Crux of World Politics," *Foreign Affairs* 25, no. 2 (January 1947): 290–302; von Papen, *Memoirs,* p. 527; Knatchbull-Hugessen, *Diplomat in Peace and War,* p. 201; Erkin, *Les Rélations Turco-Soviétiques et la Question des Détroits,* pp. 270–85. Von Papen told the writer, at Nurnberg in November 1945, that he was unaware of the character of these small warships and had been deceived by his own intelligence service.

[117]See Robert L. Wolff, *The Balkans in Our Time* (Cambridge: Harvard University Press, 1956), pp. 251–64; Stephen G. Xydis, *Greece and the Great Powers, 1944–1947: Prelude to the "Truman Doctrine"* (Thessaloniki: Institute for Balkan Studies, 1963), pp. 31–48, 54–59.

knowledge of the Department of State, agreed to the proposal on a temporary basis on June 12, 1944. When the Prime Minister conferred with Molotov and Stalin during October 9–16, the arrangement was further extended, with the result that the USSR was to have a basic predominance in Bulgaria, Hungary, and Rumania, and Great Britain in Greece, with the two sharing influence in Yugoslavia. Hull, never convinced of the utility of the agreement, felt that it had "an untoward effect" at the Yalta Conference in February 1945.[118]

At the same time, the United States and Great Britain worked definitely to bring about a complete break in Turkish–German relations, Operation OVERLORD having begun on June 6, with the Allied landings on the Normandy beaches.[119] On June 23 Lord Halifax urged that the time had come to press Turkey into a break with Nazi Germany, since Turkey's relations with the Allies had recently undergone "a considerable change for the better," and both the question of the Straits and the export of chrome had been settled and assurances had been given that Turkey wished "to cooperate wholeheartedly with the Allies." There was hope for making progress in relations with Turkey, and the time had come "to tell Turkey exactly what we are prepared to contribute to her equipment for the role in which we now propose to cast her." But Eden did not propose to go quite as far as the USSR, which had already told the Turkish government that it should break with Germany and declare war. Nevertheless, only by a complete break could Turkey clarify its policy and fill "the international position" to which it was entitled "both during the war and at the peace making," although Eden did not believe it desirable at the moment to invoke the alliance of October 1939. If it did become necessary, the Turkish government would be reminded that the only occasion on which the alliance had been invoked was when Italy came into the war on June 10, 1940 and, in default, it was suggested that it should at least break diplomatic

[118]See USFR (1944), 5: 112-27; Hull, Memoirs, pp. 1451-57; Eden, The Reckoning, pp. 533-36; Churchill, The Second World War, 6: 74-75, 77-79, chap. 16; Goodrich and Carroll, Documents on American Foreign Relations, 1944-1945, 7: 347-48; J. R. M. Butler, Grand Strategy (London: HMSO, 1956), pp. 104-05; Feis, Churchill, Roosevelt, Stalin, p. 291.

[119]Eden (The Reckoning, pp. 533, 534-35) advised on June 7 that the only practical policy to check Soviet influence in the Balkans was to consolidate the British position in Greece and Turkey and that "we should have to abandon our policy of trying to force Turkey into the war under the implied threat that, if she does not want to come in, we shall leave her to 'stew in her own juice' after the war. . . . Although the Soviet Government now take the line that they are not interested in whether Turkey comes into the war or not, they have probably never liked the Anglo-Turkish alliance, and the present deadlock in our relations with Turkey suits them very well."

relations. On the other hand, a request for a break might face the Allies with Turkish demands for assistance in the event of German retaliation, a point on which they could not commit themselves. They would have to try to persuade Turkey that the Germans would not and could not take violent countermeasures. At the moment, Eden preferred to avoid resuming military conversations, although he realized that the Turkish government might press for them as the price of a break with Germany.[120]

Steinhardt was authorized to support this British proposal, although Saracoglu was convinced that a mere break would be of little or no use, and that it would be easier to go to war, after first giving the Bulgarians an ultimatum to drive the Germans out of Bulgaria. As he cabled on June 23,[121] Knatchbull-Hugessen thought that, to achieve success, it would be necessary to supply Turkey with essential requirements. He also doubted that a complete rupture could be achieved without a commitment as to military assistance. Steinhardt agreed that it was desirable to advise the Turkish government as soon as possible of the Anglo-American objectives, since their attainment would require long discussions, especially as to severance of economic relations with the Axis, and the supplying of Turkey with basic requirements.

On June 30, when Knatchbull-Hugessen urged Saracoglu to break completely with Germany, the latter observed that this was a difficult and "dishonorable" action and that it could not be taken without the approval of the Party, the Grand National Assembly, and the country—an approval more difficult to obtain than that for entry into the war. To the observations that Turkey would probably still need an excessive amount of war material, that Allied plans did not envisage Turkey's active participation in the war, and that he knew of no plan for a major Balkan operation, Saracoglu replied that the British might now "fix what Turkey needed in the way of military equipment, the preparatory period and the date of her entry into the war." In Saracoglu's view, Turkey might issue an ultimatum to Bulgaria to drive the Germans out of the country and if it failed to do so Turkish forces, aided by Soviet troops, would drive them out. But Knatchbull-Hugessen was not authorized to discuss this matter, and he urged the Prime Minister to consider the request for a break, which he promised to do. Later, the British Ambassador agreed with the Prime Minister that he had not made his request under the alliance, although he had done so "with a view to ascertaining whether the

[120]*USFR* (1944), 5: 859–62; Hull, *Memoirs*, 2: 1373–76; Kirk, *The Middle East in the War*, pp. 461–64. Actually the alliance was not *formally* invoked in June 1950.
[121]*USFR* (1944), 5: 862–63.

alliance was still alive." If the Turkish government complied with the request, the British government "would thereafter treat Turkey as a full ally."[122]

Steinhardt, soon expected in Washington, was authorized to support the British effort, but this did not preclude pressure on Turkey to go further along the lines of the Soviet proposal that it enter the war, if it were "agreed that this course is militarily desirable in the light of present circumstances."[123] On July 1 he told Saracoglu that the war was progressing so rapidly toward inevitable Allied victory that this might be "Turkey's last opportunity" actively to "associate herself with the United Nations." The Prime Minister, however, had been hurt by the British policy of "sulking," since the departure of the military mission in February, and remarked that Turkey recently had doubted that "Britain really wanted Turkey to enter the war," although the Russians had spoken plainly on the matter. The Turks, a proud people, did not like being treated as "inferiors or colonials." The Russians had offered to declare war on Bulgaria if Turkey entered; the road to Yugoslavia would be opened, "and it would be for the British to decide whether they wished to cross the Adriatic into the Balkans." The Council of Ministers would consider the problem on July 3, and the Prime Minister added, without forecasting, that a negative reply to the specific request "would not mean that the Turkish government was not prepared to discuss Turk entry into the war along the lines outlined above." The American Ambassador was now convinced more than ever that Turkey was not only willing but anxious to enter the war in the near future, and that if such action were desirable it could be achieved "if account is taken in London of Turkish susceptibilities." By offering additional war material commensurate with operations to be undertaken, with delivery at an agreed time, assuring fighter protection of its principal cities, and obtaining Soviet assurances as to Bulgaria, Steinhardt thought Turkey would "undertake to enter the war as of an agreed date."

The Turkish Council of Ministers reached its decision on July 3, and Saracoglu told Steinhardt that within the next day or so the British and American governments would be informed that Turkey was "prepared to break off all relations with Germany immediately."[124] But Turkey wanted assurances—not "conditions"—that it would be treated by Great Britain as a "full Ally," receive assistance in surplus exports and such war material as Great Britain and the United States might regard as "necessary to protect the country against a surprise attack by Germany . . . and, should Turkey become

[122]Ibid., pp. 866–67.   [123]Ibid., pp. 868–70.   [124]Ibid., pp. 870–71.

involved in the war, to be furnished as much war material as may be deemed necessary by Britain and the U.S." But a complete break with Hungary, Bulgaria, and Rumania was not contemplated, although such action would be taken if and when requested. Although the British and Soviet governments had not yet been informed of the new position, Steinhardt judged that the rupture with Germany was viewed "as merely a step towards entering the war." Likewise, on July 3 Inönü wrote to Roosevelt of the "unswerving fidelity" of Turkey to its alliance, its "open solidarity with the cause of the Allies," and its determination at the proper time to give "more effective and tangible expression to this strong desire for cooperation."[125] The next day, the Prime Minister gave Robert Kelley, the American chargé, copies of the draft note which he hoped to receive from the British government and the draft Turkish reply.[126] The former provided the assurances; the latter, under the Anglo-Turkish alliance, announced the break with Nazi Germany. The Turkish government was anxious to avoid delay in taking the action desired by Great Britain and, while it desired "assurances," it was imposing no conditions for action. The British and American embassies were convinced that Turkey was sincerely desirous of giving much greater assistance than hitherto, and that it was fully prepared to break with Germany "in accordance with the desire expressed by the British Government," and with Bulgaria, Rumania, and Hungary if so requested.

But a Soviet *aide-memoire* of July 10 to Hull repeated the Soviet reservations to the British proposals concerning Turkish entry into the war, and on July 11[127] Hull authorized Ambassador Winant in London, subject to agreement by the military authorities, to inform the Foreign Office that the United States agreed in principle with the USSR, but that the Turkish government, by making the break with Germany a preliminary step toward early entry into the war, would be in a position to contribute toward hastening the victory over Germany, and there would be no question as to fulfillment of the Moscow and Tehran decisions. From the long-range view, it seemed likely "that a Turkey which has earned its seat at the peace table might be a useful friend." Unless a forthright reply along

---

[125]Ibid., pp. 872.
[126]Ibid., pp. 873–75. Turkey desired an assurance as to "the right of Turkey, devolving upon her as equal allied partner to take part in the settlement of all international questions at the time of the liquidation of the war and the edification of the peace." Knatchbull-Hugessen, however, pointed out that the United Kingdom could hardly agree to this sweeping request, and Saracoglu admitted that it could be changed appropriately.
[127]Ibid., pp. 875–79. Among other things, the Soviet *aide-memoire* summarized the Turkish–Soviet exchanges of May–June 1944.

these lines, worked out by the USSR and the United Kingdom, were made immediately, the Turkish government might be led to sever relations with Germany on its own, "thus pushing their alliance with Britain into the background and turning their eyes eastward."

With the Soviet armies now poised on the Rumanian frontier, Churchill considered it the last Turkish chance to join the Allies, and he felt that Turkey's entry at that stage would have a powerful influence on the future of Southeastern Europe. Moreover, Turkey now offered to go as far as breaking off relations with the Axis.[128] As he wrote to Stalin on July 11, Turkey was willing to break relations immediately, and he agreed that it ought to declare war, but feared that if it did so the demands for war material and equipment would be so high it would be difficult to supply. Churchill thought it wiser to "take this breaking off relations with Germany as a first installment." Turkey would then be assisted against a German vengeance air attack, and out of this might come Turkish entry into the war. Alluding to the Turkish-German alliance in World War I, Churchill thought a Turkish break with Germany now "would be a knell to the German soul," and it seemed "a pretty good time to strike such a knell." But the United Kingdom did not favor either the proposed Turkish exchange of notes or a request for immediate Turkish entry into the war. A break would involve no military commitments, and it would "produce very nearly the same moral effect on Germany and in the Balkans generally as would a declaration of war." Hull informed Leahy of the situation on July 13, requesting the views of the Joint Chiefs of Staff, and noting his inclination to accept the British view, provided both the Turkish and the Soviet governments understood that a break in relations was "only a first step towards active belligerency."[129] Hull similarly advised Averill Harriman in Moscow on July 14, and he thought the difference between the Anglo-American and the Soviet positions was "only one of method

---

[128]Ibid., pp. 879-81; Churchill, *The Second World War*, 6: 79-80; *Stalin's Correspondence*, 1: 235-37. Field Marshal Viscount Montgomery (*Memoirs*, p. 219), wrote in this period that Turkey had not reacted as hoped, but that it had not mattered overmuch, and the day might come when Turkey would regret its attitude, since the Allies were going to win.

[129]*USFR* (1944), 5: 882. According to Hull, among the advantages were: (1) Immediate high altitude flights over Turkey to the USSR; (2) immediate expulsion of some 2,000 German agents from Turkey; (3) immediate creation of a favorable attitude as to use of Turkish air bases; (4) immediate use of Turkish harbors, and (5) active Turkish cooperation in furthering the Allied war effort. Steinhardt told Leahy during July 12-13 that Turkey had made a "formal offer" to Great Britain to break with Germany and enter the war at an agreed time, but that the British government had not replied (Leahy, *I Was There*, p. 245).

and not of substance."[130] The Stalin reply to Churchill on July 15 was skeptical as to "half measures on the part of Turkey." He could see no benefit to the Allies, and thought it better to leave it in peace "and to her own free will and not to exert fresh pressure on Turkey," in which case it would have no claim "to special rights in post-war matters."[131] In the light of Soviet policy concerning Turkey, it is not difficult to speculate as to the essential reasons for Stalin's position. But, interestingly enough, when Marshall, in behalf of the American Joint Chiefs of Staff, replied to Hull's request for the military view, he stated on July 19: "From a military point of view the Joint Chiefs of Staff concur with the Secretary of State in the opinion that it is desirable that Turkey sever relations with Germany as soon as practicable. As to the proviso that such action be regarded as only a first step toward active belligerency, the Joint Chiefs of Staff concur therein, subject to the reservation that in taking this position, the United States should inform Turkey and our Allies, that the United States is not thereby committed to military, naval, or air support of any campaign in the Balkans."[132] The Joint Chiefs were also "definitely opposed to the diversion of any resources from the approved operations in Italy and the Western Mediterranean." Subject to these military reservations, Hull advised both the British and the Turkish governments on July 20 of the American position, noting American willingness to render financial and economic assistance to Turkey in the event of a break with Germany.[133]

A similar reply went to the USSR on July 22, indicating that Turkey's entry into the war was expected and that Turkey would not be considered an ally until it was at war with Germany.[134] At the same time, the British Ambassador replied to Saracoglu in the matter of a break in relations, and Kelley, the American chargé, was told on July 24 of the decision to submit the question to the Grand National Assembly on August 2. But the USSR persisted in its view that the Turkish action was both too late and unnecessary, as Harriman was

[130]*USFR* (1944), 5: 883–84.

[131]Churchill, *The Second World War*, 6: 80–81; *Stalin's Correspondence*, 1: 238–39.

[132]*USFR* (1944), 5: 884–85.

[133]Ibid., pp. 885–87; Hull, *Memoirs*, 2: 1375–76. On July 22 the British government expressed the hope that the United States would cooperate "in the immediate resumption of supplies to Turkey as soon as relations between Turkey and Germany have been broken."

[134]*USFR* (1944), 5: 885–92. The Turkish reply of July 22 took offense at British characterization of Turkish policy as "obscure" and "confusing," and noted: "The Turkish Government, conscious of having pursued a clear and clean-cut policy, and which, in spite of all vicissitudes, has never deviated from the line of its policy fixed for many years, considers itself entitled to point out the injustice of this characterization and to hope that the happier and more appropriate terms which have often been used in British documents and statements will be preferred to describe Turkey's policy."

informed on July 27. After discussing the problem with Vyshinsky on July 30, Harriman recommended postponement of any further discussion and concluded that the Soviet Union, which would share in any benefits from Turkish action without being under any obligation to Turkey, had "used the British and our action vis-à-vis Turkey without approval to free itself of its obligations assumed at Moscow to concert with us in dealing with Turkey." But he had no indication that the USSR had "any specific plans at present regarding Turkey which would give rise to difficulties between us." Meanwhile, Kelley cabled on July 26[135] that he was having difficulties with the Foreign Minister concerning the American reservation against military operations in the Balkans, and it was explained on August 7, five days after the formal break, that American military resources were already committed to major European campaigns, and the Joint Chiefs of Staff were unwilling to make additional commitments, although they were willing to consider "whether any resources would be diverted to the Balkans in the event a campaign developed there."

Turkey broke economic and diplomatic relations with Germany on August 2, 1944, a step which the United States and the United Kingdom welcomed. The United States considered it "as a step towards full cooperation with the United Nations in their struggle against Nazi aggression."[136] Churchill told the House of Commons on August 2 that he could not forget that "Turkey declared her alliance with us before the present war, when our armaments were weak and our policy pacific." "New life" had been infused into the alliance, and if Turkey were attacked Great Britain would make common cause. The Prime Minister hoped that the break would "contribute to the continuity of friendship of Turkey and Russia."[137] But the Soviet Union was very reserved in its position, and there were open statements in *Pravda* and *Izvestia*, along with continued attacks, that Turkish entry into the war would serve no useful purpose and was no longer desired.[138] While the Turkish government continued disturbed over attitudes reflected in the Anglo-American press, in a letter to Inönü on August 18, Roosevelt hailed the Turkish action "as a step toward cooperation in bringing this war . . . to a speedy and victorious conclusion."[139]

[135]Ibid., pp. 892-97.
[136]Ibid., p. 897.
[137]*Parliamentary Debates, House of Commons*, fifth series, 402, cols. 1459-87.
[138]See also the remarks of Vinogradov to Steinhardt on August 26: *USFR* (1944), 5: 898-99.
[139]Ibid., p. 898.

In the months which followed, the United States and the United Kingdom opened conversations with Turkey concerning passage of the Straits into the Black Sea for the purpose of sending supplies to the Soviet Union. By November 1944, as the Mediterranean route again was opened for Allied shipping, the eastern front moved westward, and by January 15, 1945, some 870,000 tons were shipped to the Soviet Union via the Persian Gulf and the Black Sea. Out of a total of 1,583,605 tons, 838,486 tons of American, and 547,937 tons of British shipping passed the Straits during 1945, much of it to the USSR. Meanwhile, Bulgaria surrendered on September 9, 1944 and Athens was liberated on October 14. The formal Turkish declaration of war came on February 23, 1945, following the Yalta Conference, and on February 27 Turkey signed the Declaration by the United Nations.

The Position of Turkey in the War: Some Summary Observations

At the intercontinental crossroads, it was very natural that Turkey should pursue a cautious, careful and realistic policy during World War II, as, indeed, it did. But the evidence indicates that Turkey remained a faithful nonbelligerent ally of Great Britain under the alliance of October 1939 and that its position served well the interests both of Turkey and the Allies against the Axis. Had Turkey acted prematurely, the entire Middle East might well have been thrown open to the armed forces of the Axis during the critical period of 1940–42.[140] Turkey did not become involved in the actual armed conflict, largely because there were no concerted or integrated plans for Turkish operations, no Balkan campaign was carried out on a scale to involve Turkish forces, and no supplies were diverted by the Western Powers for this purpose. Indeed, with the possible exception of the period when Italy entered the war in June 1940 and the winter of 1943–44, despite Churchill's position, the evidence would seem to indicate that neither the United Kingdom nor the United States nor even the Soviet Union actually desired Turkey's entry into the "shooting war." The British chiefs of staff and the war cabinet appeared skeptical as to the advantage of active Turkish participation, as compared with that already found in the Turkish position as a nonbelligerent ally, with neutral status, at the intercontinental crossroads.

[140]See, for example, Cevat Açikalin, "Turkey's International Relations," *International Affairs* 23, no. 4 (October 1947): 477–91; Kiliç, *Turkey and the World*, pp. 109–13.

The United States held firmly to the view that the knockout blow against Germany was to be delivered in the West and was not disposed to divert supplies to any secondary front. This is clear from the discussions at Quebec, Moscow, Tehran, and Cairo, where even Churchill indicated that he would settle for "strained neutrality" on Turkey's part. Despite all the talk and propaganda to the contrary, the Soviet government and Stalin did not appear much interested in Turkey's active participation, as noted especially at Tehran, because of (1) the priority of Operation OVERLORD, which "must come first"; (2) the Soviet objection to Turkish or other non-Soviet forces in the Balkans; (3) the Soviet desire for concessions at the Straits and elsewhere in Turkey; (4) the Soviet objection to Turkish representation at a postwar peace conference; and (5) the Soviet desire to "talk" and make propaganda out of Turkey's nonparticipation in the "shooting war." The Soviet position concerning Turkey during the period of Nazi-Soviet collaboration, when the Turkish government was given a very thinly veiled warning on October 31, 1939, because of its close association with Great Britain and France, throws Soviet policy relative to Turkey into sharp relief, indeed.[141] So also does Soviet policy relative to the Turkish Straits, set forth in the Berlin discussions of November 12-13, 1940, and now to be pressed vigorously in the period immediately following the war, during 1945-46.

[141]See Knatchbull-Hugessen, *Diplomat in Peace and War*, pp. 203-04; Kirk, *The Middle East in the War*, pp. 465-66.

Chapter VII
The Powers Debate the Question of the Straits (1945-1946)

The problem of the Straits, as already observed, had been discussed on a number of occasions during the war.[1] It had come up during the Hitler-Molotov-Ribbentrop interview in Berlin during November 12-13, 1940, when Foreign Minister Molotov expressed a desire, not only for greater freedom of passage for Soviet warships, but for something more than "paper guarantees" in this Soviet "security zone," including bases in the Straits. While the German government did not concede, it is interesting to observe the persistence of the Soviet position through all the strategic and tactical maneuvers as outlined in November 1940 and in discussions concerning the Straits, whether with the Turkish government or with other Powers. The United States knew little of the Soviet position until capture of German Foreign Office archives brought matters to light. The problem was also raised during the Churchill-Eden visit to Moscow during October 1944, although no definitive agreements were reached, and it was understood that detailed Soviet proposals would be forthcoming.

There was also some discussion of the issue in connection with arrangements for the meeting at Yalta.[2] Thus, on October 23, 1944,

[1]For background, see Harry N. Howard, *The Problem of the Turkish Straits*, Department of State Publication 2752, Near Eastern Series 5 (Washington, D.C.: USGPO, 1947), pp. 36 ff.; "Germany, the Soviet Union and Turkey during World War II," Department of State *Bulletin* 19, no. 472 (July 18, 1948): 63-78: Halford L. Hoskins, *The Middle East: Problem Area in World Politics* (New York: Macmillan, 1954), chap. 2.

[2]Department of State, *Foreign Relations of the United States, The Conferences at Malta and Yalta 1945* (Washington, D.C.: USGPO, 1955), pp. 11-12, 13, 21, 27-28, 34-37. Hereafter cited as *Yalta Papers*. On administrative arrangements for the Yalta meeting, see C. E. Olsen, "Full House at Yalta," *American Heritage* 23, no. 4 (June 1972): 20-25, 100-03.

Churchill advised Roosevelt that Stalin's doctors did not like to have him fly, and he presumed there "would be the same difficulties in Russian warships coming out of the Black Sea as of American and British warships coming in." Turkey might be willing to declare war and facilitate matters, but Churchill was "not at all sure that the Russians would welcome this at the present juncture," in view of the Soviet desire for revision of the Montreux Convention. As an alternative, Turkey could be asked "to waive the Montreux Treaty for the passage either way of said ships," and the Prime Minister expected that the Russians "would like" this, but he was not certain about the Turks. Prior to the Yalta meeting arrangements were made for the passage of the USS *Catoctin* and four mine sweepers into the Black Sea.

AMERICAN PREPARATIONS FOR YALTA

The U.S. Delegation came to the Yalta Conference well prepared for any discussion of the problem of the Straits. As Secretary Edward R. Stettinius had noted: "We had material ready for the President in case this question were raised at Yalta. We described the history of the Russian desire to have access through the Dardanelles to the Mediterranean. We favored holding a conference of the signatories to the Montreux Convention for revision of Turkish control of the Straits."[3]

But the United States hoped that the problem of the Straits would not be raised at Yalta because the Montreux Convention, in fact, had worked well, any major changes in the regime "probably would violate Turkish sovereignty and affect adversely the struggle and political balance in the Balkans and the Near East," and the Convention could be adapted to the emerging pattern of the United Nations. "By and large," it was stated, Turkey had "been a good custodian of the Straits." The United States could not, on the other hand, object if minor changes were proposed, either by the USSR or Great Britain, although such proposals should be "carefully considered by the Navy and War Departments." It was felt that no valid claim for altering the convention could be made regarding the passage of merchant ships, which were free to transit the Straits "subject to certain Turkish security provisions." In any event, all changes should be left until 1946, a regular period for possible revision, and could be made "within the framework of the Convention itself." However, it was

[3]Edward R. Stettinius, Jr., *Roosevelt and the Russians. The Yalta Conference*, ed. by Walter Johnson (New York: Doubleday, 1948), p. 44; James F. Byrnes, *Speaking Frankly* (New York: Harper, 1947), p. 39; Robert E. Sherwood, *Roosevelt and Hopkins: An Intimate History* (New York: Harper, 1948). pp. 864–65; *Yalta Papers*, pp. 328–29.

pointed out that "internationalization" of the Straits was "not a practical solution at this time because, if that is done, the Suez Canal and
the Panama Canal logically should receive the same treatment.
Turkey would resist such a proposal." If asked, the United States,
it was said, should consider sympathetically a proposal to participate
in a conference to revise the Montreux Convention.

The Turkish Problem at the Yalta Conference

The meeting of the "Big Three" at Yalta, February 4-11, 1945, was
the final summit conference before the end of World War II in
Europe, and it was, of course, to be the last for President Roosevelt.
In view of its importance during the war, and of the discussions concerning the problem at Casablanca, Quebec, Moscow, Tehran, and
Cairo, it was perfectly natural and, indeed, inevitable that there
should be discussion of the Turkish problem in general and of the
regime of the Straits in particular at Yalta. Churchill, Roosevelt,
and Stalin were gathered, after all, to discuss the great problem
of the war and those which would arise, once *Winged Victory* had
perched on the standards of the armed forces of the United Nations.
Turkey had not yet formally entered the war, although it was to do so
on February 23, 1945, but it had broken diplomatic and economic
relations with Germany and Japan, and it signed the United Nations
Declaration on February 27, 1945, shortly after the Yalta Conference.
Moreover, supplies had been going through the Turkish Straits to the
USSR since mid-January 1945. But there was still some question
as to the position of Turkey in the United Nations, soon to be organized at San Francisco.

TURKEY AND THE STRAITS
Eden and Stettinius talked about the problem of the Straits on
board HMS *Sirius* in Grand Harbor, Malta, on February 1, 1945.
After discussion of the Iranian problem, Stettinius observed that
Roosevelt "had in mind the question of Russian interests in a warm
water port," and inquired whether the British government had any
indication as to what the USSR wanted. Eden stated that "the Russians certainly wished to revise the Montreux Convention. We had
told them that they should put their ideas on paper. We had no clear
indication of what they had in mind, but it might be that they would
wish for a regime of the Straits similar to that of the Suez Canal
which would enable their warships to pass from the Black Sea into
the Mediterranean in time of war." Eden continued that "the Rus-

sians would be wanting a good many things, that we had not very much to offer them, but that we required a good deal from them," and he felt that "we ought to arrange to put together all the things we wanted against what we had to give."[4]

Stalin raised the more general problem of Turkey on February 8, when he inquired as to the criteria to be applied in the admission of states at the United Nations Conference on International Organization, soon to convene at San Francisco. The Soviet leader felt that there were states which had really waged war and had suffered, while others had wavered and speculated "on being on the winning side." Roosevelt remarked that only those associated nations which had declared war should be invited to the conference and suggested that the time limit should be March 1, a program which Churchill supported. He noted, however, that Egypt, although not formally at war, had wished to enter on two occasions and had been advised by the British government not to do so because it was more useful and convenient to have Egypt as a nonbelligerent in order to prevent Cairo from being bombed. While he did not include Eire among the possible candidates, he did "refer to a new one that would not be greeted with universal approbation, namely Turkey. Turkey, however, had made an alliance with Great Britain at a very difficult time, but after the war had been in progress she had discovered she would not be up-to-date for modern war. Her attitude had been friendly and helpful, although she had not taken on the chance provided them a year ago to enter the war." Stalin, thereupon, indicated that if Turkey declared war before the end of February, he agreed to her being invited to the conference, and the Prime Minister expressed his gratification. Roosevelt, of course, was in agreement.[5]

But the essential discussion of the problem of the Straits did not take place until February 10, when it was raised by Stalin, the day before the conference was to end. After a discussion of the problems of Poland, French participation in the Control Commission for Germany, Yugoslavia, the United Nations, and the question of German reparations, Stalin said that he would like "to say a few words about the Montreux Convention regarding the Dardanelles," which he regarded as "outmoded." Among other things, he remarked that Japan had played "a big part in the treaty, even greater than that of

[4]Ibid., pp. 498–506.
[5]Yalta Papers, pp. 771–82. Cf. also with Hiss note (ibid., pp. 782–85) in which Churchill is cited as having said that an invitation to Turkey would "cause universal satisfaction." See also Stettinius, Roosevelt and the Russians, pp. 201–22; Byrnes, Speaking Frankly, p. 39. At the same time the Soviet Union desired independent membership in the United Nations for the Ukraine and Byelorussia, and perhaps for one of the Baltic states.

the Soviet Union, and that the Convention was linked with the now defunct League of Nations. Speciously, he argued: "Under the Montreux Convention the Turks have the right to close the Straits not only in time of war but if they feel that there is a threat of war. He said that the treaty was made at a time when the relations between Great Britain and the Soviet Union were not perfect, but he did not think now that Great Britain would wish to strangle Russia with the help of the Japanese. The treaty needed revision." Stalin thought there would be no objection to revision of the Montreux Convention, although he did not know the manner in which it should be revised and did not wish to prejudge any decisions. But he felt that Soviet interests "should be considered," since it was "impossible to accept a situation in which Turkey had a hand on Russia's throat." Stalin added, however, "that it should be done in such a manner as not to harm the legitimate interests of Turkey." It was a question which an appropriate conference could consider, and Stalin thought that the three foreign ministers, who were to meet periodically every two or three months, might well consider it at their first meeting and report to their respective governments.[6] Roosevelt only commented on the fact that there were no armaments along the United States frontier with Canada. More to the point, Churchill recalled that Stalin had brought up the Straits problem during their meeting in Moscow in October 1944. Churchill had been sympathetic with revision of the Montreux Convention and had suggested that the Soviet government send a note on the subject. None had yet been received. Churchill thought the proposed method "wise," and the British government "certainly felt that the present position of Russia" with its "great interests in the Black Sea should not be dependent on the narrow exit." If the matter were brought up at the meeting of the foreign ministers, "he hoped the Russians would make their proposals known." In the meantime, it would be well to inform the Turks "that the matter of revision of the Montreux Convention would be under consideration." This was especially true if the Allies desired the Turks to come into the war. Eden, in turn, reminded Churchill that he had mentioned the matter of the Straits to the Turkish Ambassador in London and had said that it might be advisable to give the Turks

[6]*Yalta Papers*, pp. 897–906, 906–18; Stettinius, *Roosevelt and the Russians*, pp. 267–69. Despite Stalin's strictures against the Montreux Convention, it is curious to recall that the Soviet diplomatic history, published in 1945, declared that "despite certain faults in this Convention, its adoption had a great positive importance and constituted a great victory of Soviet diplomacy." See V. Potemkin, *Istoria Diplomatii* (3 vols.; Moscow, 1941–45). The French translation is Vladimir Potemkine, *Histoire de la Diplomatie* (3 vols.; Paris: Imprimerie de Medicis, 1946–47), 3: 586.

at the same time some assurances that their independence and integrity would be guaranteed.

Stalin, however, considered it impossible "to keep anything secret from the Turks," although such an assurance should be given. He wondered whether the problem could not be discussed when the foreign ministers met in the United States at the end of the United Nations Conference. But Churchill thought the matter affected the British position in the Mediterranean more than that of the United States and that the proper place for such a discussion would be in London, if the foreign ministers held a meeting there. He added that during 1915 "he had tried very hard to get through the Dardanelles and then the Russian Government had made available an armed force to help but it did not succeed." Stalin indicated that Churchill "had been in too much of a hurry in withdrawing his troops since the Germans and Turks were on the verge of surrender." By that time, however, as Churchill explained, he was not in office, and was not responsible for the decision.

THE YALTA DECISION ON THE STRAITS

There was no further substantive discussion of the Straits problem at Yalta, although brief reference was made at a meeting of the foreign ministers at the final session on February 11, in connection with the preparation of the communiqué and protocol, when Stettinius, as an alternative regarding the statement on the Montreux Convention, wanted to add that the Soviet Union would put forward proposals for revisions. In the end the protocol simply stated: "It was agreed that at the next meeting of the three Foreign Secretaries to be held in London, they should consider proposals which it was understood the Soviet Government would put forward in relation to the Montreux Convention and report to their Governments. The Turkish Government should be informed at the appropriate moment."[7]

While this was the substance of the discussion of the Straits problem at Yalta, it may be well to note Leahy's remark that "the real crux of this problem did not come out into the open at Yalta," and that Churchill was undoubtedly apprehensive.[8] In the weeks to come the full import of the Soviet demands became evident when on March

---

[7]*Yalta Papers*, pp. 931–33, 940, 982.

[8]Admiral William D. Leahy, *I Was There: The Personal Story of the Chief of Staff to Presidents Roosevelt and Truman* (New York: McGraw-Hill, 1950), p. 307. Charles E. Bohlen, counselor in the Department of State, who was at Yalta, denied before the Senate Foreign Relations Committee on March 2, 1953, that the United States had once asked the Turkish government to grant concessions to the USSR in the Straits. To the contrary, Bohlen stated that the United States had, of course, backed up Turkey in the rejection of Soviet demands (*New York Times*, March 3, 1953).

19, the USSR denounced the Turkish-Soviet agreement of 1925, which had been renewed as late as March 24, 1941. This step was followed on June 7, 1945 with Soviet demands to Turkey for bases in the Straits, a new regime of the Straits providing for joint Turkish-Soviet defense of the area, and cession of the Kars-Ardahan area in Eastern Anatolia as a price for Turkey's consent to becoming a Soviet satellite on the Polish model. Moreover, another chapter in the problem was to open with the discussions at the Potsdam Conference in July 1945.

The Yalta-Potsdam Interlude

The war was now clearly drawing to a victorious close and, as already noted, on February 23, 1945 Turkey formally entered with a declaration against Germany and Japan and adhered to the United Nations Declaration on February 27, after the end of the Yalta Conference. It was, therefore, to be represented at the United Nations Conference on International Organization in San Francisco (April 25–June 26, 1945). But immediately after the Yalta Conference the Soviet government engaged in a bitter press and propaganda campaign against Turkey, especially after the denunciation of the Turkish-Soviet nonaggression agreement of December 17, 1925, which was due to expire on November 7, 1945.

THE SOVIET ACTION AGAINST TURKEY

Molotov called in the Turkish Ambassador, Selim Sarper, who was soon to depart for Ankara on leave and consultation, and informed him on March 19 that the Turkish-Soviet nonaggression agreement of 1925 was no longer in accord with the requirements of the new situation created by the war and needed serious improvement. But beyond this denunciation of the treaty there was no substantive or detailed discussion of a new treaty at the time. The Turkish government was naturally much "concerned" at this development, and a polite reply expressed the Turkish desire to maintain and strengthen the ties of friendship and good neighborliness between the USSR and Turkey and declared that it accepted the proposition of replacing the denounced agreement with a new one better adapted to the mutual interests of the two countries. Turkey was ready to examine with care the suggestions which might be made by the Soviet government.

When Sarper returned to Ankara, immediately thereafter, the problem was discussed with the Turkish government, and Sarper held a number of conversations with Ambassador Vinogradov, in which he indicated the Turkish desire for another treaty of friendship, not unlike the one which had just been denounced. The Soviet Ambassador agreed that the two neighboring countries should have some kind of treaty relationship, but suggested that the matter should be discussed with Molotov and the Foreign Ministry in Moscow, a proposal which the Turkish government considered dangerous. Otherwise, Vinogradov was very evasive. Ambassador Feridun Erkin, soon to become secretary general of the Turkish Foreign Ministry, also discussed the problem with Vinogradov on a number of occasions, and the latter repeated the necessity of presenting proposals in Moscow. Erkin was also advised that the atmosphere could be improved if the alleged Turkish press campaign against the USSR could be ended and if the distinguished Turkish journalist Huseyin Cahit Yalçin could be silenced. But he did not enter into any details concerning Soviet-Turkish relations. As Foreign Minister Hasan Saka told Steinhardt on March 31, the USSR desired to make it clear to the United Kingdom that Turkish-Soviet relations fell within the framework of regional understandings, regardless of the Anglo-Turkish alliance; to serve notice to the world that the USSR regarded "the future regime of the Straits as exclusively the concern of the Black Sea powers"; to notify the British government that the USSR wanted "bilateral discussions with the Turkish Government in respect of future Turkish-Soviet relations including the regime of the Straits"; and to attempt to force bilateral discussions on the Turkish government and face the United Kingdom with a *fait accompli*. In turn, Saka advised Steinhardt that, while it had expected the denunciation, and the Turkish government was prepared to discuss revision of the Montreux Convention, it would not be intimidated. On April 4 the Turkish government stated its readiness to examine any proposals for a new treaty "better adapted to the present interests of the two countries."[9]

Meanwhile, Soviet-American relations were deteriorating seriously, and by April 2, ten days before his death, Roosevelt had sent a strong message to Stalin deploring the situation, which had centered in the Polish problem, noting that the war ties were "in grave danger of dissolution."[10] The general situation was discussed when Molotov came through Washington on April 22, on his way to the San Fran-

[9]See, especially, Feridun Cemal Erkin, *Les Relations Turco-Soviétiques et la Question des Détroits* (Ankara: Basnur Matbaasi, 1968), pp. 286–92; Department of State, *The Foreign Relations of the United States 1945* (Washington, D.C.: USGPO), 8: 1218–32, hereafter cited as *USFR*.

[10]See, especially, Walter Millis, editor, *The Forrestal Diaries* (New York: Viking, 1951), pp. 38–39; George Kirk, *The Middle East in the War 1939–1945* (London: Oxford University Press [RIIA], 1950), p. 465.

cisco Conference, to see the new President Truman. During a discussion as to Poland the next day, the conversation with Truman developed "most unsatisfactorily." Secretary Forrestal thought the Polish problem not an isolated case, "but was one of a pattern of unilateral action on the part of Russia, that they had taken similar positions vis-à-vis Bulgaria, Rumania, Turkey, and Greece," and he thought "we might as well meet the issue now as later on." The President was seeing Molotov within the hour and proposed "to put it to him quite bluntly" that the San Francisco conference would go on regardless of Soviet attendance and also to raise the question of whether Stalin intended to depart from the expressions of cooperation at Yalta.[11]

There was little discussion of the Turkish problem at the San Francisco conference, although Foreign Minister Saka talked with Molotov, who indicated that he had not had time to study the Turkish dossier and suggested that he make known the Turkish proposals for the conclusion of a new Turkish–Soviet agreement. All this signified to the Turkish government that the time had not yet come for any negotiations, although Sarper evidently reported the impression that events had taken a somewhat favorable turn which could "only presage a happy development in the future relations between Turkey and the Soviet Union." Meanwhile, Sarper carried on some conversations with Vinogradov in Ankara and the discussions "were pushed to the exploration of the possibilities of an alliance," although there was a basic question as to the object of such a treaty. All this was quite obscure and uncertain, and both parties were more interested in sounding out their respective dispositions than in entering into new formal discussions at the moment.[12]

Sarper discussed the problem of a new Turkish–Soviet treaty of friendship and nonaggression with Molotov on June 7, 1945, shortly after his return from Ankara. He suggested, among other things, that under a new treaty Turkey would be willing to seek some formula under which the USSR could consider itself "secure" in the Black Sea, but there was no question of an alliance. Sarper, however,

[11]Ibid., pp. 49–50. See also Harry S. Truman, *Memoirs. Year of Decisions* (New York: Doubleday, 1955), 1: 74–76, 79–82. Truman cites Molotov as remarking that he had "never been talked to like that in my life," to which the President rejoined: "Carry out your agreements and you won't get talked to like that."

[12]Erkin, *Les Rélations Turco-Soviétiques et la Question des Détroits*, chap. 8. See also the general remarks of Saka on May 1, 1945, at the San Francisco Conference (Department of State, *The United Nations Conference on International Organization. San Francisco, California. Selected Documents* [Washington, D.C.: USGPO, 1946], pp. 359–62; *USFR* [1945], 8: 1231–33; *USFR, Conference of Berlin [Potsdam], 1945*, 1: 1020–22. Hereafter cited as *Potsdam Conference*.)

was informed that as a price for the new arrangement, certain important concessions would have to be made. In the first place, the frontier between Turkey and the USSR, delimited in the Treaty of Kars (October 13, 1921), would have to be revised, with the Kars-Ardahan district retroceded to the Soviet Union.[13] Second, the Soviet Union would require bases in the Turkish Straits, at least in time of war. Third, it would have to have an agreement as to the principles relative to revision of the Montreux Convention, looking toward "joint" control and defense of the Straits and establishing a kind of Turkish–Soviet condominium in the Straits. Molotov then indicated that the type of treaty relationship which he had in mind for Turkey was that which the USSR had been establishing with Communist Poland and the other Soviet satellites. All this, of course, represented a reversion to and elaboration of the very propositions which Molotov had presented to Hitler and Ribbentrop in November 1940. Sarper made it very clear that the Turkish republic not only would not cede bases in the Straits or give up its territory, but had no interest at all in becoming a Soviet satellite. The conversation was substantially repeated on June 18, when Sarper, on instructions, reemphasized the Turkish rejection of the Soviet demands.[14]

DEVELOPMENT OF THE AMERICAN POSITION

The British Ambassador in Ankara was informed of the Soviet overture on June 13, and he thoroughly agreed with the Turkish position. But he indicated that the Turks were rather nervous and wondered what was likely to happen next. A few days later, on June 18, John Balfour, the British chargé, called on Acting Secretary of State Joseph C. Grew to discuss the situation, observing that the United Kingdom proposed to support Turkey, more particularly since the Molotov position appeared "to be in direct conflict with statements made by Marshal Stalin at Yalta." It was also surprising that

[13]For text see United Kingdom, Foreign Office, British and Foreign State Papers (1924), 120: 906-13. See also Treaty of Moscow, March 16, 1921, in ibid. (1923), 118: 990-96; J. C. Hurewitz, Diplomacy in the Near and Middle East (Princeton, N.J.: D. Van Nostrand, 1956), 2: 95-97. When Erkin became secretary of the Turkish Foreign Ministry immediately after the San Francisco Conference, he considered the desire to settle within a short period the "almost insoluble complex of the Turco-Soviet conflict" as a "dangerous and unrealizable dream." Erkin contends that the Kars-Ardahan region, which had come under Russian control in 1878 and had been retroceded to Turkey under the Treaty of Kars in 1921, had been Turkish territory, essentially, since the thirteenth century. He traces the Soviet position on the Straits basically to 1913-17 and could have gone back to the Russo-Ottoman treaties of 1798, 1805, and 1833. See Erkin, Les Rélations Turco-Soviétiques et la Question des Détroits, pp. 297-309.

[14]Sarper, with no special instructions, took his position on his own responsibility on June 7, but was instructed on June 18. See Potsdam Conference, 1: 1024-26; Feridun Cemal Erkin, "The Straits Question," Aylik Ansiklopedi, no. 24 (May 1946).

the Soviet Foreign Minister should have taken this action at the very
time when the United Kingdom and the United States were still
awaiting the Soviet views concerning the Straits promised at Yalta.
If Turkey had no objection to such procedure, Balfour hoped the United
States would agree to a joint Anglo–American approach along the
lines of a British *aide-memoire* presented to Grew, prior to the Potsdam Conference. Without committing himself, Grew promised immediate attention to the suggestion, stating that it would be prefer-
able to withhold action until the end of the San Francisco conference.
Balfour agreed concerning the wisdom of delay and hoped that if
the United States could not make a joint approach, it would at least
support the British action with some step of its own. Two days later,
on June 20, Ambassador Wilson in Ankara suggested that the United
States "express an interest in this matter at Moscow for the reason
that the Russian proposals to Turkey are wholly incompatible with the
spirit and principles on which we are seeking with the participation
of the Soviet Union to set up a new world organization."[15]

Since the Sarper–Molotov conversation of June 7 had taken place
in a "friendly atmosphere and was of an exploratory character," and
amounted to a "preliminary exchange of views," it was considered
that a protest to Moscow would not only be "premature," but might
create an "unfortunate background" for the prospective talks regarding the Straits among the heads of government at Potsdam. The
United States did not wish to reach a decision prior to the Potsdam
meeting and thought the best tactics would be to treat the Sarper–
Molotov conversation as one which did not call for "special attention"
for the time being. Meanwhile, the Turkish government, which had
asked for the views of the United States, was to be advsied of the hope
that future conversations would be conducted in accordance with the
principles of "the International Security Organization" to which
the United States was committed and would continue in a friendly
atmosphere.[16]

Toward the end of June the Department of State developed a more
comprehensive position concerning the problem of the Straits,
largely in connection with the preparations for the meeting at Potsdam.[17] The principles set forth indicate that the United States was
prepared to go far in meeting the Soviet position, prior to 1948, and

[15]Joseph C. Grew, *Turbulent Era: A Diplomatic Record of Forty Years, 1904-1945*
(Boston: Houghton Mifflin, 1952), 2: 1469–70; *Potsdam Conference*, 1: 1017–20,
1022–23. See also Millis, *Forrestal Diaries*, p. 71; Kirk *The Middle East in the War*,
pp. 21 ff.

[16]*Potsdam Conference*, 1: 1027–28.

[17]Ibid., pp. 1010–16, for Briefing Papers of June 24, 27, 30, 1945. Any change in (6)
as to fortifications or bases in the Straits was to be considered by the Navy and War
Departments.

its position during this period somewhat alarmed the Turkish government. The primary American interests, it was stressed, lay in (1) freedom of commerce and (2) a regime of the Straits which would appear most effectively to promote the cause of peace in accordance with the principles of the emerging United Nations. There was no justification, it was felt, for the USSR to propose changes in the Montreux Convention at Potsdam, since it had proved generally satisfactory. Moreover, any changes without Turkish consent would violate Turkey's sovereignty and might adversely affect its strategic and political position. It was also pointed out that there were adequate provisions in the convention for revision, and that it could as easily be adapted to the United Nations Charter as it had been fitted originally within the Covenant of the League of Nations. But there could be no valid claim for alteration of the provisions concerning freedom of commercial passage in the Straits. On the other hand, the United States, it was thought, might not object to minor changes proposed by the USSR, "the Great Power primarily at interest," concerning the transit and navigation of warships and their right of sojourn in the Black Sea, since there appeared to be some validity to the Soviet view that the Montreux Convention insufficiently recognized the special importance of the Straits to the Black Sea Powers. For example, the United States, it was suggested, would not oppose a revision which would make it possible that:

1. In time of peace the Straits would be open to commercial vessels of all nations.
2. In time of peace the Straits would be open for ingress and egress of war vessels of Black Sea riparian powers.
3. In time of peace there should be certain restrictions upon the aggregate strength in the Black Sea at any one time of the war vessels of non-riparian Black Sea powers.
4. During a war in which one or more of the Black Sea riparian powers is involved, no war ships of any non-riparian power shall be admitted into the Black Sea without the consent of the riparian power or powers at war, unless they are moving under the direction of the United Nations Organization.
5. During time of war, regardless of whether one or more of the Black Sea Powers is involved, the war vessels of the Black Sea riparian powers shall have free ingress and egress through the Straits in the absence of contrary directions of the United Nations Organization.
6. The American Government would have no objection to the establishment by the Soviet Union of fortifications on the Dardanelles, or to the maintenance by the Soviet Union of bases in the Dardanelles, provided these fortifications and bases are established with the free consent of Turkey.

By the end of June there was mounting evidence that Soviet ambitions went far beyond the Straits or other demands which were being made on Turkey. Saracoglu told Wilson on July 2 of his disappointment with American views concerning the Molotov-Sarper conversations. He simply could not comprehend the expressed hope for mutual Turkish-Soviet understanding, or believe that the United States desired that Turkey carry on further conversations relative to the cession of Turkish bases and territory, although he was consoled with the American confidence that neither party would act contrary to the principles of the United Nations. The Prime Minister, who considered that passage through the Straits was of more interest to the maritime powers than to Turkey, pointed toward the Soviet ambitions for world conquest, expressed his concern for Turkish security, and made it clear that Turkey would "not accept Soviet domination" and would fight to maintain its independence and sovereignty. The situation could be saved if the United States and the United Kingdom stood firm at Potsdam.[18]

This was also the burden of the Turkish position when Ambassador Huseyin Ragip Baydur called on Grew on July 7 to discuss the problem and to ascertain the American attitude concerning the situation. Grew told the Ambassador that the United States was "very definitely concerned with any threat to the peace which might fall within the purview of the United Nations organization," but he understood that for the present, "the conversations had been a friendly exchange of views and that no concrete threats had been made." Baydur asked Grew "whether, if the Soviet Government should demand that we cede to the Soviet Union the cities of Boston and San Francisco, we would not consider such a demand as a threat, and he also asked whether we felt that such a demand could be a matter for negotiation." Grew responded definitely in the negative, but wondered whether the Soviet demands were "yet of such a concrete nature as to be regarded as open threats." Baydur indicated that Molotov had stated that the Treaty of Kars had been negotiated while the USSR was weak, adding: "Now we are strong." Baydur declared categorically that "Turkey would not cede one inch of territory and that if Soviet Russia should appropriate such Turkish territory Turkey would immediately fight. A situation would thus be created which was totally contrary to the spirit and letter of all that had been achieved at San Francisco." He went on to say that strong representations by the United States in advance of possible difficulties would have "a powerful effect on the Soviet Government." Grew indicated that the United States had been following the problem with concern and hoped that the subject would be discussed at Potsdam,

[18]Ibid., 1: 1027–33.

President Truman having been fully informed as to the subject. As a friend both of the Soviet Union and of Turkey, the United States would "naturally be glad to be of assistance in arriving at a peaceful solution of the problem." Baydur understood this position perfectly, but he repeated "with all possible emphasis that Turkey would cede no territory and was prepared to fight if necessary." While Grew was sympathetic with the Turkish position, "no commitment of any kind was made or implied."[19]

The British government thought it better that the USSR be informed of its views before the Potsdam Conference, and on July 7 addressed a note to Moscow on the subject. While the United States had already expressed its views in Ankara, when he passed through London on his way home from San Francisco, Saka conferred with Ambassador Winant on July 12 concerning Turkish–Soviet relations, expressing "grave apprehensions" concerning Soviet intentions. Turkey, he said, admitted that a revision of the Turkish–Soviet nonaggression agreement was in order, but it had been surprised at the Soviet position regarding the Straits, territorial cessions, and a "political reorientation" of Turkey. He repeated that Turkey could not discuss either territorial cessions or bases in the Straits. To the Soviet position that the USSR could not leave its defense to a weak country, the Turkish government had replied that the United Nations was designed to meet such a situation. It was also stressed that the Montreux Convention was an international agreement and could only be changed through international negotiations. Saka also repeated that while Molotov's approach, initially, had been vague, it was obvious that the USSR intended to bring Turkey into the sphere of immediate Soviet influence, and the position of Poland had been used as an illustration of what was expected of Turkey. In the view both of Saka and Ambassador to the United Kingdom Cevat Açikalan the matter resolved itself into a question of "the political, economic and social integrity of Turkey," and Turkey would have no recourse "but to resist to the utmost of its ability." But world peace was really at stake in the issue, and the Turkish government looked to its ally, Great Britain, and its friend, the United States, for support. The Turkish Foreign Minister wanted no discussion of the problem of the Straits at Potsdam without an opportunity for the Turkish voice to be heard.[20]

[19]Grew, *Turbulent Era*, 2: 1470-73; *Potsdam Conference*, 1: 1044-46. Grew similarly advised Balfour, the British chargé, as to the American position, immediately after conferring with Baydur. See ibid., pp. 1046-48.

[20]Ibid., pp. 1050-51.

Two days later, Assistant Secretary of State James C. Dunn advised Permanent Under Secretary Sir Alexander Cadogan in London that the United States was pleased with the British message to Moscow, but explained that since the United States was not a signatory of the Montreux Convention and the Turkish government had not approached it, the United States had sent no similar message. Cadogan correctly assumed that in seeking passage for warships through the Straits in wartime, the primary Soviet objection was to the right of Turkey to close the Straits under the condition of "threat of war" (Article 21). He also inquired whether the bases the Soviet government was expected to demand should be placed under the United Nations.[21]

Although all the details were not clear, the basic Soviet position concerning the passage of warships through the Straits and bases in the region of the Straits was well known by this time. The United Kingdom, in principle, was not opposed to a revision of the Montreux Convention, but it did want to specify that the question of bases in the Straits was not a matter merely for Turkish–Soviet settlement. On the other hand, George V. Allen, deputy director of the Office of Near Eastern and African Affairs in the Department of State, as he observed on July 15, considered the Soviet proposal concerning passage of Soviet warships through the Straits in time of war as "fully understandable," but felt that it should apply to all Black Sea riparian powers. He also thought that it would be wise, in any revision of the Montreux Convention, to enable the Security Council of the United Nations "to restrict the passage, in either direction, of the warships of a state branded as an aggressor."[22] Allen proposed concurrence with the British position, with the addition of two provisions: (1) that the right of passage of warships be extended to all Black Sea riparian powers and (2) that a provision be included to envisage action under the direction of the Security Council.[23] Similarly, the War Department was not opposed to changes in the Montreux Convention, provided the United Kingdom agreed, although it recommended that the United States try to limit and postpone the

---

[21]Ibid., p. 1052.

[22]Ibid., pp. 1053–54. See, especially, Article 19 of the Montreux Convention for a somewhat comparable provision.

[23]Allen felt that because of bilateral arrangements for United States bases in Brazil, Ecuador, and Portugal, for example, it would be awkward to interpose objection to a genuinely friendly Turkish–Soviet arrangement concerning bases. But the United States should insist that the negotiations be "genuinely friendly" and that the USSR, in all frankness, might be advised that Turkey would be justified in referring the matter to the United Nations, which should, "take cognizance of the question in view of the important bearing of the Straits on international security."

discussion of the Straits and, in any event, insist that the final decision be delayed until the general settlement. But if the United States
were compelled to reach a settlement at Potsdam, the War Department was prepared to agree with the Department of State's position
and supported demilitarization of the Straits. Failing the latter, it
was thought that the United States "should oppose any proposals
granting a nation, other than Turkey, bases or other rights for direct
or indirect military control of the Straits."[24]

The Potsdam Conference, July 17–August 2, 1945

THE DISCUSSION AT POTSDAM

While the Turkish problem was not discussed at San Francisco, it
did enter into the deliberations at Potsdam much more than at Yalta.[25]
President Truman told Admiral Leahy on the eve of the conference
that "he considered free and equal rights of all nations to transport
on the waterways of Europe—the Rhine, Danube, Dardanelles, and
the Kiel Canal—would be advantageous if not essential to the
preservation of peace in Europe" and he decided to make such a proposal to the conference.[26] At the end of the first session at the Potsdam
Conference on July 17, Truman records his awareness that Stalin
"wanted the Black Sea straits for Russia, as had all the czars before
him," while Churchill "was determined that Britain should keep and
even strengthen her control of the Mediterranean." On July 21 it
was understood that the British delegation wanted to raise the question "of Soviet desires concerning the modification of the Montreux
Convention" and other aspects of Soviet-Turkish relations.

Churchill, who had discussed the problem in Moscow during
October 1944 and had agreed concerning the need to modify the
Montreux Convention, raised the question of the Turkish Straits at

---

[24]*Potsdam Conference*, 2: 1420–22, 1425–26. In a memorandum of July 19, Allen
agreed with the latter point, but noted that proposals for "demilitarization" or "neutralization" would not find favor in Turkey, while Turkish fortifications would be in the
Anglo-American interest.

[25]For general discussion, see Herbert Feis, *Between Peace and War: The Potsdam
Conference* (Princeton, N.J.: Princeton University Press, 1960).

[26]Leahy, *I Was There*, p. 392. The idea was not new to Truman. In his view, the
problem "was to help unify Europe by linking up the breadbasket with the industrial
centers through a free flow of trade." The Rhine and the Danube could be linked with
a canal network and provide a passage between the North Sea and the Black and
Mediterranean Seas. In addition, he thought, " it would be possible to extend the
free waterways of the world by linking the Rhine-Danube waterways with the Black
Sea Straits and making the Suez, Kiel, and Panama canals free waterways for merchant ships." See Truman, *Memoirs*, 1: 236.

the session on July 22.[27] The British government, he said, favored revision of the convention, but that could be achieved only through agreement among the signatories, with the exception of Japan. The Prime Minister had also "frequently expressed his readiness to welcome an arrangement for the free movement of Russian ships, naval or merchant, through the Black Sea and back," and therefore opened the discussion on the basis of "a friendly agreement." But he also wanted to impress on Stalin "the importance of not alarming Turkey," which had, in fact, been alarmed by strong concentrations of Bulgarian and Soviet troops in Bulgaria, by continuous Soviet press and radio attacks, and by the turn which the Molotov-Sarper discussion had taken, both in regard to the Kars–Ardahan area and the problem of the Straits. These developments had led to Turkish fears, although Churchill had understood that they were not "demands on Turkey," which had asked "for an alliance," only to be told of the Soviet conditions for such an arrangement. Mr. Churchill understood that if the Turkish government had asked for an "offensive and defensive alliance," this would be the occasion for the Soviet government to set forth its conditions.[28]

In reply, Molotov, who had indicated that the matter had been discussed in Ankara and in conversations with Sarper, both at the end of May and during two conversations early in June, declared that Turkey had taken the initiative in proposing an alliance, to which the Soviet government had had no objection. But he confirmed that the USSR had laid down two prior conditions: (1) retrocession of territory ceded to Turkey under the Treaty of March 16, 1921, and (2) preparation of a new regime of the Straits which would give adequate guarantees to the Soviet Union. If Turkey were not ready to settle both questions, the Soviet Union was prepared to make an agreement on the Straits exclusively between the Black Sea Powers. At this point the Soviet Delegation circulated a memorandum concerning the Straits which called for the abrogation of the Montreux Convention, through the "proper procedure," since it no longer corresponded "to the present conditions." The memorandum went on

[27]*Potsdam Conference*, 2: 256–59 (Thompson), 265–69 (Cohen). For accounts of these aspects on July 22 see, especially, Truman, *Memoirs* 1: 375; Leahy, *I Was There*, pp. 408 ff.; Byrnes, *Speaking Frankly*, chap. 4. For convenient texts of pertinent provisions of the Russo-Ottoman treaties of 1798, 1805, and 1833, see Howard, *The Problem of the Turkish Straits*, pp. 14–15. Strangely enough, Churchill makes no reference to the Turkish problem at the Potsdam Conference in his *Second World War*, vol. 6 (Boston: Houghton Mifflin, 1948).

[28]See Erkin, *Les Rélations Turco-Soviétiques et al Question des Détroits*, pp. 312–17. While Turkey had wanted some kind of substitute for the agreement of December 17, 1925, which the USSR had denounced, there is no evidence, of course, that it had wanted or proposed an alliance with the USSR.

to state that "the determination of the regime of the Straits—the only sea passage from and to the Black Sea," should "fall within the province of Turkey and the Soviet Union as the states chiefly concerned and capable of ensuring the freedom of commercial navigation and the security in the Black Sea Straits." Moreover, in addition to the establishment of Soviet military bases in the Straits, the memorandum stipulated that, in the "interests of their own security and maintenance of peace in the area of the Black Sea," Turkey and the USSR should prevent use of the Straits by other countries for purposes "inimical to the Black Sea powers."

Churchill considered this an important document which went far beyond the conversations which he and Eden had had with Stalin in October 1944, although Molotov explained that a Turkish–Soviet alliance had not been under consideration at that time. The Prime Minister inquired as to the meaning of "proper regular procedure," and repeated that different questions were raised in the paper, including those of bases and the proposal that the Straits be regulated solely by the USSR and Turkey. He was certain that "Turkey would never agree to the proposal that was being made." When Molotov pointed out that there had been similar treaties between the Ottoman Empire and Russia in the past (1798, 1805, and 1833), Churchill inquired whether he meant the question of a Russian base in the Straits, only to meet the Molotov reply that there had been treaties (1921, 1922) which provided for the settlement of the Straits question between the USSR and Turkey. In the end, the Prime Minister indicated that since he was unfamiliar with "these ancient treaties," he would have to ask his staff to look them up, and added that the British government was not prepared to ask the Turkish government to accept the Soviet proposals. In turn, Molotov indicated that the USSR had intended to bring up the matter at the June meeting of the foreign ministers if it had taken place. But the Prime Minister repeated that he stood by his agreement of October 1944 concerning revision of the Montreux Convention. He felt quite free, however, "with regard to these new proposals," and Stalin agreed.

Churchill adverted to the problem again on July 23, although he indicated that he had already concluded his remarks on the previous day when he had stated that he could not consent to the establishment of a Russian base in the Straits and that he did not think that Turkey would agree to that proposal. Stalin denied that there had been any threat to Turkey. As to rectification of the Turkish–Soviet frontier, Stalin had in mind, he said, not restoration of the pre-1914 frontiers, but the area of Kars and Ardahan. But even this question, he speciously remarked, would not have been brought up if Turkey had not raised the question of an alliance, since an alliance meant defense of frontiers, and there was some dissatisfaction in the USSR concerning these frontiers. Stalin then proceeded to talk about the Montreux Convention which, he argued, had been decided against the Soviet Union, which considered it "inimical." Stalin then reiterated the thesis sounded at Yalta, that the Soviet Union had been placed on the same footing as Japan, and he wondered how the British and the Americans would feel if a similar regime prevailed at Suez or Panama. The point at issue, he contended, was to give Soviet shipping the possibility to pass to and from the Black Sea freely and, since Turkey was too weak to provide effective guarantees, the Soviet Union wanted to see the Straits effectively defended.[29] When the Prime Minister appeared to misunderstand, Stalin reiterated that force was necessary for the defense of the Suez and Panama canals and declared that if the Turks rejected the idea of Soviet naval bases in the Straits, other bases should be provided where, in cooperation with its Allies, the Soviet fleet could protect the Straits.

THE TRUMAN PROPOSALS

At this point Truman explained that the United States favored revision of the Montreux Convention, but thought the Straits should be guaranteed by all. He had been convinced by historical study that many of the wars during the past 200 years had been concerned with waterways. One way of preventing them was to arrange for free passage of commerce through the Straits on a basis similar to that which prevailed on American waters. The President presented a paper outlining his views for free and unrestricted navigation of "inland waterways" under international guarantees. Very briefly, the President proposed "that there be free and unrestricted navigation of such inland waterways as border on two or more states and that the regulation of such navigation be provided by international authorities representative of all nations directly interested in navigation on the waterways concerned."[30] As an initial step, it was

[29]But see *supra*, chap. 5; Howard, *The Problem of the Turkish Straits*, pp. 1–2. Byrnes has stated (*Speaking Frankly*, p. 77): "The Soviets wanted the free navigation of the Straits guaranteed by the Soviets, or by the Soviets and Turkey. This meant their armed forces would be on Turkey's soil. We wanted the free navigation of the Straits guaranteed by the United Nations."

[30]*Potsdam Conference*, 2: 301–05, 654; Truman, *Memoirs*, 1: 377–78. Leahy (*I Was There*, p. 409) noted: "Truman's purpose was to remove one of the persistent sources of irritation in Europe and the Near East. I felt it was a wonderful idea. However, the conference turned it down. It had no effect on the Dardanelles discussion as the Soviets had no thought of giving free passage to everybody in the Straits and said so. Nor did the British take much interest in the American proposal." According to Erkin, the

suggested that interim navigation agencies for the Danube and the Rhine be established as soon as possible, and that membership include the United States, the United Kingdom, the USSR, France, and "the sovereign riparian states recognized by these Governments." But, on the other hand, President Truman believed that the question of territorial concessions was one for Turkey and the Soviet Union to settle themselves, while the question of the Straits concerned the United States and the entire·world. Churchill supported the desire for a revision of the Montreux Convention, with the object of giving security to the USSR, and he agreed with President Truman both concerning free and unrestricted navigation of the Straits under international guarantees and free navigation of the Kiel Canal and the Rhine and Danube rivers. Churchill believed that a guarantee by the Great Powers would be effective and he hoped that Stalin would consider it as an alternative to the Soviet desire for bases in the Straits. Stalin, however, was reserved and felt he would have to "study" the President's suggestions.

The problem was discussed once more on July 24, along with the American suggestions concerning "inland waterways," embodying the principle of freedom of navigation under international authorities, with membership in the control authorities to include the United States, the United Kingdom, the USSR, France, and the riparian states. Stalin did not want to consider the Straits within this broad context, as suggested by Truman, and expressed his fear that no agreement could be reached on the Straits in view of the wide divergence on the subject. Churchill, on the other hand, thought it had been agreed that freedom of navigation in the Straits should be guaranteed by the Big Three and other powers and considered the fact that the United States had offered to participate remarkable and important, and he hoped that the guarantee would be more than a substitute for fortification of the Straits. Molotov inquired whether similar principles applied to the Suez Canal and wondered if internationalization were a good rule for the Straits, why it could not be applied to the Suez Canal. Despite Churchill's assurances that it had worked well for seventy years, Molotov doubted that the Egyptians were as happy with the regime of the Suez Canal as was the British government. As the discussion continued, the Prime Minister repeated that freedom of the Straits could be guaranteed interna-

---

Turkish government had misgivings concerning the American position at Potsdam and the "internationalization of the Straits and other waterways." While the Truman formula was "ambiguous and therefore unsatisfactory," pure and simple rejection might risk isolating Turkey in the face of the Soviet Union (Erkin, *Les Rélations Turco-Soviétiques et la Question des Détroits*, pp. 312–14).

tionally without detriment to Turkey, but agreed that the discussion be postponed, hoping that the Truman proposal would not be underestimated by his Soviet colleagues. Truman, who did not want another world war in twenty-five years over the Straits or the Danube, then clarified his position by stating that by an international guarantee of freedom of the Straits, he meant that any nation should have free ingress for all purposes, and did not contemplate any fortification of any kind.

In the end, Churchill once more agreed that the USSR should not have to ask Turkey concerning passage of the Straits, while Stalin indicated that the question should be postponed, since it was not yet ready for discussion. It was also agreed that there would have to be discussions with the Turkish government, which was increasingly disturbed about the problem, and a subcommittee worked toward an agreed statement concerning the issue of waterways, British and American drafts being ready on July 25.[31] A British draft, for example, proposed that the Montreux Convention be revised and that the principle of free and unrestricted navigation of the Straits by warships and merchant vessels, in peace and war, be affirmed and guaranteed by the Three Powers. An American proposal of July 25 was similar, although the U.S. Delegation seriously questioned Soviet agreement, in that it affirmed the principle of free and unrestricted navigation of "inland waterways" such as the Kiel Canal, the Turkish Straits, and others, and provided that the Three Powers would support the policy of freedom in any revision of the Montreux Convention.

THE POTSDAM PROTOCOL

When the problem of inland waterways again came before the conference on July 31, Truman reiterated his intense interest in the subject, although he realized that there were serious complications. Stalin indicated that the question had been postponed, and Truman suggested reference to the Council of Foreign Ministers, a proposal to which Prime Minister Clement Attlee, who had now succeeded Churchill, and Stalin agreed. The Council of Foreign Ministers, in fact, considered the issue briefly on August 1. But, in view of Stalin's objection, the question of the Straits, despite the discussions—or because of them—was not mentioned in the final communiqué of the Potsdam Conference.[32]

---

[31]*Potsdam Conference*, 2: 393, 527, 1435-40. The Turkish government was especially concerned about proposals as to demilitarization and neutralization. See also Truman, *Memoirs*, 1: 384-86.

[32]*Potsdam Conference*, 2: 577, 606, 1476-98. Stalin wanted no mention of the problem in view of the lack of agreement, whatever his other reasons, and thought the best

In the end, the problem of the Straits was not noted and the United States did not make public officially the full protocol of the conference, including Section XVI on the Straits, until March 24, 1947, although the Soviet government published its version in its note to Turkey on August 7, 1946, and Foreign Secretary Ernest Bevin gave the Anglo-American text in an address to the House of Commons on October 23, 1946.[33] According to the Anglo-American version: "The Three Governments recognized that the Convention regarding the Straits, concluded at Montreux, should be revised, as failing to meet present-day conditions. . . . It was agreed that as the next step the matter should be the subject of direct conversations between each of the three Governments and the Turkish Government." But, according to the Soviet version, the three governments agreed that "as the proper course," the problem of revision of the Montreux Convention "would be the subject of direct negotiations between each of the three powers and the Turkish Government." It is evident at once that the important differences between the two versions lay in the phrases "the next step" and "direct conversations" in the Anglo-American and "proper course" and "direct negotiations" in the Soviet text. The United States, Great Britain, and Turkey, in the period which followed the Potsdam Conference, looked upon the phrase "direct conversations" as tantamount to an exchange of views prior to the calling of an international conference for revision of the Montreux Convention, not as "direct negotiations" leading to a bilateral agreement concerning the Straits between the USSR and the Turkish republic.

The Development of the American Position, August–November 1945

Discussion of the problem of the Straits continued during the months which followed the Potsdam Conference. In a report of August 9,

way to handle the matter was simply to state that there were no secret agreements. Truman wrote to Herbert Elliston in November 1955 that he had gone to Potsdam "hoping we could open some of these bottlenecks for commerce, among them the Rhine–Danube waterways through to the Black Sea Straits and the Black Sea. I presented the matter to the conference, but the Russians were not interested. They wanted to control the Danube and the Straits themselves. It is a matter of record, however, that the proposal was made to open the Kiel Canal, the Rhine-Danube, the Black Sea Straits, the Suez Canal and the Panama Canal for the free commercial use of all nations. Sometime or other it may be possible to do it." See *The Washington Post*, November 20, 1955; Truman, *Memoirs*, 1: 409 ff.

[33]For various texts see Department of State Press Release No. 238, March 24, 1947; United Kingdom, *Parliamentary Debates, House of Commons*, fifth series, 427, cols. 1500-02; Howard, *The Problem of the Turkish Straits*, pp. 47 ff.; Raymond Dennett and Robert K. Turner, *Documents on American Foreign Relations, 1945-1946*, (New York: Harper, for the Council on Foreign Relations), 8: 936.

Truman summed up the position which he had taken at the Conference, as follows:

One of the persistent causes of wars in Europe in the last two centuries has been the selfish control of the waterways in Europe. I mean the Danube, the Black Sea Straits, the Rhine, the Kiel Canal, and all the inland waterways of Europe which border on two or more states.

The United States proposed at Berlin that there be free and unrestricted navigation of these inland waterways. We think this is important to the future peace and security of the world. We proposed that regulations for such navigation be provided by international authorities.

The function of the agencies would be to develop the use of the waterways and assure equal treatment on them for all nations. Membership on the agencies would include the United States, Great Britain, the Soviet Union, and France, plus those States which border on the waterways.[34]

Foreign Secretary Bevin also referred to the Potsdam Conference in his remarks to the House of Commons on August 20, noting that there were, of course, "many serious matters left over" and still to be considered: "The internationalization of the waterways of Europe, the question of the Straits, the position of Turkey—all these matters will become the subject of very careful study during the coming weeks. . . . One of the most vital areas affecting the British Empire and Commonwealth, as indeed it affects the peace of the world, is the Mediterranean and the Middle East."[35]

Meanwhile, the Turkish government was obliged to determine its future attitude toward the USSR and, on the one hand, it had to calculate coldly the possible reactions of a power "resolved to obtain complete satisfaction of its demands" and, on the other, "to meet the wishes and gestures of goodwill" of the United States and the United Kingdom, "whose aid and assistance were indispensable to it." While the Truman formula at Potsdam was unsatisfactory, pure and simple rejection of it might risk isolating Turkey in the face of the USSR. Having weighed with care all these considerations and fully appreciating the high value and great importance of American assistance in the guarantee of freedom of passage and in the maintenance of peace in the region of the Straits, on August 25 the Turkish government made known both in Washington and in London its decision that it could agree to the suggested formula only on the condition that it would not infringe the sovereignty and the security of

[34]Department of State, *The Axis in Defeat. A Collection of Documents on American Policy Towards Germany and Japan*, Publication 2423 (Washington, D.C.: USGPO, 1945), pp. 20-21. The Potsdam Protocol on the Straits was sent to Ankara on August 9 (*USFR* [1945], 8: 1236-37).

[35]*Parliamentary Debates, House of Commons*, fifth series, 413, cols. 287-89.

Turkey and that the settlement thus envisaged would carry with it a détente in Turkish–Soviet relations.[36] As had been proposed at Potsdam, discussions were, of course, carried on with the Turkish government. On September 19, Secretary of the Navy Forrestal, who feared that the signs of the times were ominous of "disorder and destruction" in the new world, indicated that the Turkish Foreign Ministry "felt that either the 'Soviets, like Hitler, have become drunk and are embarking on world domination,' or else they were staking out huge claims all over the world in order to make good those in which they were really interested— among which Turkey probably had a top priority. To the Turks the future seemed dark, but, they said, 'we would rather die on Turkish soil than be deported to Siberia.'"[37] Ambassador Wilson, in Ankara, considered the Soviet position relative to the Straits a mere façade. What the USSR really wanted was to convert Turkey into a Soviet satellite, control the Straits, kill the Anglo–Turkish alliance, and end "western liberal influence" not only in Turkey but in the Middle East as a whole. In Moscow, George Kennan knew of nothing which would warrant the hope that any concessions would satisfy the USSR, since its aim was the establishment of a "friendly" regime in Turkey.[38]

SOVIET AMBITIONS IN THE MEDITERRANEAN

That there was some justification, both for Turkish fears and Forrestal's disquietude, to put it mildly, was strongly in evidence when the Council of Foreign Ministers convened in London in September 1945, and particularly when, on September 13, discussion began on the Italian treaty, when Molotov staked out a claim, in line with the position of Stalin in Potsdam, for an individual Soviet trusteeship over Tripolitania.[39] Bevin complained that Great Britain had recognized the interest of the Soviet Union in Eastern Europe

[36]For discussions with the British and Turkish governments during this period see *USFR* (1945), 8: 1236–45. By September 3, the United States was ready to submit its draft proposals to Turkey and the United Kingdom embodying (1) opening of Straits to commerce at all times; (2) opening to Black Sea warships at all times; (3) closure to non-Black Sea warships except with consent of Black Sea Powers; (4) Minor changes to bring the convention down to date.

[37]Millis, *Forrestal Diaries*, p. 97; Erkin *Les Rélations Turco-Soviétiques et la Question des Détroits*, chap. 8; Altemur Kiliç, *Turkey and the World* (Washington, D.C.: Public Affairs Press, 1959), pp. 122 ff.

[38]*USFR* (1945), 8: 1248–49, 1251. Wilson believed that the development of air power since World War I had fundamentally altered the question of the Straits.

[39]See especially *USFR* (1945), 2: 112 ff., 630, 632, 675; Byrnes, *Speaking Frankly*, chap. 5, especially, pp. 95–96, 97, 99; Department of State, *United States and Italy, 1936-1946. Documentary Record* (Washington, D.C.: USGPO, 1946), passim. See

and had supported Soviet claims, but "he expressed his surprise that
Russia did not recognize a similar interest on the part of his country
in the Mediterranean." When Molotov presented the Soviet position, he was "precise and specific" concerning Tripolitania, and
declared that "the Soviet Union had a sea outlet on the north . . . ,
and in view of its vast territory should have one also in the south,"
especially so since it now had the right to use Dairen and Port Arthur
in the Far East. But he went on: "The Soviet Union should take the
place that is due it. . . . and therefore should have bases in the Mediterranean for its merchant fleet. We do not propose to introduce the
Soviet system into this territory apart from the democratic order that
is desired by the people. This will not be done along the lines that
have been used in Greece."

The Soviet Foreign Minister professed surprise at Anglo-American
opposition to the Soviet request for Tripolitania, one result of which,
of course, was failure at the time to reach any agreement concerning
the Dodecanese Islands, although there was no question as to the
ethnic composition of the population. Molotov "insisted that a decision on these islands could be made only in connection with a decision on the Italian colonies." In view of the Soviet position, Byrnes
became convinced that the USSR "was determined to dominate
Europe." Taken in conjunction with Soviet policy at the time concerning Trieste, the Balkan region and Greece, to say nothing of Iran,
it was clear that Soviet policy regarding Tripolitania would give the
USSR a base in the Mediterranean on the other side of the Turkish
Straits, whatever regime might ultimately be established in that
strategic waterway. To continue the story briefly, in January 1946
Molotov, again at the Council of Foreign Ministers—although the
United Nations was holding its first sessions in London at the same
time—proposed that the Soviet Union and Italy jointly administer
Tripolitania and was countered with a British proposal that all of
Libya be given immediate independence. But it was not until June
1946 that the USSR finally agreed that the Dodecanese Islands should
go to Greece, having receded from its position on Tripolitania in
May.[40]

---

also Benjamin Rivlin, *United Nations Action. Italian Colonies* (New York: Carnegie
Endowment for International Peace, 1950); John C. Campbell, *The United States in
World Affairs* (New York: Harper, 1947), pp. 62, 112, 120.

[40]See, especially, *USFR* (1946), 2, *Council of Foreign Ministers:* 88 ff., 661, and
passim; Byrnes, *Speaking Frankly*, pp. 127, 132. Ultimately, of course, it was agreed
that the fate of Libya be settled by the United Nations General Assembly, if the powers
had not previously agreed. When Molotov finally agreed, on June 26 that the Dodecanese should go to Greece, Byrnes asked "for a minute or two to recover" from the
shock.

Meanwhile, it had been agreed not to discuss the problem of the Straits when the Council of Foreign Ministers met on September 11, and the United States had no real intention of bringing it up, although the problem of European inland waterways was on the agenda. The Turkish government continued disturbed about the Straits, and wondered why Truman had assimilated the problem to that of European waterways.[41] While there were consistent reports of Soviet military concentrations in the Balkans and in the Caucasus and Azerbaijan, few difficulties were anticipated when the 1925 Turkish–Soviet nonaggression agreement came to an end on November 7. As Ambassador Harriman reported on October 24, the agreement was out of date, and after November 7, Soviet policy toward Turkey would continue to be the result of Moscow's estimate of the need for expansion into Turkey, calculated against probable Turkish resistance and the degree of Anglo–American support.[42]

As the Soviet war of nerves continued, there were further exchanges among the United States, the United Kingdom, and Turkey, and on October 24 Ambassador Wilson was instructed to transmit the American proposals to the Turkish government. While there was no "collusion," the British and American positions were very close, although the British government was dubious about restrictions on the passage of naval vessels of non-Black Sea Powers.[43] In an address of October 27 Truman repeated his Potsdam thesis that "all nations should have the freedom of the seas and equal rights to the navigation of boundary rivers and waterways and of rivers and waterways which pass through more than one country."[44] A few days later, in an address before the Grand National Assembly on November 1, Inönü took up the Straits problem, denying any malfeasance in administering the Montreux Convention during World War II, as both the Soviet Union and the United Kingdom had alleged in 1944, and asserting that throughout the war Turkey had acted within the spirit of its alliance with Great Britain.[45]

THE BASIC AMERICAN POSITION

The American note was sent off to Ankara on October 30 and, in accordance with the agreement reached at Potsdam and the principles enunciated by the President, the United States presented it formally to the Turkish government on November 2.[46] The United

[41]USFR (1945), 2: 112 ff., 123, 318-21; USFR (1945), 8: 1242, 1246, 1250, 1253–54.
[42]Ibid., 8: 1254-62.   [43]Ibid., 8: 1258-59, 1262-63, 1264-65.
[44]Department of State Bulletin 331 (October 28, 1945): 654.
[45]Turkish Embassy, Washington, D.C., Press Release (1945).
[46]See USFR (1945), 8: 1269-73; Howard, The Problem of the Turkish Straits, p. 47; Dennett and Turner, Documents on American Foreign Relations, 1945-1946, 8:

States called attention to the Potsdam agreement that the Montreux Convention required revision and that the problem should be the subject of direct conversations between each of the three governments of the United States, the United Kingdom, on the one hand, and the Turkish government on the other. The United States hoped that the problem of the "control and use of the Straits" could be "solved in a manner which" would "promote international security," show "due consideration for the interests of Turkey and all Black Sea riparian powers," and "secure the free use of this important waterway to the commerce of all nations." The Montreux Convention was subject to revision in 1946, and the United States proposed an international conference for this purpose, indicating its own willingness to participate if invited. As a basis for an equitable solution of the question of the Straits, the following principles were set forth:

1. The Straits to be open to the merchant vessels of all nations at all times;
2. the Straits to be open to the transit of the warships of Black Sea Powers at all times;
3. save for an agreed limited tonnage in time of peace, passage through the Straits to be denied to the warships of non-Black Sea Powers at all times, except with the specific consent of the Black Sea Powers or except when acting under the authority of the United Nations; and
4. certain changes to modernize the Montreux Convention, such as the substitution of the United Nations system for that of the League of Nations and the elimination of Japan as a signatory.[47]

REACTIONS TO THE AMERICAN POSITION

Wilson gave copies of the American proposals to the British and Soviet ambassadors. Sir Maurice Peterson was pleased with the document with the exception of the provisions relative to the passage of the warships of non-Black Sea Powers into the Black Sea. Ambassador Vinogradov, on the other hand, complained that the American proposals provided inadequate security for the Black Sea Powers. The Soviet Union could not trust a weak Turkey to fulfill its

---

860-61. This note and the developments which followed in 1946 should serve to clear up the misunderstanding which some writers have had that Truman had proposed to place regulation and control of the Straits under the United Nations, although it is clear that, in the event of aggression, members of the United Nations would be concerned with the security of this important area.

[47]The Treaty of Peace with Japan, signed at San Francisco on September 6, 1951, (Article 8) provided that Japan renounce "such rights and interests as it may derive from being a signatory of . . . the Straits Agreement of Montreux of July 20, 1936." See *Conference for the Conclusion and Signature of the Treaty of Peace with Japan. San Francisco, California, September 4-8, 1951. Record of Proceedings* (Washington, D.C.: USGPO, 1951), pp. 216-17.

obligations in the Straits.[48] Feridun Erkin, the Turkish secretary-general, found three difficulties in the American proposals:

1. There was no indication as to how the Black Sea Powers were to decide whether warships of non-riparian states were to enter the Black Sea;
2. the Turks might find the entire Soviet and possibly satellite fleets in the territorial waters of Istanbul at the same time; and
3. the effect of the American proposals would be to turn the Black Sea into a Soviet naval base "from which the Soviet Navy could make hit and run expeditions into the Mediterranean without danger of pursuit.[49]

On the other hand, the Turkish government fully supported the principle of freedom of transit and navigation in the Straits, although it disagreed with the principle that the warships of Black Sea Powers should have complete freedom at all times, and did not like the restrictions as to the passage of the warships of nonriparian Powers. Erkin had also been turning over the idea of a possible Black Sea security arrangement, which would include Greece among its adherents. The Turkish government felt, in any event, that there was no point in responding until the Soviet views were known and the American proposals could be considered as a basis for discussion.[50]

While Soviet pressures on Turkey continued, there was little indication that the USSR was ready formally to present its own proposals relative to the Straits. On November 21, however, the British government presented a memorandum to the Turkish government indicating that it was agreeable to the American proposals. While a revision of the Montreux Convention was necessary, it was not "particularly urgent." But if the Turkish government or the USSR desired to call a conference, the United Kingdom would be glad to participate—it did not want to enter into detailed discussion at the moment, however.[51] The Turkish government, despite its misgivings, on December 6, accepted the American note as a basis for discussion.[52] Turkey would "participate in an international conference on the Dardanelles and accept any decisions reached there, provided Turkey's independence, sovereignty and territorial integrity are not infringed." At the same time, Prime Minister Saracoglu told a press conference in Ankara:

[48]*USFR* (1945), 8:1271–73.
[49]Ibid., pp. 1273–74; Erkin, *Les Rélations Turco-Soviétiques et la Question des Détroits*, pp. 314–17.
[50]*USFR* (1945), 8: 1274–77.   [51]Ibid., p. 1281.
[52]Ibid., pp. 1282–83. See also M. Epstein, *The Annual Register* (London: Longmans, Green, 1946), p. 215; Turkish Embassy, Washington, D.C., Press Release No. 1, February 1, 1946; Harry S. Truman, *Memoirs*, vol. 2, *Years of Trial and Hope* (New York: Doubleday, 1956), p. 96.

The best basis for reconciling Turkish security and sovereignty and the present clauses of the Montreux Convention relative to the rights of liberty of passage of war and merchant vessels in time of peace and war should be established at an international conference clearly envisaged by that convention. After the several points of view of the three interested Governments are communicated by our Government we will be able to make known our own opinions. We favorably regard in principle the American viewpoint and it goes without saying that it merits being accepted as a basis of discussion in order to study the method of its application at the appropriate time. In any event it is [the] strong desire of our Government to see the United States participate in the future conference and furthermore we consider such participation an essential.

While there was no formal discussion of the Straits problem at the Council of Foreign Ministers in Moscow during December 1945, there was some substantive discussion of the Turkish problem.[53] Bevin told Byrnes on December 17, for example, that Great Britain could not be "indifferent to a Russian threat to Turkey and would stand by her." The United Kingdom could not agree to the Soviet request for a base in the Straits or for the return of Kars and Ardahan. While Byrnes had no intention of raising the Straits question, it did come up when Bevin noted the pressures on Turkey and the Soviet war of nerves during the session of December 19. Stalin noted that there were two problems, the first of which was that of the Straits and the second that of the territorial demands of the Georgians and the Armenians. As to the Straits, he observed: "Under the Montreux Convention it was left to Turkey to decide whether there was a threat of war and whether to close the Straits and to control them. That was a difficult situation for Russia because Turkey thus had a right to hem her in and the Soviet Government wished to safeguard their liberty." Stalin repeated the Soviet position as to Turkish weakness and confirmed the desire for a Soviet base in the Straits. The important thing for the USSR was to limit Turkey's right to close the Straits on its own authority. Bevin, who was "anxious not to destroy Turkey's free and independent position," wanted to see definite proposals in order to determine whether it would be worthwhile to call a conference to deal with the problem. It was agreed, in any event, to postpone discussion, and Bevin hoped that Soviet actions "would not necessitate the continuance of Turkish mobilisation."

The pressures continued, nevertheless, and the Turkish government raised questions as to the American attitudes. The American

[53]See, especially, *USFR* (1945), 8: 1283-84; 2: 629-32, 688-91, 744. The problem of European inland waterways, of course, was much discussed during 1945 (ibid., 2: 1364 ff.).

position became increasingly clarified as the weeks went by. Truman reiterated his stand in his annual message to the Congress on the State of the Union on January 21, 1946. Indeed, the President persisted in this view, rightly or wrongly, although he was well aware of the Soviet threat to this region and complained to Byrnes, following the Moscow Conference in December 1945, not only about Iran, but about other matters:

There isn't a doubt in my mind that Russia intends an invasion of Turkey and seizure of the Black Sea Straits to the Mediterranean. Unless Russia is faced with an iron fist and strong language another war is in the making. Only one language do they understand—"How many divisions have you?" I do not think we should play compromise any longer. We should refuse to recognize Rumania and Bulgaria until they comply with our require- ments; we should let our position in Iran be known in no uncertain terms and we should continue to insist on the internationalization of the Kiel Canal, the Rhine–Danube waterway and the Black Sea Straits and we should maintain complete control of Japan and the Pacific. We should rehabilitate China and create a strong central government there. We should do the same for Korea.[54]

Soviet pressure on Turkey, however, continued, and the press and radio campaign increased in intensity in the ensuing weeks, al- though the USSR did not specifically announce its position until August 1946. During January 1946 Acting Foreign Minister Nurullah Sümer was indirectly advised that Turkish–Soviet relations would be much improved if Saracoglu were no longer prime minister. The Turkish government replied calmly to the Soviet war of nerves. Late in January 1946, Saracoglu advised a *Newsweek* correspondent in Ankara:

1. With or without the assistance of UNO, Turkey intends to protect present territory and sovereignty even if this means war.

2. Turkey will participate in an international conference on the Dar- danelles and accept any decisions reached there, provided "Turkey's independence, sovereignty and territorial integrity are not infringed."

3. The UNO can be effective in protecting peace and security only if it has the full support of the United States.[55]

---

[54]William Hillman, *Mr. President: The First Publication from the Personal Diaries, Private Letters, Papers and Revealing Interviews of Harry S. Truman* (New York: Farrar, Straus and Young, 1952), pp. 22-23; Truman, *Memoirs*, 1: 551-52. From a memorandum dated January 5, 1946, which the President said he read to Byrnes, but which the latter denied. While there was some confusion as to American policy on the Straits, it is evident that the United States did not support internationalization, al- though it did, for a while, support demilitarization (*USFR* [1945], 8: 1289-93).

[55]Turkish Embassy, Washington, D.C., Press Release, February 1, 1946. See also *USFR* (1946), 7: 801-04, 809-10, 810-13. Foreign Minister Hasan Saka told Byrnes in London on January 17 that no official demands had been made as to bases in the

Nevertheless, the Soviet propaganda campaign continued to assail the Turkish government and the "unofficial" claims, especially to the Kars–Ardahan region in Eastern Anatolia were pursued with encouragement on the part of the Soviet government.[56] At the same time, perhaps because of the failure to shake Turkey's firm resistance to pressure, Vinogradov sought to use the "method of caress," to detach Turkey from its Western ties, to smother it with "friendship and solicitude." Once completely isolated, as Molotov had observed, Turkey would be "elevated in its relations with the Soviet Union to the atmosphere of cordiality which prevailed between the Soviet Union and Poland." Evidently it was too late for Turkey to be seduced, although Turkish fears remained, and the Turkish government considered that it was necessary to approach the British Ambassador during mid–February, with a view to a reaffirmation of the Anglo–Turkish alliance of October 19, 1939.[57] There were further Soviet troop concentrations pointed toward Turkey, and the USSR complained of Turkish attitudes as reflected in the press. Moreover, Vinogradov told Wilson on February 1 that both the Straits and the claims to the Kars–Ardahan area were important, and if the Turkish government wanted to improve relations with the USSR, these issues would have to be met.

The United Kingdom was well disposed toward the American principles for revision of the Montreux Convention. Bevin, in an address of February 21, 1946, to the House of Commons, seriously questioned Soviet desires as to the eastern Turkish frontiers. Moreover, he assured the House that he was anxious that any revision of the Montreux Convention should keep the international aspect of the Straits in view, since it would not contribute to international peace and security, if "one particular Power as against another should have bases in a particular spot." In a reaffirmation of the Anglo–Turkish alliance, Bevin declared that the United Kingdom had "a treaty with Turkey." He further observed that he would like to see the Turkish–Soviet friendship agreement renewed, but dis-

---

Straits or territories, but that "new conditions" would be considered in connection with a new treaty. It was indicated that the Kars–Ardahan area should be returned to the USSR and bases in the Straits discussed.

[56]See Professor V. Kvostov in *The New Times*, February 1, 1946, for the "Armenian" claims, and L. Chairkviani, secretary of the Georgian Community party, Moscow, *Pravda*, February 25, 1946, for the "Georgian" claims. See also George Kirk, *The Middle East, 1945–1950* (London: Oxford University Press, 1954), pp. 25–27; *USFR* (1945), 8: 1285–87.

[57]See, especially, Erkin, *Les Rélations Turco-Soviétiques et la Question des Détroits*, chap. 8; Kiliç, *Turkey and the World*, pp. 126–27; *USFR* (1946), 7: 806–07, 817–18.

tinctly did not "want Turkey converted into a satellite State," models of which had been established in Eastern and Southeastern Europe. Churchill vigorously supported this position in New York on March 15. On March 25, Hector McNeil, minister of state in the Foreign Office, declared that the Anglo-Turkish alliance of 1939 obligated Great Britain to assist Turkey in the event of aggression by an European Power, although he indicated that he had no reason "to believe that any such aggression was likely to take place." But the British statements brought forth the Soviet retort that it was illogical for the United Kingdom to object to the Soviet Union's desire to control the sole entrance through the Straits to the Black Sea, when Great Britain maintained a concentration of power at both ends of the Mediterranean Sea, which it could close at will.[58]

In his Army Day address of April 6, 1946, Truman reiterated the American intention to "press for the elimination of artificial barriers to international navigation, in order that no nation by accident of geographic location, shall be denied unrestricted access to seaports and international waterways." Truman also pointedly referred to the significance of the Near and Middle East, an area which presented "grave problems":

This area contains vast natural resources. It lies across the most convenient routes of land, air and water communications. It is consequently an area of great economic and strategic importance, the nations of which are not strong enough individually or collectively to withstand powerful aggression.

It is easy to see, therefore, how the Near and Middle East might become an area of intense rivalry between outside powers, and how such rivalry might suddenly erupt into conflict.

No country, great or small, has legitimate interests in the Near and Middle East which cannot be reconciled with the interests of other nations through the United Nations. The United Nations have a right to insist that the sovereignty and integrity of the countries of the Near and Middle East must not be threatened by coercion or penetration.[59]

[58]*Parliamentary Debates, House of Commons*, fifth series, 419, cols. 1355-59; vol. 421, cols. 6-7; *USFR* (1946), 7: 815-18. See also Winston Churchill, *The Sinews of Peace* (London: Cassell, 1948; Boston: Houghton-Mifflin, 1949), p. 118; Kirk, *The Middle East*, p. 27. The Soviet pattern for satellites in Eastern and Southeastern Europe was, of course, already clear. See Howard, "The Soviet Alliance System, 1942-1948," Department of State, *Documents and State Papers* 1, no. 4 (July 1948): 219-49; "New Links in the Soviet Alliance System, 1948-1949," ibid., 1, nos. 12-13 (March-April 1949): 681-84, 727. It may be noted that the Soviet cold war offensive against Turkey stimulated Turkish attempts to create solidarity between Turkey and the Arab world, which did bring about a Turkish-Iraqi Treaty of Friendship and Good Neighborliness on March 29, 1946, although it was not ratified until June 1947. In general, see also Ferenc Vali, *Bridge Across the Bosphorus: The Foreign Policy of Turkey* (Baltimore: The Johns Hopkins University Press, 1971), passim.

[59]Department of State *Bulletin* 14, no. 354 (April 14, 1946): 622; *USFR* (1946), 7: 820-22.

Evidently the situation remained relatively unchanged, for on May 10, Inönü declared that the world situation continued "darker and even more unsettled than could have been foreseen a year ago."[60] But there appeared to be no new elements in the picture. Nevertheless, on June 4, Bevin once more discussed the Turkish problem in the House of Commons. He did not believe there was any real basis for misunderstanding or "fundamental disagreement" concerning the Straits:

We have been willing, equally with our predecessors, to consider the revision of the Montreux Convention. What we are anxious to avoid, and I emphasize this, is to do anything, or agree to anything which will undermine the real independence of Turkey, or convert her into a mere satellite state. But, with the recognition of these principles, I am convinced that these two factors are not irreconcilable. Let me go further and say that we will always welcome the mercantile fleet of the Soviet Union on all the seas of the world. We sail the Baltic, but we have not got a base and have not got a port there. We will sail to Odessa again, to the Black Sea and Constantinople, quite freely, but we do not ask for a base or military requirements to enable us to do so. Our aim, as a Government, is the free movement of shipping and the world's trade. Therefore, whatever responsibilities we undertake in the defence scheme of the world in a particular area, we give a solemn undertaking that they will be on a basis of freedom to all members of the Peace Club on equal terms. I believe that, if such an attitude is accepted all around, this great desire for bases can be considerably minimised.[61]

The Great Debate Concerning the Turkish Straits (August–October 1946)

THE SOVIET NOTE OF AUGUST 7, 1946

The substantial exchange of views concerning the problem of the Straits, however, began only on August 7, 1946, when the USSR pre-

[60]Turkish Embassy, Washington, D.C., Press Release No. 8, May 16, 1946. On February 29, Forrestal asked Byrnes if he were agreeable to the Navy preparing plans for a task force in the Mediterranean. The latter agreed, with the suggestion that it might accompany the USS *Missouri*, which was to take home the body of the late Turkish Ambassador Mahmud Mehmet Ertegun (*USFR* [1946], 7: 822–23; Millis *Forrestal Diaries*, pp. 141, 171). In June there was talk of sending "casual cruisers unannounced" to the Mediterranean, the visit of the *Missouri* having been "most effective" and having produced "most satisfactory results."

[61]*Parliamentary Debates, House of Commons*, fifth series, 423, cols. 1836–37; *USFR* (1946), 7: 824–25. A few days before the Bevin address, Stalin told the British ambassador, Sir Maurice Peterson, that it was necessary for the USSR to have complete freedom for its ships to move to and from the Black Sea and that freedom of passage through the Straits was of little value without a base somewhere in the Mediterranean.

sented a detailed note on the subject to the Turkish government.[62] The Soviet note referred to the Potsdam agreement concerning revision of the Montreux Convention, indicating that the question was to be "the subject of direct negotiations between each of the three powers and the Turkish government. It called attention to a number of incidents which had occurred in the Straits during World War II, and generally charged the Turkish government with malfeasance in the administration of the regime of the Straits. The USSR believed, therefore, that since the Montreux Convention had not, apparently, prevented the use of the Straits by enemy powers, it should be revised, as proposed at Potsdam. It was familiar with the American and British notes on the subject. For its own part, the Soviet government proposed not to revise the Montreux Convention, but to establish a "new regime" for the Straits along the following lines:

1. The Straits should be always open to the passage of merchant ships of all countries.
2. The Straits should be always open to the passage of warships of the Black Sea Powers.
3. Passage through the Straits for warships not belonging to the Black Sea Powers shall not be permitted except in cases especially provided for.
4. The establishment of a regime of the Straits, as the sole passage, leading from the Black Sea and into the Black Sea, should come under the competence of Turkey and other Black Sea Powers.
5. Turkey and the Soviet Union, as the powers most interested and capable of guaranteeing freedom of commercial navigation and security in the Straits, shall organize joint means of defense of the Straits for the prevention of the utilization of the Straits by other countries for aims hostile to the Black Sea Powers.[63]

---

[62]For text, see Howard, *The Problem of the Turkish Straits*, pp. 47–49; *USFR* (1946), 7: 827–29, 829–30. See also I. Vasiliev, *O turetskom "neitralitete" vo vtoroi mirovoi voine* (Moscow, 1951), pp. 104–08.

[63]These principles are reminiscent of the Ottoman-Russian treaties of December 23, 1798, September 23, 1805, and July 8 (Hunkär Iskelesi), 1833, and of the Treaties of Moscow (March 16, 1921) and Kars (October 13, 1921), and the Turkish–Ukraninian Treaty of January 2, 1922 (Howard, *The Problem of the Turkish Straits*, pp. 14–15, 16, 17). Note also the remarks of Friedrich Engels in his essay on "The Foreign Policy of Russian Czarism (1890)": "Czargrad as the third Russian capital beside Moscow and Petersburg—that would mean a single sovereign authority over the Black Sea, Asia Minor and the Balkan peninsula. That would mean, whenever the Czar wished it, the closing of the Black Sea to all except Russian merchant and warships, its transformation into a Russian naval base and an exclusive maneuver area for the Russian fleet, which from this secure reserve position could sally forth through the fortified Bosphorus and retreat back to it as often as it pleased. Then Russia would need to achieve only the same control, direct or indirect, over the Sound and the Danish Belts and it would be unassailable also from the sea." See P. W. Blackstock and B. F. Hoselitz,

The first three of these principles were in general consonance with the first three principles set forth in the American note of November 2, 1945. Points 4 and 5, however, called for the establishment of a new regime of the Straits by the Black Sea Powers and the development of a joint Turkish–Soviet system of defense for the Straits, on the ground that the Black Sea Powers were primarily, or even exclusively, concerned and that only a joint defense system could offer genuine security in the Black Sea area. This was substantially identical with what Molotov had demanded of Nazi Germany during November 1940, and presented to the Turkish ambassador in June 1945.

THE RESPONSE TO THE SOVIET DEMANDS

The Soviet note had been transmitted to the United Kingdom and the United States as well as to Turkey, and one of the first things done upon its receipt was "to order a respectable U.S. naval task force to the Mediterranean," the USS *Missouri* having arrived in the Dardanelles on April 5. The new aircraft carrier, the *Franklin D. Roosevelt* and two destroyers promptly weighed anchor and, after a rendezvous off the Portuguese coast with two cruisers and three destroyers, proceeded to the Mediterranean. The next step was to develop a firm position to stand resolutely with the Turkish government, whatever the consequences. Truman considered the Soviet proposal for joint Turkish–Soviet defense of the Straits especially "ominous": "This was indeed an open bid to obtain control of Turkey. If Russian troops entered Turkey with the ostensible purpose of enforcing joint control of the Straits, it would only be a short time before these troops would be used for the control of all of Turkey. We had learned from the experience of the past two years that Soviet intervention inevitably meant Soviet occupation and control. To allow Russia to set up bases in the Dardanelles or to bring troops into Turkey, ostensibly for the defense of the Straits, would, in the natural course of events, result in Greece and the whole Near and Middle East falling under Soviet control."[64]

The Turkish government, which was in constant touch with the American ambassador, Edwin C. Wilson, and Sir David Kelly, the British ambassador, sought advice concerning the Soviet overture.[65]

---

eds., *The Russian Menace to Europe by Karl Marx and Friedrich Engels. A Collection of Articles, Speeches, Letters and News Dispatches* (Glencoe, Illinois: Free Press, 1951), p. 29.

[64]Truman, *Memoirs*, 2: 96–97. See also Joseph M. Jones, *The Fifteen Weeks (February 21–June 5, 1947)* (New York: Viking, 1955), pp. 62–63; Dean Acheson, *Present at the Creation: My Years in the State Department* (New York: Norton, 1969), chap. 27, pp. 194–201.

[65]See especially *USFR* (1946), 7: 830–39.

After conferring with Acting Secretary of State Dean Acheson, Truman directed the Departments of State, War, and Navy to make a careful study of the situation. The import of the Soviet position now seemed quite evident. At a "summit" meeting at the White House on August 15, 1946, with Acheson, the Secretaries of War (Royal) and Navy (Forrestal), and Chief of Staff General Eisenhower present, the study was presented. Among other things, it noted:

When the Soviet Union has once obtained full mastery of this territory [the Near and Middle East], which is strategically important from the point of view of resources, including oil, and from the point of view of communications, it will be in a much stronger position to obtain its objectives in India and China.

We, therefore, feel that it is in the vital interests of the United States that the Soviet Union should not by force or through threat of force succeed in its unilateral plans with regard to the Dandanelles and Turkey. If Turkey under pressure should agree to the Soviet proposals, any case which we might later present in opposition to the Soviet plan before the United Nations or to the world public would be materially weakened; but the Turkish Government insists that it has faith in the United Nations system and that it will resist by force Soviet efforts to secure bases in Turkish territory even if Turkey has to fight alone. While this may be the present Turkish position, we are frankly doubtful whether Turkey will continue to adhere to this determination without assurance of support from the United States.[66]

In their view, the United States now had to decide to "resist with all means at our disposal any Soviet aggression and in particular, because the case of Turkey would be so clear, any Soviet aggression against Turkey." Indeed, "the best hope of preserving peace" was the conviction that "the United States would not hesitate to join other nations in meeting armed aggression by the force of American arms." Acheson summarized the situation:

It was the view of the State Department that the Russian note and its last three demands on Turkey reflected a desire to control and dominate that country; that acceding to these demands would be followed next by infiltration and domination of Greece by Russia with the obvious consequences in the Middle East and the obvious threat to the line of communications of the British to India. He said that he felt that this trial balloon of the Russians should be firmly resented by the President with the full realization that if Russia did not back down and if we maintained our attitude it might lead to armed conflict. The President replied that he was perfectly clear we should take a firm position both in this instance and in China; that we might as well find out whether the Russians were bent on world conquest now as in five or ten years.[67]

---

[66]Ibid., pp. 840-42; Erkin, *Les Rélations Turco-Soviétiques et la Question des Détroits*, chap. 9, pp. 343-54.

[67]Millis, *Forrestal Diaries*, pp. 192-93; Acheson, *Present at the Creation*, pp. 199-200; Jones, *Fifteen Weeks*, pp. 63-64.

Indeed, the problem was thoroughly surveyed around a map on Truman's desk, the recommendation for firm action was unanimously approved, and the decision was coordinated with the views of the United Kingdom and France. The Turkish government was advised on August 16, in view of the delicacy of the situation, "to assume a reasonable, but firm, attitude," and told orally that the American position of firm support had been "formulated only after full consideration had been given to the matter at the highest levels."[68]

The United States commented firmly on the Soviet note on August 19, substantially reiterating its position of November 2, 1945 and expressing its view that the establishment of a regime of the Straits was not the exclusive concern of the Black Sea Powers—a view which American representatives, incidentally, had set forth vigorously at the Lausanne Conference in December 1922. The United States held that Turkey should remain primarily responsible for the defense of the Straits and warned: "Should the Straits become the object of attack or threat of attack by an aggressor the resulting situation would constitute a threat to international security and would clearly be a matter for action on the part of the Security Council of the United Nations." The American note also declared that the regime of the Straits "should be brought into appropriate relationship with the United Nations" and "function in a manner entirely consistent with the principles and aims of the United Nations." In conclusion, the United States reaffirmed its willingness to participate in a conference for the revision of the Montreux Convention.[69]

The British note of August 21 expressed similar views, pointing out in particular:

that it has for long been internationally recognized that the regime of the Straits is the concern of other States besides the Black Sea Powers. His Majesty's Government cannot, therefore, agree with the Soviet view that the future regime should be the concern of the Black Sea Powers and Turkey alone.

As regards the fifth proposal that Turkey and the Soviet Union should organize the defense of the Straits by joint means His Majesty's Government consider that Turkey, as the territorial power concerned, should continue to be responsible for defense and control of the Straits.[70]

---

[68]*USFR* (1946), 7: 843–47. In view of the seriousness of the situation it was recommended that the country be informed of the background of the decision, particularly of the implications of the Soviet note, and that especially correspondents of *The New York Times* and *The Herald-Tribune* and other newspapers should be briefed on the factual backgrounds. See, especially, Truman, *Memoirs*, 2: 95–98; Acheson, *Present at the Creation*, pp. 194–96; Millis, *Forrestal Diaries*, pp. 192–93; Jones, *Fifteen Weeks*, pp. 63–64.

[69]*USFR* (1946), 7: 847–49; Howard, *The Problem of the Turkish Straits*, pp. 49–50; Hurewitz, *Diplomacy in the Near and Middle East*, 2: 268–71.

[70]*USFR* (1946), 7: 849–51; Howard, *The Problem of the Turkish Straits*, p. 50.

The Turkish government was much encouraged by the firmness of the Anglo-American position, despite its own earlier misgivings. Prior to the sending of the first Turkish reply to the Soviet government, on August 22, a spokesman for the British Foreign Office had indicated that the British government felt that there should be direct consultations between Turkey and the USSR on the subject of the Straits. But the dangerous implications of this position were pointed out to Sir David Kelly, namely, that if a Turkish foreign minister were invited to Moscow, he would have been confronted, in fact, with a meeting of the "Black Sea Powers" for negotiations on the Straits. The Turkish government, therefore, rejected the Soviet demands and demonstrated a determination to resist in the event of a Soviet resort to open violence, although the Turkish Army was poorly equipped and would have been "no match for the battle-tested divisions of the Kremlin." The Turkish reply of August 22 declared that the Turkish government had examined the Soviet note "with all the more attention," since the "international importance" of the question was "only surpassed by the vital interest" which it represented "from the Turkish national point of view." After repeating the thesis advanced in the Soviet note of August 7, the Turkish government gave a detailed answer to the charges concerning the passage of Axis vessels through the Straits. Although it could not accept the Soviet charges concerning alleged misconduct during the war, the Turkish government was prepared to admit that the definitions of warships in Annex II of the Montreux Convention and certain technical provisions had been "bypassed by events and weakened by experience," and needed "to be adapted to technical progress and present conditions." It was, indeed, prepared for a revision of the Montreux Convention through an international conference, at which the signatories and the United States of America would be represented.[71]

But the Turkish government could not accept Point 4 of the Soviet note, which called for the establishment of a regime of the Straits by Turkey and the other Black Sea Powers. Nor could it accept Point 5 as to the establishment of a joint Turkish–Soviet system of defense for the Straits. From the Turkish viewpoint, the Soviet proposal was "not

[71]*USFR* (1946), 7: 852–56; Howard, *The Problem of the Turkish Straits*, pp. 50–55; Truman, *Memoirs*, 2: 97; Erkin, *Les Rélations Turco-Soviétiques et la Question des Détroits*, pp. 343–54. It was during this period that the Soviet government published a series of captured German documents bearing on Turkey, a review of which appeared conveniently in *The New Times*, no. 16 (August 15, 1946): 26–30, and in *Pravda* on August 11, 1946. The complete publication is Foreign Ministry, *Dokumenti Ministerstva Inostranikh Diel Germanii*, Vipusk II. *Germanskaia Politika v. Turtsii Documents (1941–1943)*. OGIZ-Gospolitizdat, 1946 (French translation: *La Politique Allemande. Documents Secrets du Ministère des Affaires Etrangères d'Allemagne* (Paris, 1946).

compatible with the inalienable rights of sovereignty of Turkey nor with its security, which brooks no restriction." Moreover, it was felt that from the international point of view, the Soviet proposal raised the "gravest objections." In the Turkish view, the surest guaranty for Soviet security in the Black Sea lay "not in the search for a privileged strategic position in the Straits, a position incompatible with the dignity and sovereign rights of an independent country, but in the restoration of friendly and trusting relations with a strong Turkey," determined to inaugurate the happy era of friendly relations, "but whose efforts in this direction must be seconded by an equal good will coming from its northern neighbor." The Turkish government also felt that the security of each country was under the guaranty of the United Nations, of which both Turkey and the Soviet Union were members.

THE SECOND ROUND

Very serious questions were now being raised about Soviet intentions—questions about next steps and the implications of what might follow. On August 23, the day after the Turkish note, the American Joint Chiefs of Staff reported their consideration of "the military implications in the existing international situation concerning the Turkish Straits."[72] Among other things the Joint Chiefs of Staff observed that, since Soviet military base rights in the Straits would not provide effective defense of traffic unless "such rights were extended to include military dominance of the area for several hundred miles in all directions," "logic which would justify Soviet participation in the defense of the Dardanelles would also tend to justify further Soviet military penetration through the Aegean." Soviet participation in defense of the Straits would "project Soviet military power into an area vital to the Turks," involve "Soviet immediate military dominance of Turkey," and threaten to soften the Turkish attitude toward the USSR in a way soon to "result in reducing Turkey to a satellite Soviet State." Turkey was considered strategically "the most important military factor" in the Eastern Mediterranean and Middle East. If the USSR attained military dominance by political concessions in Turkey, there was grave doubt that in the event of a major world crisis "the Middle East and Eastern Mediterranean could be considered militarily tenable for the non-Soviet powers." It was recognized that successful opposition to the USSR rested primarily on the will of the Turkish government, that the security interests of the United Kingdom were more direct than those of the United States,

[72]*USFR* (1946), 7: 856-58.

and that the American people were not well informed regarding problems in this area. The Joint Chiefs recommended encouragement to the Turkish purchase of both economic and military supplies from the United States.

In the Turkish view the USSR had three courses open to it—to attack Turkey, which was not expected; to take steps to call a conference, also not likely; or to allow the question to remain in status quo until the time was more favorable for pressing essential Soviet claims against Turkey.[73] In any event, the Soviet note of September 24, which began the second round, substantially reiterated the position set forth on August 7. It repeated the charges concerning the violation of the Montreux Convention during the recent struggle. It also took note of Turkish acceptance of the first three Soviet principles concerning commercial freedom in the Straits, opening of the Straits to the warships of Black Sea Powers, and closure to warships of nonriparian powers "except in cases especially provided for." These principles had been enunciated in the American note of November 2, 1945. In view of Turkish objections, the Soviet note discussed points 4 and 5, involving the establishment of a regime of the Straits by the Black Sea Powers and Turkey and of a joint Turkish–Soviet system of defense in the Straits, at some length. The Soviet government reverted to an established Russian theme and invited

the attention of the Turkish Government to the special situation of the Black Sea as a closed sea. Such a situation means that the Straits of the Black Sea represent a seaway leading only to the shores of a limited number of powers, namely: to the shores of several Black Sea Powers. Therefore, it is entirely natural that the Soviet Union and the other Black Sea Powers are the most interested in the regulation of the regime of the Straits of the Black Sea and accordingly their situation in this matter cannot be compared with that of the other powers. The destination of these Straits, leading to the Black Sea which is a closed sea, differs from that of world seaways such as for example, Gibraltar or the Suez Canal, giving access not to a limited number of States, and which, as is known, are seaways of world importance. With regard to such international seaways it is indeed necessary to establish an international control with the participation of the Powers most interested, which, moreover, has not yet been realized. With regard to the Straits of the Black Sea leading into the Black Sea, which is a closed sea, it seems proper in this case to establish such a regime of the Straits which above all would meet the special situation and the security of Turkey, the U.S.S.R., and the other Black Sea Powers.

The USSR contended that Turkey had accepted the principle of the elaboration of a regime of the Straits by Turkey and the Black Sea

[73]*USFR* (1946), 7: 859–66; Howard, *The Problem of the Turkish Straits*, pp. 55–58; Erkin, *Les Rélations Turco-Soviétiques et la Question des Détroits*, pp. 354–73.

Powers in the treaties of Moscow (March 16, 1921) and Kars (October 13, 1921) and in the Turkish–Ukrainian agreement of January 2, 1922. The Soviet government also elaborated on the theme of joint Turkish–Soviet defense of the Straits, pointing, among other things, to the passage in August 1914 of the German cruisers *Goeben* and *Breslau* through the Straits, as well as to alleged incidents during World War II. The fact that the USSR had a shoreline of some 1,100 miles along the Black Sea, which gave access to important Soviet regions, was also cited as a reason for direct participation of the Soviet Union in defense of the Straits. In the Soviet view, only a joint defense could offer genuine security to the parties concerned, namely, Turkey and the Black Sea States.

The USSR considered joint defense of the Straits entirely consonant with the principles of the United Nations Charter, since the proposal was intended to serve not only the general interests of international commerce, but to create the conditions for the maintenance of the security of the Black Sea Powers and to contribute to the consolidation of the general peace. Finally, the Soviet note contended, in the light of the Potsdam agreement that the Montreux Convention should be revised to meet present conditions and that the calling of a conference for this purpose should be preceded by a discussion of the question through direct *pour-parlers* between governments.

The Soviet note was not very persuasive, and there was little or no question of changing the Anglo-American or Turkish positions during the second round.[74] Although it was not addressed to the United States, the American government again responded on October 9, reiterating its earlier position. The United States recalled "that in the Protocol of the proceedings of the Potsdam Conference . . ., the three Governments recognized that the Convention on the Straits . . . should be revised as failing to meet present-day conditions. It was further agreed . . . that as the next step the matter should be the subject of direct conversations between each of the three Governments and the Turkish Government." This repetition was, no doubt, understandable in the light of the Soviet position, and the American government understood that the three governments, in agreement with each other concerning the desirability of revision of the Montreux Convention, "mutually recognized that all three signatories of the Protocol" had "an interest in the regime of the Straits and in any change which might be made in that regime." Although the United States, in its note of August 19, had indicated that the regime of the

---

[74]*USFR* (1946), 7: 866–75; Howard, *The Problem of the Turkish Straits*, p. 59.

Straits was a matter of concern not only to the Black Sea Powers but to others, including the United States, the USSR had reiterated its position concerning the establishment of a new regime by the Black Sea Powers in its note of September 24. The American government did not believe that the Potsdam Agreement contemplated that the "direct conversations" envisaged in the protocol "should have the effect of prejudicing the participation of the other two signatory powers in the revision of the regime of the Straits." On the contrary, the Potsdam Agreement "definitely contemplated only an exchange of views with the Turkish government as a useful preliminary to a conference of all the interested powers, including the United States, to consider the revision of the Montreux Convention." Finally, it was held that "the Government of Turkey should continue to be primarily responsible for the defense of the Straits and that should the Straits become the object of attack or threat of attack by an aggressor, the resulting situation would be a matter for action on the part of the Security Council of the United Nations."

The British government also replied on October 9 and, like the United States, declared that the Potsdam agreement "laid it down that as the next step" the problem of revision should be "the subject of direct conversations between each of the three Governments and the Turkish Government." In addition, however, the British government stressed that the "next step" had already been completed "by the exchange of views which" had "now taken place between these Governments." It, therefore, saw "no need for or purpose in continuing direct correspondence on the subject." Although the British attitude toward Points 4 and 5 of the Soviet note of August 7 remained as the Foreign Office had indicated on August 21, the United Kingdom was ready to attend a conference of the Soviet Union, the United States, the United Kingdom, France, and all other signatories of the Montreux Convention, with the exception of Japan, "to consider a revision of that Convention."[75]

But the problem of the Straits also came up indirectly by this time at the Paris Peace Conference. During a discussion of the Danubian problem on October 10, Molotov observed: "At Potsdam President Truman and Mr. Byrnes had widened the scale of discussion by taking up the question of the regime for the Danube, the Rhine and the Black Sea Straits at one time. The previous Danube regime established in 1856 was the expression of imperialism and while Mr. Bevin had said that Great Britain had abandoned the imperialism of the 19th century a regime similar to the previous imperialistic re-

[75]USFR (1946), 7: 876–78; Howard, The Problem of the Turkish Straits, pp. 59–60.

gime was now put forward. It was not possible for the Soviet Union to accept this project. Why was there such concentration on nondiscrimination for the Danube when there were other important waterways, specifically, the Suez Canal and the Panama Canal?"[76] While the Soviet position was understandable, if Molotov were really speaking of political security in the region of the Black Sea, since the Straits "were considered as vital to the security of Russia as was the Panama Canal to the security of the United States,"[77] the

[76]USFR (1946), 3, Paris Peace Conference: Proceedings: 761-62; New York Times, October 11, 1946.
    [77]J. C. Campbell, The United States in World Affairs, 1945-1947 (New York: Harper, for the Council on Foreign Relations), p. 151. How old Russian policy is in this respect may be gleaned from Baron M. de Taube, La Politique Russe d'Avant Guerre et la Fin de l'Empire des Tzars 1904-1907 (Paris: Leroux, 1938); Erik Bruel, International Straits (London: Sweet and Maxwell, 1947), 2, pt. 1. See also American Journal of International Law 45, no. 2 (April 1951): 351-53, for interesting comments on the defense of the dissertation of S. V. Molodtzov on "The International Legal Regime of the Baltic Straits" at the meeting of the Learned Council of the Institute of Law of the Academy of Sciences of the USSR, as reported in the May 1950 issue of Sovietskoe Gosudarstvo i Pravo, in which the old Russian thesis of the mare clausum in the Baltic and Black Seas is firmly supported. Taking as the basis of the discussion the "fundamental decisions contained in the acts of the Soviet State concerning the question of the regime of the Baltic and Black Sea Straits, decisions which result from the essence of the peace-loving policy of the Soviet Union and which correspond to the security interests of the Baltic and Black Sea Powers," Molodtzov provided a definition of the legal status of the Baltic Straits. According to this definition, "Straits are maritime waterways, leading to the Baltic Sea which is isolated from the world sea highways; they lead to the coasts of only a few coastal Powers. From this particular position of the Baltic Sea and the Baltic straits legally results the right of the Baltic Powers to close, in the interest of security, access to the Baltic to the warships of non-Baltic Powers, as well as the exclusive right of all Baltic Powers to establish the regime of navigation in the Baltic straits, thus guaranteeing the exercise and the security of this navigation." Molodtzov concludes "that the foundation of the international regime of the Baltic straits should be built upon their effective closing to the warships of non-Baltic Powers. The Baltic States, including the great, peace-loving Power—the Soviet Union—have the right, founded on law and history, to take this step which would not preclude freedom of merchant navigation on the Baltic Sea for all countries, but which would protect the sovereignty and security of the nations populating the coasts of the Baltic." See also Kazimierz Grzybowski, "The Soviet Doctrine of Mare Clausum and Policies in Black and Baltic Seas," Journal of Central European Affairs 14, no. 4 (January 1955): 339-53. Also of interest in this connection is the statement of Senator Tom Connally, August 1, 1946, urging an amendment whereby the United States would determine that disputes essentially within the domestic jurisdiction of the United States, under Article 2(7) of the United Nations Charter, should be excepted from the compulsory jurisdiction of the International Court of Justice, referring specifically to the Panama Canal: "It [the ICJ]] might decide that the navigation of the Panama Canal was an international question. It is pretty close to it. It might decide that the regulation of tolls through the Canal was an international question." The next day Senator Connally inquired: "Do we want the International Court of Justice to render a judgment in a case involving the navigation of the Panama Canal? The Court might say, 'It is an international stream, like the Dardanelles, and the commerce of the world passes through it, and problems relative to it are international.' In the case of the Panama Canal, our treasure bought it, our blood built it, and it is ours by right of construction.

larger issues involved, unquestionably, were those of the territorial integrity and political independence of Turkey. Moreover, it may be well to note at this point, in view of the comparisons made with the Panama Canal, the Suez Canal, and other waterways of international concern, that the Soviet government and Soviet and Russian imperial spokesmen have stressed, not the similarities in these waterways, but the almost unique position of both the Black Sea and the Baltic Sea as "closed seas," and have sought, not freedom, but Soviet domination of these waters and their approaches, as part and parcel of Soviet policy throughout Eastern and Southeastern Europe and the Near and Middle East as well.

The Turkish government reaffirmed its earlier position on October 18, and once more provided a point-by-point reply to reiterated Soviet charges of alleged Turkish misconduct during World War II.[78] The note repeated that there were certain difficulties in the technical distinctions of Annex II of the Montreux Convention between commercial and war vessels. But it stressed that the "real threat to the security of the Soviet Black Sea shores came from the occupation of a large part of the shore of that sea by the German Armies, from the German possession of the Rumanian and Bulgarian fleets and from the presence of German and Italian ships sent to the Black Sea ports by rail or through the Danube." The Turkish government believed, however, that the Convention should be revised. First, Annex II, which defined warships, required technical revision. Second, the provisions relative to the League of Nations would have to give way to the system established by the United Nations in its task of maintaining world peace. Finally, Japan should be removed from the list of contracting parties, and the United States should become a signatory of the revised convention. It was within this framework that the Turkish government envisaged an eventual revision of the Montreux Convention and was willing to be represented at a conference for that purpose. Nevertheless, the Turkish government could not admit "Unfounded complaints tending to justify this revision on the

---

We do [not] propose to submit to the jurisdiction of any tribunal at any time the right to say whether a question relative to it is a domestic question" (*Congressional Record* 92, no. 153 [August 1, 1946]: 10764; no. 154 [August 2, 1946]: 10839).

[78]*USFR* (1946), 7: 479–893; Howard, *The Problem of the Turkish Straits*, pp. 60–68. See also the letter of Henry Wallace in the *New York Times*, September 18, 1946, in which he declared: "Most of us are firmly convinced of the soundness of our position when we suggest the internationalization and defortification of the Danube or of the Dardanelles, but we should be horrified and angered by any Russian counter-proposal that would involve also the internationalizing and disarming of Suez and Panama. We must recognize that to the Russians these seem to be identical situations." In fact, of course, the Soviet argument has been on a quite different basis.

basis of an alleged responsibility on its part, born of pretended viola-
tions of the regime of the Straits in the course of the Second World
War."

Once more, Turkey took special note of the Soviet contention that
the regime of the Straits should be elaborated by Turkey and the Black
Sea Powers alone, in view of their direct interests and of the fact
that, in the Soviet view, the Black Sea, like the Baltic, was a "closed
sea." But the Turkish government pointed out that the Montreux
Convention had already established a "preferential regime in favor
of the *riverain* Powers." Turkey could not accept the Soviet reasoning
based on the 1921-22 treaties, however, or the argument as to the
"closed sea." Moreover, it pointed out that, in accordance with the
Montreux Convention, revision could take place "in an international
conference uniting the contracting States and in accordance with a
procedure foreseen by the text of the Convention itself."

The Turkish government agreed with the USSR, of course, that the
Montreux Convention went further than the Lausanne Convention
and established "a sharply-defined system of preference for the benefit of the Black Sea Powers." Nevertheless, it was clear to Turkey that
the three principles for revision proposed by the United States and
supported by the United Kingdom, Turkey, France, and the Soviet
Union offered the possibility of "giving greater satisfaction to the
Soviet *desiderata*." Likewise, Turkey could not accept Point 5 regarding the establishment of a joint Turkish–Soviet defense system,
which it continued to regard "as incompatible with the sovereignty
and the security of Turkey, without previously having examined the
concrete suggestions of the Soviet Government on this subject." The
question had been discussed in the Saracoglu–Molotov conversations
in September–October 1939, when the Turkish statesman had received such cool treatment in Moscow at the beginning of the war.[79]
Acceptance by Turkey of a joint system of defense "would mean no
less than the sharing of her sovereignty with a foreign power." Turkey
was anxious for friendship with the USSR, however, and it urged
stress on the United Nations as an international agency for the
preservation of the peace and security of all nations.

Relying on these explanations, Turkey was convinced that it had
established tangible proof of its good will and of its spirit of conciliation in agreeing to participate in a conference for revision of the
Montreux Convention. It appealed to the USSR to study, in its turn,
the reflections which the Turkish proposals might evoke, with the

[79]See, for example, Michael Sokolnicki, *The Turkish Straits* (Beirut, 1950), pp. 17,
39-45.

same goodwill and objectivity. Turkey felt that the direct conversations contemplated at Potsdam had been fulfilled and doubted the usefulness and advisability of continuing to follow the same procedure as to exchange of views by correspondence. It therefore declared its readiness to attend a conference for revision of the Straits Convention, which representatives of the USSR, the United Kingdom, the United States, and France, and the signatories of the convention, with the exception of Japan, would attend.

The End of the Great Debate

By the fall of 1946 the great debate over the question of the Turkish Straits appeared to be drawing to a close, although there was no indication that the argument was really over. During the exchange, the United States had come to the considered view that the Soviet moves were "designed to weaken Turkey with the objective of bringing it under the direct influence of the USSR and enabling the Soviet Union to use Turkey both as a defense against possible outside attack from the Mediterranean and as a springboard for political and military expansion by the USSR into the Mediterranean and the Near and Middle East."[80] Execution of such a policy by the USSR, it was thought, "would have the most serious consequences." Strategically, Turkey was

the most important factor in the Eastern Mediterranean and the Middle East. By its geographical position, Turkey constitutes the stopper in the neck of the bottle through which Soviet political and military influence could most effectively flow into the eastern Mediterranean and Middle East. A Russian-dominated Turkey would open the floodgates for a Soviet advance into Syria, Lebanon, Iraq, Palestine, Transjordan, Egypt and the Arabian Peninsula, all of which are at present still relatively free from Russian activities and direct Russian pressure because of their relative remoteness from the sphere of Soviet dominance. It would also dangerously, perhaps fatally, expose Greece and Iran, two countries whose governments are already having the greatest difficulty in standing up to the Soviet Union and its agents. None of the nations mentioned has a government or social order so stable and united as Turkey, and none could be expected to stand against Soviet pressure after Turkey had gone down.

From the purely military point of view, it was the judgment of the War and Navy departments that if the Soviet Union attained military dominance of Turkey (as would be the case if it were permitted

[80]*USFR* (1946), 7: 893–97. Memorandum on Turkey Prepared in the Division of Near Eastern Affairs, October 21, 1946, drafted by John D. Jernegan.

to share in the defense of the Straits), there would be grave doubt whether the eastern Mediterranean and Middle East could be considered tenable for the non-Soviet powers. But the political consequences might be even more far-reaching:

> Because Turkey is so obviously a key point and is so obviously under powerful Soviet pressure, all other nations, large and small, which fear the spreading power of the USSR are watching the current diplomatic struggle with the most intense concern. Any weakening which resulted in even partial attainment of the Soviet objectives in Turkey would have a disastrous effect upon these nations, influencing them to come to terms with the Soviets and abandon support of the United States in its efforts to see that the principles of the United Nations are upheld throughout the world. Such a development would produce a considerable weakening in the comprehensive security situation of the United States.

While Turkey appeared to be firmly determined to resist Soviet pressures and possessed a "relatively effective military force," it was obvious that it could not "stand in the face of the USSR if left entirely alone." It was, therefore, the policy of the United States to give Turkey diplomatic, moral, economic, and military assistance.

Foreign Secretary Bevin summarized the British position as it stood after the exchange of notes which had taken place since August 7. On October 22 he advised the House of Commons of the Potsdam Agreement, adding that he thought "there should be a discussion between the Great Powers and Turkey in order to consider a revision of the Montreux Convention." The basic British position was as follows:

> At the various international conferences during the last three or four years, and in their latest correspondence with the Turkish Government, the Soviet Government have made it clear that they are anxious to obtain a base in the Straits, which would ensure, in effect, that the control of this waterway would rest in the hands of the Soviet Union and not in the hands of the territorial Power most closely concerned. His Majesty's Government have made it clear that in their view, if this were adopted, it would involve an unwarrantable interference with the sovereignty of Turkey, and the effect of it would be to put her really under foreign domination, and would also represent an improper interference with the rights of other Powers concerned. During the last two months, the Soviet Government have placed their views publicly on record in two Notes to the Turkish Government, which have received wide publicity. I repeat that His Majesty's Government do not dispute that the existing convention requires modification in certain respects to bring it into accord with present-day conditions. For instance, at present Japan is one of the signatories. The Convention itself contains a number of references to the League of Nations and the definition of warships given in an annex to the Convention is clearly out of date. We agreed at Potsdam that as a next step matters would be the subject of direct conversations between each of the three governments concerned, and the Turkish Government.

But, while recognizing that revision is necessary, His Majesty's Government are very anxious to keep the international aspect of this waterway always in view.[81]

Bevin took note of the Soviet charges that the Montreux Convention had not prevented enemy powers "from using the Straits for hostile purposes against the Soviet Union, and other Allied Powers." The United Kingdom, although it had "some differences of opinion with the Turkish Government about the interpretation of the Convention, held that, on the whole, its terms had been conscientiously observed." The British government was unable to accept the position that the regime of the Straits should be reserved to the Black Sea Powers exclusively and that Turkey and the USSR should jointly organize the defense of the Straits, as the Soviet government had been advised. Against this view, the United Kingdom had pointed out the international character of the Straits and had declared that the proposal was "not acceptable." As the territorial power, Turkey "should continue to be responsible for the defence and control of the Straits." This view was similar to that of the United States. Bevin now felt, in the light of the exchange of notes, that "any further discussions should . . . take place at an international conference." If such a conference were called, the United States, the USSR, France and all the other signatories, with the exception of Japan, would participate, and the United Kingdom would be glad to join and to strive "for an agreed solution of this difficult problem." A solution should take into account "the legitimate interests of Turkey and the Soviet Union," with both of which the United Kingdom had alliances. But any solution should also "respect the sovereignty of Turkey and the interest of other powers concerned outside the Black Sea." The Foreign Secretary believed that if the case were "not pushed unilaterally" and were "dealt with on an international basis," a solution would be found. Matters had, nevertheless, been made much more awkward by the "war of nerves" which had been carried on, and the British government was convinced that if this ceased, "a new atmosphere would be created which would enable the matter to be dealt with on a much better footing."

There was a similar note in the address of İnönü to the Grand National Assembly on November 1, 1946, in which the question of security was listed as the first among Turkish problems.[82] İnönü de-

[81]*Parliamentary Debates, House of Commons*, fifth series, 427, cols. 1500–02.
[82]Turkish Embassy, Washington, D.C., Press Release No. 13, November 13, 1946. See also the more general remarks of Ambassador Huseyin R. Baydur in the United Nations General Assembly on October 26, 1946, in which he indicated that "Arms and military might are powerful weapons, but the force of world opinion is far more potent.

sired to see the war followed by a general settlement among nations and noted especially the fact that Turkey was now faced with the question of revision of the Montreux Convention:

We agree that it is necessary to improve the Montreux Convention in a manner conforming to new conditions, in keeping with the methods and within the limits clearly foreseen by Montreux. We are considering with good-will that the Convention in question should become the subject of conversations at an international conference. We shall welcome wholeheartedly any modifications which take into consideration the legitimate interests of each of the interested parties on the basis of ensuring the territorial integrity and sovereign rights of Turkey. We are convinced with a perfectly clear conscience that, during the second World War, the Montreux Convention was applied by us with the greatest attention; and the allegation to the effect that the Montreux Convention was applied with a bias in favor of the Axis Powers is manifestly unjust. We have nothing to fear from submitting our actions to examination and decision by arbitration. Inasmuch as concerns the question of the Straits, too, we perceive in the United Nations Charter every possible guarantee for ourselves and for every other nation concerned. So long as the clauses of the United Nations Charter concerning territorial integrity and sovereign rights are respected, no obstacle should exist to prevent the adjustment and improvement of relations between ourselves and the Soviet Union. It is our well-considered and sincere desire to have friendly and confidence-inspiring relations with the Soviet Union, as befits two neighbors.

Formal discussions had now ended. On October 26, the Soviet Union advised the United Kingdom that it did not share the British view that the direct conversations envisaged at Potsdam should "be regarded as complete." But, in the Soviet view it was "premature to consider the question of calling a conference to establish a new regime for the Black Sea Straits." Indeed, the USSR had suffered a diplomatic setback, if not outright defeat, as a result of the firm stand which had been taken throughout the discussions of the problem. The Turkish government was inclined to ascribe this result to:

1. The unanimous and resolute opposition of the Turkish people to any demand contrary to the rights of national independence and sovereignty, and this in a period during which Turkey could not reasonably count on foreign or international support to sustain its cause, despite the Anglo-Turkish alliance, in the period immediately following World War II;
2. the premature revelations of the real Soviet aims concerning the Turkish Straits before the Potsdam Conference, which resulted in strengthening the patriotic sentiments of the Turkish people and in arousing the suspicions of the Governments of the United Kingdom and the United States; and

---

It may be defied for a time, but it cannot be flaunted always and forever" (*Journal of the United Nations*, no. 16 [1946], p. 89). See also Millis, *Forrestal Diaries*, p. 219.

3. the appearance of the United States as a formidable factor of order and peace on the world stage, at first underestimated by the Soviet Union, which constituted, at the time, an insurmountable obstacle in the face of the Soviet assaults against Turkey.[83]

There were no further communications on the subject of the Straits after October 26, 1946. The developments during 1946, in the view of American officials, had brought to the fore "the vital importance of Turkey in the international picture," since it was one of the few nations on the periphery of the Soviet Union which was "not under effective control of the USSR," despite the "unmistakable signs" that the Soviet government planned "to add Turkey"—along with Greece—" to its group of satellites." It was urged that the United States support Turkey and, in turn, the Turkish government, which had remained firm in face of the Soviet pressures, felt that it should adopt a reasonable posture concerning the Straits. Feridun Erkin, secretary-general in the Turkish Foreign Ministry, told Ambassador Wilson on December 30, 1946, that he was thinking of the possible development of a regional security agreement among the United States, the United Kingdom, Turkey, and the Soviet Union for the defense of the Straits in time of war. If the Soviet Union, which professed to be concerned with this aspect of the problem, proved "reasonable," one course of action would be open. If, however, there were no change in the Soviet attitude and the pressures continued, the future looked "dreary for Turkey," since the economic burdens of maintaining large military forces against Soviet threats were already creating serious problems in the country. Unless some genuine settlement could be made relieving Turkey of Soviet pressure, Turkey would have to appeal to the United States for economic assistance, since it could not continue to carry the burden indefinitely.[84]

The problem of the Straits, and especially of revision of the Montreux Convention, could have arisen in 1951, in accordance with the five-year period stipulated in the convention. As will be noted later, following the death of Stalin, namely, in May 1953, the Soviet government communicated with the Turkish government concerning the Straits, and there were hints that a new regime satisfactory to Turkey and meeting Soviet security requirements could be elaborated. Nevertheless, there was no denunciation of the Montreux Convention in November 1954, and the convention remained in force. It is perhaps noteworthy that on April 19, 1950, *Krasnii Flot*

---

[83]Erkin, *Les Rélations Turoc-Soviétiques et la Question des Détroits*, p. 369; Kiliç, *Turkey and the World*, pp. 132–33.

[84]*USFR* (1946), 7; 897–99, 899–923; Erkin, *Les Rélations Turco-Soviétiques et la Question des Détroits*, pp. 369 ff.

(Red Fleet), official organ of the Soviet Navy Ministry, in tracing the historical interest of the Soviet Union in the Black Sea, expressed the view that the Montreux Convention should be revised, since its provisions had "ceased to accord with the interests of the Black Sea Powers." Secretary of State Dean Acheson commented on April 21, 1950, reviewing the position which had been taken during 1945 and 1946, and stating that at the time, the United States, the United Kingdom, France, and Turkey had expressed their willingness to participate in a conference for revision of the Montreux Conference. He concluded: "There the matter stands."[85]

Following World War II the United States assumed a very direct interest in the problem of the Turkish Straits. At the Yalta and Potsdam Conferences and in the exchanges of notes during 1945-46, the United States joined Great Britain and France, and the Soviet Union in discussing the problem with the government of Turkey. The United States was willing to go far in meeting the Soviet position as to use and transit of the Straits and admitted the special interest of the USSR in the Straits. It maintained its position as to commercial freedom and assimilated the Straits to other waterways of international concern (President Truman's "inland" waterways) like the Rhine, the Elbe, the Danube, the Suez and Panama canals. But the United States, like the United Kingdom, rejected the Soviet position as to (1) the elaboration of a new convention of the Straits by "the Black Sea Powers" and (2) joint Turkish–Soviet defense of the Straits, which would have subverted Turkish independence. While the USSR did not formally push its case after the end of 1946, thanks partly to the American stand, the pressures on Turkey continued.

[85]Department of State Press Release No. 387 (April 21, 1950).

Chapter VIII

The Problem of the Turkish Straits in the Postwar Period

The Continuing Soviet Threat

While formal discussion of the problem of the Turkish Straits had ended in October 1946, the question remained significant and there were always possibilities that it might come up again in the future. In the view of American officials dealing with the question, as observed in chapter VII, the developments during 1946 had "brought to the fore the vital importance of Turkey in the international picture," since it was one of the few nations on the Soviet periphery which was not under the "effective control of the USSR." Turkey had refused either to cede territory in the Kars–Ardahan area to the Soviet Union, to accept effective Soviet control over the Straits, or to become a Soviet satellite. It was now urged that the United States should support Turkey and, in turn, the Turkish government, which had remained firm under constant and severe Soviet pressures, felt that it could adopt a reasonable posture concerning the Straits, in the hope of a reasonable Soviet response. But, if no change in the Soviet attitude occurred, and the pressures continued, the future might prove dreary for Turkey. The economic burden of maintaining large military forces was already creating serious dislocations in the country. In the absence of some genuine settlement and consequent relief, Turkey would be compelled to appeal to the United States for both economic and military assistance, since it could not continue to carry the burden indefinitely.[1]

Nevertheless, the Soviet pressures on both Greece and Turkey, to say nothing of Iran, remained and took on an ominous form late in 1946 and early 1947—when the USSR still considered the area south

[1]Ferenc Vali, *Bridge Across the Bosporus: The Foreign Policy of Turkey* (Baltimore: The Johns Hopkins University Press, 1971), chap. 5.

of Batum and Baku the center of gravity of its policy and interest, sought a trusteeship in Libya, and a naval and commercial base in the Mediterranean. The American response was quick and decisive. The United Kingdom advised the United States on February 21, 1947, that it could no longer bear the financial and economic burden of assisting Greece and Turkey, and the American decision to pick it up was made at the White House on February 22. As Acting Secretary of State Acheson observed at the time, Soviet pressures on Greece, Turkey, and Iran during 1946–47 had brought the Balkan and neighboring areas to the point where a Soviet breakthrough might well open Eurasia and Africa to Soviet penetration. These were the high stakes involved in the British withdrawal from the Eastern Mediterranean, as American officials saw the problem, and only the United States was in a position to contain the USSR in that area.[2] Greece made its formal appeal on March 3, and on March 12, President Truman announced that "it must be the policy of the United States to support free peoples who are resisting attempted subjugation by armed minorities or by outside pressures." Both Greece and Turkey needed assistance, and the integrity of Turkey was "essential for the preservation of order in the Middle East."[3]

THE FLARE-UP AT THE UNITED NATIONS

While Turkey had not been subject to the same kinds of pressures which had been brought to bear on Greece and Iran during the immediate postwar period, there was, nevertheless, a continuing threat which forced that country, as already observed, to keep a larger standing army than it was able economically to support. There was no indication that the Soviet Union, in any way, had altered its position as to joint defense or control of the Straits or as to the Kars–Ardahan region along the Turkish–Soviet frontier in Eastern Anatolia. Indeed, Andrei Vyshinsky, the Soviet representative at the United Nations, bitterly attacked the Turkish government, along with the United States and Western Powers, in his remarks in the Political and Security Committee of the United Nations General Assembly on September 18, and October 22 and 24, 1947, in connection with the discussion

[2]Dean Acheson, *Present at the Creation: My Years in the State Department* (New York, Norton, 1969), p. 219; Harry S. Truman, *Memoirs*, vol. 2, *Years of Trial and Hope* (New York: Doubleday, 1956), pp. 103–09.
[3]See, especially, Department of State *Bulletin Supplement*, 16, no. 409A (May 4, 1947): 827–909; *Aid to Greece and Turkey: A Collection of State Papers*. See also Raymond A. Hare, "The Great Divide: World War II," and Joseph C. Satterthwaite, "The Truman Doctrine: Turkey," in Parker T. Hart, ed., "American and the Middle East," *The Annals* of the American Academy of Political and Social Science, 401 (May 1972): 23–30, 74–84.

of "measures to be taken against propaganda and the inciters of a new war," in accordance with the Soviet pattern which was already being established. Ambassador Selim Sarper, of Turkey, replied to Vyshinsky on October 24, in no uncertain terms, pointing out that there had been no "warmongering" on the part of Turkey. "On the contrary," he remarked:

Turkey had tried to use her important geographical situation to work for peace in the hope of becoming a factor for mutual trust and confidence between East and West.

The reason for the expression of increasing resentment and indignation in the Turkish Press against the USSR was well known. The events of 19 March, 7 June and 18 June 1945 had begun a chain of events that had frustrated hopes of better relations. After these dates, the press and radio of the USSR had indulged in unparalleled libelous and threatening articles.[4]

Sarper, who had served as Turkish ambassador in Moscow at the time, was, of course, referring to the Soviet denunciation of the Soviet-Turkish nonaggression agreement of 1925 on March 19, 1945, and to the demands of a new regime of the Straits to be elaborated by the Soviet Union and Turkey, which would provide for Soviet control of land, sea, and air bases and joint defense of the area, together with the demands for cession of the Kars–Ardahan area. He then went on to cite the Soviet press and radio attacks to the effect that Turkey was becoming a tool and "stooge" of the United States and was "preparing an invasion of the Greek democracy." But he did not cite the worst of the Soviet fulminations against Turkey, because "he did not desire to cause further deterioration in the relations between Turkey and the USSR, which were far from satisfactory." Nevertheless, he complained "against the warmongering attempts by the USSR Press and radio to incite one group of Turks against another, to incite the Turkish Army to rebel against the State, to intervene in the internal affairs of Turkey, to propagate aggressive intentions against Turkish territorial integrity, to incite Turks against their neighbors and vice-versa, to incite the Soviet people against the Turks and to conduct a moral and psychological aggression and war of nerves."

Vyshinsky did not reply until the afternoon of October 24, when he admitted that *Izvestiya* had attacked Turkey, but denied that that had had anything to do with war propaganda. But, rather playfully, perhaps, with regard to "Turkish territories which were historically part of Georgia—to say nothing of the Armenian claims—Vyshinsky stated that "two Georgian academicians had merely prepared an academic thesis on the Georgian character of those territories." The Soviet Representative then went on, with a somewhat nonchalant, if complete, disregard for the facts to charge:

On the other hand, official documents of the German Foreign Ministry, seized by the Russian authorities in Berlin and published in Moscow in 1946, showed that the Turkish Government, taking advantage of its neutrality during the war, had tried to secure the support of Nazi Germany for the establishment of a Turkish State in the Caucasus, and for the extermination of half of the USSR's man-power.

Even now, there was talk in Turkey of the necessity of dropping atomic bombs on Russian territory. That, too, showed the close connection between expansionist policy and war propaganda.[5]

Following the Vyshinsky tirade, in which the United States was brought in for good measure, Sarper pointed out that the documents cited by the Soviet Representative could not be considered by themselves. He called attention "to the fact that the efforts made by France, the United Kingdom and Turkey in August 1939 to secure Russian participation in a joint plan of defence had been frustrated by the signature of the Nazi-Soviet Pact."[6] Sarper also charged that the USSR had asked German assistance "in annexing territories in North-Eastern Turkey." In any case, there was no question of the continuing Soviet threat and the necessity of meeting it.

Turkish Association with the West

NATO AND REGIONAL DEFENSE

While no official demands were made for revision of the Montreux Convention of the Straits, the Soviet Union continued to insist that the convention should be revised, since it no longer met the interests of the Black Sea Powers. Although it could have raised the question of revision in 1951, in accordance with the five-year period stiuplated in Article 29 of the Montreux Convention, the Soviet government made no effort to do so. There was little doubt that in the immediate postwar years the Soviet Union had suffered a diplomatic setback on the problem of the Straits, largely because of the unanimity with

---

[5]UN Doc. A/C.1/SR.83, pp. 217–18. The Soviet publication, which contained only thirty-six documents is The Soviet Foreign Ministry, *Dokumenti Ministerstva Inostranikh Diel Germanii*, Vipusk II. *Germanskaia Politika v. Turtsii Documents (1941–1943)* (OGIZ-Gospolitizdat, 1946), (French translation: *La Politique Allemande. Documents Secrets du Ministère des Affaires Etrangeres d'Allemagne* (Paris, 1946), published in August 1946 as part of the Soviet propaganda attack at the time that the USSR was making its demands concerning the Straits.

[6]UN Doc. A.C.1/SR.83, p. 218.

which the Turkish government and people resisted the Soviet demands, the premature revelations of the Soviet aims concerning
Turkey, and the appearance of the United States as a very formidable
factor on the world stage, with increasingly important interests in
the Eastern Mediterranean. It is also true that, whatever its short-
comings, the Montreux Convention gave to the Soviet Union its basic
requirements, whether in the Straits or in the Black Sea. Realistically,
there was little need for revision, even from the Soviet point of view,
despite some questions or reservations as to Turkey's right to take
security measures, under Article 21, in the event of danger or threat.

Although no significant problems, technically, arose concerning
the Straits in the ensuing years, there were important developments
in the realm of regional defense, which had a bearing both on American policy and interests and those of the Soviet Union. During
October–November 1951, along with France, the United Kingdom,
and the United States, Turkey proposed a project for the establishment of a Middle East Command—a regional security project which
would have included both the Arab states and Israel. The move
proved abortive, for probably understandable reasons.[7] Turkey had
participated in the proposal, evidently, only on the understanding that
it would be accepted into membership in the North Atlantic Treaty
Organization, and on February 18, 1952, on their own volition and
insistence, both Greece and Turkey became members of NATO,
guardians of the Southeastern and Eastern Mediterranean flank.

General of the Army Omar Bradley, chairman of the Joint Chiefs
of Staff, in a statement of January 15, 1952 to the Foreign Relations
Committee of the United States Senate, in this connection, made
some interesting observations concerning the military importance
of both Greece and Turkey:

> From the military viewpoint, it is impossible to overstate the importance
> of these two countries. The free nations which have joined together for
> mutual security would be strengthened considerably by their presence, and
> their presence would lend stability to an area which we consider to be ex-
> tremely vital.
> Greece and Turkey occupy strategic locations along one of the major east-
> west axes. They offer to the North Atlantic Treaty Organization large and
> capable military forces in being. Their territories are suitable for the conduct
> of defensive operations essential in the event of an aggression.
> Turkey has a common boundary with Soviet Russia and her satellite state
> of Bulgaria. Greece is situated at the southern end of the Balkan Peninsula

---

[7]The Department of State, *American Foreign Policy, 1950–1955: Basic Documents*
(Washington, D.C.: USGPO, 1957), 2: 2180–87. As Acheson commented, this was a
"political stillbirth," which only brought a sharp Soviet response. Acheson, *Present at
the Creation*, pp. 562–65.

immediately adjacent to the satellite state of Albania. Therefore, both occupy key positions in a sound Atlantic defense system.

Allied with the free nations, they would compel a diversion of the forces of Soviet Russia and her satellites in any aggressive move against the West.

Located as they are—and allied with the free nations—they serve as powerful deterrents to any aggression directed toward southern Europe, the Middle East, or North Africa.

The successful defense of those areas—any one or all of them—is dependent upon control of the Mediterranean Sea. Greece and Turkey block two avenues to the Mediterranean which an aggressor might endeavor to use should they decide upon a thrust there.

Greece, as the map will show, presents a barrier along the overland route from the Balkan States located to the north. Turkey, astride the Bosporus and Dardanelles, guards the approach by water from the Black Sea to the Mediterranean and to the Suez Canal and Egypt farther south.

Turkey, too, flanks the land routes from the North to the strategically important oil fields of the Middle East.[8]

General Bradley found evidence of the strategic significance of both Greece and Turkey "in the intensive efforts of international communism to bring Greece under Soviet domination, and in efforts of Russia, extending over almost 200 years, to gain control of the Turkish Straits." Secretary of State Acheson sounded much the same note, stressing the Soviet pressures upon both Greece and Turkey and emphasizing their strategic importance: "Turkey flanks the land route from Russia to the rich oil fields of the Middle East. The known determination of Greece and Turkey to maintain their independence and national integrity and to develop their strength has made them increasingly effective barriers to Soviet expansion in the eastern Mediterranean and the Middle East areas. Their continued alinement with the free world and the integration of their strength with that of the collective strength of the present NATO members thus has great significance in terms of their own security."[9]

A year later, on February 28, 1953, Turkey joined with Greece and Yugoslavia in a new Balkan Entente, but while a Treaty of Alliance, Political Cooperation and Mutual Assistance was signed at Bled, Yugoslavia, on August 9, 1954, the new grouping did not, in fact, prove of much significance as a regional security instrument. The so-called Baghdad Pact (CENTO), the beginnings of which went back to 1954-55, appeared, for a time, to be on sounder ground, and it became the object of bitter Soviet attack.[10]

[8]*American Foreign Policy, 1950-1955: Basic Documents,* 1: 856-58; Vali, *Bridge Across the Bosphorus,* chap. 4.

[9]*American Foreign Policy, 1950-1955: Basic Documents,* 1: 858-64, 871-73; Acheson, *Present at the Creation,* pp. 563-64, 569-70, 593, 609, 710.

[10]*American Foreign Policy, 1950-1955: Basic Documents,* 1: 1233-39; J. C. Hurewitz, *Diplomacy in the Near and Middle East* (Princeton, N.J.: D. Van Nostrand, 1956),

The New Soviet Tactics

THE POLITICS OF "RENUNCIATION"

During this period, the United States considered Turkey one of its staunchest allies, as Secretary of State Dulles observed during his visit to that country in May 1953.[11] A few days after the Dulles visit, however, on May 30, 1953, Molotov, in a new overture to Turkey, advised the Turkish Ambassador in Moscow that the Soviet government had been considering its relations with neighboring states and, among other matters, Turkish–Soviet relations. The Soviet note referred to the denunciation of the nonaggression agreement of December 17, 1925, and to the discussions which had followed, during which, on June 7, 1945, as a price for the negotiation of a new treaty, which would have converted Turkey into a Soviet satellite, the USSR had demanded the retrocession of the Kars–Ardahan district and a new regime of the Straits. As Molotov observed, "this was taken amiss by government and public circles in Turkey, which could not but be reflected to some extent in Soviet–Turkish relations." Now, however, the Soviet government felt that the Turkish government had been unduly alarmed and grieved in these matters. The governments of Armenia and Georgia had found it possible "to renounce their territorial claims on Turkey." The Soviet government had also reviewed its policy concerning the Straits and considered it possible to protect Soviet security in the region of the Straits on terms equally acceptable to both the Soviet Union and Turkey. Consequently, the Soviet Union now had "no territorial claims on Turkey."[12]

The Turkish government duly informed the United Kingdom, the United States, and France of the Soviet gesture and indicated its intention of advising the North Atlantic Council. There appeared no doubt of the Soviet intention to weaken both NATO and the new Balkan Entente (Greece, Turkey, and Yugoslavia). While the United States made no official comment on the Soviet move, on June 11 the Turkish Foreign Ministry acknowledged that it had received the Soviet note, and the Turkish press gave a resounding response. The Turkish government did not reply until July 18, expressing its satisfaction at the renunciation of territorial claims, noting that the Soviet

---

2: 415-21. See also Harry N. Howard, "The Regional Pacts and the Eisenhower Doctrine," in Hart, "American and the Middle East," pp. 85-94.

[11]*American Foreign Policy, 1950–1955: Basic Documents*, 2: 2168-75.

[12]For the Turkish-Soviet exchange, see, especially, Council on Foreign Relations, *Documents on American Foreign Relations 1953*, pp. 165-69. See also Feridun Cemal Erkin, *Les Rélations Turco-Soviétiques et la Question des Détroits* (Ankara: Başnur Matbaasi, 1968), pp. 410 ff.

concern for good relations corresponded with its own desires, and stressing that "the question of the Black Sea Straits," as the Soviet government well knew, was "regulated by provisions of the Montreux Convention." To keep the discussion going, evidently, on July 20 the Soviet government sent another note to Ankara, which had a special bearing on Turkish–American relations, for it complained concerning the prospective visit, during July 22–27, of 10 U.S. warships to Istanbul, to be followed by a visit, during July 27–August 3, of 22 British naval vessels, which the Soviet government considered a "kind of military demonstration." But, on July 24, the Turkish government observed that these were all courtesy visits, under Articles 14 and 17 of the Montreux Convention, and their frequency was but a "happy evidence of the friendly ties uniting Turkey with countries to which the invited fleets" belonged. The Soviet government reiterated its position on July 31, when it pointed out that 33 warships of 197,000 tons displacement had visited Turkey in 1950, 49 (378,000 tons) in 1951, and 69 (587,727 tons) in 1952, to say nothing of the 60 (300,000 tons) which had passed the Straits during the first seven months of 1953.[13]

There was no special response to the Soviet note, but on August 8, 1953, Premier Malenkov reiterated the Soviet renunciation of territorial claims and stressed the desire for good neighborly relations with Turkey.[14] The Soviet government took no steps to denounce the Montreux Convention, as it could have done, on November 9, 1954, with the result that in accordance with Article 28, that instrument was to endure until two years after any specific date of denunciation by any of the signatories. It may be assumed that the Soviet government refrained from such action because it had substantially what it required under the Montreux Convention, despite its complaints during 1945–46, because it could not necessarily achieve its additional *desiderata* through the convening of an international conference either to revise the Montreux Convention or to elaborate a new regime, particularly as to conversion of the Black Sea into a Soviet *mare clausum* or the establishment of joint Turkish–Soviet defense of the Straits, and also because the region of the Straits could be controlled effectively with the new weaponry and missiles.

[13]See Republique Turque, Ministère des Affaires Estrangères, *Rapports Annuels sur le Mouvement des Navires à Travers les Détroits*, 1946 ff., for detailed data.

[14]Council on Foreign Relations, *Documents on American Foreign Relations 1953*, pp. 138–39. Malenkov said that the renunciation created "the essential prerequisites for development of good-neighborly relations if, of course, the Turkish side in its turn makes due efforts in this direction." Improvement in relations "would undoubtedly be to the benefit of both sides and make an important contribution to strengthening security in the Black Sea area."

Few questions have arisen technically since that time concerning the Straits and there have been few pronouncements. While the Turkish government supported the American position as to a form of international control over the Suez Canal during the Suez crisis and conflict in 1956, in view of its own "nationalization" of the Straits in 1936, perhaps, and of the possibility that it wanted no reflection on that basic fact, Turkey raised no question of principle following Egyptian nationalization of the Suez Canal Company.[15] In 1957 the Turkish government fully supported the Eisenhower Doctrine for defense of the Middle East, in line with its consistent policy up to that time.[16] During the Syrian crisis of August–October 1957, Turkey was once more under severe Soviet pressure, not dissimilar to that which had been applied in reference to the Straits during 1945–46, as Secretary of State Dulles had pointed out.[17] The Turkish government became somewhat concerned with the elaboration of principles pertaining generally to the regime of the high seas during 1954–56 by the International Law Commission, in view of the suggestions concerning transit and navigation of straits, and it may be noted that the later Conference on the Law of the Sea, 1958–60, failed to reach basic agreement, especially as to territorial waters.[18]

Despite Soviet warnings, Turkey entered into a defense agreement with the United States on March 5, 1959, under the Eisenhower Doctrine and in connection with CENTO, under which the United States undertook to take appropriate action, including the use of armed force, in the event of aggression against Turkey, and reaffirmed its promise of economic and military assistance.[19] There appeared to be no basic changes in policy or interest relative to the Straits in Turkish–American relations in the later years, whether be-

[15]Department of State, *The Suez Problem, July 26–September 22, 1956* (Washington, D.C.: USGPO, 1956), pp. 120–23.

[16]Department of State, *American Foreign Policy: Current Documents 1956*, p. 837.

[17]Ibid., pp. 1046–48.

[18]See, especially, UN Doc. A/2934: *Report of the International Law Commission Covering the Work of its Seventh Session, 2 May–8 July 1955*; Department of State, *American Foreign Policy: Current Documents 1958*, pp. 249–91. For American views, see also *Sovereignty of the Sea*. Geographic Bulletin No. 3 (revised October 1969). Office of the Geographer, Department of State (1969) "U.S. Draft Articles on Territorial Sea, Straits, and Fisheries submitted to U.N. Seabeds Committee; statement by John R. Stevenson and Texts of Draft Treaties," Department of State *Bulletin* 45, no. 1680 (September 6, 1971): 261–68.

[19]See, for example, the *New York Times*, May 23, 27, 29, 1960. It may be observed that, during 1946–62, American assistance to Turkey totaled no less than $3,869,300,000, with $1,581,300,000 in economic and $2,288,000,000 in military assistance. By 1971, total assitance was approximately $5,700,000,000 with $135,667,000 allocated in 1971 and $148,170,000 in 1972. See also *American Foreign Policy: Current Documents 1959*, pp. 1020–23.

fore or after the *coup d'état* of May 1960. There were, no doubt, differences concerning strategic concepts, the problem of NATO bases, and Polaris submarines, to say nothing of missiles and military installations.[20] While there appeared little doubt that in the nuclear age of instantaneous communications the Straits no longer had quite the importance they possessed during the nineteenth and early twentieth centuries, there was also no doubt that they remained of vital significance to Turkey, its independence and its territorial integrity.[21] There also appeared to be little question as to the vital significance of the Straits to the Soviet Union.

TURKISH CAUTION

Turkish foreign policy in the later years continued to develop in the direction of independence, based on highly realistic considerations in a very strategic area of the world at the intercontinental crossroads.[22] Although the trends had earlier roots, anti-American and neutralist sentiments began to develop in Turkey especially by 1964. While the American position on the sensitive problem of Cyprus stood out as one of the most significant factors, other elements included the presence of a large number of American troops on Turkish soil, Turkish dissatisfaction with the USAID program, alleged CIA attempts to intervene in Turkey's domestic affairs, and Soviet receptiveness to Turkish moves toward a more "friendly" relationship.[23] But there was an ingrained caution in Turkish policy toward the Soviet Union, based on a well-founded sense of realism. The development of the Soviet Mediterranean fleet, with its base largely in the Black Sea, did not go unnoticed in Ankara. The fact that there was such a fleet, with an announced intention to remain in the Mediterranean as a counterweight to the U.S. Sixth Fleet, made its inevitable impact. Following the Soviet invasion of Czechoslovakia in August 1968, Turkey reaffirmed its basic position in both NATO and CENTO. President Cev-

[20]On May 23, 1963, the USSR sent notes to the United States, the United Kingdom, Turkey, and fourteen Mediterranean countries urging that the Mediterranean be declared a nuclear-free zone, well-timed for the opening of the North Atlantic Council in Ottawa, Canada. See *New York Times*, May 22, 1963.

[21]See *Washington Post*, March 24, April 23, May 9, 1963; London *Economist*, February 9, 1963.

[22]Vali, *Bridge Across the Bosporus*, chaps. 3, 5, 8, especially.

[23]The fact that Turkey was a major source in the opium traffic to the United States was a serious irritant. President Nixon announced on June 30, 1971, that Turkey had agreed to eliminate by 1972 its production of opium poppies, which accounted for two-thirds of the illegal heroin reaching the United States. *New York Times*, July 1, 1971. See also Vali, *Bridge Across the Bosporus*, chap. 4: A. H. Ulman and R. H. Dekmejian, "Changing Patterns in Turkish Foreign Policy, *1959-1967*," *Orbis* 11, no. 3 (Fall 1967): 772-78; *United States Foreign Policy. A Report of the Secretary of State* (Washington, D.C.: USGPO, 1972), pp. 106-08.

det Sunay observed on August 30, 1968 that in the interest of maintaining its own independence and sovereignty, Turkey would have to fulfill its "mutual pledges and commitments," recent events having proved once more "the necessity for and use of our alliances." In turn, it was noteworthy that the NATO Council, during November 15-16, 1968, observed that "the new uncertainties resulting from Soviet actions" extended to the Mediterranean basin, and warned that "clearly any Soviet intervention directly or indirectly affecting the situation in Europe or the Mediterranean would create an international crisis with grave consequences."

The Turkish Straits Today

If, as has been suggested, the Bolshevik Revolution of November 1917 did not alter the significance of the region of the Black Sea and the Turkish Straits, it may be added now that the period since World War II has shown a continued growth and development of that region and the use of the waterway both for commercial and naval purposes. The great development of Odessa and other Black Sea ports, as already observed, dates from the early nineteenth century, as does the basic development of Russian commerce passing from the Black Sea into the Mediterranean and the open sea. Similarly, the Russian position as to the security of the Straits and the assertion of Russia's vital security interest in the area goes back at least to this period. By 1914 some 50 percent of Russia's total export maritime commerce went out to the West via the Black Sea and the Turkish Straits, at the very time when the area was considered the "key" to Russia's Black Sea shores.

THE COMMERCIAL SIGNIFICANCE OF THE STRAITS
The period following World War II well illustrates the development of Soviet and other commerce operating in the region of the Straits. By 1973, some 50 percent of the total Soviet commercial tonnage sailed from Black Sea ports, and 40 percent of the ships operating in or transiting the Straits and 43.1 percent of the tonnage were of Soviet registry. By 1973, no less than 19,658 ships of 83,293,840 tons had passed the Straits, as compared with 13,150 ships (101,391,132 tons) transiting the Panama Canal (1969) and 21,250 ships (274,250,000 tons) transiting the Suez Canal (1966).[24]

---

[24]See Appendix 5 for tables illustrating commercial use of the Straits, compiled from Republique Turque, Ministère des Affaires Etrangères, *Rapports Annuels sur le Mouvement des Navires à Travers les Détroits Turcs (1946-1972).* The Turkish

The steady development of Soviet commercial shipping in the Turkish Straits is evident throughout the post-World War II period, and particularly since 1955, when the tonnage increased from some 1,200,000 to more than 26,365,000 in 1969, 29,054,266 in 1971, and 30,296,084 in 1973. As already observed, by 1973 Soviet commercial vessels constituted some 40 percent of the ships and 43.1 percent of the tonnage. With ships of Bulgarian and Rumanian registry, Black Sea ships constituted about 50 percent of the total and 50 percent of the tonnage. While this heavy percentage underlines the regional significance of the Straits, it may be well to observe that Mediterranean commercial shipping (primarily Greece, Italy, Yugoslavia, and France) made up some 25 percent of the ships and 26 percent of the tonnage. The primary Western European users of the Straits are Norway, the United Kingdom, Sweden, and West Germany, with about 5 percent of the ships and 7 percent of the registered net tonnage. In Eastern Europe, the primary users are Finland, Poland, and East Germany, with about 5 percent of the ships and tonnage. Among the Arab states, ships of Lebanese registry are of primary interest, with 1,312,916 tons in 1962, and an annual average of some 400,000 tons over the past several years. From south Asia, Indian ships have averaged an annual 350,000 tons or more, as have ships of Japanese registry. Another element of great interest, however, is the fact that American shipping has generally ranked well in the tonnage which has passed the Straits. Thus, between 1945 and 1947, American commercial tonnage surpassed all other shipping, as it did in 1949, while it was exceeded by that of the United Kingdom and the USSR in 1948, Italy in 1950 and 1951, and the USSR and Greece in 1952. While American tonnage reached an all-time high level of 1,449,389 tons in 1964, in the later years it was outranked, not merely by the USSR, but by Greece, Italy, Yugoslavia, Norway, and France. During 1972, 198 American vessels, of 908,408 tons passed the Straits. American tonnage would, of course, be much higher if ships of Panamanian (1,130,647 tons in 1972) and Liberian (3,466,239 tons in 1972) registry, often of American ownership, flew the American flag. British shipping, which played a leading role during the interwar period of 1919–39, declined after World War II (994,701 tons in 1972). The total amount of commercial shipping using the Straits, with the exception of the war and immediate post-World War II years, showed a rather steady increase from 6,500,178 tons during 1923 to 12,322,012 in 1935, and 70,295,878 in 1972. These data, of course, leave aside Turkish domestic shipping which sails these waters.

---

merchant marine, which is not listed in the *Rapports Annuels*, consists of some 298 ships, with 648,171 gross tons.

Insofar as the Soviet Union is concerned, the significance of the Black Sea and the Straits may be measured in other ways. For example, it appears that *Soviet Far Eastern* lines comprise some 35 percent of Soviet shipping and 23 percent of the deadweight tonnage, the *Baltic* lines about 23 percent of the shipping and 19 percent of the tonnage, and the *Arctic* merchant fleet only 2 percent of the shipping and 8 percent of the tonnage. By contrast, the *Black Sea* merchant fleet comprises 31 percent of the shipping and 50 percent of the tonnage. On an average day, it is estimated, some 250 Soviet merchant vessels ply Mediterranean ports. As a whole, the Soviet merchant fleet, which is now carrying some 75 percent of the total Soviet maritime foreign commerce (1970), advanced from 21st in rank in 1950 to 5th place by 1968. By 1970 it was carrying an estimated 186,700,000 tons of cargo in 1970, as compared with 144,000,000 tons in 1967. The value of annual foreign trade increased from some $5,000,000,000 in 1962 to no less than $18,000,000,000 in 1968. By 1980 Soviet officials hope that cargoes from developing countries will be worth some $11,000,000,000, much of which will, of course, go through the Black Sea and into the Straits and the Mediterranean.[25]

NAVAL USE OF THE STRAITS

Naval passage of the Straits increased significantly after World War II, and this was especially true of the Soviet fleet after 1964, when a Mediterranean squadron came into being, and particularly so after 1967. Problems as to naval passage after 1946, however, were not of overriding significance under the terms of the Montreux Convention. A problem did arise concerning the passage of three Italian warships which were to be transferred to the Soviet Black Sea fleet. It may be recalled that according to Annex B of the Treaty of Peace with Italy, signed on February 10, 1947, the Italian government was to place certain warships at the disposal of the Soviet Union, the United Kingdom, the United States, and France.[26] Ultimate disposition was finally made, with the *Giulio Cesare* and two submarines assigned to the USSR in 1948. The question then arose as to the passage of these ships from the Mediterranean, through the Turkish Straits and into the Black Sea port of Odessa, since an Italian vessel, the *Giulio Cesare*, of 23,622 tons, exceeded the tonnage permitted to

---

[25]The Center for Strategic and International Studies, *Soviet Sea Power* (Washington, D.C., 1969), pp. 73–91. The Soviet Union maintained a merchant fleet of some 14,832,000 tons in 1970. Through the canal shuttle system (Volga–Don and Volga–Baltic canals) ships of up to 5,000 tons could shuttle from the Caspian and Black Seas to the Baltic. On the development of the Soviet merchant fleet, see "Under the Soviet Flag: Our Correspondent Interviews Victor Bakayev, Minister of the Soviet Merchant Marine," *Culture and Life*, no. 10 (1968): 11–15.

[26]See *Treaty of Peace with Italy* (1947), pp. 22, 92–94.

pass under Article 14 of the Montreux Convention (15,000 tons). Since this limitation, however, did not apply to the Black Sea Powers under Article 11, the three vessels which were transferred to the USSR were placed under Soviet crews and under the Soviet flag and passed through the Straits during February 23-25, 1949.[27] A second problem, having to do with the removal of Japan as a signatory of the Montreux Convention, as already observed, constituted no basic issue or difficulty. In signing the treaty of peace on September 6, 1951, at San Francisco, Japan renounced such rights and interests as derived from being a signatory.[28]

While there were no special, technical problems concerning transit and navigation of the Straits, whether by commercial or naval vessels, following World War II, it is of interest to note the increasing use of the Straits by the Red Navy in the later years, as compared with other fleets. For example, some 90 Soviet warships passed the Straits in 1964 and 307 transits occurred in 1971 (691,261 tons). The steady decline of American naval use, even granted the alliance with Turkey under NATO, is illustrated by the fact that only 22 American warships (53,350 tons) transited the Straits in 1971 (54 ships of 865,648 tons in 1957).[29]

Naval courtesy visits continued to play a role in the Straits during the post-World War II era, and they are without limit as to tonnage. For example, in 1947, 2 American cruisers and 2 destroyers (41,400 tons) paid a courtesy visit to Istanbul, as did 9 British warships, 2 cruisers, with accompanying destroyers (64,700 tons), and an Argentinian cruiser (7,500 tons). As already observed, the USSR protested the courtesy visits of 10 American and 22 British warships during July-August 1953. While fewer American warships transited the Straits after 1962, there were courtesy visits, for example, in 1963, when 7 American warships (165,000 tons) visited Istanbul. Fifteen American warships visited in 1964 (163,500 tons) and 16 in 1965 (158,856 tons), while 34 paid a visit in 1966, 10 in 1967, and 16 in 1968. Partly, no doubt, in view of increasing difficulties around Istanbul, American courtesy visits were much reduced during 1969-71, with only 5 paying courtesy calls in 1969, 6 in 1970, and 5 in 1971. There is,

[27]The *Giulio Cesare* was renamed the *Novorossisk*, while the two submarines were the M41 (971 tons) and M42 (643 tons). The USS *Missouri*, 45,000 tons, bearing the body of Ambassador Mehmet Munir Ertegun, passed the Straits on April 4, 1946, returning on April 9, but this was a courtesy visit, in which the element of tonnage was not involved (see Department of State *Bulletin* 14, no. 350 [March 17, 1946]: 447).

[28]See *Conference for the Conclusion and Signature of the Treaty of Peace with Japan. San Francisco, California, September 4-8, 1951*, Record of Proceedings (Washington, D.C.: USGPO, 1951), pp. 216-17.

[29]See Appendix 5 for detailed statistical data.

on the other hand, no record of a courtesy visit by units of the Soviet fleet, despite the dominant Soviet position in the Black Sea, the constant use of the Straits, and its significant activities in the Mediterranean.

Throughout the postwar period the USSR sought to establish the principle of the *mare clausum* in the Black Sea. Not until January 1962 did it bother to report to the Turkish government, under Article 18 of the Montreux Convention, its naval tonnage in the Black Sea, when it listed 95,000 tons of warships in that sea. These figures have remained constant in the ensuing years. Bulgaria and Rumania began reporting in 1964, with figures which have also remained constant: Bulgaria 7,000 tons and Rumania 3,881 tons.

The Soviet Union continued to frown upon the entry of American warships into the Black Sea. The United States asserted its right to send its ships into the Black Sea in accordance with the provisions of the Montreux Convention and maintained this right, usually by sending two destroyers or frigates in the spring and fall of each year. Other considerations aside, the obvious purpose of these semiannual visits appeared to be the maintenance of the principle of freedom of transit and navigation through the Straits and into the Black Sea, in accordance with the American–Ottoman treaties of 1830 and 1862 and with the principles enunciated in May 1871.[30] The Soviet position was well stated, albeit unofficially, in *Krasnaya Zvezda*, on September 3, 1966,[31] when it commented on the announced visit of the USS *Pratt* in the Black Sea and charged that since it was armed with rockets, its entry into the Black Sea would constitute a violation of the Montreux Convention. The urgency of the question of the illegality of the entry of the *Pratt*, or of other warships of non-Black Sea Powers carrying similar weapons, it was said, arose from the necessity of protecting Black Sea states whose peoples could not "remain indifferent to the type of warship entering the Black Sea or to the aims of

[30]The destroyers *Johnston* and *Perry* entered and left the Black Sea on October 4, 1963 (3,500 tons each); the destroyers *Luce* and *Corry* entered and left on September 22, 1965; the guided missile frigate *Yarnell* and the destroyer *Forrest Royal* entered and left on January 13, 1966; the destroyers *Goodrich* and *Wood* visited the Black Sea on November 18, 1967; the destroyers *Cecil* and *Norris* visited on June 10, 1968, and the *Turner* and *Dyess* on December 12, 1968. The destroyers *Perry* and *Norris* paid visits during June, August, and September 1969 and the *Roberts* and *Strong* during December. The *Perry* and *Sumner* visited the Black Sea during March 1970, the *O'Hare* and *Mullinix* durig May and August, and the *Perry* and *Strong* in December. The pattern was repeated during 1971, with visits of the *New, Rich, Steinaker,* and *Wood* during April 16-21, the *Wood, Rich,* and *New* during July 1-4, and the *Hawkins, O'Hare,* and *Wilson* during November 20-29.

[31]Cited in Walter Laqueur, *The Struggle for the Middle East* (New York: Macmillan, 1969), pp. 348-50. See also Ferenc Vali, *The Turkish Straits and NATO* (Stanford, California: The Hoover Institution, 1972), pp. 99-107.

their passage." While the Straits might be utilized in the interest of strengthening friendship, that waterway could not be used "to the detriment of the security of states situated in this area." In the interests of all the Black Sea states, the Black Sea "must remain a sea of peace and friendship."

Granted the use of the region of the Straits and the Black Sea by the Soviet Navy, which now maintains a substantial squadron of some 60 ships in the Mediterranean, it would appear that the region remains vital to the security of the Soviet Union, as it was to Imperial Russia, and for the same reasons, whatever the changes in military technology. The Imperial Russian government maintained this position throughout its history, as it sought to maintain the principle of the *mare clausum* in the Black Sea, while attempting to achieve freedom for its warships to pass through the Straits into the Mediterranean and return. It was also the position of the USSR in the demands made upon the Nazi government in November 1940 and in those made upon Turkey during 1945–46. From the evidence available, it appears to be the position of the Soviet government today, despite the developments in the new weaponry and missiles, even though in wartime it is doubtful that any foreign fleet would attempt to or need to utilize the Straits for war operations against the Soviet Union.[32]

---

[32]The distribution of the principal surface vessels among the four Soviet fleets appears to be as follows: (1) the *Pacific fleet*, from 4 to 6 cruisers and at least 30 destroyers, with frigates and escort vessels; (2) the *Northern fleet*, at least 3 cruisers and some 35 destroyers, frigates, and other vessels; (3) the *Baltic fleet*, 4 or more cruisers and some 25 destroyers and other combat ships; and (4) the *Black Sea fleet*, about 7 cruisers, at least 50 destroyers, frigates and escorts, and two helicopter carriers (*Moskva* and *Leningrad*). The Mediterranean squadron is composed primarily of ships from the Black Sea fleet. A number of ships move between fleet areas on the high seas, but interfleet transfer over internal Soviet waterways is possible, of course, only for small vessels. Some 140 Rumanian and Bulgarian warships could add strength to the Soviet Black Sea fleet. The Mediterranean squadron has been as large as 61 vessels, although its size and composition change from time to time. See also Drew Middleton in *New York Times*, March 25, 1973, p. 16.

The official formation of the Mediterranean squadron of the Black Sea fleet probably came in 1964, when the *Mikhail Kutuzov* and other vessels under the command of Admiral S. Y. Chursin cruised the Mediterranean at length, and as many as 15 Soviet warships transited the Straits. The number and radius of activity increased during the next two years. During 1966, submarine tenders, rocket-firing destroyers, submarine chasers, and other ships participated and visited in Ethiopia, Port Said, and Toulon. By the end of 1966 the USSR maintained some 25 ships in the Mediterranean. Several destroyers, including the *Naporisty, Plamenny, Gnevny,* and *Boiky,* participated in operations, and in 1967 some 157 Soviet warships passed into the Mediterranean and only 91 returned. Among the 66 which remained, 21 were mine layers and 21 torpedo boats. The fleet grew to 45 ships in 1968, including one 19,000-ton cruiser and one or two 5,200-ton rocket cruisers. The squadron was reinforced in 1968 with one or two 20,000-ton carriers of the Moskva class, which carry up to 36

The Soviet Union, the United States, Turkey, and the Global Picture

If one looks at the grand Soviet strategy, it would appear that the USSR is attempting to control the Baltic and the Black seas, as in the past, and, ultimately, to exercise a dominant influence in the Mediterranean Sea, together with their approaches, and it is still seeking to become the dominant power in the Turkish Straits, through which its warships must pass from the Black Sea into the Aegean and the Mediterranean. One of the world's two superpowers, the USSR has built a superfleet, and its Mediterranean squadron is now five times larger than it was a bare eight years ago.[33] In conjunction with land-based air power, the Soviet fleet poses a serious political threat in the Mediterranean and an increasing politico-naval challenge to the American Sixth Fleet in the inland sea. In the Indian Ocean, even with the Suez Canal barred to traffic, the Soviet Navy is establishing its presence, where there is no western force, with the exception of very small units of the United States Navy. With the opening of the Suez Canal, the Turkish Straits should take on even more significance, for very obvious reasons. On the other hand,

the land-locked nature of the Soviet Union provides the United States with the choice of maintaining barrier defenses across narrow sea approaches to such Soviet fleet areas as the Greenland, Iceland and Faeroe Island gaps, the entrances to the Baltic, the Mediterranean and the Black Seas and the exits from the sea of Japan and the Tartar Strait. In case of war geography thus gives the United States the advantage of blocking fleet movements into the high seas. The very factor of geography requires the Soviets to keep up four distinct naval fleets. This strategic handicap, with the limited outlet to warm-water ports, is compounded by the need to operate in ice-blocked seas.[34]

---

helicopters and marines. By 1970 the Black Sea fleet was said to include 9 missile, light and heavy cruisers, 14 guided missile destroyers, 15 conventional destroyers, 299 patrol craft and other minor surface ships, and 28 conventionally powered submarines, the grand total being some 398 combat vessels of varying types.

(See, especially, The Center for Strategic and International Studies, *Soviet Sea Power* 39-40, *Time* 99, no. 5 [January 31, 1972]: 28-33; Gover Heiman, "Mediterranean Bid," *Armed Forces Management* [January 1969]: 46-48; David Fairhall, *Russian Sea Power* [Boston: Gambit, 1971], passim; Lawrence L. Whetten, "The Military Consequences of Mediterranean Super Power Parity," *New Middle East*, no. 38 [November 1971]: 14-25; Robert G. Weinland, *The Changing Mission Structure of the Soviet Navy*, Professional Paper No. 80, November 1971, Center for Naval Analyses [1971]. For American and NATO concern over Soviet naval buildup, see *New York Times*, May 29, July 1, 5, 1971; *Washington Post* November 15, 1970.)

[33]See, especially, *Jane's Fighting Ships 1971-1972* (London: St. Giles House, 1973), pp. 590-659.

[34]The Center for Strategic and International Studies, *Soviet Sea Power*, p. 29 and passim.

After building up its naval forces for some twenty years after World War II, the USSR has recently engaged in showing the Red flag in the Mediterranean, the Red Sea, the Indian Ocean, and the Far East. A significant portion of the fleet, as already observed, is in the Mediterranean and includes some of the Soviet Union's largest, newest and most sophisticated units. The Soviet Union has used its Mediterranean squadron politically, with units moving into facilities at Port Said and Alexandria, and calling regularly at Latakia in Syria and at Mersel-Kabir in Algeria. As the Soviet foreign minister, Andrei Gromyko, remarked on May 12, 1968: "Being a Black Sea Power, and consequently a Mediterranean Power, the Soviet Union is interested in peace and security in that area which is in direct proximity to the USSR's southern borders. We have always stood for turning the Mediterranean Sea into a sea of peace and a zone free of nuclear weapons. The presence of the Soviet ships in the Mediterranean is a factor facilitating the safeguarding of the security of the entire Mediterranean zone."[35] Moscow announced on October 12, 1968, that a "new power" had appeared in the Mediterranean—the Soviet Union—and that its presence had both "political and military importance." Its influence was to be felt in the Middle East, along the shores of North Africa, and of Southern Europe. Ultimately, it appeared that the Soviet aim was to overshadow and, perhaps, to deny the American naval presence in the Mediterranean and then to open up a secure passage through the Suez Canal to the Red Sea, the Persian Gulf, and South Asia. It is also conceivable, if improbable in the near future, that the development of Soviet naval strength in the Mediterranean—to say nothing of increasing Soviet commerce—may encourage the Soviet Union not merely to seek formal changes in the Montreux Convention of the Straits, but to seek to loosen further the Turkish ties to the West under the North Atlantic Treaty Organization and to neutralize it.[36] In broad and summary terms, the basic interests which have led the USSR to

[35]Moscow TASS International Service, in English, May 12, 1968.

[36]See, especially, *Soviet Involvement in the Middle East and the Western Response*, Joint Hearings before the Subcommittee on Europe and Subcommittee on the Near East of the Committee on Foreign Affairs, House of Representatives, Ninety-Second Congress, First Session, October 19, 20, 21; November 2 and 3, 1971 (Washington, D.C.: USGPO, 1971); *A Sino-Soviet Perspective in the Middle East*, Hearing before the Subcommittee on the Near East of the Committee on Foreign Affairs, House of Representatives, Ninety-Second Congress, Second Session, April 26, 1972 (Washington, D.C.; USGPO, 1972); *The Middle East in Crisis: Problems and Prospects*, Report of the Subcommittee on the Near East of the Committee on Foreign Affairs, House of Representatives, December 21, 1971 (Washington, D.C.: USGPO, 1971). See also Vali, *Bridge Across the Bosporus*, chap. 5; Lord Chalfont, "Russia and the Indian Ocean: New Attitudes to Sea Power," *New Middle East*, no. 44 (May 1972): 4-6; D. C. Watt, "The Persian Gulf—Cradle of Conflict," *Problems of Communism* 21, no. 3 (May–June 1972): 32-40.

take its actions concerning the Mediterranean squadron center around (1) its ambitions for a secure outlet to the open sea for Soviet military and commercial operations; (2) its struggle for "legitimacy" and its desire to achieve it through the unequivocal establishment of the Soviet Union as a world power, with world wide interests; (3) its desire for participation in the Middle Eastern oil industry;[37] (4) its desire to keep its ideological competitors, the Chinese, out of the Middle East; and (5) its ambition to control the Turkish Straits, the Suez Canal, and the southern entrance of the Red Sea.

That these developments in Soviet policy and interest have been and remain matters of serious concern to American policy-makers and to NATO is all too obvious. The United States and Turkey have been in alliance—sometimes "troubled"—under NATO for more than twenty years. Despite occasional strain, the alliance has served the mutual interests of the two countries. Like other nations, the United States continues interested in access to the Eastern Mediterranean and the Middle East, access to Middle Eastern oil, and in prevention of Soviet dominance in the area. While there has been a weakening of NATO ties with Turkey as a consequence of the Cyprus problem, as already observed, following the Soviet invasion of Czechoslovakia in August 1968 and the enunciation of the "Brezhnev Doctrine," the alliance was reaffirmed, with special reference to the uncertainties in the Mediterranean. Concern over the Mediterranean continued, and in his report for 1969-70, Secretary of State William Rogers observed that relations with Turkey were "firmly grounded in our membership in NATO, our cooperation in CENTO, and our pattern of close bilateral economic and military cooperation for more than 20 years." Important security interests were involved in American relations with Turkey, whose political and military strength was considered essential to the protection of NATO's southeastern flank and, in addition, Turkey's strength provided "a vital measure of stability to the eastern Mediterranean area." The increasing Soviet naval activities in the Mediterranean underscored the importance of the southern flank of NATO. In his own report to the Congress on foreign policy in 1970, President Nixon observed that the United States would view any effort by the USSR to seek predominance in the Middle East "as a matter of grave concern."[38]

[37]George Lenczowski, *Soviet Advances in the Middle East* (Washington, D.C.: American Enterprise Institute, 1971), passim; John A. Berry, "Oil and Soviet Policy in the Middle East," *Middle East Journal* 26, no. 2 (Spring 1972): 149-60; Thomas C. Barger, "Middle Eastern Oil Since the Second World War," *Annals* 401 (May 1972): 31-44.

[38]See, especially, *United States Foreign Policy, 1969-1970. A Report of the Secretary of State* (Washington, D.C.: USGPO, 1971), pp. 87-88; *United States Foreign Policy, A Report of the Secretary of State. 1971* (Washington, D.C.: USGPO, 1972), pp. 106-08;

The problem of the Turkish Straits and of the Middle East as a
whole—and American interest and policy—must be seen both in its
historical and contemporary setting. The United States has had long-
standing and wide-ranging interests in the area, going back to the
beginning of the nineteenth century, although its enduring politico-
strategic interests date only from World War II. Turkey has played a
central role in American policy in the area as a key to the northern
tier of the Middle East and the Eastern Mediterranean. While the
American interest in the Turkish Straits down to the post-World War
II years was primarily commercial in character, the politico-strategic
interest in the Straits was stressed under the Soviet threat to Turkey
in the immediate postwar years. There has been a basic consistency
in American policy since the beginning of the nineteenth century
in the insistence on freedom of commerical passage and on the open
character of the Black Sea. Granted the contention of Laurence
Martin that the Middle East is "a declining asset" to the West in its
"traditional role of line of communication," it is not for the Soviet
Union, for which, indeed, the area has taken on an increasing
interest, with Turkey and the Straits as key points in the situation,
"as a way to break out finally from its long encirclement." If the USSR
is really seeking and developing its strength to enhance its status
and position as a global power, with Turkey and the Middle East as
one of the avenues by which to achieve that end, it is doubtful that the
United States can afford to ignore or neglect the totality of its own
interests in the area.[39]

U.S. Foreign Policy for the 1970's. A New Strategy for Peace. A Report to the Congress
by Richard Nixon, President of the United States. February 18, 1970 (Washington, D.C.:
USGPO, 1970), pp. 77–83: Building for Peace . . . February 25, 1971 (Washington, D.C.:
USGPO, 1971), pp. 121–34; . . . The Emerging Structure of Peace . . . February 9, 1972
(Washington, D.C.: USGPO, 1972), pp. 133–40. As an attestation of the importance
which the United States has attached to Turkey, it may be observed that since World
War II it extended more than $2,500,000,000 in economic and $3,000,000,000 in grant
military assistance.
[39]See J. C. Hurewitz, ed., Soviet–American Rivalry in the Middle East (New York:
Praeger, 1969), p. 61; J. C. Hurewitz, Changing Military Perspectives in the Middle
East (Santa Monica, California: RAND, 1971); William B. Quandt, United States Policy
in the Middle East: Constraints and Choices (Santa Monica, California: RAND, 1970);
George Lenczowski, project director, United States Interests in the Middle East
(Washington, D.C.: American Enterprise Institute, 1968); John C. Campbell and Helen
Caruso, The West and the Middle East (New York: Council on Foreign Relations, 1972).
For an estimate of NATO concern with the Mediterranean and Soviet policy in the
Middle East, see Cyrus L. Sulzberger, New York Times, June 18, 1972. See also George
S. Harris, Troubled Alliance: Turkish American Problems in Historical Perspective,
1945–1971 (Stanford, Calif.: Hoover Institution; Washington, D.C.: American Enter-
prise Institute, 1972).

Annotated Bibliography

1. DOCUMENTARY SOURCES

France

Documents Diplomatiques. Conférence de Lausanne sur les Affaires du Proche-Orient (1922–1923). Recueil des actes de la conférence. Paris: Imprimerie Nationale, 1923. Premiere serie. Volume I contains protocols of first commission; volume IV documents on negotiations of February 1 to April 22, 1923. Deuxième série, volume I, proces-verbaux and documents on second part of conference, April 23–July 24, 1923. Volume II contains final acts of conference. 6 vols.

Germany

Die Grosse Politik der euroäischen Kabinette, 1871–1914. Berlin, 1922–27. 40 vols.

Department of State. *Documents on German Foreign Policy, 1918–1945.* Series D (1937–45). Washington, D.C.: USGPO, 1949 ff. 13 vols.

The Soviet Foreign Ministry. *Dokumenti Ministerstva Inostranikh Diel Germanii,* Vipusk II, *Germanskaia Politika v. Turtsii (1941–1943).* OGIZ-Gospolizdat, 1946. [French translation, Madeline and Michel Eristov, trans., *La Politique Allemande (1941–1943). Documents Secrets du Ministère des Affaires Étrangères d'Allemagne. Turquie.* Paris: Dupont, 1946, 136 pp.] Documents found by Soviet authorities and published for propaganda purposes.

Montreux Conference

Actes de la Conférence de Montreux Concernant lé Regime des Détroits. 22 Juin–22Juillet 1936. Compte Rendu des Séances Plénières et Proces-verbal des Débats du Comité Technique. Paris, 1936. 310 pp. Official records of the conference.

Russia (Soviet Union)

E. A. Adamov, editor. *Evropeiskie derzhavi i Gretsia v epokhy mirovoi voini.* Moscow, 1922. Russian documents dealing with Greece during World War I. 239 pp.

———. *Konstantinopol i Prolivy.* Moscow, 1922–26. 2 vols. Authoritative Russian source on the cession of Constantinople and the problem of the Straits during World War I. [French translation: *Constantinople et les Détroits.* Paris: Les Editions Internationales, 1930. 2 vols.]

281

————. *Razdel Aziatskoi Turtsii.* Moscow, 1924. 383 pp. Partition of Asiatic Turkey according to secret documents of the Imperial Russian Foreign Ministry.

René Marchand, editor. *Un Livre Noir. Diplomatie d'Avant Guerre d'Après les Documents des Archives Russes.* Paris, 1922–24. 3 vols.

Turkey

Tevfik Rüştü Aras, *10 Ans sur les Trace de Lausanne.* Istanbul: Akşam Matbaasi, 1935. 284 pp. Official addresses of the Turkish Foreign Minister.

Cemil Bilsel. *Türk Bogazlari* [*The Turkish Straits*]. Istanbul: Ismail Akgün, 1948. Documents and texts of Soviet and Turkish diplomatic exchanges relative to the Straits.

A Speech delivered by Ghazi Mustapha Kemal [*Atatürk*], *President of the Turkish Republic.* October 1927. Leipzig: K. F. Koehler, 1929. 724 pp.

Gasi Mustafa Kemal Pascha [Atatürk]. *Die Dokumente zur Rede.* Leipzig: K. F. Koehler, 1929. Documentary appendix to the great six-day speech. 279 pp.

United Kingdom

Documents on the Origins of the War, 1898–1914. Edited by G. P. Gooch and H. W. V. Temperley. London: HMSO, 1924–26. 11 vols. The official British documents for the period.

Documents on British Foreign Policy, 1919–1939. First Series. Edited by E. L. Woodward and Rohan Butler. London: HMSO, 1952 ff.

Turkey No. 1 (1923). Lausanne Conference on Near Eastern Affairs, 1922–23. Cmd. 1814. The records of proceedings and the draft terms of peace. The British records, official only for the British Delegation, do not go beyond the first phase of the conference, February 1923.

Treaty Series No. 16 (1923). Treaty of Peace with Turkey, and Other Instruments Signed at Lausanne on July 24, 1923. Cmd. 1929.

Turkey No. 1 (1936). Convention regarding the Regime of the Straits with Correspondence relating thereto. Montreux, July 20, 1936. Cmd. 5249.

United States

Department of State. *The Foreign Relations of the United States.* Washington, D.C.: USGPO, 1861 ff. Special documentary volumes on *The Paris Peace Conference (1919)* (1942–47), *Conferences at Washington, 1941–1942, and Casablanca 1943* (1968), *The Conferences at Cairo and Tehran,* 1943 (1961), *The Conferences of Malta and Yalta* (1955), and *The Conference of Berlin (Potsdam)* (1960) are particularly important.

————. *American Foreign Policy: Basic Documents, 1950–1955.* Washington, D.C.: USGPO, 1957. 2 vols. *Current Documents* after 1955. Essential for contemporary developments. *A Decade of American Foreign Policy; Basic Documents, 1941–49,* prepared at the request of the Senate Committee on Foreign Relations by the Staff of the Committee and the Department of State; appeared in 1950.

Committee on Foreign Relations, United States Senate. *A Select Chronology and Background Documents Relating to the Middle East*. First revised edition. May 1969. Washington, D.C.: USGPO, 287 pp. Comprehensive chronology and documentary collection for period of ca. 1946–69.

Other Documentary Sources

Jacob C. Hurewitz, editor. *Diplomacy in the Near and Middle East*. Vol. I, 1535–1914; Vol. II, 1914–56. Princeton: D. Van Nostrand, 1956. A collection of basic documents on the Middle East, its history and development, especially in the field of international relations. Now under revision and expansion.

Ralph H. Magnus, editor. *Documents on the Middle East: United States Interests in the Middle East*. Washington, D.C.: American Enterprise Institute, 1969. 229 pp. Comprehensive selection of documents.

David Hunter Miller. *My Diary at the Conference of Paris, with Documents*. New York: Appeal Printing Co., 1928. 22 vols. An authoritative documentary source, now somewhat superseded by the Department of State's thirteen volumes.

The Royal Institute for International Affairs. *Documents on International Affairs*. London: Oxford, 1928 ff. Annual volumes which serve as companions to the annual *Surveys of International Affairs*.

World Peace Foundation and Council on Foreign Relations. *Documents on American Foreign Relations*. 1938 ff. Published by the World Peace Foundation originally. After 1952 the series was continued annually by the Council on Foreign Relations as a companion volume to the annual volumes on *The United States in World Affairs*.

II. SELECTED BOOKS

Abrevaya, Juliette. *La Conférence de Montreux et le Régime des Détroits*. Paris: Editions Internationales, 1937. 137 pp. Brief treatise.

Anderson, M. S. *The Eastern Question*. New York: St. Martin's, 1966. 475 pp. Following the model of Sir John A. R. Marriot's *The Eastern Question*, Professor Anderson covers the period of 1774–1923. The author makes much use of Russian materials and gives ample consideration to the problem of the Straits.

Brüel, Erik. *International Straits: A Treatise in International Law*. Vol. I. *The General Legal Position of International Straits*; Vol. II. *Straits Comprised by Positive Regulations*. Copenhagen: Nyt Nordisk Forlag, 1947. 278 pp. London: Sweet and Maxwell, 1947. 426 pp. A comprehensive discussion of Straits. The problem of the Turkish Straits is covered in Vol. II, Pt. IV. Excellent discussion by a Danish scholar.

Campbell, John C., and Caruso, Helen. *The West and the Middle East* (New York: Council on Foreign Relations, 1972), 71 pp. Council Papers on International Affairs 1. Brief, succinct study dealing with security, the Arab-Israeli conflict, and oil.

Daniel, Robert L., *American Philanthropy in the Near East, 1820–1960.* Athens: Ohio University, 1970. 322 pp. Scholarly, objective treatment of the missionary-educational-philanthropic enterprise in the Middle East, ranging from Greece and the Balkans to the Turkish and Arab portions of the area. Excellent delineation of long-standing and wide-ranging American interest.

DeNovo, John A. *American Interests and Policies in the Middle East, 1900–1939.* Minneapolis: University of Minnesota, 1963. 447 pp. Excellent general survey of the development of American policies and interests. First of a trilogy.

Djonker [Conker], M. C. *Le Bosphore et les Dardanelles: Les Conventions des Détroits de Lausanne (1923) et Montreux (1936).* Lausanne: Held, 1938. 164 pp. Succinct treatise by a Turkish writer.

Erkin, Feridun Cemal. *Les Rélations Turco-Soviétiques et la Question des Détroits.* Ankara: Başnur Matbaasi, 1968. 540 pp. A comprehensive treatise by the former foreign minister of Turkey. Bibliography and documentary appendix.

Evans, Laurence. *United States Policy and the Partition of Turkey, 1914–1924.* Baltimore: The Johns Hopkins University Press, 1965. 437 pp. Excellent survey of problems in the period of World War I, the Paris Peace Conference, and the Lausanne Conference.

Field, James A. *America and the Mediterranean World, 1776–1882* (Princeton, N.J.: Princeton University Press, 1969). 485 pp. Best single, historical account of the early American concern and interest in the Mediterranean world and the Middle East. Covers naval, diplomatic, and missionary activity.

Finnie, David H. *Pioneers East: The Early American Experience in the Middle East.* Cambridge: Harvard University Press, 1967. 333 pp. Chapters 2, 3, and 4 are especially important for early American-Ottoman relations.

Fisher, Sydney N. "Two Centuries of American Interest in Turkey," *Festschrift for Frederick B. Artz.* Durham, N.C.: Duke University, 1964, pp. 113–38.

Foreign Area Studies, American University. *Area Handbook for the Republic of Turkey.* Washington, D.C.: USGPO, 1969. 438 pp. Useful handbook, prepared by the Systems Research Corporation for the use of the U.S. Army.

Fuad, Ali. *La Question des Détroits: Ses Origines, Son Evolution, Sa Solution a la Conférence de Lausanne.* Paris: Pierre Bossuet, 1928. 187 pp. An analysis by a Turkish writer.

Gordon, Leland. *American Relations with Turkey, 1830–1930: An Economic Interpretation.* Philadelphia: University of Pennsylvania Press, 1932. 402 pp. General survey of American-Ottoman relations, with ample consideration of American policy relative to the Straits.

Goriainov, Serge. *Le Bosphore et les Dardanelles. Étude Historique sur la Question des Détroits. D'Après la Correspondence Diplomatique Déposée aux Archives Centrales de Saint-Petersbourg et à Celles de l'Empire*. Préface de M. Gabriel Hanotaux, de l'Academie Française. Paris: Librairie Plon, 1910. With all its errors of fact and judgment, still a classic work.

Grabill, Joseph L. *Protestant Diplomacy and the Near East: Missionary Influence on American Policy, 1810-1927*. Minneapolis: University of Minnesota Press, 1971. 395 pp. The American conern with the missionary-educational enterprise; the impact of the missionary establishment on American policy.

Harris, George S. *The Troubled Alliance: The United States and Turkey: Their Problems in Historical Perspective, 1945-1971*. Stanford, California: Hoover Institution Press, 1972. A survey of the problems involved in the Turkish–American relationship.

Hart, Parker T., special editor. *America and the Middle East. The Annals of The American Academy of Political and Social Science*, vol. 401 (May 1972), 142 pp. An excellent, succinct series of papers dealing with the various facets of American policy and interest in the Middle East. Should be read by all students of the area.

Helmreich, Paul C. *From Paris to Sèvres: The Partition of the Ottoman Empire at the Peace Conference of 1919-1920*. Columbus: Ohio State University Press, 1974. 376 pp. Detailed study based on much archival material.

Hoskins, Halford L. *The Middle East: Problem Area in World Politics*. New York: Macmillan, 1954. 311 pp. Chapter II contains a brief treatment of the Straits problem.

Howard, Harry N. *The Partition of Turkey: A Diplomatic History, 1913-1923*. Norman: University of Oklahoma Press, 1931; New York: Howard Fertig, 1966. 486 pp. Discussion of partition of Ottoman Empire, with development of the Straits problem and consideration of the policies of the Powers.

——, *The Problem of the Turkish Straits*. Department of State Publication 2752, Near Eastern Series 5. Washington, D.C.: USGPO, 1947. 68 pp. Covers backgrounds, analyzes Montreux Convention, discusses exchanges of 1945-46, with texts of notes, and gives texts of treaties and conventions, 1774-1936.

——, *The King Crane Commission: An American Inquiry in the Middle East*. Beirut: Khayats, 1963. 369 pp. A study of the peace-making in 1919 relative to the Middle East. Ample coverage of the Straits problem.

James, Robert. *Gallipoli: The History of a Noble Blunder*. New York: Macmillan, 1965. 384 pp. A brilliant history of the Gallipoli campaign, devoted almost entirely to military aspects.

Jelavich, Barbara. *The Ottoman Empire, the Great Powers and the Straits Question, 1870-1887*. Bloomington: Indiana University Press, 1973. 209 pp. Excellent treatment of period.

Jones, Joseph M. *The Fifteen Weeks (February 21-June 5, 1947)*. New York: Viking, 1955. 296 pp. Revealing account of the origins of the Truman Doctrine and of developments looking toward the Marshall Plan. Special reference to aid to Greece and Turkey.

Joshua, Wynfred. *Soviet Penetration into the Middle East.* New York: National Strategy Information Center, 1971. 57 pp. Useful summary of situation.

Khadduri, Majid, ed. *Major Middle Eastern Problems in International Law.* Washington, D.C.: American Enterprise Institute, 1972. 139 pp. Chapter V is especially on passage through international waterways.

Kirk, George E. *The Middle East in the War, 1939–1946; The Middle East, 1945–1950.* London: Oxford [RIIA], 1953, 1954. 511 and 338 pp. A comprehensive work, indispensable for the period.

Lenczowski, George, editor. *United States Interests in the Middle East.* Washington, D.C.: American Enterprise Institute, 1968. 132 pp. Succinct statement covering politico-strategic, economic, and cultural interests.

———. *Soviet Advances in the Middle East.* Washington, D.C.: American Enterprise Institute, 1971. 176 pp. A very useful, well-documented study. Chapters III (Turkey), VIII (Soviet arms and military presence), and IX (Summary and conclusions) are especially pertinent.

Mandelstam, Andre N. *La Politique Russe d'Accès á la Méditerranee au XXème Siècle.* Academie de droit international à la Haye Recueil des cours. Vol. 47 (1934, I), 6030798. Excellent presentation of Russian policy by a former Dragoman of the Imperial Russian Embassy at Constantinople (1898–1914).

Mischef, P. *La Mer Noire et les Détroits de Constantinople.* Paris, 1899. Concentrates on Russian policy and interest.

Moorehead, Alan. *Gallipoli.* New York: Ballantine, 1956. 314 pp. An excellent account of the Gallipoli campaign, by the Australian journalist.

Mosely, Philip E. *Russian Diplomacy and the Opening of the Eastern Question in 1838–39.* Cambridge: Harvard University Press, 1934. 178 pp. Excellent, brief study.

Papadopoulos, G. S. *England and the Near East, 1896–1898.* Thessaloniki: Institute for Balkan Studies, 1969. 300 pp. A study of Lord Salisbury and the changes in British policy at the turn of the century.

Phillipson, Coleman, and Buxton, Noel. *The Question of the Bosphorus and Dardanelles.* London: Stevens and Haynes, 1917. 264 pp. A classic British treatise.

Polmar, Norman. *Soviet Naval Power: Challenge for the 1970s.* New York: National Strategy Information Center, 1972. 106 pages. Useful summary.

Potemkin, V. P. *Istoria Diplomatii.* Moscow, 1941–45. 3 vols. French translation, *L'Histoire de la Diplomatie.* Paris: Librairie de Medicis, 1946–47. 3 vols. Very interesting reflections on the Montreux Conference.

Psomiades, Harry J. *The Eastern Question: The Last Phase: A Study in Greek–Turkish Diplomacy.* Thessaloniki: Institute for Balkan Studies, 1968. 145 pp. Centers on the period of 1919–23.

Puryear, V. J. *England, Russia and the Straits Question, 1844–1856.* Berkeley: University of California Press, 1931. 481 pp. Centers on the period of the Crimean War.

———. *France and the Levant*. Berkeley: University of California Press, 1941. 252 pp. French policy to the mid-nineteenth century.

———. *Napoleon and the Dardanelles*. Berkeley: University of California Press, 1951. 437 pp. French policy and action in the era of Napoleon.

———. *International Economics and Diplomacy in the Near East: A Study of British Policy in the Levant, 1834-1853*. Stanford: Stanford University Press, 1935. 264 pp.

Shotwell, James T., and Deak, Francis. *Turkey at the Straits*. New York: Macmillan, 1940. 164 pp. A short history of the problem; useful as an historical outline of the subject.

Taube, Baron M. d. *La Politique Russe d'Avant-Guerre et la Fin de l'Empire des Tsars (1904-1907)*. Paris, 1928. Observations on Baltic and Black Sea policy.

Trask, R. R. *The United States Response to Turkish Nationalism and Reform, 1914-1939*. Leiden: Brill, 1971. 294 pp. Analyzes the course of American-Turkish relations from World War I to World War II.

Thomas, Lewis V., and Frye, Richard N. *The United States and Turkey and Iran*. Cambridge: Harvard University Press, 1951. 291 pp. Pp. 1-170 deal with Turkey.

Trumpener, Ulrich. *Germany and the Ottoman Empire, 1914-1918*. Princeton: Princeton University Press, 1968. 433 pp. Excellent discussion, based on German archival materials.

Ulam, Adam B. *Expansion and Coexistence: The History of Soviet Foreign Policy, 1917-1967*. New York: Praeger, 1968. 768 pp. Brief discussion of the problem of the Straits.

Vali, Ferenc A. *Bridge Across the Bosphorus: The Foreign Policy of Turkey*. Baltimore: The Johns Hopkins Press, 1971. 410 pp. Chapters IV-VI are of special interest on the problem of the Straits.

———. *The Turkish Straits and NATO*. Stanford, California: The Hoover Institution Press, 1972. 350 pp. Treats of the strategic, political, and legal significance of the Turkish Straits to NATO and the Soviet naval penetration of the Mediterranean Sea. An appendix of 33 documents.

Vere-Hodge, Edward R. *Turkish Foreign Policy, 1918-1948*. Ambilly-Annemasse; Imprimerie Franco-Suisse, 1950. Interesting outline of Turkish policy.

Warsamy, Georges D. *La Convention des Détroits (Montreux 1936)*. Preface de M. N. Politis. Paris: Pedone, 1937. 159 pp. Legal analysis of the Montreux Convention.

Weber, Frank G. *Eagles on the Crescent: Germany, Austria and the Diplomacy of the Turkish Alliance, 1914-1918*. Ithaca, N.Y.: Cornell University Press, 1970. 284 pp. Well-prepared study, based on archival materials.

Whetten, Lawrence L. *The Soviet Presence in the Mediterranean*. New York: National Strategy Information Center, 1971. 52 pp. Useful summary.

Xydis, Stephen G. *Greece and the Great Powers, 1944-1947: Prelude to the "Truman Doctrine."* Thessaloniki: Institute for Balkan Studies, 1963. 758 pp. A basic of the period based, in part, on Greek archival materials.

III. SELECTED PERIODICALS

Açikalin, Cevat. "Turkey's International Relations." *International Affairs* 23 (1947): 479 ff.

Bilsel, Cemil. "International Law in Turkey." *American Journal of International Law* 38, no. 4 (October 1944): 553-56.

_____. "The Turkish Straits in the Light of Recent Turkish-Russian Correspondence." ibid. 41, no. 4 (October 1947): 727-47.

Esmer, Şükrü. "The Straits: Crux of World Politics." *Foreign Affairs* 25, no. 2 (January 1947): 290-302.

Harris, George S. "The Role of the Military in Turkish Politics." *Middle East Journal* 19, no. 1 (Winter 1965): 54-66; no. 2 (Spring 1965): 169-76.

Howard, Harry N. "The United States and the Question of the Turkish Straits." *Middle East Journal* 1, no. 1 (January 1947): 58-72.

_____. "Germany, The Soviet Union and Turkey During World War II." *Department of State Bulletin* 19, no. 472 (July 13, 1948): 63-78.

_____. "The United States and the Problem of the Turkish Straits: The Foundations of American Policy (1830-1914)." *Balkan Studies* 3, no. 1 (1962): 1-28.

_____. "The Entry of Turkey into World War II." *Belleten* 31, no. 122 (April 1967): 221-75.

_____. "The Turkish Straits after World War II: Problems and Prospects." *Balkan Studies* 11, no. 1 (1970): 35-60.

Hurewitz, J. C. "Russia and the Turkish Straits: A Revaluation of the Origins of the Problem." *World Politics* 14, no. 4 (July 1962): 605-32.

_____. "The Background of Russia's Claims to the Turkish Straits." *Belleten* 28, no. 111 (1964): 459-503.

Kerner, Robert J. "The Mission of Liman von Sanders. I. Its Origin." *Slavonic Review* 6, no. 16 (June 1927): 12-27; II. "The Crisis," ibid. 6, no. 17 (December 1927): 344-63; III. ibid. 6, no. 18 (March 1928): 543-60; IV. "The Aftermath", ibid. 8, no. 19 (June 1928): 90-112.

_____. "Russia, the Straits, and Constantinople, 1914-1915." *Journal of Modern History* 1, no. 3 (September 1929): 400-15.

_____. "Russia and the Straits, 1915-1917." *Slavonic Review* 8, no. 24 (March, 1930): 589-593.

Langer, William L. "Russia, the Straits Question and the Origins of the Balkan League, 1908-1912." *Political Science Quarterly* 43, no. 3 (September 1928): 329-37.

Mamopoulos, Pierre. "La Convention de Montreux." *Les Balkans* 8, nos. 1-8 (September 1936): 2-26.

Sadak, Necmeddin. "Turkey Faces the Soviets." *Foreign Affairs* 27, no. 2 (April 1949): 449-61.

Shatzky, B. E. "La Question de Constantinople et des Détroits." *Revue d'Histoire de la Guerre Mondiale* 4, no. 4 (October 1926): 289-311; vol. 5, no. 1 (January 1927): 19-43.

Smith, C. J., Jr. "Great Britain and the 1914-1915 Straits Agreement with Russia: The British Promise of 1914." *American Historical Review* 70, no. 4 (July 1965): 1015-34.

Turlington, E. W. "The American Treaty of Lausanne." *World Peace Foundation* 12, no. 10 (1924): 565-602.

Zotiades, George B. "Russia and the Question of Constantinople and the Turkish Straits During the Balkan Wars." *Balkan Studies* 11, no. 2 (1970): 281-98.

Appendix I

Treaty of Commerce and Navigation between the United States and the Ottoman Empire, signed at Constantinople, May 7, 1830

Article VII.—The merchant vessels of the United States, either in balast or laden with the productions of their countries or with productions and merchandise not prohibited of the countries of the Ottoman Empire, may pass from the waters of the Imperial Residence and go and come in the Black Sea like the aforesaid nations [most-favored nations].

   (D. H. Miller, *Treaties and Other International Acts of the United States of America* 3 [no. 69], p. 549.)

Appendix II

Treaty of Commerce and Navigation between the United States and the Ottoman Empire, February 25, 1862. Proclaimed July 2, 1862

Article I.—All rights, privileges, and immunities, which have been conferred on the citizens or vessels of the United States of America by the treaty already existing between the United States of America and the Ottoman Empire, are confirmed, now and forever, with the exception of those clauses of the said treaty which it is the object of the present treaty to modify; and it is moreover expressly stipulated that all rights, privileges, or immunities, which the Sublime Porte now grants, or may hereafter grant to, or suffer to be enjoyed by the subjects, ships, commerce, or navigation of any other foreign Power, shall be equally granted to and exercised and enjoyed by the citizens, vessels, commerce, and navigation of the United States of America.

   (W. M. Malloy, *Treaties, Conventions, International Acts, Protocols and Agreements between the United States of America and Other Powers, 1776-1909* [Washington, 1910], II: 1321–28.)

Appendix III

The Convention Regarding the Regime of the Straits, signed at Montreux, July 20, 1936. Entered into force November 9, 1936

Article 1.—The High Contracting Parties recognise and affirm the principle of freedom of transit and navigation by sea in the Straits.

The exercise of this freedom shall henceforth be regulated by the provisions of the present Convention.

SECTION I.—*Merchant Vessels*

Article 2.—In time of peace, merchant vessels shall enjoy complete freedom of transit and navigation in the Straits, by day and by night, under any flag and with any kind of cargo, without any formalities, except as provided in Article 3 below. No taxes or charges other than those authorised by Annex I to the present Convention shall be levied by the Turkish authorities on these vessels when passing in transit without calling at a port in the Straits.

In order to facilitate the collection of these taxes or charges merchant vessels passing through the Straits shall communicate to the officials at the stations referred to in Article 3 their name, nationality, tonnage, destination and last port of call (provenance).

Pilotage and towage remain optional.

Article 3.—All ships entering the Straits by the Aegean Sea or by the Black Sea shall stop at a sanitary station near the entrance to the Straits for the purposes of the sanitary control prescribed by Turkish law within the framework of international sanitary regulations. This control, in the case of ships possessing a clean bill of health or presenting a declaration of health testifying that they do not fall within the scope of the provisions of the second paragraph of the present Article, shall be carried out by day and by night with all possible speed, and the vessels in question shall not be required to make any other stop during their passage through the Straits.

Vessels which have on board cases of plague, cholera, yellow fever, exanthematic typhus or smallpox, or which have had such cases on board during the previous seven days, and vessels which have left an infected port within

Turkey No. 1 (1936). Convention Regarding the Regime of the Straits with Correspondence relating thereto, Montreux, July 20, 1936. CMD 5249; 173 *League of Nations Treaty Series* 213.

less than five times twenty-four hours shall stop at the sanitary stations indicated in the preceding paragraph in order to embark such sanitary guards as the Turkish authorities may direct. No tax or charge shall be levied in respect of these sanitary guards and they shall be disembarked at a sanitary station on departure from the Straits.

Article 4.—In time of war, Turkey not being belligerent, merchant vessels, under any flag or with any kind of cargo, shall enjoy freedom of transit and navigation in the Straits subject to the provisions of Articles 2 and 3.

Pilotage and towage remain optional.

Article 5.—In time of war, Turkey being belligerent, merchant vessels not belonging to a country at war with Turkey shall enjoy freedom of transit and navigation in the Straits on condition that they do not in any way assist the enemy.

Such vessels shall enter the Straits by day and their transit shall be effected by the route which shall in each case be indicated by the Turkish authorities.

Article 6.—Should Turkey consider herself to be threatened with imminent danger of war, the provisions of Article 2 shall nevertheless continue to be applied except that vessels must enter the Straits by day and that their transit must be effected by the route which shall, in each case, be indicated by the Turkish authorities.

Pilotage may, in this case, be made obligatory, but no charge shall be levied.

Article 7.—The term "merchant vessels" applies to all vessels which are not covered by Section II of the present Convention.

SECTION II.—*Vessels of War*

Article 8.—For the purposes of the present Convention, the definitions of vessels of war and of their specification together with those relating to the calculation of tonnage shall be as set forth in Annex II to the present Convention.

Article 9.—Naval auxiliary vessels specifically designed for the carriage of fuel, liquid or non-liquid, shall not be subject to the provisions of Article 13 regarding notification, nor shall they be counted for the purpose of calculating the tonnage which is subject to limitation under Articles 14 and 18, on condition that they shall pass through the Straits singly. They shall, however, continue to be on the same footing as vessels of war for the purpose of the remaining provisions governing transit.

The auxiliary vessels specified in the preceding paragraph shall only be entitled to benefit by the exceptional status therein contemplated if their armament does not include: for use against floating targets, more than two guns of a maximum calibre of 105 millimetres; for use against aerial targets, more than two guns of a maximum calibre of 75 millimetres.

Article 10.—In time of peace, light surface vessels, minor war vessels and auxiliary vessels, whether belonging to Black Sea or non-Black Sea Powers, and whatever their flag, shall enjoy freedom of transit through the Straits without any taxes or charges whatever, provided that such transit is begun during daylight and subject to the conditions laid down in Article 13 and the Articles following thereafter.

Vessels of war other than those which fall within the categories specified in the preceding paragraph shall only enjoy a right of transit under the special conditions provided by Articles 11 and 12.

Article 11.—Black Sea Powers may send through the Straits capital ships of a tonnage greater than that laid down in the first paragraph of Article 14, on condition that these vessels pass through the Straits singly, escorted by not more than two destroyers.

Article 12.—Black Sea Powers shall have the right to send through the Straits, for the purpose of rejoining their base, submarines constructed or purchased outside the Black Sea, provided that adequate notice of the laying down or purchase of such submarines shall have been given to Turkey.

Submarines belonging to the said Powers shall also be entitled to pass through the Straits to be repaired in dockyards outside the Black Sea on condition that detailed information on the matter is given to Turkey.

In either case, the said submarines must travel by day and on the surface, and must pass through the Straits singly.

Article 13.—The transit of vessels of war through the Straits shall be preceded by notification given to the Turkish Government through the diplomatic channel. The normal period of notice shall be eight days; but it is desirable that in the case of non-Black Sea Powers this period should be increased to fifteen days. The notification shall specify the destination, name, type and number of the vessels, as also the date of entry for the outward passage and, if necessary, for the return journey. Any change of date shall be subject to three days' notice.

Entry into the Straits for the outward passage shall take place within a period of five days from the date given in the original notification. After the expiry of this period, a new notification shall be given under the same conditions as for the original notification.

When effecting transit, the commander of the naval force shall, without being under any obligation to stop, communicate to a signal station at the entrance to the Dardanelles or the Bosphorus the exact composition of the force under his orders.

Article 14.—The maximum aggregate tonnage of all foreign naval forces which may be in course of transit through the Straits shall not exceed 15,000 tons, except in the cases provided for in Article 11 and in Annex III to the present Convention.

The forces specified in the preceding paragraph shall not, however, comprise more than nine vessels.

Vessels, whether belonging to Black Sea or non-Black Sea Powers, paying visits to a port in the Straits, in accordance with the provisions of Article 17, shall not be included in this tonnage.

Neither shall vessels of war which have suffered damage during their passage through the Straits be included in this tonnage; such vessels, while undergoing repair, shall be subject to any special provisions relating to security laid down by Turkey.

Article 15.—Vessels of war in transit through the Straits shall in no circumstances make use of any aircraft which they may be carrying.

Article 16.—Vessels of war in transit through the Straits shall not, except in the event of damage or peril of the sea, remain therein longer than is necessary for them to effect the passage.

Article 17.—Nothing in the provisions of the preceding articles shall prevent a naval force of any tonnage or composition from paying a courtesy visit of limited duration to a port in the Straits, at the invitation of the Turkish Government. Any such force must leave the Straits by the same route as that by which it entered, unless it fulfils the conditions required for passage in transit through the Straits as laid down by Articles 10, 14, and 18.

Article 18.—(1) The aggregate tonnage which non-Black Sea Powers may have in that sea in time of peace shall be limited as follows:

(a) Except as provided in paragraph (b) below, the aggregate tonnage of the said Powers shall not exceed 30,000 tons;

(b) If at any time the tonnage of the strongest fleet in the Black Sea shall exceed by at least 10,000 tons the tonnage of the strongest fleet in that sea at the date of the signature of the present Convention, the aggregate tonnage of 30,000 tons mentioned in paragraph (a) shall be increased by the same amount, up to a maximum of 45,000 tons. For this purpose, each Black Sea Power shall, in conformity with Annex IV to the present Convention, inform the Turkish Government, on the 1st January and the 1st July of each year, of the total tonnage of its fleet in the Black Sea; and the Turkish Government shall transmit this information to the other High Contracting Parties and to the Secretary-General of the League of Nations.

(c) The tonnage which any one non-Black Sea Power may have in the Black Sea shall be limited to two-thirds of the aggregate tonnage provided for in paragraphs (a) and (b) above;

(d) In the event, however, of one or more non-Black Sea Powers desiring to send naval forces into the Black Sea, for a humanitarian purpose, the said forces, which shall in no case exceed 8,000 tons altogether, shall be allowed to enter the Black Sea without having to give the notification provided in Article 13 of the present Convention, provided an authorisation is obtained from the Turkish Government in the following circumstances: if the figure of the aggregate tonnage specified in paragraphs (a) and (b) above has not been reached and will not be exceeded by the despatch of the forces which it is desired to send, the Turkish Government shall grant the said authorisation within the shortest possible time after receiving the request which has been addressed to it; if the said figure has already been reached or if the despatch of the forces which it is desired to send will cause it to be exceeded, the Turkish Government will immediately inform the other Black Sea Powers of the request for authorisation, and if the said Powers make no objection within twenty-four hours of having received this information, the Turkish Government shall, within twenty-four hours at the latest, inform the interested Powers of the reply which it has decided to make to their request.

Any further entry into the Black Sea of naval forces of non-Black Sea Powers shall only be effected within the available limits of the aggregate tonnage provided for in paragraphs (a) and (b) above.

(2) Vessels of war belonging to non-Black Sea Powers shall not remain in the Black Sea more than twenty-one days, whatever be the object of their presence there.

Article 19.—In time of war, Turkey not being belligerent, warships shall enjoy complete freedom of transit and navigation through the Straits under the same conditions as those laid down in Articles 10 to 18.

Vessels of war belonging to belligerent Powers shall not, however, pass through the Straits except in cases arising out of the application of Article 25 of the present Convention, and in cases of assistance rendered to a State victim of aggression in virtue of a treaty of mutual assistance binding Turkey, concluded within the framework of the Covenant of the League of Nations, and registered and published in accordance with the provisions of Article 18 of the Covenant.

In the exceptional cases provided for in the preceding paragraph, the limitations laid down in Articles 10 to 18 of the present Convention shall not be applicable.

Notwithstanding the prohibition of passage laid down in paragraph 2 above, vessels of war belonging to belligerent Powers, whether they are Black Sea Powers or not, which have become separated from their bases, may return thereto.

Vessels of war belonging to belligerent Powers shall not make any capture, exercise the right of visit and search, or carry out any hostile act in the Straits.

Article 20.—In time of war, Turkey being belligerent, the provisions of Articles 10 to 18 shall not be applicable; the passage of warships shall be left entirely to the discretion of the Turkish Government.

Article 21.—Should Turkey consider herself to be threatened with imminent danger of war she shall have the right to apply the provisions of Article 20 of the present Convention.

Vessels which have passed through the Straits before Turkey has made use of the powers conferred upon her by the preceding paragraph, and which thus find themselves separated from their bases, may return thereto. It is, however, understood that Turkey may deny this right to vessels of war belonging to the State whose attitude has given rise to the application of the present article.

Should the Turkish Government make use of the powers conferred by the first paragraph of the present article, a notification to that effect shall be addressed to the High Contracting Parties and to the Secretary-General of the League of Nations.

If the Council of the League of Nations decide by a majority of two-thirds that the measures thus taken by Turkey are not justified, and if such should also be the opinion of the majority of the High Contracting Parties signatories to the present Convention, the Turkish Government undertakes to discontinue the measures in question as also any measures which may have been taken under Article 6 of the present Convention.

Article 22.—Vessels of war which have on board cases of plague, cholera, yellow fever, exanthematic typhus or smallpox or which have had such cases on board within the last seven days and vessels of war which have left an infected port within less than five times twenty-four hours must pass through the Straits in quarantine and apply by the means on board such prophylactic measures as are necessary in order to prevent any possibility of the Straits being infected.

Section III.—*Aircraft*

Article 23.—In order to assure the passage of civil aircraft between the Mediterranean and the Black Sea, the Turkish Government will indicate the air routes available for this purpose, outside the forbidden zones which may be established in the Straits. Civil aircraft may use these routes provided that they give the Turkish Government, as regards occasional flights, a notification of three days, and as regards flights on regular services, a general notification of the dates of passage.

The Turkish Government moreover undertakes, notwithstanding any remilitarization of the Straits, to furnish the necessary facilities for the safe passage of civil aircraft authorized under the air regulations in force in Turkey to fly across Turkish territory between Europe and Asia. The route which is to be followed in the Straits zone by aircraft which have obtained an authorization shall be indicated from time to time.

Section IV.—*General Provisions*

Article 24.—The functions of the International Commission set up under the Convention relating to the regime of the Straits of the 24th July, 1923, are hereby transferred to the Turkish Government.

The Turkish Government undertakes to collect statistics and to furnish information concerning the application of Articles 11, 12, 14 and 18 of the present Convention.

They will supervise the execution of all the provisions of the present Convention relating to the passage of vessels of war through the Straits.

As soon as they have been notified of the intended passage through the Straits of a foreign naval force the Turkish Government shall inform the representatives at Angora of the High Contracting Parties of the composition of that force, its tonnage, the date fixed for its entry into the Straits, and, if necessary, the probable date of its return.

The Turkish Government shall address to the Secretary-General of the League of Nations and to the High Contracting Parties an annual report giving details regarding the movements of foreign vessels of war through the

Straits and furnishing all information which may be of service to commerce and navigation, both by sea and by air, for which provision is made in the present Convention.

Article 25.—Nothing in the present Convention shall prejudice the rights and obligations of Turkey, or of any of the other High Contracting Parties members of the League of Nations, arising out of the Covenant of the League of Nations.

SECTION V.—*Final Provisions*

Article 26.—The present Convention shall be ratified as soon as possible.

The ratifications shall be deposited in the archives of the Government of the French Republic in Paris.

The Japanese Government shall be entitled to inform the Government of the French Republic through their diplomatic representative in Paris that the ratification has been given, and in that case they shall transmit the instrument of ratification as soon as possible.

A *proces-verbal* of the deposit of ratifications shall be drawn up as soon as six instruments of ratification, including that of Turkey, shall have been deposited. For this purpose the notification provided for in the preceding paragraph shall be taken as the equivalent of the deposit of an instrument of ratification.

The present Convention shall come into force on the date of the said *proces-verbal.*

The French Government will transmit to all the High Contracting Parties an authentic copy of the *proces-verbal* provided for in the preceding paragraph and of the *proces-verbaux* of the deposit of any subsequent ratifications.

Article 27.—The present Convention shall, as from the date of its entry into force, be open to accession by any Power signatory to the Treaty of Peace at Lausanne signed on the 24th July, 1923.

Each accession shall be notified, through the diplomatic channel, to the Government of the French Republic, and by the latter to all the High Contracting Parties.

Accessions shall come into force as from the date of notification to the French Government.

Article 28.—The present Convention shall remain in force for twenty years from the date of its entry into force.

The principle of freedom of transit and navigation affirmed in Article 1 of the present Convention shall however continue without limit of time.

If, two years prior to the expiry of the said period of twenty years, no High Contracting Party shall have given notice of denunciation to the French Government the present Convention shall continue in force until two years after such notice shall have been given. Any such notice shall be communicated by the French Government to the High Contracting Parties.

In the event of the present Convention being denounced in accordance with the provisions of the present article, the High Contracting Parties agree to be represented at a conference for the purpose of concluding a new Convention.

Article 29.—At the expiry of each period of five years from the date of the entry into force of the present Convention each of the High Contracting Parties shall be entitled to initiate a proposal for amending one or more of the provisions of the present Convention .

To be valid, any request for revision formulated by one of the High Contracting Parties must be supported, in the case of modifications to Articles 14 to 18, by one other High Contracting Party, and, in the case of modifications to any other article, by two other High Contracting Parties.

Any request for revision thus supported must be notified to all the High Contracting Parties three months prior to the expiry of the current period of five years. This notification shall contain details of the proposed amendments and the reasons which have given rise to them.

Should it be found impossible to reach an agreement on these proposals through the diplomatic channel, the High Contracting Parties agree to be represented at a conference to be summoned for this purpose.

Such a conference may only take decisions by a unanimous vote, except as regards cases of revision involving Articles 14 and 18, for which a majority of three-quarters of the High Contracting Parties shall be sufficient.

The said majority shall include three-quarters of the High Contracting Parties which are Black Sea Powers, including Turkey. . . .

Appendix IV

Comparative Charts of the Conventions Regulating the Turkish Straits

I. CONVENTIONS OF THE STRAITS IN THE NINETEENTH CENTURY

Types of ship		1840	1841
Signatories		Great Britain, Austria, France, Prussia, Russia, Ottoman Empire	Great Britain, Austria, France, Prussia, Russia, Ottoman Empire
I.	THE STRAITS		
A.	Merchant ships		
1.	*Time of peace*	Free passage under earlier treaties	Free passage under earlier treaties
2.	*Time of war*	Under Ottoman control	Under Ottoman control
B.	Warships:		
1.	*Time of peace*	Closure to foreign warships "at all times"	Closure to foreign warships "at all times." So long as Porte at peace, no foreign warship in Straits. Signatories to conform to rule. Light vessels for missions to pass
2.	*Time of war*	On demand of Sultan, signatories agree to secure Constantinople and Straits *vs.* aggression of Mehemet Ali	Control of Ottoman Government, whether neutral or belligerent
II.	BLACK SEA		
A.	Merchant ships		
B.	Warships		

1856	1871	1878
Great Britain, Austria, France, Prussia, Russia, Sardinia, Ottoman Empire	Great Britain, Austria, France, Germany, Italy, Russia, Ottoman Empire	Great Britain, Austria, Hungary, France, Germany, Italy, Russia, Ottoman Empire
Free passage under earlier treaties Under Ottoman control	Free passage under earlier treaties Under Ottoman control	Free passage under earlier treaties Under Ottoman control
Closure to foreign warships "at all times." So long as Porte at peace, no foreign warship in Straits. Signatories to respect rule. Light vessels for missions and Danube *stationnaires* to pass	Closure to foreign warships according to rule of 1856, with power of Sultan to open Straits in peace to warships of allied and friendly powers, if necessary to execute provisions of 1856 treaty	Closure to foreign warships according to rule of 1856, with power of Sultan to open Straits in peace to warships of allied and friendly powers, if necessary to execute provisions of 1856 treaty
Control of Ottoman Government, whether neutral or belligerent	Control of Ottoman Government, whether neutral or belligerent	Control of Ottoman Government, whether neutral or belligerent
Commerce subject only to health, police, customs regulations. Open to merchant marine of all nations	Commerce subject only to health, police, customs regulations. Open to merchant marine of all nations	Commerce subject only to health, police, customs regulations. Open to merchant marine of all nations
Black Sea demilitarized, flag of war prohibited in perpetuity. Contracting parties to have two *stationnaires* at mouth of Danube. Turkey and Russia to have six 800-ton steam vessels, four 200-ton ships	Remilitarization of Black Sea. Rebuilding of fortifications, naval forces permitted	Same as in 1871

II. CONVENTIONS OF THE STRAITS IN THE TWENTIETH CENTURY

Types of ship	Convention of Sèvres August 10, 1920 (not in operation)
Signatories	British Empire, France, Italy, Japan, Greece, Armenia, Belgium, Hejaz, Poland, Portugal, Rumania, Yugoslavia, Czechoslovakia and Turkey
I. THE STRAITS A. Merchant ships: 1. *Time of peace*	Freedom of commerce to all flags (art. 37)
2. *Time of war*	Freedom of commerce, any flag; no blockade except under decision of League Council; no belligerent rights or acts except under League Council decision (art. 37)
Time of war, Turkey, neutral or non-belligerent	
Time of war, Turkey belligerent	
Turkey under threat of war	
B. Warships: 1. *Time of peace*	Freedom of passage, any flag (art. 37)

Convention of Lausanne July 24, 1923	Convention of Montreux July 20, 1936
British Empire, France, Italy, Japan, Bulgaria, Greece, Rumania, Russia, Yugoslavia, and Turkey	Bulgaria, France, Great Britain, Greece, Japan, Rumania, Turkey, U.S.S.R., and Yugoslavia

General principle of freedom of transit and navigation by sea and air (art. 1, 2). Annex: merchant vessels, including hospital ships, yachts, fishing vessels, nonmilitary aircraft have complete freedom of passage, day or night, any cargo subject to sanitary provisions, no tax or charge except for direct services. Communicate particulars

Principle of freedom of transit and navigation by sea in Straits affirmed (art. 1); without limit of time (art. 28). Exercise of freedom regulated by Convention. Complete freedom day and night, any flag, any cargo. Ships communicate particulars, to facilitate collection taxes, charges. Pilotage, towage optional. Sanitary inspection, if necessary (sec. I, art. 2)

Complete freedom, day or night as in peace. Turkey to take no action interfering with navigation thru Straits, whose waters, with air above, remain entirely free. Pilotage optional.
Freedom for neutral ships and non-military aircraft, if no assistance to enemy, carry contraband, etc. Turkish right to search and right to apply measure to enemy ships allowed by international law. Turkish right to prevent enemy use of Straits, not to interfere with free passage of neutral ships

Complete freedom, any flag, any cargo as in peace (art. 4). Pilotage optional

Merchant vessels of country not at war with Turkey enjoy freedom of transit and navigation on condition of not assisting enemy (art. 5). Such ships enter Straits by day and transit indicated by Turkish authorities

Turkey threatened, free passage as in peace, except that ships must enter Straits by day and transit by route indicated by Turkish authorities (art. 6)

Warships (including fleet auxiliaries, troopships, aircraft carriers and military aircraft) enjoy freedom of passage, day or night, any flag. Maximum force any *one* non-Black Sea power may send into Black Sea not to exceed most powerful Black Sea fleet. Right to send into Black Sea, in any case, force of not more than 3 ships, none to exceed 10,000 tons. Straits Commission to keep informed by reports as to Black Sea fleets. Naval force sent into Black Sea

Light surface vessels, minor warships, auxiliaries belonging either to Black Sea or non-Black Sea powers, any flag, have freedom of transit (art. 10). Black Sea powers may send through Straits capital ships of more than 15,000 tons if pass singly, escorted by not more than 2 destroyers; right send submarines through Straits constructed or repaired outside Black Sea. Turkey to be informed, vessels travel by day, on surface, pass Straits singly (arts.

II. CONVENTIONS OF THE STRAITS IN THE TWENTIETH CENTURY *(Cont.)*

Types of ship	Convention of Sèvres August 10, 1920 (not in operation)
2. *Time of war*	Freedom of passage, any flag. Waters not subject to blockade except under League Council decision. No hostile acts except under League Council decision. Belligerent warships not to revictual or repair except as strictly necessary, under Commission control. Passage without delay or interruption, 24-hour delay in case of distress; 24-hour interval between hostile warships. Further regulations subject to League Council. Prizes subject to same control as warships. No disembarking of troops, except when necessary. Nothing to limit powers of belligerents acting under Covenant of League (arts. 37, 56, 57, 58, 59, 60)
Time of war, Turkey, neutral or non-belligerent	

Convention of Lausanne July 24, 1923	Convention of Montreux July 20, 1936
calculated on number and type of warships in active service only. Passage of Straits by submarines must be made on surface. Military and non-military aircraft freedom to fly over strip 5 km. wide on each side of narrow part of Straits. Can light on coast or in territorial waters if forced. Warships except for damage, remain only time for passage. Turkey to regulate number of warships and military aircraft any one power may send to visit Turkish ports at one time, duration of stay. Danube *stationnaires* counted as additional to warships. Right of Turkey to move fleet freely in Turkish waters not infringed by Convention (art. 17)	11, 12, 14). *General Rules for Passages:* 1. Notification: normal period 8 days, 15 days desirable for non-Black Sea powers; 2. Maximum tonnage: not to exceed 15,000 tons, except for Black Sea powers, over-age Japanese training ships. Forces not to include more than 9 ships. Courtesy visits not included in tonnage calculation. Damaged ships not calculated in tonnage, but subject to Turkish security regulations; 3. Use of aircraft forbidden; 4. Period of transit: except in case of damage, not to remain longer than necessary for passage; 5. Courtesy visit: nothing to prevent naval force of *any* tonnage or composition from courtesy visit of limited period at Turkish invitation, but force must leave by same route of entry unless: (*a*) it is composed of light surface ships, minor warships, and auxiliary ships, in time of peace, belonging to either non- or Black Sea power; (*b*) in time of peace, force composed of not more than 9 ships, or over-age Japanese training ships (annex III) or have suffered damage in passage of Straits; or (*c*) fall within limitations of tonnage non-Black Sea powers may have in Black Sea (arts. 13–18)
Complete freedom as in peace. Limitation not applicable to any belligerent to prejudice of rights of belligerent in Black Sea. Rights and duties of Turkey	Complete freedom of transit and navigation under articles 10–18, as in peace (art. 19). Ships belonging to belligerents not to pass Straits except: 1. In cases of

II. CONVENTIONS OF THE STRAITS IN THE TWENTIETH CENTURY *(Cont.)*

Types of ship	Convention of Sèvres August 10, 1920 (not in operation)
Time of war, Turkey belligerent	
Turkey under threat of war	
Special sanitary regulations for warships	Enforced by the Commission of the Straits

Convention of Lausanne July 24, 1923	Convention of Montreux July 20, 1936
as neutral not authorize measures interfering with navigation in Straits, air above, which must remain free. No capture, visit, search, other hostile act. Thirteenth Hague Convention (1907) as to revictualling and repairs. Military aircraft receive similar treatment as warships, pending conclusion of convention regulating aircraft	assistance rendered to victim of aggression in virtue of mutual assistance pact binding Turkey, under article 25 of League Covenant, providing that nothing in Convention prejudices rights and obligations of Turkey or other signatories as members of League (art. 19). In this case, limitations of arts. 10–18 not applicable. Notwithstanding prohibitions above, warships belonging to belligerents, Black Sea or not, separated from bases, may return thereto. No capture, search, visit, or other hostile acts permitted (art. 19)
Complete freedom for neutral warships, under same conditions as in peace. Turkish measures to prevent enemy passage not to prevent passage of neutral ships and aircraft, instructions or pilots to be assigned. Neutral aircraft make passage at own peril, submitting to examination	Provisions of arts. 10–18, governing passage, not applicable. Turkey has discretion as to passage of warships through Straits (art. 20)
Security Provisions: Signatories, in any case, France, Great Britain, Italy, Japan, acting together, if Straits violated, attacked, threatened, to act by all means League Council decides. Straits regime applied again after trouble. Provisions (art. 18) not prejudice rights and obligations of signatories under League Covenant	Under threat, Turkey has right to use own judgment as to passage of warships; nevertheless ships which have passed Straits before Turkey has made use of powers, may return to bases, but Turkey may deny this right to warships belonging to state, attitude of which has given rise to suspicion. Use of powers must be notified to high contracting parties and to League of Nations. If League Council decides by two-third majority measures unjustified, and if opinion is upheld by majority of signatories, Turkey to discontinue measures under art. 21 as applied to warships and under art. 6 as applied to merchant vessels
Warships with plague, cholera or typhus, within 7 days, or have left infected port within less than 120 hours must pass Straits in quarantine and apply measures to prevent infection of Straits region. Same rules apply to merchant vessels with doctor on board, if passing in transit without stopping. If no doctor on board, to comply with international sanitary regulations. Warships and merchant ships calling at Straits ports subject to sanitary regulations	Warships with plague, cholera, yellow fever, exanthematic typhus or smallpox, or have had cases within 7 days, or have left infected port within 120 hours, must pass Straits in quarantine and apply prophylactic measures to prevent infection of Straits region (art. 22)

II. CONVENTIONS OF THE STRAITS IN THE TWENTIETH CENTURY (*Cont.*)

Types of ship	Convention of Sèvres August 10, 1920 (not in operation)
C. Civil aircraft	
D. Demilitarization of the Straits	Straits region under complete control of Inter-Allied Commission (art. 39)
E. Commission of the Straits:	
1. *Composition*	British Empire, France, Italy, Japan, Greece, Rumania, United States (if and when willing), Russia, Turkey, Bulgaria (if and when members of League). Great powers 2 votes each
2. *Jurisdiction*	Over all waters between Mediterranean mouth of Dardanelles and Black Sea mouth of Bosporus, and waters within 3 miles of each mouth
3. *Functions*	(1) Works for improvement of channels or harbors; (2) lighting and buoying; (3) pilotage and towage; (4) control of anchorages; (5) control to assure application in Constantinople and Haidar Pasha; (6) wrecks and salvage; (7) control of

Convention of Lausanne July 24, 1923	Convention of Montreux July 20, 1938
	To assure passage of civil aircraft through Straits, Turkish Government to indicate routes, outside forbidden zones to be established. Civil aircraft use routes, provided they give notification of 3 days for occasional flights, and general notification of dates of passage for flights on regular service. Turkish Government, despite remilitarization of Straits, to furnish necessary facilities for safe passage of civil aircraft, routes to be indicated from time to time (sec. III)
Region of Straits (Dardanelles, Sea of Marmara, Bosporus) demilitarized to depths varying from 3 to approx. 15 miles. Islands of Marmara, exception of Emir Ali Adasi, Aegean Islands of Samothraee, Lemnos, Imbros, Tenedos, and Rabbit Islands demilitarized. No fortifications, artillery organization, submarine engines of war aside from submarines, no military air organization, or naval base in demilitarized zone. No armed force except police and gendarmerie. Turkish Government right of observation balloons and planes over Straits, with right to land. No submarine engines of war, other than submarines in Marmara. No battery or torpedo tubes, interfering with passage of Straits, in coastal zone. Garrison of 12,000 at Constantinople, arsenal and naval base. If Greece and Turkey at war, provisions of demilitarization modified, must revert on peace	Right of Turkey, in sovereign control of region of Straits, to re-fortify zone, fully recognized
Turkey (President), France, Great Britain, Italy, Japan, Bulgaria, Greece, Rumania, Russia, Yugoslavia, United States (on accession); other Black Sea states on accession. One vote each	
Over the waters of the Straits (Dardanelles, Marmara, Bosporus)	Under Turkish Government's jurisdiction
(1) Enforcement of provisions relating to passage of warships and military aircraft are executed, as laid down in pars. 2, 3, 4, of annex to art. 2; (2) under League, reports, information, etc.	Functions transferred to the Turkish Government, which is to collect shipping data, supervise execution of all provisions relative to passage of ships through Straits, and make annual report to the signatories and to the League of Na-

II. CONVENTIONS OF THE STRAITS IN THE TWENTIETH CENTURY (*Cont.*)

Types of ship	Convention of Sèvres August 10, 1920 (not in operation)
	lighterage; (8) assurance of freedom of passage of Stratis; (9) acquisition of property; (10) enforcement of sanitary provisions; (11) police functions
II. Black Sea	Presumable free entry, any tonnage, on part of non-Black Sea powers
III. Final Provisions: 1. *Accession*	United States, Russia, Bulgaria, and Turkey might accede

Convention of Lausanne July 24, 1923	Convention of Montreux July 20, 1936
	tions, giving details of movement of warships through Straits, and, generally, all information useful to commerce and navigation, by sea and air, for which Convention makes provision (art. 24). Nothing in Convention prejudices rights and duties of Turkey or signatories under League Covenant (art. 25)
Maximum force any *one* non-Black Sea power may send into Black Sea not to be greater than most powerful fleet in Black Sea at time of passage, but powers, in any case, have right to send force of not more than 3 ships, none to exceed 10,000 tons. Naval force sent into Black Sea calculated only on number and type of warships in active service	In general, aggregate tonnage of non-Black Sea powers in Black Sea not to exceed 30,000 tons in time of peace. May be increased to 45,000 tons if Soviet fleet exceeds by at least 10,000 tons tonnage of Soviet fleet at date of signature of Montreux Convention. Annex V provides for annual report of Black Sea fleets. Tonnage any *one* non-Black Sea power may have in Black Sea, in general not to exceed 20,000 tons. If at any time Soviet fleet in Black Sea exceeds by at least 10,000 tons tonnage of Soviet fleet at time of signature of Montreux Convention, individual tonnage of non-Black Sea power may be increased to 30,000 tons (art. 18). For humanitarian purposes, one or more non-Black Sea powers may send into Black Sea naval force not to exceed 8,000 tons altogether after giving notification (generally 15 days); tonnage limitation not to exceed either 30,000 or 45,000 and will not be exceeded by dispatch of new forces; if tonnage has already been reached and would be exceeded, Turkish Government will notify Black Sea powers of request, and if no objection forthcoming in 24 hours, Turkish Government, within 24 hours at latest, will inform interested powers of reply to request. Any further entry into Black Sea of naval forces of non-Black Sea powers only to be effected within limits of aggregate tonnage of 30,000 to 45,000 tons. Warships of non-Black Sea powers not to remain in Black Sea longer than 21 days, whatever object of presence
Other powers might accede to Convention (art. 19)	Others might accede (art. 27) Italy did so on May 2, 1938

II. CONVENTIONS OF THE STRAITS IN THE TWENTIETH CENTURY (*Cont.*)

Types of ship	Convention of Sèvres August 10, 1920 (not in operation)
2. *Ratification*	Part of general Treaty of Sèvres
3. *Duration*	
4. *Denunciation*	
5. *Amendment or revision*	

(From Harry N. Howard, *The Problem of the Turkish Straits*, Department of State Publication 2752, Near Eastern Series 5 [Washington, D.C.: USGPO, 1947], pp. 29–35.)

Convention of Lausanne July 24, 1923	Convention of Montreux July 20, 1936
Subject to ratification (art. 20). Signed Aug. 14, 1923 by Soviet Union, but not ratified	Ratification as soon as possible (art. 26)
	Twenty years, provisions of freedom of commerce without limit of time (art. 28)
	If, two years prior to expiry, no signatory gives notice of denunciation to French Government, convention in force until two years after such notice shall have been given. Any such notice communicated to signatories by French Government. If denounced, signatories agree to hold conference for concluding new convention (art. 23)
	At expiry of each 5-year period from entry into force, each of signatories entitled to initiate proposal for amendment. To be valid, any request for revision formulated by one of signatories must be supported, in case of modification of arts. 14–18

Appendix V

Statistics Concerning Shipping
in the Turkish Straits*

TABLE 1
REGISTERED NET TONNAGE (1913-1923)[1]

Flag	1913[2]	1920[3]	1921	1922	1923
American		266,679	300,277	589,778	222,481
Austro-Hungarian	1,615,293				
Belgian	295,038				
British	5,370,781	557,353	204,065	1,488,171	1,994,689
Dutch	199,034	46,419	121,488	210,754	380,817
French	572,730	231,318	500,062	644,073	632,087
German	733,600		38,508	38,311	167,651
Greek	1,958,201	331,203	559,338	614,804	276,283
Italian	370,302	329,491	385,684	759,062	1,513,180
Norwegian	288,203				
Rumanian	350,302	138,537	172,885	284,925	457,564
Russian	1,428,435	256,375	64,371	31,042	68,498
Turkish	906,416	77,331	18,453	29,668	296,322
Other		238,109	360,277	473,162	490,606
Total	13,412,065	2,472,815	2,725,408	5,164,650	6,500,178

*Harry N. Howard, "Germany, The Soviet Union, and Turkey, during World War II," *Department of State Bulletin* 19, no. 472 (July 18, 1948): 73-76.

[1]These statistical data have been gathered from the following sources: (1) *Rapport de la Commission des Détroits à la Société des Nations* (1924-1935); (2) République turque. Ministère des Affaires etrangères. *Rapport Annual sur le Mouvement des Navires à Travers les Détroits et des Aéronels Civils entre la Méditerranée et la Mer Noire* ((1936-1941); (3) *T. C. Istanbul Ticaret ve Sanayi Odasi Mecmuasi* (*Bulletin de la Chambre de Commerce et d-Industrie d' Istanbul*, 1941; (4) Basvekalet Istatistik. Umum Mudurlugu (Republique turque. Presidence du Conseil. Office central de statistique). *Istatistik Yilligi* (*Annuaire Statistique*), vol. 12, no. 194, 1940-41 (Ankara, 1941).

[2]From Phillipson and Buxton, *The Question of the Dardanelles and Bosphorus*, pp. 232-33. In 1911 the number of vessels passing the Bosphorus was 34,562, with a total tonnage of 19,968,409; in 1912 there were 34,577, with a total tonnage of 15,298,537, and in 1913 there were 34,826 vessels, with a total tonnage of 13,412,065.

[3]From G. B. Ravndal, *Turkey: A Commercial and Industrial Handbook*, Bureau of Foreign and Domestic Commerce, Trade Promotion Series 28, p. 60.

TABLE II
REGISTERED NET TONNAGE (1924-1938)

Flag	1924	1925	1926	1927	1928	1929	1
General							
American	169,938	154,000	126,941	166,809	203,110	287,187	4(
British	1,984,783	2,242,000	2,499,471	2,080,330	1,915,053	2,778,946	3,6(
Dutch	396,799	323,000			397,654	422,436	5!
French	570,412	627,000	825,039	831,429	866,010	897,847	8(
German	260,863	469,000	464,337	540,817	576,943	643,566	8(
Italian	1,518,052	1,802,000	2,463,861	2,624,822	2,214,586	3,538,205	4,5!
Norwegian	112,773	169,000	362,186		689,853	905,048	1,1(
Polish	5,191	9,000			6,335	7,197	
Regional							
Bulgarian	87,183	92,000	83,701	87,041	103,509	117,673	(
Egyptian	48,876	151,000			106,509	112,402	1(
Greek	827,000	1,270,000	2,122,861	1,592,795	779,950	1,243,082	3,4(
Palestinian							
Rumanian	364,134	479,000	550,873	432,331	468,183	489,164	54
Russian	172,402	196,000	188,022	295,004	468,891	572,095	6(
Turkish[1,2]	715,103	774,000					
Yugoslav	36,173	31,000	143,154	91,422	22,780	64,948	1(
Total	7,646,550	9,178,000	10,643,812	9,897,579	9,218,371	12,767,012	17,8(

[1]The figures for Turkey; which are not included after 1925, do not include sailing vessels and coasting vessels from the Sea of Marmara, amounting to about 500,000 tons.

[2]The figures for Turkey, 1936-41, are taken from *T. C. Istanbul Ticaret ve Sanayi Odasi Mecmuasi (Bulletin de la Chambre de Commerce et d'Industrie d'Istanbul).* They are not included in the total figures for the years indicated.

[3]There was no report, apparently, for the months of January to August 1936, since the Commission of the Straits ceased to function in the fall of 1936. The monthly figures in *Bulletin de la Chambre de Commerce et d'Industrie d'Istanbul* make a total of 18,219,990 tons for the entire year 1936, Turkish shipping included.

	1932	1933	1934	1935	1936[3] Aug. 15– Dec. 31, 1936	1937	1938
802	196 717	175,850	147,048	189,252	108,512	207,013	275,545
,132	2,847,770	2,616,755	2,586,817	1,986,232	923,796	2,601,497	2,890,184
,618	503,676	562,884	423,356	353,357	152,852	569,165	372,842
469	1,011,056	524,625	518,136	394,250	291,201	1,261,999	408,073
,099	619,064	655,566	573,083	452,073	373,323	754,434	627,384
,973	4,230,477	4,160,918	3,414,456	2,527,164	799,156	2,167,770	1,604,666
,169	2,104,843	2,232,632	2,165,998	968,032	229,480	959,658	743,700
					235,264	187,289	196,998
		91,143	130,873	135,792	133,022	180,379	154,413
		103,406	73,454	45,619	24,881	30,304	22,881
,389	2,469,396	2,974,505	2,294,990	1,861,400	341,929	1,648,211	1,576,094
					58,964	75,584	
,816	643,038	770,399	749,895	654,788	474,059	709,536	647,391
,472	752,340	985,951	912,792	1,614,564	338,410	1,111,351	740,098
					2,315,981		2,875,777
		124,841	101,906	6,080		57,438	67,040
,346	17,514,641	17,445,427	15,504,374	12,322,012	4,781,232	12,957,364	10,762,266

TABLE III
COMMERCIAL SHIPPING IN THE MARMARA REGION (1939-1945)[1]

N—Number of ships
T—Net Tonnage

Country		1939	1940	1941	1942	1943	1944	1945
Turkey	N	34,397	33,567	29,407	30,460	25,363	25,646	32,793
	T	4,273,136	4,369,125	4,645,182	4,671,998	4,095,023	4,766,453	5,616,509
France	N	41	59				2	
	T	121,075	102,553				26	98
Great Britain	N	360	245	52				
	T	775,952	542,818	69,887				565,208
Italy	N	506	377	11		6		
	T	715,941	268,263	23,598		11,652		
Greece	N	684	664	294	8	1	11	125
	T	227,811	247,481	25,038	438	54	136	13,464
Germany	N	188	32	21	11	14	15	
	T	330,638	29,637	20,994	4,423	15,373	6,458	
Belgium	N	2						
	T	2,664						
United States	N	91	52					
	T	471,119	168,143					
Soviet Union	N	74	60	24	3		1	191
	T	157,318	128,025	53,813	8,061		45	841,766
Rumania	N	201	162	58		4	2	5
	T	528,452	498,465	120,476		13,288	7,836	19,093
Netherlands	N	90	26					3
	T	103,184	29,035					10,839
Norway	N	45	3					14

Country		1	2	3	4	5	6	7
(continued)	T	20,486	2,282					
Bulgaria	N	95	54	24	9	14	34	34
	T	126,919	47,865	14,673	402	9,106	1,206	1,206
Hungary	N	32	32	11		4		
	T	13,824	12,871	4,413		1,232		
Egypt	N	15	7					
	T	22,822	13,249					
Poland	N	8						
	T	8,928						
Spain	N		6		23			
	T		7,194		38,107			2,200
Finland	N	6						
	T	6,386						
Japan	N	5	3					
	T	19,443	9,678					
Sweden	N	86	10				3	14
	T	96,864	13,743				2,513	21,613
Yugoslavia	N	28	18	2		1		1
	T	49,914	24,480	4,528		91		1,558
Others	N	54	53	31				2
	T	29,529	29,126	9,947				7,494
Total foreign shipping	N	2,625	1,865	528	54	44	68	487
	T	3,906,395	2,185,178	347,367	51,431	50,796	18,220	1,557,834
General total	N	35,432	37,022	29,935	30,514	25,407	25,714	33,280
	T	6,554,303	8,179,531	4,992,549	4,723,429	4,145,819	4,784,673	7,174,343

¹Republique turque. Présidence de Conseil. Office central de statistique, *Annuaire Statistique* (1942-1945), Vol. 15, p. 518.

TABLE IV
COMMERCIAL SHIPPING IN THE STRAITS, 1946[1]

Country	Operating at Istanbul	Ships in transit	Total	Tonnage (Reg. net)
United States	109	72	181	797,126
Soviet Union	57	120	177	495,843
Great Britain	42	11	53	151,307
Greece	67	12	79	142,950
Rumania	17	7	24	94,293
Yugoslavia	14	22	36	81,360
Norway	28	1	29	72,399
Sweden	45	1	46	57,072
Netherlands	12	7	19	21,789
France	1	8	9	20,613
Italy	25	10	35	19,538
Denmark	4	3	7	15,563
Canada	1	3	4	12,219
Lebanon	7		7	11,273
Union of South Africa	4		4	10,832
Belgium	8		8	9,235
Panama	4	2	6	9,196
Bulgaria	12		12	8,821
Honduras	1		1	4,381
Poland	1		1	4,278
Palestine	1		1	3,425
Spain	1		1	1,037
Egypt	5		5	570
Hungary	1		1	518
Total	467	279	746	2,045,638

[1]République turque, Ministère des Affaires Etrangères, *Rapport Annuel ur le Mouvement des Navires à travers les Détroits* (Dixième Année—Janvier 1947) (Ankara: Disisleri Bakanligi Basimevi, 1947), p. 9.

TABLE V
COMMERCIAL SHIPPING IN THE STRAITS, 1947[1]

Country	Operating at Istanbul	Ships in transit	Total	Tonnage (Reg. net)
United States	118	62	180	787,495
Soviet Union	111	106	217	739,706
Great Britain	75	17	92	228,173
Greece	52	30	82	142,546
Italy	128	8	136	127,755
Norway	39	16	55	125,256
Panama	31	15	46	109,995
Sweden	74	12	86	102,464
Rumania	15	14	29	94,073
Yugoslavia	22	15	37	77,700
Netherlands	17	11	28	46,735
Denmark	13	3	16	28,887
Lebanon	9	8	17	27,443
Canada	4	1	5	18,920
Bulgaria	44	33	77	17,431
Spain	6		6	13,088
Hungary	12	7	19	12,430
Belgium	11	1	12	11,900
Argentina	1	1	2	10,112
Honduras	3		3	6,927
Java	1		1	4,236
Egypt	8	3	11	4,302
Poland	2	1	3	3,818
Syria	1		1	365
Saudi Arabia	1		1	240
Total	798	364	1,162	2,741,997

[1]République turque, Ministère des Affaires Étrangères, *Rapport Annuel sur le Mouvement des Navires à travérs les Détroits* (Onzième Année—Janvier 1948), p. 9.

APPENDIX V

COMPARATIVE TABLE ILLUSTRATING
COMMERCIAL SHIPPING OF BLACK SEA STATES
IN THE TURKISH STRAITS (1946-72)*

	Numbers of ships					
	Operating at Istanbul			Transit		
	Bulgaria	Rumania	USSR	Bulgaria	Rumania	USSR
1946	12	17	57		7	120
1947	44	15	111	33	14	106
1948	45	26	5	44	7	259
1949	3	33		78	15	114
1950	51	9	1	106	107	266
1951	57	7	2	100	151	255
1952	24	10	1	122	126	268
1953	28	3		105	178	282
1954	40	13		93	158	330
1955	74	15	4	103	142	473
1956	21	13	4	91	128	864
1957	57	13	22	116	42	1,536
1958	65	14	56	44	133	2,165
1959	17	12	75	59	162	2,424
1960	88	11	85	230	157	2,279
1961	68	5	141	278	195	2,562
1962	87	14	91	323	221	2,852
1963	135	45	174	346	151	3,106
1964	153	88	245	305	348	3,902
1965	167	108	267	480	449	4,636
1966	225	129	356	638	469	5,421
1967	252	152	355	656	460	5,837
1968	355	138	402	656	491	5,783
1969	378	138	460	726	519	5,812
1970	431	99	376	879	564	6,695
1971	344	100	335	851	569	6,960
1972	315	113	516	1,039	670	6,841

*Data on Turkish shipping in the Straits are not given in the *Rapports Annuels*.

	Total		Registered Net Tonnage		
Bulgaria	Rumania	USSR	Bulgaria	Rumania	USSR
12	24	177	8,821	94,293	495,843
77	29	217	17,431	94,073	739,706
89	33	264	25,178	126,513	766,606
81	48	114	28,243	95,843	387,892
157	116	267	54,667	390,257	596,638
157	158	257	72,292	392,792	577,888
146	136	269	65,007	176,698	533,814
133	181	282	109,075	250,253	649,990
133	171	330	68,398	267,926	827,549
177	157	477	106,759	143,802	1,207,741
113	141	868	91,672	105,472	2,390,625
173	55	1,558	197,149	122,862	4,647,107
109	147	2,221	173,238	173,346	6,323,958
76	174	2,499	221,011	223,554	6,865,018
318	168	2,364	215,146	219,055	6,884,358
346	200	2,703	297,256	236,772	8,668,596
410	235	2,942	342,785	430,564	9,570,006
481	296	3,280	463,508	642,500	12,156,452
458	436	4,147	613,180	916,754	16,443,196
647	557	4,903	1,027,292	995,655	21,160,967
863	598	5,597	2,031,256	1,089,181	24,813,076
908	612	6,192	2,019,910	1,262,019	26,631,409
1,011	629	6,183	1,725,968	1,520,168	25,704,615
1,104	657	6,272	2,188,905	1,991,993	26,365,346
1,310	663	7,071	2,885,933	2,444,410	29,337,803
1,195	669	7,295	2,773,331	1,719,377	29,054,266
1,354	783	7,357	4,894,082	2,278,190	19,732,778

APPENDIX V

COMPARATIVE TABLE ILLUSTRATING COMMERCIAL SHIPPING OF
MEDITERRANEAN STATES IN THE TURKISH STRAITS
(1946–1972)

	Numbers of Ships				
	Greece	Italy	Yugoslavia	France	Spain
1946	79	35	36	9	1
1947	82	82	37		6
1948	106	300	37		1
1949	60	330	16		2
1950	177	445	14	2	2
1951	231	510	23		
1952	249	698	29		9
1953	190	650	80	17	12
1954	295	929	107	65	30
1955	413	890	134	65	15
1956	609	960	200	69	9
1957	199	814	359	105	10
1958	688	729	405	89	55
1959	931	1,031	521	63	10
1960	1,332	1,242	436	105	17
1961	1,841	1,464	593	148	28
1962	2,015	1,349	662	129	19
1963	1,282	1,324	623	158	6
1964	2,431	1,192	621	185	19
1965	2,446	1,163	664	233	9
1966	2,846	1,271	646	277	15
1967	3,162	1,500	600	314	73
1968	3,182	1,297	654	193	92
1969	3,037	1,301	578	190	83
1970	3,171	1,181	531	116	53
1971	3,343	1,071	542	207	78
1972	3,375	973	508	140	80

Registered Net Tonnage				
Greece	Italy	Yugoslavia	France	Spain
142,950	19,538	81,360	20,513	1,037
142,546	127,555	77,700		13,088
320,654	571,619	62,667		1,747
168,823	411,823	15,595		3,494
457,947	705,508	12,578	10,500	2,384
383,154	732,774	15,613		
482,881	1,092,441	24,292		13,485
270,133	995,334	67,686	57,097	20,474
441,019	1,624,003	85,584	272,948	47,798
573,745	1,541,685	154,199	289,535	29,078
770,961	2,390,625	415,216	332,061	15,614
520,325	1,304,502	701,313	467,411	16,936
708,774	1,186,981	772,357	312,882	16,733
1,673,898	2,900,354	1,122,754	317,749	23,799
3,340,771	4,509,650	1,142,200	315,460	21,955
5,682,039	6,007,775	1,398,888	569,529	80,720
6,593,756	5,552,456	1,476,298	489,949	45,014
7,193,281	5,060,821	1,437,064	595,174	76,876
6,066,083	5,213,809	1,258,787	961,293	58,914
5,710,336	5,313,275	1,533,273	1,371,069	26,307
5,048,658	6,128,803	1,488,048	1,828,860	40,065
6,410,381	6,995,163	1,407,780	2,146,068	204,147
6,334,980	6,075,927	1,155,576	1,415,786	293,070
6,026,180	7,710,850	1,558,590	1,223,974	244,877
7,171,092	5,697,020	1,357,536	1,024,616	156,074
8,954,795	5,401,221	1,327,545	1,531,759	180,163
9,601,675	906,598	1,409,715	1,083,124	329,682

Appendix VI

American Principles and Proposals, 1945–1946

1.
THE AMERICAN AMBASSADOR IN TURKEY TO THE
TURKISH MINISTER OF FOREIGN AFFAIRS

ANKARA, *November 2, 1945*

EXCELLENCY:

I have the honor, under instructions of my Government, to inform Your Excellency as follows:

The American Government has given careful consideration to the Turkish Government's note of August 20, 1945, together with the *aide-memoire* attached thereto, concerning the question of the Straits.

The Turkish Government is no doubt aware that at the recent conference in Berlin, the President of the United States concurred with Premier Stalin and Prime Minister Attlee (1) that the convention of 1936 signed at Montreux regarding the regime of the Straits should be revised to meet present day conditions and (2) that the matter would be the subject of direct conversations between each of the three governments and the Turkish Government. It is the earnest hope of the Government of the United States that the problem of the control and use of the Straits can be solved in a manner which will promote international security, will show due consideration for the interests of Turkey and all Black Sea riparian powers, and will assure the free use of this important waterway to the commerce of all nations.

It is the understanding of the Government of the United States that the Montreux Convention is subject to revision in 1946. This government suggests that an international conference be held for the purpose of revising the convention in order that the regime of the Straits may be more in harmony with changed world conditions. The United States, if invited, would be pleased to participate in such a conference.

The Government of the United States is of the opinion that a revision of the Montreux Convention undertaken to meet changed world conditions should be based on the following principles:

(1) The Straits to be open to the merchant vessels of all nations at all times;

(2) The Straits to be open to the transit of the warships of Black Sea powers at all times;

(3) Save for an agreed limited tonnage in time of peace, passage through the Straits to be denied to the warships of non-Black Sea powers at all times, except with the specific consent of the Black Sea powers or except when acting under the authority of the United Nations; and

(4) Certain changes to modernize the Montreux Convention; such as the substitution of the United Nations system for that of the League of Nations and the elimination of Japan as a signatory.

The British and Soviet Governments are also being informed of the American Government's views set forth above.

Please accept [etc.]

EDWIN C. WILSON

His Excellency
HASAN SAKA
Minister of Foreign Affairs, Ankara.

2.

THE ACTING SECRETARY OF STATE TO THE
SOVIET CHARGÉ AT WASHINGTON[1]

August 19, 1946

SIR:

I acknowledge receipt of your note of August 7, 1946 which sets forth the text of the note addressed on the same day by the Government of the Union of Soviet Socialist Republics to the Government of the Republic of Turkey and express the appreciation of this Government for the courtesy of the Soviet Government in making this information available.

It will be recalled that the American Embassy in Moscow made available to the Soviet Government in November 1945 a copy of the note which the American Embassy in Ankara delivered to the Turkish Government on November 2, 1945.

---

[1]Copies of this note have also been transmitted to the Governments of the United Kingdom, France, Turkey, Greece, Yugoslavia, and Rumania, which were among the signatories of the Montreux Convention of July 20, 1936.

This Government has given careful study to the views expressed by the Soviet Government in its note to the Turkish Government. It would appear from a comparison of this Government's note of November 2, 1945 with the Soviet note to the Turkish Government of August 7, 1946 that the views of the Governments of the United States and of the Soviet Union, while not in entire accord, are in general agreement with regard to the three following proposals set forth in the Soviet note:

"1. The Straits should be always open to the passage of merchant ships of all countries.

"2. The Straits should be always open to the passage of warships of the Black Sea powers.

"3. Passage through the Straits for warships not belonging to the Black Sea powers shall not be permitted except in cases specially provided for."

The fourth proposal set forth in the Soviet note does not appear to envisage a revision of the Montreux Convention as suggested in our note to the Turkish Government of November 2, 1945, but rather the establishment of a new regime which would be confined to Turkey and the other Black Sea powers. It is the view of this Government that the regime of the Straits is a matter of concern not only to the Black Sea powers but also to other powers, including the United States. This Government cannot, therefore, agree with the Soviet view that the establishment of the regime of the Straits should come under the competence of the Black Sea powers to the exclusion of other powers.

The fifth proposal set forth in the note of the Soviet Government was that Turkey and the Soviet Union should organize joint means of defense of the Straits. It is the firm opinion of this Government that Turkey should continue to be primarily responsible for the defense of the Straits. Should the Straits become the object of attack or threat of attack by an aggressor the resulting situation would constitute a threat to international security and would clearly be a matter for action of the part of the Security Council of the United Nations.

It is observed that the note of the Soviet Government contains no reference to the United Nations. The position of the Government of the United States is that the regime of the Straits should be brought into appropriate relationship with the United Nations and should function in a manner entirely consistent with the principles and aims of the United Nations.

The Government of the United States reaffirms its willingness to participate in a conference called to revise the Montreux Convention.

Accept [etc.]

DEAN ACHESON
Acting Secretary of State

3.

THE AMERICAN AMBASSADOR IN THE SOVIET UNION TO THE SOVIET COMMISSAR OF FOREIGN AFFAIRS

Presented October 9, 1946[1]

I have the honor to inform Your Excellency that my Government has studied carefully the contents of the note of the Soviet Union to Turkey of September 24 relating to the regime of the Straits.

In pursuance of its policy of making clear to all interested parties its views on matters relating to the Straits, my Government has instructed me to inform you that after examining the note referred to above it continues to adhere to the position outlined in its note of August 19, 1946 to the Soviet Government.

It will be recalled that in the Protocol of the proceedings of the Potsdam Conference, signed by the U.S.S.R., Great Britain and the United States, the three Governments recognized that the Convention on the Straits concluded at Montreux should be revised as failing to meet present-day conditions. It was further agreed in the Protocol that as the next step the matter should be the subject of direct conversations between each of the three Governments and the Turkish Government.

It has been the understanding of my Government that the three Governments, in agreeing with one another that the regime of the Straits should be brought into accord with present-day conditions by means of a revision of the Montreux Convention, mutually recognized that all three signatories of the Protocol have an interest in the regime of the Straits and in any changes which might be made in that regime. My Government furthermore informed the Soviet Government in its note of August 7 to Turkey that "the establishment of a regime of the Straits . . . should come under the competence of Turkey and the other Black Sea powers". My Government does not consider that it was contemplated at the Potsdam Conference that the direct conversations which might take place between any one of the three signatory governments and the Turkish Government with regard to the regime of the Convention of the Straits concluded at Montreux should have the effect of prejudicing the participation of the other two signatory powers in the revision of the regime of the Straits. On the contrary, my Government considers that the Potsdam Agreement definitely contemplated only an exchange of views with the Turkish Government as a useful preliminary to a conference of all of the interested powers, including the United States, to consider the revision of the Montreux Convention. As stated in its note of August 19, my Government stands ready to participate in such a conference.

---

[1]Copies of this note were distributed on Oct. 10, 1946 to the representatives in Washington of the following signatories to the Montreux Convention: France, Greece, Rumania, Turkey, the Union of Soviet Socialist Republics, the United Kingdom, and Yugoslavia.

My Government also feels that it would be lacking in frankness if it should fail to point out again at this time, in the most friendly spirit, that in its opinion the Government of Turkey should continue to be primarily responsible for the defense of the Straits and that should the Straits become the object of attack or threat of attack by an aggressor, the resulting situation would be a matter for action on the part of the Security Council of the United Nations.

Index

THE JOHNS HOPKINS UNIVERSITY PRESS

This book was composed in Baskerville text and display type
by Jones Composition Company from a design by Susan Bishop.
It was printed on 60-lb. Warren 1854 regular paper and bound
in Kivar fabric by The Maple Press Company.

Library of Congress Cataloging in Publication Data
Howard, Harry Nicholas, 1902–
    Turkey, the straits and U. S. policy.

    "Published in cooperation with the Middle East
Institute."
    Bibliography: p.
    1. Straits question. 2. United States—Foreign
relations—Turkey. 3. Turkey—Foreign relations—
United States. I. Title.
D465.H66   327.73′0561   74-6826
ISBN 0-8018-1590-8

Kirtley Library
Columbia College
8th and Rogers
Columbia, MO. 65201

DATE DUE